SUMATRA

Edited by

ERIC M. OEY

PERIPLUS
EDITIONS
BERKELEY - SINGAPORE

Medan

North Sumatra

Aceh

West Sumatra

South Sumatra

Riau

Bengkulu

Jambi

Lampung

Printed in the Republic of Singapore
ISBN 0-945971-13-3

Publisher: Eric Oey
Design: Peter Ivey
Production: Ricky Kong
Cartography: Mary Chia

Distributors:
United States of America
Passport Books/NTC, 4255 W. Touhy Avenue
Lincolnwood [Chicago], Illinois 60646

UK/Europe (except Benelux)
Robertson McCarta Ltd.
17/18 Angel Gate, City Road, London EC1V 2PT

The Netherlands
Nilsson & Lamm bv
Postbus 195 1380 AD Weesp

Indonesia
C.V. Java Books
P.O. Box 55 JKCP Jakarta 10510

Singapore and Malaysia
Periplus (Singapore) Pte Ltd
78 Queen's Road Singapore 1026

Cover: A warrior from the archaic island of Nias, 125
km off Sumatra's west coast. Photo by Kal Muller.

Pages 4-5: Rafting the Alas River in Western Aceh
province. Photo by Kal Muller.

Pages 6-7: An elephant safari in Way Kambas
Reserve, Lampung Province. Photo by Alain Compost.

Pages 8-9: Woman praying at the back of Banda
Aceh's Grand Mosque. Photo by Kal Muller.

Frontispiece: A Minang woman in traditional *adat*
costume. Photo by Alain Compost.

Periplus Travel Guides

SUMATRA

JAVA

BALI

KALIMANTAN
Indonesian Borneo

SULAWESI
The Celebes

EAST OF BALI
From Lombok to Timor

MALUKU
The Moluccas

IRIAN JAYA
Indonesian New Guinea

UNDERWATER INDONESIA
A Guide to the World's Best Diving

EAST MALAYSIA
and Brunei

WEST MALAYSIA
and Singapore

DEDICATION

*The editor dedicates this book to his parents, Tom
and Berenice, whose support and love have been
a constant source of encouragement, and also to
Oom Tjie Soe and Tante Siew Eng in Pekalongan.*

Contents

14   CONTENTS

CONTENTS 15

PART I

Island of Adventure

Sumatra, fabled "Land of Gold" of the ancients, is unlike any other tropical island on earth. It is neither the largest landmass in the Indonesian archipelago (Irian Jaya and Kalimantan are larger), nor the most populous (Java has three times as many people), but by most accounts it is the most varied and interesting island to visit. Sumatra indeed has something for everyone—lush rainforests, exotic flora and fauna, cascading rivers, sparkling crater lakes, shimmering white sand beaches and an incredibly diverse array of traditional ethnic groups who inhabit some of the most spectacular volcanic landscapes in the world.

Straddling vital waterways at the western end of an immense island chain, Sumatra is a kind of anchor for the rest of the archipelago. It is truly continental in scope: vast lowland rainforests and coastal wetlands are cut by a network of broad, silt-laden rivers that snake across the island for up to 800 km before emptying into the South China Sea. Unlike all the other islands of a similar scale, however, Sumatra is also volcanic—its lofty range of western peaks forming a longitudinal "spine" dotted with lakes and fertile upland valleys.

The island is extremely rich in natural resources. Its coal, tin, bauxite, oil, gold, natural gas, timber, rubber, tea, palm oil, cacao and coffee together account for over half of Indonesia's export income, while its long coastline is dotted with harbors giving access to seas teeming with tropical marine life.

As a result, Sumatra has played a major role in Indonesian history. The first large kingdom in these islands—the Buddhist state of Srivijaya—had its capital on the Musi River near what is now Palembang, and from here controlled a massive volume of trade passing through the Malacca and Sunda straits for over 300 years—conquering all other ports around the coasts and maintaining direct links with harbors in faraway India and China.

Indian civilization, which was to have such a far-reaching cultural impact in the region, entered Indonesia through Sumatran ports in the first millennium AD. In the second millennium the same story was repeated—as Islam arrived from the west along the trans-oceanic trade routes, established a foothold in the ports of northeastern Sumatra, and spread from here to the neighboring islands.

Sumatra was of course inhabited long before the arrival of these foreign priests and traders. Well over a dozen major ethnic groups live on the island, speaking more than 25 different languages and hundreds of dialects. Sumatra today supports 40 million people—over 20 percent of Indonesia's huge population—with a size and density similar to that of California, though far less urbanized.

Found here are some of Indonesia's most dynamic peoples. The Acehnese of the north, for example, are fervent Muslims renowned for their fierce resistance to Dutch rule. The Minangkabau of West Sumatra have migrated throughout Indonesia and today form the economic and intellectual elite in many areas. Sumatra's largest group, the Malays, were the great seafaring traders of Asia in pre-modern times, and their tongue forms the basis for the national languages of Indonesia and Malaysia. Last but not least, the Bataks of the northern highlands around Lake Toba are the nation's most resourceful and flamboyant group.

As a travel destination, Sumatra thus has few peers. Its natural habitats possess an unparalleled variety of wildlife—from elephants and rhinos to the world's largest flower (the foul-smelling rafflesia) and the most expensive aquarium fish (the golden *arowana* or "dragon fish")—while the island's traditional peoples are as fascinating as they are warm and hospitable. In short, Sumatra combines most of the incomparable attractions of the Indonesian islands all rolled into one!

— *Eric Oey*

Opposite: *View of Mt. Singgalang from Panorama Park in Bukittinggi. Photo by Coen Pepplinkhuizen.*

GEOGRAPHY

A Vast Island of Dramatic Contrasts

Sumatra is the fourth largest island in the world after Greenland, New Guinea and Borneo, with a land area of some 473,481 sq km —roughly the size of California or Spain. It is an island of enormous regional diversity, that for administrative purposes has been divided into eight large provinces. To some extent, these divisions have been made along ethnic, and not geographic lines. The provinces of Aceh and Lampung at Sumatra's northern and southern tips, for example, are home to the Acehnese and Lampung peoples, while North and West Sumatra are the Batak and Minangkabau homelands, respectively. Other provincial boundaries, however, have been determined more by the island's lofty central mountain range and the large river systems flowing eastward from it. Sumatra's largest province is South Sumatra, which encompasses a major slice of territory on the east coast and the large islands of Bangka and Belitung.

Migrating continents

Contrary to earlier beliefs, recent geological research has demonstrated that Sumatra once formed part of the great southern continent called Gondwanaland, and not part of Asia. About 160 million years ago it broke away and began to migrate northwards— eventually lodging, with Malaya, Thailand and Burma, against what is now Indochina.

About 40 million years later, India started its own northward journey, crashing slowly but powerfully into Tibet some 80 million years later. The dense oceanic plate on top of which India rested then nudged eastward against the relatively light and rigid Sunda Plate. This caused massive buckling, faulting and shearing—resulting in the formation of a series of small islands to the west of Sumatra, as well as of Sumatra's central Barisan Range and the valleys in between.

Today, part of the Indian Ocean plate continues to slide below the west of Sumatra, causing frequent but minor earthquakes, eruptions and landslides. The stress and shearing has been relieved by a long rift valley stretching from Semangko Bay at the island's southern tip, north through Lake Kerinci, Bukittinggi and the Alas Valley to Banda Aceh. The most famous section of this rift is Bukittinggi's Ngarai Sianok Canyon.

All along its length, the rift has been filled

ALAIN COMPOST

in by some 65 volcanic peaks, several of which are still active. The fault continues southward into the straits between Sumatra and Java, where it has created the most infamous of Indonesia's many volcanoes—the mighty Krakatau.

Parallel slices

The physical geography of Sumatra is best considered as a series of parallel longitudinal slices running northwest to southeast along the main axis of the island. In the extreme

west is a sparsely inhabited chain of islands —from Simeulue in the north to Enggano in the south—that is separated from Sumatra by a submarine trench which plunges to depths of 2,000 meters.

The western fringe of Sumatra itself is a narrow but complex coastal strip, alternating between fertile alluvial soils where rice is grown, and inhospitable swamps that are gradually being drained for agriculture. Rugged foothills rise steeply from this coastal fringe to the mighty Barisan Mountains— several of which tower above 3,000 meters. The highest non-volcanic peaks (about 3,400 meters) lie within the Gunung Leuser National Park in the northern part of the island. Sumatra's highest volcano is Mt. Kerinci—at 3,800 meters, the highest Indonesian mountain outside of Irian Jaya.

Also found along this central axis is dramatic Lake Tujuh—a spectacular crater lake, 5 sq km in area, perched at an altitude of 2,000 meters atop Mt. Tujuh. It is best seen from the southern slopes of adjacent Mt. Kerinci, but can also be reached directly from the town of Sungaipenuh. Impressive mountains are also found in the limestone areas around Bukittinggi and Payakumbuh in West Sumatra, and in the Lhoknga area of Aceh. These are not particularly high, but the unusual karst formations with steep sides, often studded with caves, are very interesting.

East of the Barisan Range lie irregular foothills and broad, dry lowlands which have seen rapid development in this century as plantations and as urban and agricultural centers. These lowlands are now also the focus of industrial development based on food processing and fossil fuels.

As you approach the coast, particularly in the central and southern regions, the dry land turns to various types of swamps—the largest extent of swamplands in Indonesia outside of Irian Jaya. These swamps are crisscrossed by large, meandering rivers. Where the peat is not too thick, the land has been cleared for rice cultivation; where it is thicker, pineapples and coconuts grow. Where the peat is really thick—and it can reach an incredible 22 meters in parts of Riau—agricultural crops cannot be grown. Logging continues, however, and land drainage in other areas threatens to eliminate many of these magnificent raised swamps.

Further east, off the central and southern coasts, are the low-lying eastern islands at the southern end of the Malacca Strait. Here, extensive areas are mined for bauxite and tin, but Batam Island is also being developed now as a leisure, business and industrial alternative to Singapore—with everything from industrial estates to luxury beach resorts.

Far out in the South China Sea about 500 km from the mainland are the Natuna Islands. These have little agricultural potential but are important strategically, as well as possessing important fishing grounds and rich reserves of oil and natural gas.

Riches of the earth

Sumatra is extremely rich in fossil fuels—oil, gas and coal. Oil is found mainly in the east, from Riau to South Sumatra, both on land and offshore. New technologies had to be

Opposite: *The jungle-clad slopes of Mt. Marapi (2,891 m), in the heart of the Minang Highlands.*
Above: *Rimbo Panti Reserve near Bukittinggi.*

km, compared with just 0.6 cubic km for the much-publicised eruption of Mt. St. Helens in Washington State, USA. Because of the massive quantity of ejecta, the empty cone soon collapsed in on itself to form the world's largest caldera. This became an ancient lake, which was itself destroyed about 30,000 years ago when a second, much smaller eruption occurred. The island of Samosir in the center of the lake, and the lake's eastern shore—the main tourist centers today—are all that remain of the shattered cone.

developed to tap this wealth, especially to facilitate drilling in the thick peat deposits of coastal Riau. Roads there are built on top of floating plastic carpets, and derricks perch atop tall piles reaching down to the bedrock below. Almost all of the oil from this central basin is pumped to the port of Dumai on the east coast. In southeast Aceh is the enormous Arun gas field, which ranks as one of the world's most productive. In South Sumatra, at Muaraenim, is a very large open-cast coal mine. The coal is taken from here by rail south to Teluk Betung and thence to Java.

Small amounts of gold are mined, though the important metals are aluminum (bauxite) and tin. Bauxite is mined on Bintan, one of the Riau Islands, then shipped to Japan for processing into alumina, then back to Sumatra again, where it is smelted into aluminium at the Inalum plant on the coast of North Sumatra.

Sumatra's 'big bang'

Huge Lake Toba in North Sumatra is Southeast Asia's largest lake, covering 1,146 sq km, and so far defying efforts to measure its depth—though it is known to be deeper than 450 m. It occupies the caldera of a massive volcano which exploded some 100,000 years ago in the most powerful volcanic eruption ever known. Early man was probably living in Sumatra at the time, and the scale of devastation caused by the explosion is hard for us to imagine— equivalent to hundreds of hydrogen bombs detonating simultaneously.

Shortly before the eruption, a giant boil of a mountain grew above the increasing quantities of molten material below. When the solid ground finally gave way, a searingly hot plume of ash was thrown into the sky—its remains can be traced today over an area of 20-30,000 sq km. Around the volcano the ash settled in a layer more than 600 m thick. This eruption set the world record for the quantity of material ejected—some 1,500-2,000 cubic

The first Europeans to see Lake Toba were a pair of British missionaries, Messrs Burton and Ward, who traveled here in 1824. They were told that the lake level rose and fell like the sea. Although much of the area was already deforested and under rice cultivation, one area on the eastern shore was still covered with jungle. At the time, the lake's outlet was unknown, but eventually it became clear that the Asahan River flowed out through a "spirit-filled" forest at what is now Porsea on the southeastern shore.

One reason for the forest's mystique may have been the impressive 100-meter Siguragura waterfall, which races through a narrow gorge—now rendered somewhat less dramatic by the presence of a hydroelectric dam. A short distance downstream is the 150-meter Sampuran Harimau waterfall which cascades into a large natural amphitheater near Tangga. Tumbling into this spectacular gorge is Sumatra's highest waterfall, at a point where the small Ponot River drops 280 meters from the mountains above and joins up with the Asahan River below. Although the falls are now used for hydroelectric power to supply the massive Inalum plant, the natural beauty of the area has not been lost. On a clear day these falls can be seen from the windows of

Above, left: *A tea plantation near Lake Kerinci.*
Above, right: *Oil palms are a common sight throughout Sumatra.*

jets plying the Medan-Jakarta route.

The climate of Sumatra has changed dramatically over the past million years. During the ice ages, glaciers covered the higher peaks in the north, in what is now Gunung Leuser National Park. The largest glacier on Mt. Leuser covered some 100 sq km.

Sea levels have also been as much as 50 meters higher and 180 meters lower than they are at present. As a result, the low lying eastern swamps and plains have been inundated and exposed several times. At times of low sea levels, land bridges connected Sumatra with Peninsular Malaysia, Borneo and Java, and the estuaries of large rivers such as the Musi, the Kampar and the Indragiri were situated some 700 km farther east from the present-day coastline, near what are now the Natuna Islands.

Fierce tropical storms

The western parts of Sumatra are by far the wettest; few areas here receive less than 4,000 mm of rain per annum, quite evenly distributed throughout the year. The wettest spots are the hills behind Padang, which receive 5,000 mm, and the northern Bengkulu mountains, which are drenched with more than 6,000 mm (about 10 times the rainfall of London!). The driest places are on the east coast and in the central rift valley, but even most of these receive more than 2,000 mm.

Although the difference between seasons is not very distinct, dry periods often occur in the early part of the year and in June and July. During these periods, wild fires occur, often started by farmers clearing patches of land. The problem is growing worse because the changing world climate is prolonging the dry seasons. Logging has also opened up the moist forests, allowing forested areas to dry out—as have drainage schemes on the east coast, which dry out the peat deposits, causing them to burn out of control. It is not unusual for air traffic approaching Singapore to be re-routed because of the smoke from fires in southern Sumatra.

While there is considerable local variability, winds in Sumatra generally blow from the north between December and March, and from the south between May and September. Many of the seasonal winds are particularly fierce, and have been given names by the local residents. A stormy wind that occurs in the region of Lake Tawar, in Aceh, is given the name Angin Depik—after the *depik* fish that is easily caught in the lake around this time. There are also two warm, dry winds —the Angin Bohorok which blows eastwards from the mountains behind Bohorok (in North Sumatra) and the Angin Padang Lawas which blows east of Padang Sidempuan (in West Sumatra)—which often damage crops and make agriculture in some regions almost impossible because the soils become so dry.

— *Anthony Whitten*

The Sunda Shelf

Malay Peninsula

SOUTH CHINA SEA

STRAITS OF MALAKA

SUNDA

Sumatra

SHELF

Kalimantan (Borneo)

MAKASSAR STRAIT

Sulawesi

INDIAN OCEAN

SUNDA STRAITS

JAVA SEA

Java

Lesser Sunda Islands

Land height more than 450 meters (1,500 ft.)

Sea depth less than 200 meters (650 ft.)

WILDLIFE

Beasts of the Tropical Jungle

Sumatra's wildlife is the stuff of adventure books. Huge elephants, large skulking cats and elusive rhinos inhabit dense tropical forests amidst a tangle of enormous trees, twisting lianas, and weird and wonderful flowers. Massive human-like apes and beautiful shimmering birds—glimpsed but for a moment —make Sumatra a truly exciting place for naturalists and nature-lovers.

One should not expect the drive-up-and-snap ecotourism of East Africa, however. Good sightings of animals are the result of patience and a considerable investment of time. The ideal way to go about it is to wander slowly through the forest, or find a suitable spot and sit quietly and wait—or rise before dawn and go into the forest with a flashlight.

Sumatra's remarkable biological wealth is partly due to the island's great size and diversity of habitats, and partly to its periodic con-

nections with the Southeast Asian mainland during the past few hundred thousand years. The island has no fewer than 196 different species of mammals—nearly three times the number in Great Britain—20 of which are found nowhere else. These include several species of bats, five primates, the Sumatran rabbit, various squirrels and the elegant Sumatran weasel.

The wide rivers of the east coast are home to dozens of large fish, including a giant catfish that grows to 2 meters in length, and the world's most expensive aquarium fish—the golden *arowana* or dragon fish. Many types of fishes may be seen in the marketplaces in the early morning. Some air-breathing, "walking" species are kept damp and sold alive.

Smaller rivers yield many more species of aquarium fish—heavily striped tiger barbs, the pink-and-brown Kuhl's loach, the orange-and-black clown loach, silver "sharks," half-beaks, gouramis and a variety of rasbora. The guppy was introduced to the region in 1929 by an aquarist in Bandung, West Java, when he accidentally let some escape. Today the guppy is found in ditches and rice fields in most rural areas.

Regional variation

Excavations on Java, where conditions for fossil preservation are better than on Sumatra, have revealed that about 70,000 years ago the Indonesian archipelago was home to many large mammals that are now extinct. Eight species of elephant, a giant pangolin, several pigs, wild dogs, saber-toothed cats, hyenas and a hippopotamus have all left their remains in the fossil record.

Several other species have disappeared more recently—the last confirmed shooting of a Javan rhinoceros on Sumatra was in 1928. The disappearance of the leopard, which still survives in Peninsular Malaysia and Java, is more of a mystery, as it is well-adapted for mountains, forests or plains—with their abundance of monkey and deer.

Sumatra's wildlife is not uniformly distributed throughout its regions. The islands of Simeulue and Enggano—respectively at the top and bottom of the island chain west of Sumatra—have very impoverished wildlife. It is possible that neither has ever been connected to the mainland. Neither island has

Left: *The Sumatran tiger.* **Right:** *Sumatran elephants, found in abundance in the southern provinces, have been herded into reserves. Some are being trained to be economically productive.*

any species of squirrel (the main island has 24), but Simeulue has distinctive forms of the long-tailed macaque and forest pig, 3 endemic snakes and 20 endemic subspecies of birds.

The massive explosion of Lake Toba in North Sumatra (see "Geography") may have had an important influence on the distribution of animals in Sumatra, because it spread a broad barrier of dry volcanic material across thousands of square kilometers, forming a kind of barrier. There are clear differences between the mammals found to the north and south of this area. To the north live white-handed gibbons, Thomas' leaf-monkeys, orangutans, the Sumatran wren babbler, Schneider's pitta and the bronze-tailed peacock pheasant. To the south live the agile gibbon, banded leaf-monkey, tarsier, tapir and blue-masked leafbird.

A forgotten eden

More than half a million years have passed since the Mentawai Islands, which lie 100 km off the coast of West Sumatra, were connected with the main island of Sumatra. This long isolation has allowed the evolution of endemic species and the survival of primitive (or relict) species in this region.

Eighty percent of the Mentawai's mammals are endemic. These special Mentawai animals include three species of monkey and a gibbon. Two of the monkeys—the *joja* and the *simakobu*—are unique among monkeys

in the Old World in that they live (as the gibbons do) in small family units comprising the mother, father and offsprings.

The people of these islands have a story which tells how humans came into being. At a conference of the *bilou* gibbons, it was agreed that their trees were becoming too crowded. So half the gibbons left the trees to live on the ground, and in time became people. This kind of story represents the closeness felt by the traditional people for their land and its animal inhabitants.

'Men-of-the-forest'

There is an awesomeness and splendor about the primary forest that is difficult to describe in words. The Sumatran forests are disappearing fast, and a walk in one of them should be on every traveler's itinerary.

The easiest forest to reach for the casual visitor is the one at Bukit Lawang on the edge of the Gunung Leuser National Park in North Sumatra, a two-hour ride from Medan. Here captured orangutans (literally meaning "men-of-the-forest") are trained to return to the wild, and it is possible to see these splendid, tousled, russet-colored beasts being educated to adopt a forest lifestyle, though occasionally the forest area near the rehabilitation station is closed to visitors during the time that feeding is stopped to encourage the young animals to find their own food.

Other forest areas are quite easy to reach

ALAIN COMPOST

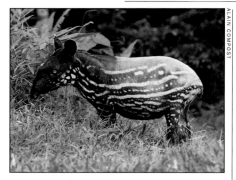

from Bengkulu, Banda Aceh, Blangkejeran, Kabanjahe, Sidikalang, Pematang Siantar, Bukittinggi, Tebingtinggi and Padang. The basic principle in any of these places is simply to head for the hills.

Mountains and parks

As one climbs a Sumatran mountain, the environment becomes cooler and more exposed. The trees and their leaves become smaller, the boughs and branches become covered in moss. Colorful rhododendrons and other familiar temperate zone plants grace the upper slopes. These plants are found only at the higher elevations, and some bird and other animal species are found only here too.

More adventurous and independent travelers could explore the mountains of Gunung Leuser National Park. Allow at least four days to climb Mt. Kemiri, one of the more accessible peaks, and plan your ascent well. Surprisingly, you will need a number of helpers, and do not forget that temperatures at the peak are only a degree or two above freezing at night.

The mountains are the place where you are most likely to see signs of rhinos and tigers. A word of warning—in this tiger country do not squat down at night to perform your ablutions; women are particularly vulnerable to attacks at night.

The clearance of large areas of lowland forest in recent years has led to conflicts between people and large forest animals such as pigs, long-tailed macaques, bears and elephants. Elephants, which cause the most local damage, have been confined to smaller and smaller areas of the forest as agricultural development and new roads have advanced. These roads often cross traditional elephant migration routes to and from areas with mineral-rich soils. Some populations of elephants are now living at higher densities in Sumatra than anywhere else in the world.

Elephants may be seen in spectacular con-

centrations in the Way Kambas National Park in Lampung province, and in the Air Sugihan Reserve. The reason for this is that elephant drives have been conducted—using helicopters blaring loud rock music, guns firing blank ammunition, and hordes of willing villagers—to persuade the elephants to move from agricultural areas into the reserves. These reserves consist largely of secondary forest, scrub and grasslands which elephants prefer, because their foodplants are more abundant there.

The plight of the elephants symbolizes the plight facing much of Sumatra's wildlife—how to survive when even the forest areas set aside for conservation are facing constant attrition? An attempted solution to the elephant's plight is to take young elephants into "training schools" and to teach them to be economically productive. The oldest of the schools is in the Way Kambas National Park.

Stinking giants

Among the records Sumatra can boast of is the possession of the largest and the tallest flowers in the world. The largest is the peculiar rafflesia, and its size is by no means its only unique feature. It is in fact a parasitic plant that has no leaves, no stem and no roots. It grows on the stem and roots of a particular climbing vine, and apart from the flower it consists only of a few strands of tissue inside the vine. Flower buds, looking like small red cabbages, emerge on the stem but develop slowly—a bud 10 cm in diameter will take about 5 months to open.

When the flower does eventually open there is a powerful smell of rotting meat. Singularly unpleasant to humans, the smell

Above, left: *The tapir, a distant cousin of the rhino.* **Above, right:** *A flying lizard swishes through the air.* **Right:** *A baby orangutan and its mother at the Bukit Lawang rehabilitation station.*

attracts flies and beetles that pollinate the flowers. Since the male and the female flowers may grow some distance apart and remain open for only a week, the odds are clearly stacked against successful pollination. After flowering they decompose and the very small, ripe fruit has to accidentally get caught in the feet of small forest animals so that some of the seeds may happen to be dropped on a vine stem where they can grow. Again, the odds are not exactly in its favor!

The small reserve of Batang Palupuh just outside Bukittinggi in West Sumatra is one of the best places to see this plant. While it is a seasonal plant, it is probably worth visiting at anytime of year—you may never get a chance to see even a Rafflesia bud again!

Another enormous flower with an impressive name is *Amorphophallus titanum*, a type of giant arum lily, of which generally only the leaves are seen. These leaves feed an underground tuber that, when large enough, produces a flower stalk as tall as a man. As with all other lilies, the blossoms are small and packed together on a central spathe.

Like the Rafflesia, the flowers smell of rotting meat and are pollinated by beetles and flies. You have to be lucky to see this plant in full flower, but chances are best in the forests around Mt. Kerinci. The local name is *bunga bangkai*, "corpse flower"—a name that is applied to the *Rafflesia arnoldi* as well on account of the overpowering stench.

And what of tomorrow?

In the forests of Sumatra, the echoing sounds of timber being chopped down at an amazing speed are now as common as the *"ku-ow"* calls of the Argus Pheasant or the drumming of the coucal. The shouts of timbermen are immediately followed by the rustling of a thousand leaves tearing through the forest canopy, and then the ground shudders as the trunk of a centuries-old tree slams to the ground, while the animals shriek with fear. Minor forest products such as rattan, tree gums, etc., are taken away with scant regard to replanting or to future harvests. Tigers, Sumatran rhinos and other game are still shot to provide pleasure for a few hunters, and to appease local villagers. The remaining patches of forest are dwindling fast.

So get out there and explore—climb the mountains, tramp the hills, and enjoy what remains. Take care not to add to the damage, and encourage others to do the same. Sumatra's wildlife is grand and very special, even though time, a certain determination, and a little bit of luck are required to see it. If you are patient and persistent, the rewards are great. But even if all that you can see is the blurred shapes of monkeys crashing through the canopy above you, you will have witnessed at least something of Sumatra's fast-disappearing wildlife.

— *Anthony Whitten*

ALAIN COMPOST

BIRDS

Rare, Colorful Denizens of the Forest

With some 600 species, Sumatra is second only to Irian Jaya in the sheer variety of its birdlife. Fully three quarters of these birds are resident, though only 17 are unique. Sadly, many species are endangered by clearing of land for settlement, logging and hunting, and some are now sighted only rarely.

Calls of the wild

Majestic hornbills attract your attention with their noisy wingbeats and loud calls. Particularly spectacular is the Rhinoceros Hornbill *Buceros rhinoceros*. The male is 1.2 m long, with a huge reddish, up-turned casque and loud honking call. The call of the Long-tailed Helmeted Hornbill *Rhinoplax vigil* consists of a long series of "*hoop*" notes gradually quickening in tempo, then rapidly building to a crescendo, climaxing in a cackling laugh.

Another common call of the forest is the loud "*ku-ow*" of the great Argus Pheasant *Argusianus argus*. When its decorative wing and tail plumes are fully developed, the male pheasant reaches a length of nearly 2 m. Like so many secretive forest birds, you must be very fortunate to see it in the wild.

The colorful kingfishers are mostly inconspicuous forest-dwellers, but the White-throated Kingfisher *Halcyon smyrnensis* lives in open country. This bird was first spotted in 1921 near Medan, but has subsequently spread throughout the island. Along swamps and rivers, watch out for the huge Stork-billed Kingfisher *Pelargopsis capensis*—with its loud, wailing cries.

Mixed dinner parties

If you are lucky enough to chance upon a fruiting fig tree, you will probably see a host of pigeons, hornbills and barbets—all so intent on gorging themselves that they ignore the observer standing below in a shower of discarded fruit debris. Occasionally shattering the cathedral stillness of the noon-time forest, a flock of birds will sweep down upon you, excitedly searching for food. This "feeding party" ranges from woodpeckers, jays and trogons to drongos, bulbuls and babblers. Such parties are believed to be a spontaneous response to food shortages in the dry season. The birds' frenzied activity drives insects from every nook and cranny, to be gobbled up greedily. After just a few minutes, the flock moves on, leaving the equally frenzied birdwatcher frantically trying to remember each species as the last bird departs.

Montane birds

Hill forests are the best birdwatching regions for the casual visitor. Many are accessible, the climate is comfortable, and the birds are less secretive. Here you will hear the rapid, monotonous, three-note call of the Black-browed Barbet *Megalaima oorti* and the curious buzzing note of the Fire-tufted Barbet *Psilopogon pyrolophus*. The lucky birdwatcher will also find the distinctive Yellow-naped Woodpeckers *Picus flavinuchus* and *Picus chlorolophus*, or a party of colorful but secretive Green Magpies *Cissa chinensis*.

Prominent calls are those of the large Cuckoo-dove *Macropygia unchall*, the Mountain Imperial Pigeon *Ducula badia*, and the White-crested Laughing Thrush *Garrulax leucolophus*, with its distinctive hopping gait and beautiful call, which builds to a maniacal climax. The Bronze-tailed Peacock Pheasant *Polyplectron chalcurum* and the Salvadori's

ALAIN COMPOST

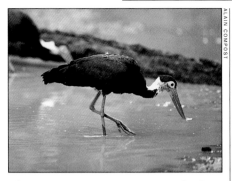

Pheasant *Lophura inornata* are endemic to the mountains of Sumatra. The latter was not seen for several decades, but has been sighted recently on Mt. Kerinci in West Sumatra.

Lowland forests

The most popular lowland area for birdwatching in Sumatra is Way Kambas Reserve in Lampung, easily accessible on a weekend trip from Jakarta. A majority of lowland forest species have been recorded here, including the hornbills. Further up the east coast are extensive expanses of swamp forest, but the remaining dryland forests here are greatly in demand for agriculture, and it is increasingly difficult to find good birdwatching localities within easy access of the main roads. It is essential to reach the forest soon after dawn in order to catch the peak activity.

In Way Kambas, the birdwatcher may happen upon a party of Crested Fireback Pheasants *Lophura ignita*, or see the huge White-bellied Woodpecker *Dryocopus javensis*. The Black-and-yellow Broadbill *Eurylaimus orchromalus* is a common songster, with its trilled notes on one pitch that steadily gather speed to a cicada-like buzz.

The best songster of the lowland forest is undoubtedly the long-tailed, scarlet, black and white Shama *Copsychus malabaricus*, a secretive robin of the deep forest. The Eared Nightjar *Eurostopodus temminckii* is also a favorite, with its "*tok-tedau*" calls uttered in flight just above the canopy of trees precisely at dusk and dawn.

The lowland forests have the greatest variety, but even the brightly colored birds are not found easily. A dedicated birdwatcher requires not only skill and patience but also a considerable degree of luck to sight some of the birds mentioned.

Left: *A Red-crowned Barbet.* **Above:** *Storm's Storks looking for fish in a swampy river along the coast.* **Right:** *A Buffy Fish Owl* (ketupa ketupa*).

Wetlands

The remote and muddy east coast is a major wintering and transit zone for over 100,000 palaearctic waders from some 25 species. The 4,000 Asian Dowitchers *Limnodromus semipalmatus* sighted here are most exciting, as they represent about half of the world's population of this rare bird.

The Asian Wetlands Bureau is anxiously trying to locate the breeding colonies of Sumatra's 3,000 Milky Storks *Ibis cinereus*, in order to protect this endangered species. The wetlands are also home to large numbers of egrets and herons, Lesser Adjutant Storks *Leptoptilos javanicus*, Black-headed Ibis *Threskiornis melanocephalus*, and a tiny relict population of Spot-billed Pelicans *Pelecanus philippensis*.

Two wetland birds are high on the endangered list. Sumatra and Kalimantan are home to most of the world population of Storm's Stork *Ciconia stormi*—a forest bird of the swamps and rivers. Sumatra is also one of the main strongholds of the forest-dwelling White-winged Wood Duck, whose range formerly extended from Northeast India south to West Java. It is now confined to scattered relict populations. One such population lives in southeast Sumatra, but the wetlands here now possess only a fraction of their former wealth due to human population pressures.

— *Derek Holmes*

PREHISTORY

From Flaked Glass to Iron and Bronze

We know little of Sumatra's role in the evolution of modern humans. Its forested equatorial landscape has not preserved the same kinds of lake and river-laid deposits which have yielded so many early human fossils in the drier climatic zone of central and eastern Java. Early humans probably avoided the humid rainforests and instead occupied the fertile mountain valleys which run along Sumatra's mountainous spine. Perhaps one day their remains will be found, but so far the record is circumstantial.

The earliest inhabitants

Sumatra, like Java, was joined by dry land to the Malay Peninsula for most of the past million years. Sea levels were generally lower, owing to the great volumes of water trapped in the Pleistocene glaciers. The western part of the Indonesian archipelago has only existed in its present form for the past 6,000 years and for brief intervals during the warmest interglacial periods; the previous interglacial occurred some 120,000 years ago.

Humans probably first entered Sumatra one million years ago across the land bridges of the Pleistocene era (1.6 million to 10 thousand years ago). Archaeological evidence of human activity in Sumatra dates back only 10,000 years. Flake tools of a black volcanic glass called obsidian have been excavated from layers of this age in the cave of Tianko Panjang near Lake Kerinci.

But the most famous remains of the early, pre-agricultural period are gigantic middens of discarded marine shells, animal bones and stone tools once found (most are now destroyed) along the east coast plain between Lhokseumawe and Medan. Little is known of the people who made these mounds, but their skulls suggest that they were of Australomelanesian (similar to the native inhabitants of Australia and inland New Guinea) instead of Mongoloid (East Asian) appearance. They hunted deer, pig, elephant, honey bear and rhinoceros and made their stone tools by flaking one side of a large oval river pebble. Their cultural re-mains are called "Hoabinhian." Similar materials dating back 4,000-13,000 years, but without such large shell middens, also occur in the Malay Peninsula, Thailand and Vietnam.

Austronesian agriculturalists

All the peoples of Sumatra speak Austronesian languages. They are closely related biologically—all belonging to the "Southern Mongoloid" population which now occupies most of Southeast Asia. The Austronesian language family includes almost all indigenous languages of island Southeast Asia and the Pacific islands beyond the Solomons. Starting about 4,000 BC, Austronesian-speaking people began to spread southwards from Taiwan, reaching Sumatra around 2,500 BC.

Most Sumatrans speak dialects of the Malay language, or very closely related languages such as Minangkabau. Languages outside this Malayic group include Gayo and Batak, and the languages spoken in the islands off Sumatra's west coast—Simeulue, Nias, Mentawai and Enggano.

Little archaeological research has been carried out in Sumatra—far too little to allow any useful statements to be made about the prehistoric relationships among these peoples. However, two important observations can be made. First, there is evidence from lakes and swamps in the highlands around Mt. Kerinci and Lake Toba that forest clearance, probably for agriculture, was underway at least 4,000 years ago—perhaps by as much as 7,000 years ago. The evidence comes from palynology: the study of pollens preserved in cores drilled from the ground. It is possible that this forest clearance reflects the arrival of Austronesian-speaking peoples in Sumatra, unless there were other (Austroasiatic-speaking?) agricultural peoples living before them. This is still one of the big unknowns of the Sumatran past.

The second observation is that languages outside the Malayic group—Gayo and Batak, Simeulue, Nias, Mentawai and Enggano—probably represent localized descent from the initial Austronesian languages established in their respective areas. Acehnese—which is related to the Chamic languages of southern Vietnam—may be an exception.

Right: *A kora-kora outrigger, perhaps similar to the crafts used by ancient Austronesian mariners to settle the islands of Indonesia and the Pacific.*

But the Malayic languages, which also occur in Peninsular Malaysia and coastal Borneo, seem to reflect a later period of cultural and linguistic expansion, perhaps due to the rise of Srivijaya in the late 7th century. This Buddhist kingdom was focused around the area which is now Palembang in South Sumatra. The Malayic languages, therefore, may have replaced older Austronesian languages.

Malay is spoken along the entire eastern lowlands of the island south of Medan—even by the nomadic Kubu peoples. The Kubu foragers, who are of Southern Mongoloid origin, speak a language so closely related to their agricultural neighbors that it is possible that sometime in the recent past their ancestors turned from agriculture to foraging—a reverse of the most commonly-assumed direction of cultural development.

The age of bronze and iron

Like Java, Sumatra has no detailed pre-Bronze Age archaeological record. Our picture for the island really only comes into focus from about 2,000 years ago, when knowledge of bronze casting and iron smelting arrived with the massive bronze drums of Vietnamese ("Dongson") origin.

These drums, with their elaborate surface decorations of boats, raised-floor houses, animals, birds and human warriors have been found at several places in Sumatra—some of these artifacts have been found near Lake Kerinci, in Lampung, in South Sumatra, and near Bengkulu.

The famous Batugajah stone in the Pasemah Highlands of South Sumatra shows a Dongson drum being carried on the back of a man who is apparently subduing an elephant. The Batugajah stone was originally located near Pagaralam in West Sumatra, but is now kept in the museum in Palembang. This carved boulder is one of the fascinating complex of carved megalithic monuments found in the fields around Pagaralam. The bas-relief carvings on these stone monuments show men riding elephants or buffaloes, helmeted human heads, humans wrestling with snakes. There are also many stone mortars, which may have had ritual uses.

Massive underground tombs constructed of large slabs of rock have produced Metal Age artifacts such as glass beads and items made of bronze, iron, and even sometimes gold. Some were painted inside in red, black and white with schematic motifs of horned buffaloes, felines, monkey-like figures and humans. In one case two humans (or possibly a human and a giant cat) are shown holding a Dongson drum. Examples of these grave paintings can be seen in the National Museum in Jakarta. These megalithic carvings and slab stone graves were probably both made during the earlier part of the first millennium AD.

—Peter Bellwood

EARLY HISTORY

Svarnadvipa: The Ancient Island of Gold

Sumatra crept slowly and tentatively onto the historical stage. The Indian *Ramayana* epic (3rd century BC) mentions a Svarnadvipa or "Gold Island" which is probably Sumatra, for the island has rich gold deposits that have been mined since antiquity. A Greek scholar of the first century AD named Claudius Ptolemy wrote that cannibals lived on the five Barousai Islands east of India. This is probably a reference to northwest Sumatra—the port of Barus on this coast was famous in later centuries as a source of camphor.

Until about AD 600, foreign writers thought of Sumatra as a forbidding wilderness, inhabited by fierce cannibalistic tribes and wild beasts, but enticingly rich in mineral and botanical wealth. One trading port, located somewhere in the southeast coast, stood out as an isolated outpost of civilization in a savage land. This port, known to the Chinese as

Gantoli, maintained diplomatic relations with China between AD 441 and 563.

By the end of the 7th century, several Sumatran kingdoms had established contact with China. These Sumatran courts sent diplomatic missions to China, and Chinese Buddhist monks undertook the hazardous 40-day sea voyage to Sumatra en route to India, bringing back with them glowing descriptions of these kingdoms as flourishing centers of trade and scholarship.

The empire of Srivijaya

The greatest name in ancient Sumatran history is Srivijaya ("Glorious Victory"). In the late 7th century, this kingdom rapidly expanded from its capital near present-day Palembang in southeastern Sumatra, and gained control over the neighboring ports. For the next 400 years Sumatra's history is essentially the story of Srivijaya's golden age.

The name Srivijaya first appeared in AD 671, when a famous Chinese monk, I Ching (also known as Yijing) sojourned in Palembang for six months on his way to India. Palembang was then an active center of Buddhist learning and trade. Yijing states that there were more than 1,000 Buddhist monks in the city, and advised other Chinese monks to go to Srivijaya to study Sanskrit before proceeding to India. Yijing sailed from China to India and back on Srivijayan ships, which were the chief means of transport and communication over this vast distance.

Almost all our accounts of Srivijaya come from records left by foreign visitors. Srivijaya must have had written records, but these would have been written on strips of *lontar* palm leaves, and none has survived. Faint echoes of Srivijayan voices are recorded on a few stone inscriptions found around Palembang and other sites in South Sumatra. Most were written during a critical period between AD 682 and 686 when the kingdom was expanding fast and consolidating its power.

The Srivijayan inscriptions are all similar in content—containing oaths of loyalty to the king coupled with threats of divine retribution against rebels and troublemakers. One inscription from the island of Bangka mentions a military expedition about to depart for Java. Another from Talang Tuo, west of Palembang, commemorates the founding of a park by the ruler—a Buddhist act of virtue

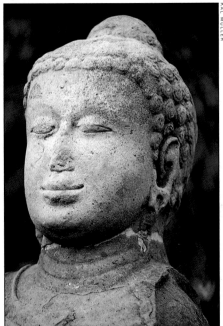

KAL MULLER

Left: *Srivijayan statue of a boddhisatva, an enlightened being whose every act was designed to contribute to the welfare of all living creatures.*

commited to earn merit for all creatures.

These inscriptions indicate that Srivijaya had a government divided into at least two levels—a central ruler and subordinate governors in outlying districts. They also reveal a complex hierarchy of officials, including generals, tax collectors and scribes attached to the central court.

Srivijayan inscriptions have been found as far north as southern Thailand, and in its heyday the empire seems to have extended all around the coasts of Sumatra, the Malay Peninsula and perhaps western Borneo. Yet these far-flung trading outposts were probably held together by nothing more elaborate than a set of loose ties of loyalty and tribute between the maharaja at Palembang and local rulers who controlled the various ports.

Buddhism and trade

The Palembang inscriptions show that Srivijaya's elite practiced an esoteric form of Buddhism imbued with magical practices. The rulers probably modelled themselves on the Buddhist concept of the *bodhisattva*, an enlightened being whose every act was designed to contribute to the welfare of living creatures. Sumatran, Chinese and later Arab sources paint Srivijaya as a wealthy and powerful kingdom, aggressively pursuing a monopoly over the trade in oriental luxuries passing along the coasts of the island. The hinterlands were never a target for direct control, since their products had to pass through Srivijayan-controlled territory along the coast anyway.

This trade was not a trifling matter. During the first few centuries AD, the Straits of Malacca became an important alternative to the better-known Silk Route across the deserts and mountains of central Asia, linking China with India and the Mediterranean World. Located half way along the sea route, Sumatra furnished products such as spices, ivory, rhinoceros horn and incense which were greatly prized in India and China. Control over this trade was worth fighting for.

In the early 7th century there were other ports in Sumatra, each seeking to attract foreign trade. The most important of these was Malayu on the Batang Hari River in the province of Jambi. By AD 700 Srivijaya had forced them all to submit. No foreign traders were allowed to enter the ports without special permission. For the next 300 years, Srivijaya monopolized the rich maritime trade of Asia. Its wealth became proverbial even among the sophisticated courtiers of China and Persia.

Although Srivijaya was a highly cultured center of trade and scholarship, its capital does not seem to have been a densely populated urban area, but a single row of houses which stretched for several kilometers along the banks of the Musi River. Only when the Chinese began to emigrate to Southeast Asia in the late 11th century, did the first Suma-

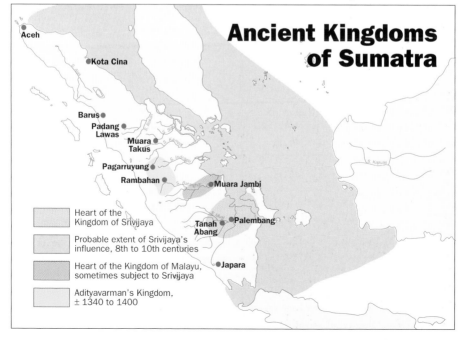

Ancient Kingdoms of Sumatra

Aceh
Kota Cina
Barus
Padang Lawas
Muara Takus
Pagarruyung
Rambahan
Muara Jambi
Tanah Abang
Palembang
Japara

Heart of the Kingdom of Srivijaya

Probable extent of Srivijaya's influence, 8th to 10th centuries

Heart of the Kingdom of Malayu, sometimes subject to Srivijaya

Adityavarman's Kingdom, ± 1340 to 1400

tran towns start to appear.

The rise of Malayu (Jambi)

Srivijaya reached the height of its prosperity around AD 1000. Chinese and Indian sources record that the rulers of Srivijaya sponsored the construction of temples in both these countries, and even densely-populated Java seems to have come under Sumatran influence at this time.

Then disaster struck from an unexpected quarter. In 1025 the mighty Chola kingdom of southern India launched a devastating raid against Srivijaya, from which the kingdom never recovered. An inscription on the wall of a temple at Tanjore in India records that an Indian armada sailed down the straits and

subdued one Srivijayan port after another, including the capital itself. The Indian motive for this act—the only such expedition on record in the annals of Indian relations with overseas countries—has never been understood. We can only speculate that Indian merchants traveling this way found Srivijaya's exactions too onerous.

The destruction of Srivijaya brought about important changes in the Sumatran scene. Tamil merchant guilds became active in Sumatra; one set up an inscription in Barus in 1088. Other Sumatran ports—older kingdoms like Malayu as well as several new ones—began to attract international trade. In 1080 Srivijaya's ancient rival Malayu succeeded in reversing their relationship, reducing

Srivijaya to vassal status. Plentiful archaeological remains from Muara Jambi on the Batang Hari testify to Malayu's political and economic domination of Sumatra during the 12th and 13th centuries. By contrast, there are few remains at Palembang from this period.

Malayu's supremacy lasted for 200 years. Few historical sources exist for this period, and we can only assume that Sumatra was peaceful and prosperous, with few disruptions to mar the placid conduct of commerce. This long period of relative stability would have been pleasant to live through, but does not make for interesting history writing.

This extended period of calm ended in the late 13th century. The first blow fell in 1278, when the kingdom of Singhasari in East Java launched a successful expedition against Malayu. According to Javanese sources, a Sumatran princess was taken back to Java, where she married a Javanese prince. In time she gave birth to a son named Adityavarman.

By 1340, this half-Sumatran, half-Javanese noble was living in his mother's ancestral homeland in the Batang Hari lowlands, perhaps sent there to serve as a vassal ruler by the Javanese prime minster Gajah Mada. One of his earliest acts in Sumatra was to set up a statue of monstrous size, depicting himself as a Bhairava, or Tantric Buddhist deity, standing on a pile of human skulls.

Withdrawal to the highlands

Adityavarman broke with tradition by moving his residence into the highlands along Sumatra's west coast, in the area now occupied by the Minangkabau people. Why did he take this radical step? Two theories have been proposed, and both may be correct. First, Adityavarman seems to have severed his ties with Java and set himself up as an independent sovereign. From his home in Sumatra's mountain fastness, he could have defied any Javanese attempt to punish him. Second, the site of his capital is the center of a gold mining region, and in one of his inscriptions he styles himself Kanakamedinindra, "Lord of the Gold Lands." Perhaps he located his palace as near to the mines as possible so as to control this supply of wealth.

Adityavarman left many inscriptions—more than all other rulers of Sumatra put together. These should ensure that his reign would be much better understood than the shadowy ages which preceded him. Unfortunately this is not so. Few of his inscriptions have been transcribed, let alone properly translated and interpreted. One reason for this is that his inscriptions use an odd language combining Old Malay with ungrammatical Sanskrit. This is a marked decline from the standard of composition which prevailed in 7th century Srivijaya, and demonstrates that the ancient traditions of classical learning were on the wane.

The few inscriptions which have been studied do tell us, however, that Adityavarman tried to establish his court in a region which, to our knowledge, had no previous direct contact with the outside world, and no form of government above the level of a federation of neighboring villages. No doubt he struggled hard to recreate the glory of the court life in which he grew up in Java. Fragments of sculpture and architecture remain as mute testimony to his effort, and legends still popular in West Sumatra about contests between champions of autocracy and democracy may echo attempts to superimpose a Javanese-style system of aristocratic rule upon an egalitarian village society.

Adityavarman's last words were inscribed around 1374, when one of his monuments mentions a crown prince, Ananggavarman. After this, a veil of silence descends over West Sumatra, only to lift when Europeans penetrated the area some 300 years later. What happened to this prince? Perhaps he ascended the throne but could not keep alive the traditions his father had tried to transplant. By the 17th century, the West Sumatran political system bore little resemblance to the court system depicted in the classical inscriptions of Srivijaya, Malayu and Java.

A Chinese pirates' nest

Even after its political eclipse in the 11th century, Palembang continued to be an important port. During the 14th century, its Malay subjects chafed under Javanese overlordship. In 1370 Palembang took advantage of the rise of the new Ming dynasty in China by sending a mission to Beijing to request diplomatic recognition. The Ming emperor dispatched envoys to Palembang with documents recognizing Palembang as a Chinese vassal, but the envoys were waylaid and taken to Java, where they were murdered.

In 1392 the ruler of Palembang, a prince whom we know as Parameswara, tried to assert his independence, but a Javanese fleet destroyed the villages on Bangka which constituted his main source of naval strength. He fled to Singapore, where he tried to set up a new Malay stronghold, but he was driven out again in 1397 by an attack by the Siamese. In

1400 Parameswara finally succeeded in establishing a new base at Malacca, which in the 15th century became what Malayu and Palembang had been earlier—the focal point of a triangular trade between the Indonesian archipelago, China and India.

Even then Palembang did not die. According to accounts brought back to China by naval expeditions sent to Southeast Asia in the early 15th century, the Chinese inhabitants of Palembang, several thousand strong, remained behind when Parameswara fled. Left without a local ruler, they chose one from among themselves. Soon his position was usurped by a Chinese ruffian who turned Palembang into a pirates' nest. A Chinese naval expedition attacked Palembang and captured the

pirate leader, who was taken back to Beijing and publicly strangled in the marketplace.

After 1430 China turned inward, and contact with Palembang was broken off. When we next glimpse the town, in the early 1500s, it was no longer a Chinese enclave but an important port dominated by Javanese culture. It would be fascinating to know how this transition took place, but unfortunately Sumatra's ancient history resembles less a continuous line than a series of brief dashes separated by broad, gaping spaces.

—John Miksic

Opposite: *A 7th-century Srivijayan inscription.*
Above: *The giant statue of Adityavarman as a Tantric deity standing on a pile of skulls.*

ISLAMIC KINGDOMS

The Rise of Coastal Sultanates

The year AD 1300 saw the beginning of a shift in political and cultural importance from the south to the north of Sumatra, linked with the arrival of a new religion—Islam. Until the 14th century, the great kingdoms of Sumatra had been located at Palembang or Jambi. Now, a number of small Islamic kingdoms began to appear at the mouths of the short, fast-flowing rivers which disgorge into the Straits of Malacca on the northeast coast of the island. It was in these kingdoms that the Malay language, the Islamic religion and a literary tradition using the Arabic script were first elaborated. Yet in the interior of Sumatra, protected by the marshes to the east and the mountains to the west, people continued to speak a dozen mutually unintelligible languages and retained their own religious and cultural traditions.

Along the northern coasts of Sumatra are numerous small rivers where ships from India and the Middle East called for food and water. In the 13th and 14th centuries, trading ports began to appear on the banks of these rivers, and it was in these ports that Islam first gained a foothold in the Indonesian archipelago.

Up to this time, the island of Sumatra had been called "Jawa" or Java Minor by travelers and traders, but now the whole island took on the name of one of the flourishing ports of the northeast, known as Samudra (Sanskrit for "ocean")—or Sumatra.

In 1292, the Venetian traveler Marco Polo sojourned at Samudra for five months waiting for the monsoon to change before continuing his journey back to Europe. His expedition disembarked, and "for fear of these nasty and brutish folk who kill men for food we dug a big trench round our encampment, and within these fortifications we lived for five months." In Marco Polo's time, Samudra was a small kingdom practicing the same shamanistic animism as the peoples of the interior. He reported, however, that the neighboring kingdom of Peurlak (near modern Langsa) had already become Muslim, "owing to contact with Saracen merchants, who continually resort here in their ships."

An Islamic trade network

Ibn Battuta, an Arab traveler, also visited Samudra in 1323. By then it had become a sophisticated Muslim sultanate, trading with places as distant as south India and China. Many south Indian Muslim traders made their home in the city. Under its preferred Muslim name of Pasai, its rulers issued gold coins, and a system of writing Malay using the Arabic script was developed. Pasai was the earliest center of Islamic scholarship in Southeast Asia. Later sultanates, such as Malacca (on the Malay peninsula), Patani, Aceh and Johor, regarded it as a model of Islamic learning and behaviour.

From Samudra-Pasai, Islam traveled with Muslim traders down the east and west coasts of Sumatra, as well as to the Malay Peninsula and to the trading ports of the north coast of Java. By the 16th century, all the important Sumatran ports were under Islamic authority, and Islam had begun to make inroads in the Minangkabau region, the heavily-populated, gold-producing area in the central mountains where the half-Javanese, half-Sumatran Adityavarman (1356–1375), claiming descent from both Majapahit and Srivijaya, had established his own Tantric Buddhist kingdom.

Sumatran rulers eagerly accepted Islamic legends woven around Alexander the Great, who for Muslims was the world-conquering hero Iskandar Zulkarnain (or "Alexander the two-horned"). Soon after adopting Islam, the kings of Pagarruyung in the Minangkabau highlands elaborated the theory that Alexander had sent his three sons to rule the world—one in China, one in "Rum" (the Roman/Byzantine empire, and its heir in Ottoman Turkey), and the third in Minangkabau.

The Chinese imperial eunuch Cheng Ho (himself a Muslim!) visited Samudra with a huge fleet of ships in the early 15th century, and it may have been the information supplied by him regarding China's needs which prompted Sumatrans to introduce the cultivation of pepper from India. By the late 15th century, Sumatra was the main exporter of pepper to China. Pepper remained Sumatra's principal export until the 19th century, and for much of this period it was the world's major supplier.

The politics of pepper

Samudra-Pasai was just one of the kingdoms on the northern coast of Sumatra. When the Portuguese arrived in Southeast Asia in 1509, there were independent states at Barus, Daya

and Lamri (near modern Banda Aceh), Pidië (near Sigli), Pasai and Aru (near Medan). After conquering Malacca and driving out its Muslim merchants, the Portuguese attempted to gain influence in Pasai and Pidië by intervening in their frequent succession disputes. The effect of this was to drive wealthy Muslim merchants to Aceh, where a new and virulently anti-Portuguese sultanate formed at the beginning of the 16th century, on the ruins of the ancient kingdom of Lamri. With the wealth generated through trade, Sultan Ali Mughayat Syah—the first ruler of this new kingdom—was able to conquer Daya, Pidië and Pasai, drive the Portuguese out of northern Sumatra, and begin a century of bitter conflict with the Christian intruders.

Portuguese attacks against Muslim trade, and Aceh's hostile response, introduced an element of holy war into the expansion of Islam in Sumatra. From 1540 to 1630, Aceh launched more than a dozen large expeditions against the Portuguese at Malacca. During one siege in 1547, St. Francis Xavier galvanized Malacca's defenders and was credited with miraculously prophesying the Portuguese naval victory.

The last and greatest of the fleets sent against Malacca contributed to the decline of both powers. In 1629, the Aceh fleet of 19,000 men and several hundred ships was trapped and destroyed by a Portuguese fleet which arrived unexpectedly from Goa in India. Few

LE ROY D'ACHEM.

Left: *An early map of Aceh, whose harbor then supplied half the world's pepper.* **Right:** *The Acehnese sultan seen through European eyes.*

of these ships returned after the fight and the hostile weather encountered on the way. Aceh never fully recovered from this blow.

Aceh's golden age

During the latter half of the 16th and early part of the 17th century, Aceh was supplying Europe with half its pepper. Venetian envoys in Cairo and Constantinople noted with satisfaction—and the Portuguese with dismay—that ships from "Assi" were arriving regularly in Jiddah or Suez laden with pepper. Aceh was then known as the "doorstep to Mecca" (*serambi Mekkah*), because it was from here that Muslim pilgrims from all countries "below the winds" (i.e. Southeast Asia) embarked for their voyage to the Holy Land.

Because of Aceh's abundant pepper, and its known aversion to the Catholic Portuguese, Protestant Europeans made the sultanate their first Asian port of call. The Dutch were welcomed in 1598 and the English in 1600. Mounted on elephants for their official reception at the palace, they were honored with gifts of sarongs and krisses. However, relations between the Dutch and the Acehnese were not always smooth; as an example the first Malay dictionary and phrasebook was written during a year's captivity in Aceh by the Dutch Admiral de Houtman.

Aceh reached its peak of power and wealth under the brilliant but ruthless Sultan Iskandar Muda ("the young Alexander," 1607-

1636). Throughout the first half of the 17th century, Aceh's court astonished visitors with its lavish feasts and public rituals. Hundreds of richly-caparisoned elephants and thousands of pikemen accompanied the sultan in the weekly Friday procession from the palace to the great mosque. On the major Islamic feast days and at receptions for foreign guests, the processions were even grander —there were contests between pairs of fighting elephants, buffaloes and rams.

In the early 17th century, Aceh was one of the major powers in Asia. Its effective authority stretched along the coast to Padang in the west and Tanjung Balai (on Karimun Island) in the east. Acehnese viceroys were appointed to rule over the Karo and Simalungun Batak and the Minangkabau. In the Malay peninsula, Aceh ruled Kedah and Perak, and conquered states as far away as Johor and Pahang. Victorious naval expeditions brought back thousands of captives to populate the city, man the war galleys, and carry out heavy construction work in the capital. Three thousand women waited on the sultan in his palace, and meals were served on plates of gold.

Warfare and the impermanence of building materials have left little trace of this former splendor. The city was never walled, a fact which an Acehnese chronicler attributed to the bravery of its people and the ferocity of its war elephants. In 1874, the palace complex was destroyed by the invading Dutch, and the great mosque, which was built of wood, was also destroyed. All that now remains is the curious limestone *gunongan* and *pintu khob*, ornaments built in the 1630s as part of the royal pleasure garden along the banks of the Krueng Daroy, just south of the palace. Today, the style of the perished great mosque can be seen in the mosque of Indrapuri, originally built in the period of Sultan Iskandar Muda, about 20 km upriver from Banda Aceh.

Iskandar Muda's declining years were marked by signs of madness. He killed many of those closest to him, including his own son. His son-in-law, Iskandar Thani, succeeded him in 1636, but died in 1641. A violent succession dispute arose, and the leading men of the kingdom decided to place on the throne Iskandar Muda's daughter (Iskandar Thani's widow), Taj al-Alam ("Crown of the World," 1641-75). During her reign, the stern personal autocracy instituted by her father was relaxed. Traders enjoyed more predictable conditions in the capital, and local lords were able to establish hereditary lineages throughout the country.

Despite being at odds with Islamic law and tradition, the experiment with female rule was deemed so successful that three more queens were successively placed on the throne. As an English visitor explained, "the very name of a kinge is long since become nauseous to them through the Tyrannical Government of their last kinge." Not until 1699, when one of the factions was able to produce a decree from Mecca judging female rule unacceptable to Islam, was a king again on the throne of Aceh.

After the defeat that destroyed its entire fleet at Malacca in 1629, Aceh went into a slow decline. The Dutch were able to prise from Aceh's control both the pepper-growing areas on the west coast of Sumatra and the tin-producing areas on the Malay Peninsula. The major sources of Aceh's continued wealth were then the items that had once been regarded as non-exportable royal treasures—gold and elephants.

Literature and theology

Malay was the language spoken in the cities of Aceh in the 17th century, and it was here that much of the best classical Malay literature was written. The earliest Muslim Malay *syair* (poetry in 4-line verses) still extant is the work of Hamzah Fansuri (Hamzah of Fansur, i.e. Barus) who lived and worked in the late 16th century. Syech Syamsuddin of Pasai, who was the chief *kadi* (Muslim judge) of Aceh until his death in 1630, was influential with Iskandar Muda. Both he and Ham-

zah were adherents of the *wujuddiya* school of mysticism, which in the eyes of its critics so emphasized union with God that it erased the distinction between God and man.

In the reign of Iskandar Thani, a rigidly orthodox current of thought gained the upper hand, the works of Hamzah and Syamsuddin were burned and several of their adherents were executed. This orthodox reaction was led by the most prolific of classical Malay writers, Nuruddin ar-Raniri (of Ranir, in Gujerat), who wrote numerous theological works, and the greatest encyclopedic work of politics and history in Malay, the *Bustan al–Salatin*. He was unpopular with the people of Banda Aceh, and when his patron Iskandar Thani died, ar-Raniri was chased out of Aceh by an angry crowd.

The most influential religious scholar of the second half of the century, Abdur'rauf of Singkel, managed to combine orthodoxy with a tolerant approach to pre-Islamic beliefs and mystical ideas, and today he is revered as the greatest of Acehnese saints. His tomb at the mouth of Aceh river is still honored and he is remembered as Syech Kuala (the Syech of the river mouth). Aceh's state university is named in his honor.

Economic decline

World demand for pepper reached a peak in the middle of the 17th century. From 1650 onwards, the port-states which had dominated Sumatra since the 15th century began to decline along with the trade which had sustained them. Aceh embarked on a long period of internal conflict, and the *uleëbalang* (local chiefs) who controlled the river-mouths of Aceh coast became virtually independent of the capital. Acehnese gradually replaced Malay as the language of literature, and the weight of state authority was lightly felt by the majority of highland Sumatrans.

The lack of any major political authority encouraged adventurers such as the Bugis from South Sulawesi, the Arabs from Hadhramaut, and the Minangkabau from West Sumatra to seize power by warfare, by marrying into the ruling families, or by strategic alliances. Increasingly, European and south Indian merchants were appointed as *shahbandars* or trade officials in the island's ports. By the 18th century, the Europeans emerged as the biggest economic powers while Sumatra was an economic backwater.

—Anthony Reid

Opposite: *A royal tiger hunt.*

IMPACT OF THE WEST

Gunboats, Garrisons and Guerrillas

By the 18th century, the decline in world demand for pepper had deprived the rulers of ports such as Aceh and Palembang of the means to dominate their hinterlands. The biggest economic powers in Sumatra were now European—the Dutch established their headquarters at Padang in 1663, and the British at Bengkulu in 1685. Each became a center of rival networks of trade along the west coast, but they were militarily vulnerable. Local Sumatrans drove the British out in 1719 and held Bengkulu for many years. These lonely European outposts also attracted the attention of the French. Admiral Comte d'Estaing occupied Bengkulu for several months in 1760; Admiral Linois pillaged the fort and town in 1803. Dutch Padang was equally vulnerable, falling to the British in 1781-1784 and 1795-1816, and to a French privateer for two months in 1793. During this period Dutch influence was virtually eliminated from Sumatra.

British officials of the Bengkulu administration were the first to give detailed accounts of the Batak interior of northern Sumatra (Holloway and Miller, 1772), and the island of Nias (Jack and Prince, 1819). Raffles himself visited the Minangkabau capital of Pagarruyung in 1818. A great opponent of slavery, Raffles was nevertheless enthusiastic about Nias—"the finest people, without exception, that I have yet met with in the East." He was outraged that the island was a major supplier of slaves to Aceh, the Dutch and the French colonies, and even to the British settlements in Bengkulu and Penang. Raffles proclaimed British sovereignty over the island in 1820, but this was disallowed by London.

Pepper, coffee and tin

A new phase of commercial expansion affected Sumatra from about 1780. British and Tamil traders came from India, British and Chinese traders arrived from the new British port at Penang (founded 1786), and Americans from Salem, Providence and New London. The Americans found willing pepper suppliers in local chiefs on the west coast between Sibolga and Meulaboh, a frontier region beyond the reach of Acehnese authority in the north and the English Company in the south. More than 5,000 tons a year were exported from this region alone in the early

19th century, primarily by Americans. In the Minangkabau area, cassia (a substitute for cinnamon), gambir (used for tanning leather), and from 1790, coffee, became attractive new crops. At the beginning of the 18th century, Chinese miners began to exploit the tin deposits in Bangka.

With the decline of authority, first of the Sumatran rulers, then of the Dutch Company, Sumatra became once again an economic frontier, as colonists from settled areas flocked to new regions to grow export crops. The absence of major powers suited foreign traders, but when commercial disputes escalated into violence they appealed for vengeance to their respective navies. The Americans began this gunboat diplomacy by destroying coastal Acehnese villages in 1826 and 1838, and then French fleets did the same in 1839 and 1840.

The Dutch had to start almost from scratch when their prewar possessions were returned by Britain after the Napoleonic Wars in 1816. Economically on their knees and militarily tied down by the Java War (1825–1830), the Dutch were obliged to accept that others would dominate Sumatra's trade. Meanwhile, they moved slowly, using their limited military force to annex one river port a time, trying to ensure that no other Europeans staked a political claim to any part of the island. Sumatrans did not accept the extension of Dutch authority without a fight.

Anglo-Dutch squabbling over their respective rights following the founding of Singapore was temporarily resolved in 1824, when the British withdrew all claims to Sumatra, in return for the Dutch doing the same on the Malay Peninsula. In 1825, the Dutch seized control of Palembang and the tin-bearing islands of Bangka and Belitung. The Dutch also inherited a British conflict with a militant Islamic movement known as "Paderi" in the Minangkabau highlands, a conflict which dragged on until 1837, when the Paderi's leader, Imam Bonjol was finally killed. (See "History" in WEST SUMATRA.)

Dutch conquests

The Paderi movement disturbed the Batak as well as the Minangkabau areas. A conquest of the southern Batak areas in the 1820s was carried out from the Paderi commercial stronghold of Bonjol in northern Minangkabau. The key leader of the holy war to the north was Tuanku Rao, a Batak who had converted to militant Islam. He led a Paderi force forcing most of the Mandailing and Angkola areas of South Tapanuli to accept Islam. Tuanku Rao appears to have taken his troops even farther north, and tried unsuccessfully to convert the Bataks around Lake Toba.

Opposite and below: *Dutch forces under Colonel van Heutsz finally managed to defeat the Acehnese only after 30 years of bitter fighting.*

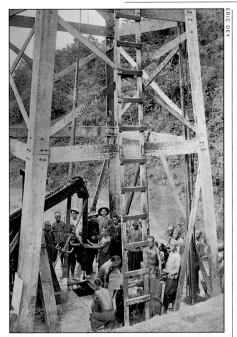

ERIC OEY

Java, where education was limited to the aristocracy. This first generation to be literate both in Jawi (Malay-Arabic) and Latin script provided Sumatra—and the rest of Indonesia—with a large number of its clerks, schoolteachers, journalists and political activists in the 20th century.

Dutch progress on the east coast of Sumatra was hampered by constant protests by British merchants in Singapore and Penang. A Dutch expedition was sent to Siak in 1858 to throw out an English adventurer, and another to the small northern states of Langkat, Deli, Serdang and Asahan in 1865, to establish Dutch rights against claims of Acehnese suzerainty and British commerce.

These small states proved a rich prize, thanks to the volcanic soil which proved ideal for growing tobacco. The pioneer Dutch planter, Jacobus Nienhuys, had moved to Deli (the region around Medan) ahead of Dutch troops, in 1863, and within a decade had established its reputation for growing the world's finest cigar wrapper-leaf. British objections were overcome by opportunities to provision this growing plantation economy.

In the 1870s and 1880s, 20,000 Chinese laborers were brought in each year to cut down the forests and tend the tobacco plantations. Later, the planters turned to cheaper and more tractable Javanese labor. In the 1920s, just before the system of indentured labor was ended, partly due to American pressure, a total of 260,000 Javanese worked on the plantations. Prosperous new towns grew up at Medan, Binjai, Pematang Siantar and Tanjung Balai. The insignificant coastal rajas who controlled the river mouths became enormously wealthy on the royalties from plantation land and (in Langkat after 1890) from oil.

There is a story that Tuanku Rao invited the tenth Singamangaraja (a Toba Batak priest-king who lived west of the lake) to meet him in the market place at Butar, and there killed him. Other Batak stories say that Tuanku Rao enjoyed extraordinary military success because he was the abandoned nephew of the magical Singamangaraja. European attempts to Christianize the Batak were less successful. It was not until the mid 19th century that any real progress was made. (See "The Batak" in NORTH SUMATRA).

Over two decades, from 1820 to 1841, the Dutch gradually conquered the Minangkabau area and built a series of strategic forts in the highlands. This made the most densely-populated region of Sumatra also the principal Dutch stronghold. The expenses of the garrisons were met by the forced delivery of coffee at fixed prices. There was however enough land to enable the enterprising Minangkabau to take advantage of improving communications and expanding markets to grow their own coffee, tobacco, sugar, cassia and gambir, giving rise to a prosperous, commercially-oriented middle class.

The same group responded enthusiastically to the token efforts the Dutch made to provide modern secular schools for Indonesians. In the 1840s they began funding their own district schools. By 1872 there were almost 1,200 Minangkabau children in school —a proportion several times higher than in

The Aceh wars

The biggest challenge to Dutch colonialism in Sumatra was Aceh, which never signed unequal treaties with the Dutch. It had wealth, arms and foreign contacts from its pepper and betelnut trade. Aceh also had a treaty of mutual defence with the British, arranged by Raffles in 1819, and a guarantee of Aceh's independence was incorporated in the 1824 Anglo-Dutch Treaty, which divided the Malay-speaking world into two halves. It was only in 1871 that British objections were overcome, clearing the way for a more vigorous Dutch approach.

The first Dutch attack was ill-prepared, brought on hastily by energetic Acehnese attempts to form defensive alliances with Turkey, France and the United States. The US Consul in Singapore agreed to forward a draft Aceh-US Treaty to Washington, though it received no support from the State Department. A Dutch force of 3,000 men attacked the Acehnese capital in April 1873, but withdrew three weeks later having lost its commander and 80 men. Humiliated, the Dutch recruited the largest force they had ever assembled in the Indies, and landed 10,000 men the following December. The Acehnese citadel was taken six weeks later amidst a cholera epidemic that wiped out at least a thousand on each side. This was, however, only the first chapter in a war which was to last until 1903, tying up Dutch resources, men and money, and sapping morale for 20 years, leaving a legacy of bitterness in Aceh.

By the mid-1880s, the leadership of Acehnese resistance passed to the *ulama* (religious scholars) who preached the necessity of a holy war at any cost. The Dutch graveyard in Banda Aceh is a monument to more than 10,000 soldiers who died of wounds or disease on the Dutch side. For the Acehnese, who lost at least 5 times as many, their enduring monument is the memory of countless dead heroes, some now officially recognized as Indonesia's national heroes. Among these are the west coast *uleëbalang* (district chief) Teuku Umar, who defected in 1896 after acting as the principal Dutch ally. Others include

Teuku Umar's gallant wife Cut Nyak Dien and *ulama* leader Cik di Tiro, who defiantly called on the Dutch governor to embrace Islam if he wished to avoid the inevitable destruction awaiting the infidels. Right to the end of Dutch rule, Aceh remained an occupied province. At the approach of the Japanese in 1942, the province rebelled and drove out the remaining Dutch forces.

On the Dutch side, the eventual success was credited to two men in particular. Colonel J.B. van Heutsz, military governor of Aceh from 1898 to 1904, adopted an uncompromising policy of relentless pursuit, and was rewarded by being named governor-general (1904-9). His invaluable key adviser was the Islamic specialist Christiaan Snouck Hurgronje, author of a Dutch strategy of tolerating or even encouraging Islam in what was held to be the religious domain, but resolutely crushing any sign of Islamic political assertion. After 1904 the policies of these two men were extended throughout the Indies. Dutch troops penetrated every corner of Sumatra, and by 1910 the whole island was for the first time under a single authority; but one that did not enjoy much love from its people.

—*Anthony Reid*

Opposite: Oil was discovered in northern Sumatra in the 1890s. **Above:** A plantation economy based on coolie labor made Sumatra the most profitable region in the Indies in the early 20th century.

MODERN HISTORY

Nationalism, Revolution & Independence

The Dutch conquest resulted in the development of a common education and administrative system throughout Sumatra. Together with Islam, this laid the foundation for the emergence of common national sentiment. This first made itself felt through the mass Muslim organization Sarekat Islam, which tapped the suppressed resentment at alien domination. Jambi witnessed a small rebellion in 1916. Aceh was disturbed by riots in 1918–1919, and the Minangkabau developed a radical Islamic movement in the same years. In 1926, the Indonesian Communist Party launched a quixotic revolution; paradoxically, it was some of the relatively commercialized Muslims of Minangkabau who fought hardest for it.

In 1917 the first generation of Sumatrans to have enjoyed Dutch education formed the Young Sumatran League. Support came from Minangkabau clerks, teachers and traders all over Sumatra. Toba Batak students established their own organization in the 1920s, and by 1926 these groups had been incorporated into the National League of Indonesian Students. Sumatran figures such as Mohammad Hatta (later Vice-President) and Soetan Sjahrir (Indonesia's first prime minister) contributed greatly to developing Indonesia's national consciousness.

Sumatra's role in developing a national literature was even more important. Malay had always been the principal written language for most Sumatrans, and its adoption as Bahasa Indonesia, the language of nationalism, involved no linguistic conflict as it did for Javanese and Sundanese. Hence the first writers to adopt Malay to modern literary uses were virtually all Sumatran. In the early twenties, the political activists Mohammad Yamin, Sanusi Pane, and Mohammad Hatta were the first to write Malay poetry in a modern spirit, while the Langkat prince Amir Hamzah and the revolutionary Chairil Anwar wrote the finest Indonesian poetry of the 1930s and

1940s. The development of the modern Indonesian novel in the 1920s and 1930s was almost entirely a Minangkabau affair.

It is not surprising, considering this strong contribution to Indonesian nationalism, that Sumatra rejected all attempts to separate it from Java in the turbulent 1940s. The Japanese invasion in March 1942 caused greater upheaval than in Java. In Aceh the Japanese were assisted by an armed rebellion against the retreating Dutch, whose leaders wanted to end the dominance of the *uleëbalang* (district chiefs). The Japanese initially suppressed all these movements, and forbade any nationalist activity. However, the Japanese gave the nationalists access to the state-controlled media in order to mobilize the population for war purposes. When the war ended, two rival elites—nationalist and traditionalist—eyed each other with mistrust.

The Japanese belatedly fostered the idea of an independent Sumatra in 1945, establishing a powerless consultative council and a secretariat in Bukittinggi. In 1947, the returning Dutch set up federal states in the areas they controlled in East Sumatra and South Sumatra. The following year they encouraged a Sumatran umbrella organization for these and other states, but the idea gained little interest. Sumatrans had already decided in the 1920s that they could only bring together their diverse ethnic groups at a national level.

Independence was declared in Jakarta three days after Hiroshima, but the revolution in Sumatra did not begin until October, when allied troops arrived to accept the Japanese surrender. Young activists, some with Japanese military training, fought against the defeated Japanese for arms, then against the British who occupied parts of Medan, Padang, and Palembang, and finally against the Dutch forces which replaced the British at the end of 1946.

Most of the violence was internal. In Aceh the *uleëbalang* were overthrown by a Muslim-led coalition in December 1945, at the conclusion of a bloody civil war. Three months later, the east coast Malay sultans and Simalungun rajas were overthrown in what was dubbed a "social revolution." These spontaneous movements led to a breakdown in central authority, especially in East Sumatra, where semi-military groups of young men, formed to fight the Japanese and Dutch, became a law unto themselves, funding themselves by sell-

Right: *The oil boom of the 1970s and 1980s has made Sumatra a major world producer.*

ing the produce of the plantations they controlled to Singapore merchants. When the Dutch occupied the plantation area around Medan, and the oil installations of Palembang in mid-1947, these armed groups fought among themselves in Tapanuli.

The vast island was far from integrated politically or economically when the revolution ended with transfer of full sovereignty to Indonesia in 1950. Each former residency had its own battle-hardened military force reluctant to return to civilian life, and each felt it had earned the right to play a part in the Republic on its own terms. Moreover, the rewards of the smuggling trade to Singapore, which had seemed patriotic during both the Japanese occupation and the revolution, were not easy to give up to an impoverished central government in Jakarta which had little to offer in return.

The first post-independence crisis occurred in Aceh, when Muslims objected to being incorporated with Christian Bataks into the province of North Sumatra, and to the failure of the government to declare Indonesia a Muslim state. In 1953, Aceh revolted against Jakarta, and declared Aceh part of Dar al-Islam (the Islamic world). Troops sent from Java quickly re-occupied the Acehnese towns, but the hinterland remained largely in rebel hands until peace was eventually negotiated in 1959. Aceh was then granted autonomous status. Meanwhile Toba Batak

and Minangkabau military leaders joined national politicians dissatisfied with the centralism, corruption and pro-communist policies of the central government, to form the Revolutionary Government of the Republic of Indonesia (PRRI) in February 1958. The central government reacted by bombing Padang and Bukittinggi and sending a large force from Java. The fighting was over within six months, but it left West Sumatra feeling like an occupied province in which locals were no longer trusted with high military or civilian office. If Sumatrans had been over-represented in national leadership before these events, they were under-represented thereafter.

Under President Suharto's New Order government which took power in 1966, regional discontents have eased. Firstly, the government's anti-communist and free-market policies are those which the PRRI had advocated. Secondly, the central government has provided roads, electricity, schools, hospitals and other infrastructural facilities, which have helped transform the economy. Large multi-ethnic provinces were broken up until all except North Sumatra (pre-war East Sumatra plus Tapanuli) were back to the boundaries of the old Dutch residencies, and the army's presence became less obvious. If one still hears grumbles about the *pusat* (center), these are now no different from those heard in every Indonesian province.

—*Anthony Reid*

HANS HOEFER

PEOPLES OF SUMATRA

A Mélange of Ethnic Groups and Religions

More than 40 million people live in Sumatra —one-fifth of Indonesia's huge population— making this the second most populous island in the archipelago, after Java. Four large ethnic groups—the Malay, the Minangkabau, the Acehnese and the Batak—form the vast majority of the island's indigenous population, but over a dozen smaller ethnic groups are also represented, each speaking a different language and possessing a distinct history and culture.

In recent centuries, there has been a significant influx of outsiders to Sumatra as well. The Javanese, who came by the thousands as plantation workers at the beginning of this century, continue to arrive through Indonesia's ambitious transmigration program. The Chinese, who first came as debt-bonded plantation coolies and tin miners in the 19th century, now dominate the wholesale and merchandising sectors of all major Sumatran towns. And a smattering of peoples from other islands of Indonesia and abroad now live and work on the island as civil servants and in the booming oil industry.

Islamic strongholds

Sumatra is among the most thoroughly Islamic regions in the archipelago. History states that Islam first came to Southeast Asia at a town on Sumatra's northeast coast, variously referred to as Samudra or Pasai. From here, the religion spread around both coasts of Sumatra and across to neighboring islands and the Malay Peninsula—largely through an Islamic trading network established by Malay merchants at Malacca in the 15th century. For many centuries the term "Malay" was indeed synonymous throughout Indonesia with "Muslim."

The Malays have a long and illustrious history dating back to the days when the Buddhist Malay kingdom of Srivijaya dominated the straits from a base at what is now Palembang, in South Sumatra, from the late 7th until the 11th centuries. For many centuries thereafter, the figure of the Malay raja embodied the highest cultural ideals of gentility, grace, eloquence, learning and Muslim piety throughout the Malay World. While fishermen and farmers could never match the raja's refinement, they modelled their best behavior on the ideals he represented.

Today the Malays are Sumatra's largest ethnic group, numbering more than 13 million people and inhabiting most of the southern and eastern coasts and lowlands of the main island, as well as the smaller islands offshore. Another 8 million people in neighboring Malaysia also consider themselves to be Malay—though many are descendants of Minangkabau, Cham and Javanese migrants. Even in Sumatra itself, many people of Batak descent call themselves "Malay," so that in fact a tremendous linguisitic and cultural variety is encompassed by this ethnonym.

The second largest ethnic group in Sumatra, and the one most closely related to the Malays in terms of language and culture, are the Minangkabau of the western central highlands. They now number about 5 million, and are known as staunch Muslims, while at the same time retaining vestiges of an unusual matrilineal kinship system that predates their conversion to Islam. This means that the traditional Minangkabau longhouses, fertile ricelands, and positions of leadership within the clan are all transmitted to the next generation through women. While men hold public positions of leadership, they inherit these through their mothers—and when they retire they are replaced by their sisters' sons.

A third major Islamic group inhabits Sumatra's strategic northern coast. The Acehnese, who number about 3 million today, also speak a language related to Malay, and are best known for their fierce resistance against the Dutch during a 30-year *jihad* (holy war) from 1873 to 1903. Long before this, in the 17th century, Aceh was in fact the most powerful Islamic kingdom in the region. Today, Islam still rules the hearts of the Acehnese, and on Fridays the faithful fill Banda Aceh's stately Grand Mosque while the town's shops are shuttered tight. Just as among the Minangkabau, and despite Islam's favoring of males, Acehnese village life revolves around women. Upon marriage, a man usually moves to his wife's village, where her family provides them a house.

Overleaf: *A Karo Batak festival ca. 1920. Photo courtesy of Antiquariaat Acanthus, Utrecht.*

In the highlands of central Aceh live the Gayo, all of whom are Muslim. Their language, like that of the Acehnese, is remarkable for its many borrowings from Mon-Khmer, a language group of mainland Southeast Asia. Unlike the Acehnese, however, the Gayo are patrilineal, and in the majority of cases, a bride moves to her hudband's village. Gayo who live around the edges of Lake Tawar harvest carp and a minnow-like fish called *depik* from the lake; coffee and tea are other major products from this region.

The Gayo fight with words. Poetic duels, *didong*, were once performed at weddings between pairs of speakers representing the families of bride and groom. Later, *didong* helped defuse hostilities between villages, and more recently men have turned this verbal art into a competition between clubs or teams composed of lead singers supported by an encircling chorus.

Christian converts

While the coastal and urban areas of the island are predominantly Muslim, large areas of Sumatra are now mainly Christian, and in fact more Christians live on this island than any other in Indonesia. German Lutheran missionaries working with the Toba Batak enjoyed early and widespread success. Today, the Toba Batak church is the largest Christian body in Indonesia.

In contrast, the Dutch Reformed missionaries who worked in the nearby Karo Batak region met decades of resistance. As a result, the Christian Karo have become a majority only since the 1950s, when an indigenous church emerged. The Simalungun Batak, once part of the Toba church, have separated into their own ethnic denomination.

The hymns and the liturgy in all these ethnic Batak churches are in the vernacular languages, but just as throughout Indonesia, these ethnic churches face competition from Catholic and Pentecostal denominations which operate through the medium of Indonesian, and whose congregations are ethnically mixed.

Ethnic Groups of Sumatra

Acehnese
Gayo
Malay
Sichule
Batak (six groups)
Niha
Orang Laut (scattered settlements)
Minangkabau
Malay
Kerinci
Kubu
Malay
Mentawai
Rejang
Malay
Komering
Enggano
Lampung

About 10 percent of the Angkola Batak who live to the south of the Toba are also Christian, but the majority, like the Mandailing Batak to the south in South Tapanuli, are Muslim. Other pockets of Christianity include the islands of Nias and Mentawai off the west coast, and some of the original inhabitants of the island of Enggano.

A patchwork of peoples

While most of Sumatra's people live as farmers, small groups such as the Kubu of Jambi Province and the Sakai of the Riau Islands live mainly by fishing and hunting along swampy southern rivers. Another group, the Orang Laut—literally "sea people" but often called sea gypsies or even sea pirates—live in boats among the hundreds of small islands in the Riau Archipelago.

Lake Kerinci, surrounded by wet rice terraces in the highlands of western Jambi Province, is home to the Kerinci people. Lacustrine fishing and tea cultivation supplement a rice economy. Like the Minangkabau, the Kerinci are matrilineal and construct longhouses for matrilineally extended families, but their longhouses are unique in the archipelago for having no communal passage or gallery linking the family apartments. While a man attaches himself to his wife's family, he retains membership in his natal family and lives partly at his own longhouse, where he helps to manage his lineage property and the affairs of his sister's children.

Bengkulu Province is home to the Rejang, who call themselves "We the People of Jang." Their mythical ancestor, Jang, was reputed to be of the royal family of Java's Majapahit kingdom. He is said to have settled in Sumatra in the 14th century, and had four sons who became the ancestors of the four patrilineal clans that today constitute Rejang society, a people numbering around 200,000. The Rejang region spans a diverse terrain, from the coast up gentle foothills to highland peaks covered in tropical rainforest.

Rejang was one of the last regions in Sumatra to accept Islam, so the pre-Islamic focus on ancestor spirits remains strong. Each of Rejang's clans claims dominion over its own territory. The oldest village in each of these territories contains a sacred shrine associated with its founding ancestor. Villages and lineages also have their ancestral shrines, so pilgrimage to the principal clan shrine occur only for extremely important purposes.

To the west of Palembang, near the town of Lahat, the Pasemah Highlands contain megalithic remains dated to AD 100. This statuary, the most extensive of its kind in the archipelago, consists of many animal and human figures as well as dolmens, menhirs and stone cist graves. Although the Pasemah people converted to Islam in the early 20th century, they continue to visit these shrines, and others on Mt. Dempo, to redeem ancestral

ALAIN COMPOST

vows. Although similar to the Rejang in their social organization and even their founding mythology, the Pasemah were bitter enemies of the Rejang, and the lowland Malays as well, in the precolonial era.

The Lampung region at Sumatra's southern tip contains several ethnic groups with different cultural histories, including many Javanese who have migrated here in large numbers, both spontaneously and through the government's transmigration programs. One of the most numerous indigenous peoples of this region, the Abung, say they originated in the mountains to the west where, in the 15th century, they maintained a megalithic culture similar to that of Nias. Headhunting and human sacrifice brought them into conflict with neighboring peoples, especially lowland Malays, who finally drove them into their current setting around 1450.

Abung society is composed of numerous patrilineal clans. Each clan maintains a separate house, occupied most of the time by only a few elderly people. Villages contain as many as 3,000 people and 120 clan houses, but working adults and children spend most of their time in small seasonal settlements outside the village, maintaining their swidden gardens. They return to the village for initiation ceremonies or other special events. Initiations usher men into a series of ranks that indicate their wealth. Formerly, headhunting was a precondition for the highest rank, and initiates to this rank were enthroned on a dolmen of stone.

Although the Dutch attempted to stop their headhunting and human sacrifices, the Abung continued these practices surreptitiously into the 19th century. Like all their neighbors in the region, the Abung are now Muslims. In their modern version of initiation rites, called *papadon*, dancing substitutes for headhunting, and a buffalo is sacrificed instead of a human.

Into the modern world

In the last 20 years, Sumatra's natural resources—particularly oil and natural gas—have helped fuel Indonesia's rapid economic growth. This growth has resulted in a new emphasis on education and on highway construction, which together with newspapers, films and television are increasingly drawing the peoples of Sumatra into a national community and into the world economy. Signs of this emphasis—from the newly-completed Trans-Sumatra Highway running the length of the island, to the puffing gas and oil refineries of Lhokseumawe and Palembang—are everywhere to be seen.

— *Rita Smith Kipp*

Opposite: *A couple in Palembang display the traditional Malay wedding costume, imitating the style of ancient Srivijayan Malay royalty.*
Below: *A wedding celebration in Lampung.*

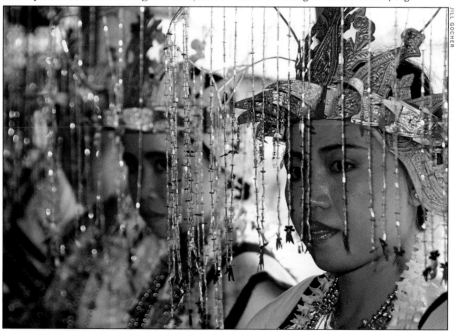

JILL GOCHER

ARCHITECTURE

ARCHITECTURE

The House with Horns and a Tail

The island of Sumatra contains some of Indonesia's richest and most fascinating traditions of vernacular, or domestic, architecture. Even the most casual observer can hardly fail to be impressed by the imposing scale of these buildings, by their ingenious nail-free construction and by the vigor and delicacy of their carved and painted decorations.

The diversity of traditional house styles found on the island is truly astounding. Around Lake Toba alone, for example, are to be found several distinctive styles belonging to the Toba, Karo and Simalungun Batak peoples—while the houses of the Mandailing Batak to the south are different again. The traditional homes of the Minangkabau of West Sumatra are equally unique—renowned for their beautiful floral carving and elegant, soaring eaves.

The Gayo people to the north of Lake Toba formerly dwelt in large multifamily houses holding up to 60 people. Each family had an apartment in the center of the house, with a men's gallery at the front and a women's gallery at the back. Acehnese houses, found along the island's north coast, are airy and well-ventilated, with large shuttered windows and elaborate woodcarving.

But perhaps the most breathtaking Sumatran architecture is found on the island of Nias. Houses stand in rows beside long, stone-paved streets, dominated—as in the famous village of Bawömataluo—by a massive chief's house resting on vertical and diagonal pillars fashioned from the trunks of giant ironwood trees.

Ancient origins

The observer of this astonishing architectural heritage will ask why so many of these houses—particularly the Batak and the Minangkabau—appear stylistically related, not only to each other but to the houses of other Indonesian peoples, such as the Toraja of Sulawesi. The most notable shared features are the pile foundations, the extended or saddle-shaped roof ridge, and the decorative, horn-shaped gable finials. What ancient historical link explains the origin and spread of this remarkable style?

The earliest surviving images of pile-built structures with saddle roofs are engraved on bronze drums found in the area of Dongson

KAL MULLER

in what is now northern Vietnam. The culture associated with these drums dates from ca. 500 BC–AD 100, and Dongson drums were traded throughout the archipelago as prestige items. Early theories about "waves" of Dongson migration into Indonesia have now been discounted, however, and it is unlikely that an architectural style could have been spread simply by pictures on drums. Much more probable is that the style was already old when the drums were cast, and that the images are simply its earliest surviving representations.

House styles ancestral to those you see today in Sumatra were probably developed in ancient times by Austronesian-speaking migrants. The Austronesians—ancestors of most modern-day Indonesians—originated from a homeland somewhere in southern China and began to migrate into these islands from Taiwan and the Philippines 6,000 years ago. Subsequently, they colonized the islands of the Pacific, and reached as far as Madagascar by AD 400, bringing with them their distinctive building style. Pile buildings with saddle roofs are found as far east as Micronesia, an area settled by Austronesians some time after 2000 BC, and saddle roofs, often of impressive proportions, are a feature of men's houses in New Guinea.

The survival of this ancient style of architecture seems to rest on its aesthetic or symbolic appeal, rather than a commitment to a particular mode of construction. Minangkabau and Batak houses, for example, both have pointed eaves and extended ridge lines, but these are produced by quite different building techniques.

In the Toba Batak house, the living space is essentially created by the roof, which rests on top of very low walls. The rafters are angled outward to produce the projecting gable, and strengthened by means of diagonal ties. In the Minangkabau house, on the other hand, the living space is formed by the walls, which are much taller in proportion to the roof than in Batak houses. The roof sits on top of this space, supported by a truss and crossbeam structure and built up into tall points by means of many small rafters and battens.

Symbolic Acehnese houses

Acehnese homeowners are women. If they can afford it, the parents provide each of their daughters with a house when she marries—otherwise they simply present their own house to a married daughter and move into the kitchen. During the day the house is the woman's domain. Men spend most of their time in public places, or migrate (*merantau*) to earn a living through trade, re-

Opposite: *The elegant, upward-sweeping eaves of a traditional Minangkabau house in Pandai Sikat.* **Below:** *Toba Batak houses on Samosir Island.*

KAL MULLER

turning home only at long intervals.

Though subdued in their outward form, Acehnese houses are rich in cosmological and symbolic significance. The front verandah is the most public and formal part. Here men sit. The rear is private, containing the kitchen and the women's entrance. Male and female are symbolically united in the central room, which has the highest floor level, and contains the two main house posts—called "prince" and "princess"—against which the bride and the groom are seated on their wedding day. This is also where the newly-married couple sleeps. At the top of the house, beneath the gable, is a platform for storing family valuables and heirlooms. Outside at floor level runs a skirting-board, often elaborately decorated. The wall separating the verandah from the inner part of the house may also be decorated with intricate woodcarving.

Monumental Nias villages

South Nias has produced some of Indonesia's most astonishing architecture. In the 19th century, the area was ruled by a warlike aristocracy which enriched itself by raiding outlying districts for slaves. The nobles staged elaborate feasts by which they raised their status on the social ladder. The greatest of such feasts entitled a chief to construct a great house (*omo sebua*).

A stunning example dating from 1863 survives today in Bawömataluo village in South Nias. It is 22.7 m tall, and is ornamented inside with carved ebony wall panels depicting ancestral thrones, male and female ornaments, animals and birds, and even a Dutch steamship mounted with cannons.

South Nias villages are remarkably large, with up to 6,000 inhabitants, as slave-raiding and headhunting made smaller communities too vulnerable. Most villages have a single main street paved with stone, sometimes crossed by a shorter street at the top forming a giant "T." Some settlements are approached by huge flights of stone stairs. The bowed fronts of the houses—reminiscent of Dutch galleons—form a continuous line on both sides. Stone monuments, commemorating past feasts and important funerals, stand before the houses of the nobility.

A distinctive feature of the houses are the massive ironwood foundation pillars, both vertical and diagonal. The diagonal pillars give added stability to the tall house structure in this earthquake-prone region. The flexibility of the house in tremors is enhanced by the fact that the piles rest on top of their foundation stones, a feature also found elsewhere in the archipelago.

The founding ancestors of South Nias communities originally came from central Nias. Here can be seen houses of an older and plainer style, without the projecting curved front, as well as different kinds of worked stone monuments. You will need the help of a guide to visit this remote area, and you should check on the weather—rivers become impassable in the rainy season.

Houses of North Nias are unusual in having an oval plan. They are less monumental in scale, but share certain features such as the use of diagonal piles, and the cutting of flaps in the roof, which can be propped open to serve as windows. Graves, now Christian in style, continue to be located next to the houses in the traditional manner.

Batak houses

The countryside around lake Toba is dotted with traditional Toba, Karo and Simalungun Batak villages as well as elaborate concrete tombs in the form of houses. The tombs are built with great ceremony and expense to house the remains of the deceased ancestors of a particular family. This traditional concern for the dead remains of great importance to the Toba, and has been integrated with Christian practice. Older sarcophagi of carved stone may also be seen on Samosir Island in Lake Toba.

COEN PEPPLINKHUIZEN

Toba houses stand on foundations of piles braced with cross-beams, forming a space beneath the house where buffaloes were once stalled. The walls are covered with graceful flowing and spiral decorations—unbroken lines are thought to provide protection to the occupants. Friezes with figures may also be seen, and three-dimensional carved protective "monsters" are found at the corners and top of the facade.

On the northeastern shore of the lake stands Pematang Purba, site of the palace of the former rajas of the Simalungun Batak, now a museum. The impressively long house has a realistically modelled buffalo-head on the front gable-end, and a tail made of the tough black fibre of the sugar-palm at the rear. Inside is the raja's private apartment, and ten separate hearths, each formerly the domain of one of his wives. Nearby is a council house with an elaborately carved central pillar, against which the ruler used to sit while giving judgement.

The Karo people living on the north of the lake developed an interesting variation on the extended ridge line, with multiple decorative gables topped by realistically-modelled buffalo heads which protected the occupants from harm. Some fine examples survive in villages around Berastagi, such as Lingga. Traditionally, houses were occupied by four or eight related families, each with its own hearth. A distinctive structure is the *geriten* or "head-house," a miniature house to store the skulls of revered ancestors.

The Minangkabau house

The Minangkabau people are well-known for their matrilineal kinship system. This means that houses and rice fields are passed down from mother to daughter. A typical Minangkabau compound will consist of an older, original house surrounded by others that have been added by married sisters and daughters of the parent family.

The elegant, sweeping eaves of traditional houses are a common sight amidst the lush green Minangkabau landscape. These pointed eaves, locals say, remind them of the legendary "victorious buffalo" (*menang kerbau*) from which their name is said to derive. On larger buildings the roof is tiered to form a series of four or six points, often with an additional peak over a porch set at right angles to the main structure. In the past, huge *rumah gadang* or "great houses" accommodated up to 100 people related to a single female ancestor. Inside was an open gallery with separate sleeping apartments off it. A surviving example—64 m long!—can be visited at the hilltop village of Sulitair, near Lake Singkarak.

Minangkabau rice barns and council houses (*balairung* or *balai adat*) are also built with pointed eaves. The ancestral village of Pariangan in the Tanahdatar valley, contains some very old examples, as does nearby Pagarruyung—site of the former palace of the Minangkabau rajas. The original palace was unfortunately destroyed by fire in 1976, but it has now been rebuilt (on a somewhat enlarged scale) as a museum.

—*Roxana Waterson*

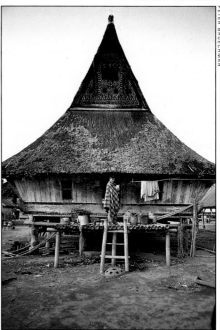

Left: *The chief's house in Bawömataluo, South Nias (1863).* **Above:** *A carved panel from the same house, depicting animals and a Dutch warship.* **Right:** *A Karo Batak house, with its pointed eaves, low walls and outwardly angled rafters.*

LANGUAGE & LITERATURE

Court Malay to Bahasa Indonesia

Sumatra's great size and cultural diversity is reflected in its wealth of languages, which range from the elegant and elaborate court Malay still spoken in the former palace centers of Palembang and Riau, to the rapidly vanishing dialects spoken by a few coastal, boat-dwelling *orang laut* (sea nomads). Most of Sumatra's languages are closely related, and belong to the huge family of Austronesian languages which stretches in a great island arc from Madagascar on the African coast to Easter Island in the eastern Pacific.

Northern Sumatra is dominated by the 1.5 million speakers of Acehnese, who surround a much smaller pocket of Gayo speakers. To the south, around Lake Toba, lie the Batak heartlands, with their many Batak dialects, some so different as almost to constitute separate languages. The most widely-spoken dialect is Toba Batak, followed by Karo, Ang-

BODLEIAN LIBRARY, OXFORD

kola, Mandailing, Dairi, Simalungun and Alas. Four million Minangkabau speakers—the second largest linguistic group on the island—are found in the fertile highlands of West Sumatra, while moving farther south, the provinces of Riau, Jambi and South Sumatra are home to numerous dialects of Malay. Rejang is spoken in parts of Bengkulu, and Lampung is spoken on the southern tip of the island. Several distinct languages are found in the four island groups along the west coast of Sumatra—Simuelue, Nias, Mentawai and Enggano.

Attached like a single-hued lining to this linguistic coat of many colors is the Malay language—for centuries the *lingua franca* of the archipelago, and forerunner of the national language, Bahasa Indonesia. Spoken as a mother tongue by about 11 million Sumatrans, Malay is indigenous to the east of the island but has spread throughout the archipelago as the language of trade and Islam, superseding local languages as a literary and courtly medium in the kingdoms of Aceh, West Sumatra and Riau.

When Sultan Iskandar Muda of Aceh corresponded with King James I of England in 1615, he wrote in Malay, not Acehnese. At the other end of the social scale, Malay has long served as the language of the market place in Sumatra's cosmopolitan port cities. The first Malay phrasebook for foreign merchants, printed in Amsterdam in 1603, contains sample conversations for purchasing provisions, weighing pepper and extracting funds from a recalcitrant debtor, as well as colorful phrases for driving a hard bargain.

Traditional literature

Traditional Sumatran scripts can be divided into two types—those that trace their origin to a South Indian script, and those that derive from a Persian-Arabic script. The earliest example of the latter is an Old Malay stone inscription from 7th century Srivijaya (Palembang). The ravages of the tropical climate have left no traces of texts on more perishable materials from this period, but the Batak and Lampung scripts also belong to this Indic group, and are still in occasional use. The arrival of Islam led to the development of a modified form of the Arabic script known as Jawi—used to write Malay, Acehnese and Minangkabau until the early decades of this century.

Manuscripts from Sumatra come in all shapes and sizes, and use bamboo, tree-bark, palm leaf and bone as well as paper. Sumatra's most important literature is written in the Malay language. Prose works include histories and romances; tales of the Prophet and Muslim heroes, like Alexander the Great (known in Malay as Iskandar Zulkarnain, the "two horned"); and theological, legal, moral treatises. The *Hikayat Raja-raja Pasai*, which relates the coming of Islam to the north coast of Sumatra in the 13th century, is the oldest known Malay history.

The two main genres of Malay poetry are the narrative *syair* and the *pantun*. The four-line stanzas of the *syair* with their a-a-a-a end-rhyme are believed to be the creation of Hamzah Fansuri, a mystic poet who lived in Barus in the 16th century. The *pantun* is a quatrain with an a-b-a-b rhyme in which the first couplet contains a veiled allusion, the meaning of which is usually elaborated in the final couplet. Written literatures also exist in Acehnese—in prose (*haba*) and poetry (*hikayat*)—and in Minangkabau, where the most important epic is the *Kaba Cindur Mata*.

In Sumatra, as in many parts of Indonesia, the dividing line between written and oral literature is blurred, for in semi-literate societies texts were usually composed and written down to be recited to an audience. Professional Sijobang singers in West Sumatra are still in demand at weddings, circumcision ceremonies and other feasts, where recitations of the adventures of Prince Anggun Nan Tungga last all night. (Sijobang performances

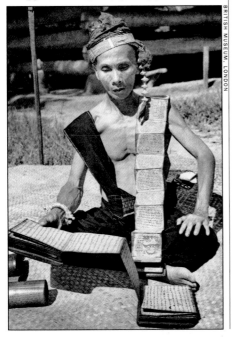

BRITISH MUSEUM, LONDON

are now also marketed on cassettes.) Sumatran peoples have a rich stock of folklore, including proverbs, mantras and animal fables—the mousedeer being the hero.

One of the most intriguing written traditions of Sumatra are *pustaha*, the bark books of the Batak. These concertina-shaped books are concerned solely with magic, divination and medicine, and were used as *aide-mem-oires* by apprentice sorcerers during their period of study with a Batak priest or *dato*. Amongst their contents might be oracles for reading the entrails of a chicken, or for divining the portents of the time of day of a child's birth ("a boy-child born at a certain moment will die in war or of smallpox; if it is a girl, she may die of suicide," etc.), as well as recipes for love philtres and poisons.

Modern literature

By the beginning of the 20th century, increasing Western influence manifested itself in a growing popular literature in Malay. Medan became a center for the publishing of "penny dreadfuls," the melodramatic romances, adventures and detective booklets owing much to the stories of Jules Verne and Arthur Conan Doyle.

In the 1920s, when Balai Pustaka—the Dutch colonial government publishing house in Batavia—began to issue novels in Malay, the earliest works were by Minangkabau writers. Many novels centered on the cultural clash between the modernizing influence of Western education and the strictures and arranged marriages of traditional Minang society. Both in the period before Independence and afterwards, Sumatran writers have been in the forefront of modern Indonesian literature.

Armijn Pane's *Belenggu* (Shackles), published in 1940, has been hailed as the first Indonesian psychological novel, and poets like Chairil Anwar and Rivai Apin were influenced by T.S. Eliot and W.H. Auden. Yet the homeland of Sumatran writers often shines through their work—from the forests of Mochtar Lubis' childhood, which form the backdrop to his novel *Harimau* (Tiger), to the images of Lake Toba which permeate the existentialist poetry of Sitor Situmorang.

—*Annabel Teh Gallop*

Opposite: *A letter from Sultan Iskandar Muda of Aceh to King James I of England, one of the earliest extant examples (1615) of Malay written with the use of Arabic script.* **Left:** *A Batak* dato *priest consults his* pustaha *bark books.*

FOOD

The Art of Sumatran Cooking

As the 17th century traveler Sir John Chardin noted, religion—as well as history and geography—has always played an important role in determining a people's diet. And so it is in Sumatra. Pork is the major dietary barrier separating the island's Muslim majority from the Christian minority. Christian Bataks around Lake Toba and elsewhere in North Sumatra eat pork (sometimes also dog), and in their village settlements they often keep pigs. For Muslims, however, the pig is ritually unclean, and may only be eaten if one is faced with starvation.

Muslims nevertheless enjoy many other meats—including the flesh of buffaloes, goats, ducks, lambs, chickens and fish—as well as eggs, fruits and vegetables. Since the 1970s, however, many Sumatran Muslims have developed an additional concern for whether or not the meat they are served is *halal*—slaughtered according to Islamic law by cutting the animal's throat while uttering the name of Allah.

History and geography are also important, of course. After centuries of trading contacts, Sumatran cooking now reflects influences from all around the archipelago (Java, Manado, Bali) as well as from abroad (India, Middle East, China, Holland). In the North Sumatran capital of Medan, for example, you will find several dishes that show a distinct Indian and Arab influence alongside the usual Indonesian dishes. This can be seen in the use of dried seeds and aromatic spices such as coriander, cumin, fennel, cardamom and cinnamon in the preparation of goat dishes. *Gulai kumah* and *gulai bagar* are two goat curries which are rich in flavor, but unlike native Sumatran dishes not particularly spicy.

Near the coasts, seafood features prominently on most restaurant menus. One of the most popular dishes in Palembang, South Sumatra, is *empek-empek*—a fish dumpling (sometimes also stuffed with egg) served hot with a bowl of spicy sauce made of chilli, garlic, dried prawns, palm sugar, soya sauce and vinegar. In addition, Palembang is known throughout Indonesia for the quality of its *kerupuk* (deep-fried tapioca crackers flavored with seafood and spices), since the *kerupuk* made here have a higher proportion of fish or prawn than those produced elsewhere in the archipelago.

Some like it hot!

Sumatra has many regional cooking styles, however the best-known is undoubtedly *masakan padang*—the fiery-hot cuisine of the Minangkabau of West Sumatra, named after the provincial capital of Padang. Padang-style restaurants are found throughout Indonesia, and a number of Padang dishes have achieved national and even international popularity. Today, the famous meat dish known as *rendang* is served in restaurants as far afield as Tokyo, New York and London, and can be found in almost every Dutch town.

Rendang is usually made with beef, cut up into cubes and cooked in coconut cream with a spice mixture of garlic, shallots, chillies, turmeric, galangal, green ginger (all finely ground), lemon grass, kaffir lime leaves, turmeric leaves and salt. Special care and attention are required during cooking so the mixture does not curdle or the pieces of meat disintegrate. Once the coconut cream reaches boiling point, the heat is reduced and the cooking continues until the mixture thickens. When finished, the *rendang* sauce turns to a rich, dark brown residue, but the pieces of meat should still be intact and slightly crisp on the outside.

The prolonged cooking and the spices, especially the chillies, preserve the meat, and it is common for *rendang* to be taken along on long journeys, such the pilgrimage to Mecca. *Rendang* is then both a reminder of home and a handy dish that saves time—as no cooking is needed apart from boiling the rice to eat with it! Solicitous Sumatran mothers cook, pack and send it to their children studying or working in the outer islands. If you eat *rendang*—and you should be sure not to miss it—be warned not to put a whole piece in your mouth at once. It is far too rich and spicy to be eaten whole. Break off a small part, then fold it into a spoonful of rice if you want to enjoy it. One should treat all spicy meat dishes with similar respect.

Padang restaurants, wherever you find them, have a unique way of serving their dishes which never fails to intrigue visitors from abroad. There is no need to order—soon after you sit down, the waiter arrives at your table with an array of small dishes precariously poised along both arms, and deposits them all on the table. You eat whatever you fancy from among these many dishes—sampling the curried eggs, fish, vegetables, chicken and meat, knowing you will only be charged for the number of pieces of egg, fish, chicken or meat that you eat. The sauce is free, and there are stories of skinflints who take a spoonful of sauce from each dish to flavor their rice to have a cheap meal!

Opposite: *Chilli paste, an important ingredient in most Sumatran food.* **Below:** *Spicey Padang food sold at an open-air lepau in Bukittinggi.*

ALAIN COMPOST

Experienced Padang restaurant-goers know exactly which dishes go well together, and make their choices accordingly. Those who are less experienced may find they end up with a plate full of clashing flavors. If in doubt, ask the proprietor for a *nasi rames*. This is a plate of white rice with several bits of meat and vegetable on top, sprinkled with gravy and *serundeng* (grated coconut, roasted with peanuts) and topped off with a *kerupuk*. It generally ends up being cheaper than getting the whole smorgasboard.

As is the custom throughout Indonesia, you eat with your right hand by compressing a bit of rice, meat and curry together with the tips of your fingers and pushing it into your mouth. Forks and spoons are also often provided now, but it is very bad form to stick the spoon you use for eating into the dishes of curry. Use a separate spoon for this!

The normal evening meal for a middle class family consists of four or five dishes and rice. These may include one or two meat dishes—say *gulai ayam* (curried chicken soup) and *dendeng* (sun-dried spicy beef)—as well as a vegetable dish, such as cucumber salad, and a selection of condiments such as *sambal* (chilli paste), pickles (*acar*) and *kerupuk*. The rice supplies the bulk of the meal, and its blandness is ideal for absorbing and combining the flavors of the various dishes.

Of course not all Padang cooking is hot. Try *opor ayam* (chicken simmered in corian-

der and coconut cream), *ayam goreng* (crisp fried chicken), or—a dish that all foreigners like—*pergedel* (meat and potato croquettes). Other dishes are prepared with only small amounts of chilli, such as *gado-gado* (vegetable salad with peanut sauce), and *sate*. The latter is found all over Indonesia and consists of pieces of meat marinated in spices and placed on bamboo skewers, then grilled over a bed of charcoal and served with sweet-spicy ground peanut sauce.

A special type of *sate* prepared in Padang needs a chapter all by itself. It consists of pieces of heart, tongue and tripe boiled in finely ground spices—coriander, cumin, galangal, turmeric, ginger, garlic, chilli and shallots—plus kaffir lemon leaf, lemon grass and salt. The meat is then cut into small pieces and threaded onto skewers. The broth of the meat is thickened with rice flour to make a pale yellow sauce. Sprinkled with fried onions, *sate padang* is a feast for the eyes as well as the stomach!

Vegetarians will delight in the variety of *tempe* dishes found in West Sumatra. *Tempe* is a kind of soybean cake prepared from boiled beans which are allowed to ferment, a process that takes three days. The finished product is firm and compact—the beans tightly bound together and covered evenly with a light coating of white mold, with an aroma reminiscent of fresh mushrooms. *Tempe* is a very cheap source of high-quality protein and is crunchy and tasty when fried. It may also be curried or stir–fried with vegetables, potatoes and chilies.

Drinks and snacks

Beer goes very well with most Sumatran dishes—the high-quality Bir Bintang and Anker produced in Indonesia is brewed according to traditional Dutch methods. The religious prohibition against imbibing alcoholic beverages does not command universal observance in Sumatra, and foreigners drinking beer generally do not cause offense. Locals, however, usually prefer to drink weak plain tea or iced water with their meals.

There is, incidentally, one locally produced food which is mildly alcoholic. Sumatrans are very fond of between-meal snacks, and one of the favorites is *tapai*, sometimes spelled *tapé*. Sumatran *tapai* is prepared from boiled or steamed black glutinous rice. Once the rice is cooled, it is sprinkled with a special yeast called *ragi tapé*; two tablets are needed for each kilo of rice. The rice then is placed in a basin with a lid, and wrapped in cloth and left in a warm place for three or four days to ferment.

When it is ready, the mixture is slightly effervescent and has a port-like fragrance. It is usually served with *lemang*—white glutinous rice cooked in a bamboo container lined with young banana leaves in thick, salted coconut cream. (Surprisingly, *tapai* also goes very well with vanilla ice cream!). It is available everyday in central Sumatra, but is especially popular during the fasting month, and around Idul Fitri (the festive celebration of the end of the fasting month).

Another popular snack specific to the region is *dadih* (buffalo yoghurt). It is sold in a small bamboo container and served with *emping*—glutinous rice flakes rinsed with boiling water to soften them—topped with freshly grated coconut and brown palm sugar. It is a very filling meal. *Dadih* is sold in almost every *kedai* or *lepau* (foodstall) all over the island.

On the road

When you travel by bus in Sumatra, foodsellers swarm around at every stop and bus terminal, calling out their wares. In their baskets are hard-boiled, salted duck eggs, tasty maize fritters, crispy fried banana slices (*rakik*), pieces of chopped sugarcane, and a variety of sweetmeats in banana leaves.

Practically every bus stop in Sumatra has one or two local specialities, and the same

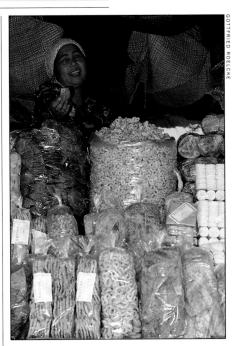

goes for train stations. Local women who are traveling on the buses will often buy a selection of these as gifts (*oleh–oleh*). When they visit relatives, it is unthinkable to arrive at a house empty-handed—one must have something to "open the door," as they say. There are always children around, and small gifts for them are always warmly welcomed.

The all-purpose banana leaf

Banana leaves, which can be found in abundance everywhere throughout the archipelago, are indispensable in all kinds of situations. They are tough, but when heated, are pliable and easily folded. They are mostly used to wrap food for steaming or cooking over charcoal, and as a wrapper for take-away food bought at a *kedai* or *lepau*. Small items and vegetables bought at the local market, such as *tapai*, bean sprouts or chillies, are usually wrapped up in banana leaves.

At a local *lepau* or *kedai* (foodstall), banana leaves may also serve as disposable plates or plate covers. They meet many needs for which we in the West use cling-wrap or aluminium foil. May they never give way to plastic which cannot be disposed of easily. Banana leaves are bio-degradable and a renewable resource!

—*Yohanni Johns*

Opposite: *Padang waiters showing off their skills.*
Above: *A woman selling snacks sold in her kedai.*

TRANS-SUMATRA HIGHWAY

The Great Traveling Road Show

The recently-completed Trans-Sumatra Highway runs the length of one of the world's largest islands—a distance of over 2,500 km. The journey from Bakauheni in the south to Banda Aceh in the north is truly one of Indonesia's great travel experiences, both for the stunning scenery you pass through and for the people you meet along the way.

However, the trip can equally become a nightmare of frustrations and uncomfortable conditions. Much depends on careful preparation, on having enough time, and on your response to the inevitable delays and minor irritations which all travelers experience in Indonesia. Patience and tolerance are invaluable qualities when traveling here, and will help ensure that your journey through some of the wildest and the least populated regions of the country will be an experience long remembered.

Only as a test of endurance should you take the highway straight through all the way from Jakarta to Banda Aceh. It is possible to do this—the journey takes about 60 hours and costs only $50. The old days of untold delays caused by collapsed bridges and washed-out roads are over. Today, the highway is paved, though your journey could come to a screeching halt if a landslide occurs, especially during the rainy season. But you will not be delayed for long. Maintenance crews show up promptly, as the highway is too important to the national economy for it to be closed more than a few hours.

Setting off: Lampung

Setting off from the south, the first leg of the Trans-Sumatra Highway runs 99 km from the Java-Sumatra ferry landing at Bakauheni, on the island's southeastern tip, up to Bandar Lampung—the capital of Lampung Province. Leaving the ferry landing, the road climbs up around Mt. Rajabasa, giving fine views of island-strewn Lampung Bay. Strands of clove trees line the hillsides, distinctive clumps of conical light green foliage.

A little over 60 km from Bakauheni, the road drops down to the coast, giving a tantalizing glimpse of Lampung Bay, its bright blue surface broken by several steep-sided islands and fishing platforms hovering over the water like giant water-spiders. Houses on stilts line the water's edge, separated from the road by a thin strip of mangrove swamp. A rail head heralds your entry into the provincial capital, and in a short while you find yourself among huge warehouses and docks.

The next stage of your Trans-Sumatra journey northward takes you 385 km in 9 hours to Muaraenim, through foothill plains skirting the eastern edge of the Bukit Barisan mountain range. The road cuts through rubber and oil palm plantations and fields of corn. There are lots of river crossings—all rivers flow eastward from the Bukit Barisan to the sea.

Stunning emerald-green *sawah* by the roadside are dotted with huts where watchmen stay to keep wild animals at bay. Your bus might have to make several stops to let long "coal trains" by. The red-tiled raised wooden houses, some sitting on ironwood logs two meters off the ground, are traditional Lampung or South Sumatra *rumah limas*, formerly fastened with ropes, not nails.

South Sumatra and Jambi

The highway continues northwest out of Muaraenim, crossing the Lematang River several times before reaching Lahat. Just after Muaraenim, you get a panoramic view of the Lematang River against a backdrop of a primary forest. In the early morning and late afternoon, herds of water buffalo and cattle compete for road space with buses and trucks. Look for an unusually shaped mountain, Bukit Serelo—a bare, finger-like projection on top of a steep-sided hill, standing apart from the foothills of the Bukit Barisan.

Lahat is the place to get off to explore the Pasemah Highlands. However, if you get off the bus here, getting a good seat for the next stage of your journey is a matter of luck. The highway north of Lahat offers plenty of swaying curves and, if the weather is clear, glimpses of the Bukit Barisan range to the west. This is landslide country during the rainy season, but bulldozers quickly clear the road. Coffee is grown on the steep hills and a rubber plantation stretches for several kilometers by the roadside. The next town is Tebingtinggi ("high embankment"), which sits above the Musi River—one of the largest and most important rivers in Sumatra.

The highway then straightens out, and you speed along to Lubuklinggau, on the junction of the main road west to Bengkulu. The tin-roofed houses whiz by your bus window with monotonous regularity for the next 248 km until you cross a bridge over the Merangin River, just outside Bangko. You are now in Jambi Province, and a sideroad to the west from Bangko leads you into the dense jungle and tea plantations of the Kerinci-Seblat National Park around Lake Kerinci.

The next stage, 92 km from Bangko to Muarabungo, seems to take no time at all. Muarabungo is the jumping-off point for Jambi, a long 212 km to the east.

Outside Muarabungo, the bridge over the Tebo River at Telukpanjang offers a view of a riverside mosque. Fifty km further on, the wide Batang Hari River provides irrigation for extensive *sawah* and you are now in West Sumatra. Along the roadside, you begin to see your first Minangkabau style roofs.

West Sumatra

After Kiliranjao the scenery at last improves as the highway winds up into the Bukit Barisan mountains. Here are stunning limestone formations (called "karst towers") and *sawah* which go right up to the edge of the jungle. The tall, white trunks of the primary forest match the pale white outcroppings of limestone. In places, the vegetation grows right from a vertical cliff! The first of the karst towers, small but impressive, rears up on your right at Sungai Langsat. There are five larger

GOTTFRIED ROELCKE

Opposite: *Road conditions have improved considerably since this photo was taken, ca. 1920, but most roads were first built in the colonial period.*
Right: *A winding stretch of road near Bukittinggi.*

ones ahead—awesome oval, dome and stupa-shaped freaks of nature. During the rainy season there are frequent landslides, and your vehicle might have to stop for a couple of hours while bulldozers clear the way.

Having passed through the mountains, you enter a more hospitable landscape of rice fields, small Minang houses and hillsides covered in ferns, before entering a gorge leading into the busy commercial town of Solok.

The next stretch, 53 km from Solok to Padangpanjang, follows the banks of the Sumani River north to Lake Singkarak, a huge and immensely scenic crater lake. The highway hugs the eastern lakeshore all the way to a bridge over the Umbilin River, which drains Lake Singkarak.

At the northern end of the lake, the highway rises to offer some good views before cutting north and east through fertile rice fields to Pandangpanjang. To your right is Mt. Marapi, an active volcano which sometimes emits puffs of smoke, and Mt. Singgalang. Both are about the same height —just a bit under 2,900 m.

Break your journey at Bukittinggi; this is the place to spend a few days recuperating. It's about halfway up or down the island, and there are lots of good hotels, restaurants and pleasant sidetrips to be made in the area (see WEST SUMATRA).

After Bukittinggi, the next leg of the Trans-Sumatra Highway is a grueling 500-km run up to Prapat—the gateway to Lake Toba and Samosir Island, in North Sumatra. It's a long trip, about 15 hours, and if you can afford the time, it is better to break the journey in Padangsidempuan or Sibolga, so as to cross over the Bukit Barisan mountains again in daylight.

The road is paved all the way, but it's narrow and there are lots of curves. Even with a good driver, the crossing can be hair-raising, as you twist and wind up the mountain pass, barely missing oncoming lorries and coaches. Fortunately, there's not much traffic on the road and the coach can't go much faster than 40 km per hour.

Try to be awake at the town of Bonjol, home of the famous Muslim leader of the Padri wars, Imam Bonjol. There's a large, sabre-wielding statue of him in town on a horse—look to the right. Just out of Bonjol, there's a monument marking the equator.

From Bonjol the road climbs up to Lubuksikaping, then descends into a long river valley with rice fields to the right. There are no more steep descents but plenty of jungle-clad

gorges as you wind your way down to Muarasipongi and Kotanopan, where your eyes are soothed by rice fields dotted with neat little huts and bridges by the river. You are now in North Sumatra.

North Sumatra

From Muarasipongi, the road follows the Batang Gadis River past Kotanopan. The Purba Baru village area here is the center of a huge *pesantren* or Islamic koranic school, the largest in Indonesia, with students from all over the country. Hundreds of tiny huts house boys, aged six to twelve, who spend their primary school years here.

Traditional Minangkabau houses are very few now since you are in Batakland. The people of this region are Mandailing Bataks, forcefully converted to Islam more than one and a half centuries ago.

Panyabungan is a crowded market town which bustles with activity on Monday, market day. Gaudy *becak*s, vegetable-laden housewives, and motorized *becak mesin* all add noise and color to the market scene. As you leave Panyabungan, you see tranquil white mosques set in the middle of rice fields. A stretch of brick factories follows, then the large town of Padangsidempuan greets you by nightfall. This is a good place for an overnight stay, or a change of bus for the one and a half hour drive to Sibolga.

Aside from a few hair-raising bends, the

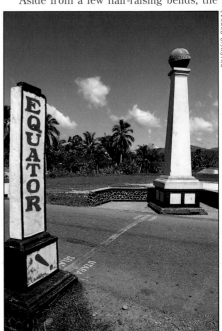

EVRARD DIJKSTRA

next stage, to Prapat and Lake Toba, is a pleasant 5-hour ride. The first part, to Tarutung, takes about 3 hours, past roadside markets and denuded hills with isolated stands of pine. After an hour or so, a pass below Mt. Sibualbuali (with a large hotel) marks the division between the Muslim and Christian Bataklands, and churches begin to replace mosques along the roadside.

It's a short half-hour hop on a straight road from Tarutung to the busy market town of Siborongborong. A little way further on

you start winding down to Lake Toba past spectacular rice fields and impressive graves crowned with figures of wide-eyed men on white stallions, elders in *adat* costume, and traditional Toba Batak houses—including one almost big enough to live in. The massive sepulchre on the right, a short way off the road past Balige, is that of the Batak ruler Raja Tano. From here the road winds around lakeside hills to emerge at Prapat.

From Prapat to Medan, the journey takes 4-5 hours. As the road climbs up from Prapat, there are magnificent views of Lake Toba. Then the road winds down through the mountains on a long, gentle slope to the sea via Pematangsiantar and Tebingtinggi. Lush rice fields and estates of rubber and oil palm line the road, while churches are gradually replaced again by mosques.

The final leg: Aceh

The long, 600-km ride from Medan to Banda Aceh takes 14 hours. There's plenty of good scenery, but the only logical place to break up the journey is at Bireuen, about two-thirds of the way up, for a side trip up to Lake Tawar. At Sabat, 17 km out of Medan, the road crosses a wide river and the traffic starts to thin. The road now passes large oil palm plantations and ageing rubber estates. Keep an eye out for a superb mosque on the left just before Tanjungpura. The scenery alternates between broad rice fields (some

stretching two km from the road), coconut groves, single and triple domed mosques, large rivers, bridges over estuaries overgrown with mangroves and nipah palms. Canoes, small boats and houses perched on stilts crowd around the estuary bridges. Further ahead are the grass-covered foothills of the hazy Bukit Barisan range.

The town of Lhokseumawe, which is set a couple of kilometers off the highway, boasts huge banks, government buildings, shopping centers, satellite dishes and five-star hotels and restaurants alongside a small, prosperous "downstream" area of small open shops. Back on the highway heading out of town, you can see several large LNG storage tanks, and flares from oil wells.

Traveling further into the province of Aceh, you will see more the girls wearing the *kerudung* or *jilbab*, the Muslim head scarf which leaves only the face exposed. These girls attend Islamic schools. Mosques here are often roofed with ironwood shingles.

Throughout much of Aceh, the Trans-Sumatra Highway follows the tracks of a long-abandoned Dutch railway. Though much of the tracks remain, most of the bridges have fallen into the river.

On the last leg of the highway, the road leaves the rice fields and coastal towns to cut across the northernmost section of the Bukit Barisan mountains. There are lots of curves as you ride over hills covered with grass, scrub; and later you pass through tall, deserted pine forests. Then, mercifully, the bus stops swaying as the road straightens out to follow the river and fertile rice valley which leads to Banda Aceh at the northernmost tip of Sumatra.

—*Kal Muller*

Opposite: *The equator marker in Bonjol, West Sumatra.* **Above, left:** *A heavily-laden intercity bus squeezes under a low-lying railway bridge.* **Above, right:** *At a crossroads in West Sumatra.*

PART II

Introducing Medan

Medan, the provincial capital of North Sumatra, is a cosmopolitan city of over 2 million inhabitants and a booming commercial center for the region's huge oil and agro-businesses. As a result of major international investments in plantation agriculture from the 1870s onward, it grew from a tiny village to a prosperous colonial city of some 60,000 people by 1943. Following independence, the population exploded at an even more rapid rate, with a dramatic influx of various Batak and other groups from all over Sumatra and Indonesia. Today it is by far the largest city on Sumatra, and the fourth largest in the nation—after Jakarta, Surabaya and Bandung.

Medan's inhabitants are notoriously forward and commercially astute, and physically the city has little to recommend it. Although numerous improvements have been effected in recent years, it has been difficult to sustain an adequate infrastructure to support such a large and growing urban population. Medan, like Topsy, "just growed"—and there have been major problems with electricity, water, drainage and pollution, many currently being tackled by the city's administration and all requiring urgent attention. Lower-lying parts of the city are increasingly subject to flooding due, at least in part, to the deforestation of the hinterland.

Early trading settlements

Some 10,000 years ago, neolithic hunters and gatherers of the "Hoabinhian" stone tool complex settled in the swampy estuarine areas around what is now Medan, accumulating enormous mounds of discarded shells from the seafood they consumed. These shell middens provide us with one of the few tantalizing glimpses of neolithic habitation in western Indonesia, but sadly they have been all but destroyed by commercial lime burners.

By the early second millennium AD—but probably much earlier—Arab, Indian and Chinese traders arrived on these coasts in search of valuable aromatic tree resins from the valleys and slopes of the Bukit Barisan —resins such as camphor (*kapur barus*) and benzoin (*kemenyan*) that were much in demand by the peoples of Asia for medicinal and ritual purposes. Traces of an early trading settlement has been found at Kota Cina near Belawan, the port north of Medan.

In subsequent centuries, riverine communities of traders and seafarers established themselves along the coast under the leadership of Islamic Malay rulers, to take advantage of an increasingly profitable international trade. By the early 16th century, a struggle for the rich resources of the hinterland (especially pepper) ensued between the rulers of Aru—a Malay kingdom based at Deli Tua, near modern-day Medan—and the kingdom of Aceh at Sumatra's northern tip.

The Acehnese attacked and subdued Aru in 1536, and a Portuguese adventurer by the name of Pinto tells of the attack and the struggle of Aru's queen against Aceh. This may also be reflected in the Malay (and Karo) legend of Puteri Hijau, the "Green Princess." Aru was finally conquered by Aceh in the early 17th century, and Aceh thereafter controlled the coasts of both eastern and western Sumatra until the early 19th century.

The wealth and independence of Deli and other Malay polities in the area increased dramatically during the 19th century with the development of a lucrative pepper trade with the British, even though the authority of their rulers was largely confined to areas immediately around the river mouths. The Sultan of Deli, for example, controlled an area extending along the lower reaches of the Deli River, from its mouth to Deli Tua, and only "as far as a cannon shot on either side." The hinterland areas, by contrast, were at

Overleaf: *Medan's Royal Mosque. Photo by Kal Muller.* **Opposite:** *The Sultan of Deli's ceremonial palace umbrella. Photo by Peter Bruechman.*

this time peopled almost exclusively by Karo Bataks. The Karo lived under their own independent chiefs in the four *urung* (village federations) of Sunggal (Serbanyaman), Hamperan Perak, Senembah and Sukapiring. Due to the influence of the increasingly prosperous Malay rulers of Deli, several chiefs converted to Islam in the early 19th century, and by about 1870 many Karo villagers living in the coastal area had also adopted Islam and Malay culture (*masuk Melayu*).

The plantation boom

The modern history of the Medan area begins in 1862 when a Dutch entrepreneur, Jacob Nienhuys, recognised the potential of the rich volcanic soils of the area and per-

suaded the Sultan of Deli to grant a concession for the growing of tobacco. Deli wrapper leaf for cigars rapidly became world famous, and from the late 19th century onward, foreign capital flooded into the area.

Thus began the dramatic transformation of a region that was at this time still largely virgin rainforest—rich in elephants, deer, wild pigs, tigers, flying squirrels, monkeys and a host of other creatures. Access to the hinterland was quite arduous in those days —involving travel upriver by *perahu* then on foot along narrow jungle tracks up into the foothills and across a series of passes onto the Karo plateau and the Simalungun Batak areas to the southeast.

Approached by a steady stream of Euro-

pean entrepreneurs, the Sultan of Deli proceeded to grant concessions of land to which he had no traditional right, consequently alienating the predominantly Karo inhabitants of the area. This highhanded action led to the Sunggal War of 1872-1897, but with Dutch military help the Karo were put down.

Here too, were the beginnings of the modern Indonesian oil industry. In 1883, following observations of surface oil seepages, a certain Mr. Zijlker was granted an exploratory concession in the Sungai Lipan area by the Sultan of Langkat. This venture was so successful that in 1890 the Koninklijke Nederlandsche Maatschappij tot het Exploiteeren van Petroleum—precursor to Royal Dutch Shell—was formed with a capital of Dfl. 1.1 million, a considerable sum in those days.

International investments were much larger here than in any other area of the archipelago in the pre-war period, as capital for plantation and other development poured in from the United States, Britain, Belgium, Germany, Scandinavia, Switzerland, Japan and Holland. As the indigenous inhabitants were few in number and had no wish to work for European masters, thousands of immigrant laborers were brought in to work the plantations, initially from China and India, but later from Java and Madura. The population of the so-called Cultuurgebied plantation area around Medan subsequently rose ten-fold, from 120,000 in 1880 to 1.2 million in 1920.

The cultivation of tobacco reached boom proportions by 1890, and was followed in turn by rubber, oil palms, sisal and tea. By 1925, over a million hectares of jungle had been cleared and cultivated. The east coast sultans of Deli, Langkat, Serdang and Asahan waxed fat on the incomes of their leased concessions in this period—their splendid courts rivaling those of the Malay Peninsula and Java. This ended abruptly in 1946 with a "cultural revolution" instigated by young rebels, in which many of the Malay aristocracy, including the brilliant Malay poet Tengku Amir Hamzah, were brutally murdered.

Events following Independence upset the status quo in the east coast areas. A rapid influx of Batak settlers into the rich plantation areas caused major demographic changes. From then on the population was no longer predominently Malay, Javanese and Chinese, but was dominated by Batak peoples from the highlands.

— *E. Edwards McKinnon*

Above: *The Sultan of Deli and his consort.*

Medan

to Belawan

JL. LABORATORIUM

JL. GETAH

JL. PUTRI HIJAU

JL. GUDANG

JL. SENA

JL. RAMBLING?
JL. MAJANG

JL. RAMBUTAN

JL. GELUGUR BYPASS

JL. WARINGIN

JL. JENDERAL
GATOT SUBROTO

to Berastagi

JL. KARO

JL. TEMBAKAU

Deli Plaza

PTP IX Building

JL. TEMBAKAU DELI

KLM

Hotel Dharma Deli

Bank Indonesia

Bank Negara Indonesia

Town Hall

JL. RADEN SALEH

Mosque

Baron MacKay's Plaque

JL. MAYJEN SITOYO SISWOMIHARJO

Hotel Dirgha Surya

Hotel Danau Toba

Governor's Office

JL. CANDI KALASAN

JL. CANDI MENDUT

JL. CANDI PRAMBANAN

JL. C. PENGADILAN

JL. CANDI BIARA

JL. TARUNA

Bank Bali

JL. KH ZAINUL ARIFIN

JL. IMAM BONJOL

JL. TEUKU UMAR

JL. MAYJEN S. PARMAN

JL. TEUKU CIK DITIRO

JL. HANG TUAH

JL. LISKU P. AGUNG

JL. DIPONEGORO

JL. WALIKOTA

JL. LINGGAR JATI

JL. M.S. KARIM

JL. SLAMET RIYADI

JL. A. RIVAI

JL. RATULANGI

JL. JENDRAL SUDIRMAN

JL. IMAM BONJOL

Bakeries

Maternity Hospital

JL. CUT MUTIA

Garuda Airlines

JL. CUT MUTIA II

Hotel Tiara

JL. R. A. KARTINI

JL. TENGKU DAUD

Immanuel Church

Bukit Barisan Museum

JL. PALANG MERAH

Buddhist Temple

Malaysian Airlines

SMAC Airlines

Hotel Polonia

Singapore Airlines

St. Elizabeth Hospital

Hotel Pardede International

JL. JUANDA

JL. SUPENA

JL. SURYO

JL. WOLTER MONGISIDI

JL. DR. CIPTO MANGUNKUSUMO

JL. JENDRAL SUDIRMAN

Vihara Gunung Timur

Deli Plaza

Former DSM Railway Office

Post Office

Railway Station

Bank Central Asia

JL. BUKIT BARISAN

JL. BALAKOTA

Padang
(town square)

London Sumatra Building

JL. JEND. AHMAD YANI

Panin Bank

Bank Kesawan

Tjong A Fie Mansion

Tip Top Rest.

Bank Duta

JL. USKUP AGUNG WIRJOPRANOTO

JL. KOPELNI

ALS

JL. KOLONEL SUGIONO

Bank Niaga

AVROS Building

JL. ALIMIN

JL. LETJEN SUPRAPTO

JL. MULTATULI

JL. SAMANHUDI

JL. KAPT. TENDEAN

JL. JUANDA

JL. WARNI

Maimoon Palace

Mesjid Raya

JL. BRIGJEN KATAMSO

JL. PROF. H. M. MUHAMAD YAMIN S. H.

JL. SULAWESI

JL. BELITUNG

JL. LOMBOK

JL. SIAK

JL. BEDAGAI

JL. LANGKAT

JL. TAMRING

JL. ASAHAN

JL. SUMBA

JL. SEIKERA

JL. SERAM

JL. DR. SUTOMO

JL. MADURA

JL. VETERAN

Everprompt

Pasar Pusat
(Central Market)

JL. RIAU

Edelweiss

JL. DR. SUTOMO

JL. JAMBU

Olympia Theater

JL. LETJEN. M.T. HARYONO

JL. IRIAN BARAT

JL. SURABAYA

JL. SUKAHARTA

JL. SEMARANG

JL. BOGOR

JL. PANDU

Cantik

JL. SISINGAMANGARAJA

Hotel Garuda Plaza

Bengawan

Hotel Dhaksina

JL. MANTRI

Merpati Airlines

to Tebing Tinggi, Pematang Siantar, Prapat

Mandala Airlines

Indah

Polonia Airport

to Delitua

0 1 1.5 2 km

N

MEDAN SIGHTS

Vestiges of a Plantation Boomtown

Medan has changed considerably over the past several decades. Before the war this was a small but fabulously wealthy plantation city with some 60,000 inhabitants. Today it is a sprawling and bustling metropolis—its busy streets are lined with new office and shopping blocks and thronged with minibuses and noisy motorised *becak* that produce voluminous clouds of thick, acrid smoke. The pre-independence population of Chinese, Indians, Javanese and Europeans has been swamped by an influx of indigenous Sumatrans—predominantly Bataks, but also Acehnese, Malays and Minangkabau.

Medan, like Jakarta, is a hot and crowded city, and most visitors rush straight through on the way to the cooler and more scenic highlands. It is in fact quite a shock to land here, especially if you are visiting Indonesia for the first time. On the other hand, Medan has pleasant hotels and well-preserved colonial buildings, a lovely palace and mosque, and numerous fascinating temples, markets and ethnic quarters. A day or two can profitably be spent sightseeing; the best way to get around is to hire a car or motorised *becak* (see "Medan Practicalities").

The old planters' town

Most visitors arrive by air at Polonia International Airport, once the city's racetrack and before that a Polish-owned tobacco plantation. The Deli River flows past the northern end of the runway, marked by a line of coconut trees, with the dome-shaped roof of the Sultan of Deli's palace visible in the distance. Polonia was the fashionable colonial residential neighborhood, and lavish villas still line its broad, shady boulevards.

The colonial period main street, **Jalan Jenderal Ahmad Yani**, with its many European style buildings, is still known locally as Kesawan, the road to the *sawah* or rice fields. Here, behind an iron grill fence alongside numerous Chinese shops, is the mansion of the former millionaire Kapitan Cina or head of the Chinese community, Tjong A Fie, who made and lost a fortune in the booming plantation world of the 1920s and '30s. Opposite his house is the Cafe Tip Top, once a favorite haunt of Medan's colonial society and still in almost original condition—where one can sit beside the sidewalk sipping iced Vienna coffee and nibbling on some of their Dutch-style *koekjes* as the world goes by.

At the northern end of Jl. Ahmad Yani are the offices of London-based Harrisons and Crosfield Ltd., built of Aberdeen granite imported as ballast during the 1920s, and now occupied by P.T. London Sumatra, the British Consulate and the British Council Library. Just behind the London Sumatra building, at the junction of Jl. Kesenian and Jl. Hindu, is a plaque laid by Baron MacKay, former *burgemeester* (mayor) of Medan, in 1926. East on the opposite side of Jl. Hindu, at Gang Bengkok, is a small mosque with an ancient well—reputedly the oldest in Medan—possibly that mentioned by Anderson in 1823.

Around the *padang* or town square to the north of Jl. Ahmad Yani are several colonial buildings, notably the old town hall, the Bank of Indonesia building (formerly the Javaasche Bank), the Bank Negara (formerly the exclusive Witte Societeit club, built in 1879), and the Hotel Dharma Deli, which incorporates the old Hotel DeBoer—made famous by the Ladislao Székely novel, *Tropic Fever*, which describes the experiences of a young European planter in Sumatra in the early years of this century. The old train station has gone, but the *jembatan gantung*, the original suspension bridge over the railway, remains.

On the corner of Jl. Puteri Hijau, the colonial era Post Office stands virtually unchanged, with the Nienhuys fountain just outside—dedicated to the man responsible for the Medan area plantation boom. Just around the corner on Jl. H.M. Yamin (formerly Jl. Serdang), one may walk against the flow of one-way traffic to see the former DSM (Deli Spoorweg Maatschappij) railway office adjacent to a one-meter gauge railway that still carries the bulk of North Sumatra's plantation produce, linking the harbor of Belawan-Deli with Pematang Siantar and Rantau Prapat to the south. On nearby Jl. Tembakau Deli is the former VDM (Vereenigde Deli Maatschappij) building built by Nienhuys in 1869, now headquarters of PTP IX, a state-owned plantation company.

One block from the southern end of Jl. Ahmad Yani is the former AVROS (Algemeene Vereeniging van Rubberplanters ter Oostkust van Sumatra) building, now the Sumatra Planters' Association, with its green-tiled dome and dark teak-panelled boardroom.

Maimoon Palace

Directly to the south is Istana Maimoon, the ceremonial palace of the sultans of Deli, with its yellow trim (yellow is the color of Malay royalty) and typical east coast Malay architecture. It was actually designed by an Italian architect and completed in 1888. The audience hall, with portraits of the Deli royal fam-

Opposite: *The former VDM building, constructed by Nienhuys in 1869.* **Below:** *Maimoon Palace.*

STEVE TEO

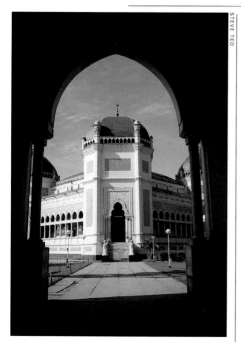

STEVE TEO

The Deli family is related by marriage to Malay royal houses in Malaysia.

Beside the Istana is a Karo Batak style *balai* or open pavilion, built to house the *meriam puntung*—the stub of an ancient iron cannon. This is associated with the legendary Puteri Hijau, the "Green Princess," heroine of Deli's wars against Aceh in the 16th century. She is said to have come from Siberaya in the Karo Highlands and thus reflects Deli's close association with the Karo Batak. The cannon is named Indera Sakti and is said to have been one of the princess's two brothers—the other was a *naga* or snake of enormous proportions ("*naga yang mengamuk*") who assisted her in the fight against the Acehnese. This legend may have its origin through Tamil contacts with the Madras area of South India, where there is a similar tale of a Green Goddess.

One block to the east across the single track railway, on Jl. Sisingamangaraja (named after the powerful Batak priest-king killed by the Dutch in 1907), is the **Mesjid Raya** or Great Mosque, with its imposing tiled archway, royal burial ground and adjacent *kolam* or tank across the road. From here, looking back along Jl. Sisingamangaraja one may see also the tall water tower adopted as a symbol of the municipality of Medan.

The Polonia area

A walk from the AVROS building westwards along Jl. Suprapto into the Polonia area adjacent to the airport will give an impression of what the colonial Medan lifestyle was like in the '20s and '30s. This walk leads over the Deli River past the former HVA (Handels Vereeniging Amsterdam) building, now used as a police headquarters, and past St. Elizabeth Hospital. Broad, tree-lined avenues with their tall, red-flowered spathodeas and bungalow-style houses set well back from the road in colorful shrub-lined gardens imparts a feeling of security and affluence. Most of the Medan expatriate population still live here, though as in the rest of the town, changes are visible and numerous architectural alterations have been undertaken to suit modern Indonesian taste.

At the corner of Jl. Imam Bonjol and Jl. Sukamulia, in the courtyard of the Danau Toba Hotel, with its traditional Batak-style entrance, is the former Dutch Assistant Resident's house, now part of the modern hotel complex. Next door on Jl. Imam Bonjol is the Buddhist Vihara Borobudur temple.

Further west on Jl. Diponegoro is the Provincial Governor's office, a single-storey shut-

ily, old Dutch furniture and a few weapons, is open to the public. It has patterned tiles and elegant moorish archways supported by large pillars covered in floral patterns. Malay dance performances, accompanied by traditional music, are held here to accompany weddings and other festivities. The sultan now lives in Jakarta, where he is a member of parliament; the palace living quarters are occupied by the sultan's brother.

During the late 19th and early 20th century, Malay royalty lived with great pomp in splendid style. With the establishment of Dutch suzerainty and the completion of the new palace in Medan they left their old timber-built home at Labuan Deli. Malays conceptualized riches in political terms; a rich ruler was one with many subjects, whose duties were primarily ceremonial. The revenue from plantations enabled the sultans to support a large retinue of followers, to make trips to Europe, and to send their children to Dutch or British schools.

The Deli sultans are reputedly descended from Mohammed Dalek Sri Paduka Gocah Pahlawan, a nobleman of Indian descent, appointed governor and first ruler of the state of Deli by the Sultan of Aceh around 1630. Deli was then conquered by Siak in 1770. In 1814, Mangidar Alam, the Raja of Deli, was awarded the full title of Sultan Panglima Mangidar Alam Syah ("Sultan Warrior who Encircles the World") by the Sultan of Siak.

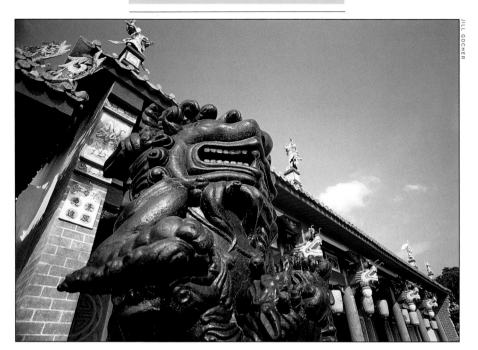

JILL GOCHER

tered colonial structure with neo-classical pillars, originally the Deli Tabaksproefstation. Immediately behind this, the Medan Club, with its fine timber pillars and open design, was built by Allied prisoners-of-war as a Shinto temple for use by officers during the Japanese occupation.

To the south, overlooking the Babura River, is the **Vihara Gunung Timur**. This is the largest Chinese temple in Medan, perhaps in Indonesia. Nearby is the Immanuel Protestant Church, built in 1921—a fine example of art-deco colonial architecture.

To the north along Jl. Imam Bonjol is another square dominated by the modern Batak-style Provincial Assembly building, the Benteng Restaurant and Convention Hall built on the site of the original military barracks, and the Dirga Surya Hotel, with a line of evening foodstalls in front.

Nearby **Kampung Keling** (Jl. Zainul Arifin), a busy commercial center, is, as its name implies, the original center of Medan's Indian community. Its high-walled Sri Mariamman temple devoted to the goddess Kali was built in 1884; the entrance is topped by a small *gopuram* or ornamental pyramidal gateway. The Medan Indian community are mainly descendents of South Indians who came to work on plantations in the late 19th and early 20th centuries. A second though less impressive Sri Mariamman temple on Bekala Estate, off the road to Pancurbatu some 11 km south

of Medan near the Sepit River, was established in 1876 and is the site of the Hindu Theemithi fire-walking ceremony during the annual Thaipusam festival—one of the few places where it is still held.

Medan's Chinatown

East of the railway, centered on Jl. Sutomo, is Medan's Chinatown, the heart of North Sumatra's wholesale trade—with shops selling everything from heavy machinery to toiletries. Here are Medan's two main markets, Pasar Hongkong and Pasar Sentral—havens for local pickpockets. This area has changed dramatically in recent years as the streets have been widened for ease of access. Unfortunately, most of the old shopfronts have been cut off as a result, though you can still see many shops and small Chinese restaurants run in the traditional manner.

During the durian season, heaps of fruit are offered for sale throughout the area (bargain hard!). Here too, in the evening, you will find colorful Chinese and seafood stalls lining Jl. Selat Panjang. Medan can offer a wide variety of delicious food, from roadside foodstalls serving basic Padang or Chinese meals, to plush, air-conditioned restaurants serving expensive Chinese and European banquets.

— *E. Edwards McKinnon*

Opposite: *Mesjid Raya, the Great Mosque.*
Above: *Vihara Gunung Timur Buddhist temple.*

Historic Sites Along the Deli River

A number of day excursions may be made to places around Medan. All main roads in the area are in quite good condition, but many secondary (*kabupaten*) roads, although asphalted, are still rough and uneven. Off the beaten track it is advisable to use a jeep-type vehicle with rugged suspension. Organized tours with a car and guide are available to any of these places through agents in Medan (see "Medan Practicalities").

Old Deli

Deli Tua or Old Deli (also known as Benteng Puteri Hijau, the "Fortress of the Green Princess") is the ancient site of the Aru court, overlooking the west bank of the Deli River (Lau Petani) about 10 km upstream from Medan, opposite Pasar Deli Tua. The area may be reached by going south from the Maimoon Palace (Jl. Brigjen Katamso) toward

Namorambe. Along the way you can stop at the Research Institute of the Sumatra Planters' Association (RISPA) at Kampung Baru—a good example of prewar colonial architecture—and at **Taman Margasatwa**, Medan's zoo, to see the Sumatran tigers and a range of birds and other animals.

Just before Deli Tua, a small road to the right leads across the river, and further south are tracks leading to two sets of ramparts overlooking the Deli River—one site occupied by the modern Karo village of Deli Tua Lama, the rest given over to the cultivation of cassava gardens. This was once the seat of the piratical kings of Aru who harassed Malacca during the late 15th and early 16th centuries. It is closely associated with the legend of the "green princess" from Siberaya, in Tiga Panah district on the Karo Plateau. Despite Portuguese assistance, Deli Tua was destroyed by the Acehnese in 1536.

According to one version of the story, the Acehnese fired cannon loaded with thousands of small gold coins called *dirham* into the bamboo *pagar* defences, and then withdrew. When the men of Aru cut down the bamboo to recover the gold, the Acehnese attacked, causing a rout.

Belawan and Kota Cina

Medan's port of Belawan, the third largest in Indonesia, is situated in the opposite direction, downstream from Medan, on a man-

ALAIN COMPOST

grove-lined estuary at the confluence of the Belawan and Deli rivers. Extensive cargo and passenger terminals and palm oil storage facilities have been completed in the past decade to ease what had become a major bottleneck in Indonesia's effort to increase exports. Here also is the giant Ivomas palm oil refinery and oleo-chemical plant, and the nearby archaeological site of Kota Cina.

Belawan is some 25 km north of the city. Most of Medan's new industrial development is sited along the old Belawan road, which was built in the late 19th century and follows the course of the Deli River. Along the way it passes through Pulau Brayan (Tanjung Mulia area), once known as Kota Jawa—where vestiges of a 14th century earthen rampart are visible in a graveyard to the left of the road—then through Kota Bangun and Labuhan. The latter was Medan's first port and consists of a ramshackle street of wooden buildings, now bypassed by the road and by time.

The opening of the Belawan-Medan-Tanjung Muara toll road to the east of the old road means that much of the heavier traffic can now bypass the Belawan town center. The name Belawan derives either from the name of a type of tree found here (*Terminalia citrina*, Roxb.), or from the Karo *dusun* word *erbulawan*, meaning to make an agreement on oath—as here an ancient shrine is associated with the "Green Princess" of Karo legend, and oaths were once made.

There are several good evening seafood restaurants and a flourishing market for modern Chinese-style ceramics. Passenger connections are available to Jakarta, Bintan Island opposite Singapore, Padang and by ferry to Penang. Elaborate bamboo fishtraps line the channel to the sea, and long elevated walkways lead to rows of Malay houses perched on stilts above the water.

Nearby **Kota Cina** is the site of an 11th to 14th century South Indian and Chinese trading settlement, with its adjacent harbor of Paya Pasir. It may be reached from the old Belawan road by turning left at Titipapan (km 16), past the jail on the left and over the Deli River, proceeding about 2 km toward Hamparan Perak and turning right along a track to Rengaspulau and Kota Cina, two typical Malay villages. A caretaker, whose house is adjacent to the village primary school, is usually present.

Evidence suggests that Kota Cina was linked with places as far afield as Java, south China, Sri Lanka, India and the Persian Gulf through a complex web of regional and international trade routes in ancient times. At Paya Pasir, the wrecks of ten ancient ships constructed with the Southeast Asian lash lug technique were discovered by accident when sand was being dug for the construction of the Belawan-Medan toll road. This former harbor site is now, unfortunately, almost totally destroyed due to commercial sand exploitation, and only limited excavation work could be undertaken. Buddha and Vaisnavite images from a brick Buddhist *asrama* and other artifacts from Kota Cina are now in the North Sumatra Provincial Museum in Medan.

Bukit Lawang (Bohorok)

The Bukit Lawang Orangutan Rehabilitation Station, established in 1973 (see following article for more details), is some some 76 km and 3 hour's drive west of Medan (4 hours by bus). About 6 km out of town, you may or may not want to stop at the **Crocodile Farm** at Sunggal—the largest in Indonesia, with some 1,500 reptiles packed in like sardines. From here, the road leads west through Binjai to Belarang—famous for its juicy, grapefruit-like pomelos (*jeruk bali*)—and on to Kuala, railhead for the one-meter gauge North Sumatra railway system. Along the way you pass through vast rubber and oil palm plantations, now obscured by roadside development.

Bohorok was the former seat of the Malayized Kejuruan Langkat, and formed the upper limit of Malay cultural influence on the Wampu River. The Langkat Ulu (upper Langkat) area is, however, essentially a Karo *dusun* area with a sizeable number of Javanese settlers who originally came to work on the plantations. The last stretch along the Bohorok River to Bukit Lawang leads through a lovely irrigated rice area.

At **Bukit Lawang** there are basic bamboo chalets for those who wish to stay overnight by the river at the edge of the forest. Although the elevation, is not high—only about 90 m above sea level—the evenings can be quite cool. Good *durian* and *rambutan* are available in season and Tertiary limestone caves are found in the immediate vicinity, with a pre-Tertiary carboniferous formation around Bohorok. A sidetrip from Bohorok for the fit and adventurous leads to **Pintu Angin**, the "door of the wind"—a hole in the limestone walls near the village of Batukatak, about 5 km upstream from Bohorok. An underground river flows nearby.

— *E. Edwards McKinnon*

Opposite: Malay villages on stilts at Belawan.

GUNUNG LEUSER PARK

A School For Orphaned Orangutans

Gunung Leuser, established in 1980, is one of Indonesia's oldest national parks. It straddles the border between Aceh and North Sumatra, covering an area of some 8,000 sq km and encompassing some of the most spectacular montane and equatorial forests in Asia. Its wildlife includes most of Sumatra's extensive range of mammals—including elephants, rhinos, tigers, sun bears, gibbons, macaques, tapirs, squirrels, clouded leopards and orangutans. Also found are about 500 bird species, notably the hornbills and argus pheasant.

As with any Southeast Asian rainforest, the principal difficulty in Gunung Leuser is in finding a way to get in and out without slogging uncomfortably for hours through damp, leech-ridden jungle. The other problem, of course, is to see something once you are there. Fortunately, this park is easily accessible at the Orangutan Rehabilitation Station at **Bukit Lawang**, 9 km past Bohorok and about 76 km west of Medan. Here, young orphaned orangutans are trained to live in the wild, and since its establishment in 1973 over 150 have been returned to the forest.

Visiting the park

A 3-hour journey from Medan (see "Medan Sidetrips") brings you to the village of Bukit Lawang, where permits to visit the center can be obtained upon showing your passport. From here, a rocky 2-km path leads to the banks of the Landat River past cacao plantations and a limestone cave.

The path ends at a bend in the river and one has to cross over here to reach the station, which discourages too many people from entering. In order to cross you have to attract the attention of the park wardens, who ferry you in a cable-and-pulley driven dugout canoe. Make sure you find out the current feeding times in Bukit Lawang before walking to the station, because the wardens are very strict about not letting people cross at other times. Normal feeding times are in the early morning and afternoon, but they are periodically stopped to encourage the orangutans to become more independent.

Once across the river, a steep muddy trail through the forest leads to a platform above the station where the young orangutans are fed their twice-daily ration of bananas and milk. Some of these animals have been deliberately orphaned by hunters who illegally shot their mothers in order to sell them as pets, while others became homeless when their habitat was destroyed by loggers.

New arrivals are kept in quarantine for 3 to 4 months to reduce the risk of passing infections to the wild population. During this period, they are introduced to some of the things every young orangutan should know: how to eat leaves and fruit and how to build a comfortable sleeping nest by bending branches together.

The next stage is to introduce the young orangutans gradually to life in the wild. Park wardens carry the apes piggy-back up to the feeding platform, so they can practice clambering about the branches and make the acquaintance of the other orangutans. After a couple of weeks, they are left at the feeding platform to begin to fend for themselves. Some, pining for human company, return to the station, but most quickly learn the pathways through the forest, and the places to find wild fruits.

The steady diet of bananas at the station is deliberately monotonous to encourage the animals to forage for themselves and find more interesting food. Gradually, the orangutans return less frequently to be fed, and after six months or so they disappear into the vast forests of Gunung Leuser. Most are never seen again, but occasionally one will be spotted in the forest, sometimes with her own baby—a sign of the program's success.

Adventurous types might like to try the speedy route back to Bukit Lawang by hiring an inflated inner tube in the village and riding the rapids downriver from the end of the path opposite the orangutan station. Once back at Bukit Lawang, good food and accommodation are available and there is an excellent visitors' center with displays and slide-shows about the wildlife and ecology of the park.

It is difficult and dangerous for the uninitiated traveler to head off alone into the forest from here because of the dense vegetation, steep terrain and absence of clearly-marked trails, and it is therefore a good idea to join

Right: *Feeding time at the Bukit Lawang station.*

one of the hikes organized by the staff at the visitors' center. These can range from a few hours to several days, depending on the visitors' inclination. One option is to walk right through the national park across the mountains to Kutacane, which takes 3 or 4 days.

The Alas River valley

Bohorok and its immediate hinterland lie in the province of North Sumatra, but most of Gunung Leuser lies in the province of Aceh. The park's administrative center is here, at **Kutacane** (pronounced: KU-ta-CHA-nay) in the Alas River valley, a 6-8 hour drive from Medan. Permits can be obtained for entry into the park on production of photocopies of your passport, but once again, the difficulty is in finding an interesting route into the jungle. One solution is simply to walk along the road running northwest from Kutacane to Blangkejeren. This road bisects the park, and although the area is inhabited it also passes through dense forest. Without the worry of path-finding or attacks from wild tigers, it is possible to concentrate on observing the birds and other wildlife from the road. It is even possible to walk to Blangkejeren in a couple of days, sleeping in villages along the way. There is little traffic, but you may be passed by the occasional minibus which will pick you up if you are tired of walking.

Not far from Kutacane the road passes the scientific research center at Ketambe, but the scientists do not welcome casual visitors and travelers should definitely not plan on staying there. The road to Blangkejeren runs for part of its length along the Alas River, which offers another excellent way to travel through the park, by taking a white-water rafting trip (see "Medan Practicalities" and "Western Aceh" for more details).

Alternatively, you can set out through the jungle with guides and porters hired at Kotacane. The danger from tigers here is probably exaggerated, but be careful; it is said that women squatting in the forest at night are particularly vulnerable. Fieldworkers, however, consider themselves fortunate to catch the merest glimpse of one fleeing from them. Hikers are much more likely to see a wild orangutan or other primates. The graceful dark grey and cream Thomas's leaf-monkey and the more prosaic long-tailed macaques are frequently encountered—a crashing in the branches often indicates the presence of a troop of one of these species.

One of the most exciting experiences of the forest is to see and hear a family of white-handed gibbons or the larger black siamangs, as their whooping calls ring out across the hills and valleys. The white-handed gibbons call in a series of high yells, while the siamangs have a deeper, bubbling whoop backed by a booming sound made by their inflatable throat pouches.

— Janet Cochrane

ALAIN COMPOST

Medan Practicalities

Telephone code is 061. All prices US dollars. S = Single, D = Double, AC = air-conditioned.

Medan is the principal city of North Sumatra. It is also the chief port of entry for those visiting Toba, Nias, Aceh and other points around the island. With a recently expanded municipal area of nearly 300 sq km, and a population of over 2 million, this is a big city with an extremely diverse population—Karo, Toba, Mandailing, Simalungun and Pakpak Bataks as well as Malays, Javanese, Minang, Acehnese, Indians, Chinese and virtually every other ethnic group in the country. Given that North Sumatra is one of the most important economic areas in Indonesia, producing a major portion of the national income from oil and plantation exports, Medan is developing fast. With some patience, you'll discover the city has much to offer.

GETTING THERE

BY AIR (international). Daily flights arrive from Singapore (Garuda and Singapore Airlines, $200 RT) and Penang (Malaysian Airlines, $125 RT). Once a week there is a joint KLM/Garuda flight from Amsterdam en route to Bali.
Local offices: Garuda: Jl. Cut Mutia, tel: 25809, 516871. KLM: Jl. Balai Kota 2, tel: 327011, 327999. Malaysian Airlines: Jl. Imam Bonjol 17, tel: 519333, 517992. Singapore Airlines: Jl. Jend. Sudirman 24, tel: 325300.
BY AIR (domestic). Four daily jet flights by Merpati connect Medan with Jakarta, $140. Mandala flies reconditioned Elektra propjets on this route, which are 10 percent cheaper and OK in good weather, but subject to delays and cancellations otherwise. A new private airline called Sempati is also operating jets from Medan to Jakarta twice a day, at the same fares as Merpati. Merpati flies here daily from most major Sumatran cities as well.
Local offices: Mandala: Jl. Brigjen Katamso 37E, tel: 513309, 519983. Merpati: Jl. Brigjen. Katamso 41, tel: 514102. Sempati: Polonia airport. SMAC: Jl. Imam Bonjol 59, tel: 516934, 516617.
BY SEA. You can get to Medan from Penang (Malaysia) now via a fast hydrofoil, the Gadis Langka Suka—a joint venture between Malaysian and Indonesian companies. It runs twice weekly and docks at Belawan, Sumatra's port on the Malacca Straits, taking a mere 5 hours as opposed to the previous 15 hours for the crossing. One-way fare is $40. Office in Medan is Jl. Brigjen Katamso 62A, tel: 515562.

Two large cruise ships, the Rinjani and the Kambuna, run by the state shipping company PELNI, sail to Jakarta every other week, one of them leaves Jakarta every Saturday afternoon, arriving in Medan Monday morning. The ships are large and comfortable in the upper classes. Fares are $84 first class (2 per cabin), $62 second class (4 per cabin), $45 third class (6 per cabin), $35 fourth class (8 per cabin) and $22 deck class. Food is included, and though there is little to do on the ship (no pool, video in first class cabins and dining rooms, band and dancing at night in the first class dining room), the upper class rooms are well appointed, with AC and hot showers, and the trip on the straits is calm and relaxing. Unfortunately tickets must be purchased at the point of departure, and can only be one way, not round trip. The PELNI office in Medan is at Jl. Kol. Sugiono 5, tel: 518899.

Bargain hard at Belawan for the bemo trip to Medan. Cost is about $1.
BY BUS. The alternative for adventurous souls wishing to see the countryside on a budget, is to travel the length of Sumatra by bus from Jakarta (or from Padang or Palembang). The most reliable bus line is ALS, with offices at Jl. Amaliun 2A in Medan (tel: 22014), which also has ticketing offices in all cities it services. Approximate cost Jakarta-Medan in an AC coach is $30. In the other direction, ALS can book you all the way direct to Yogya or Solo. Just around the corner from ALS, in a row of shops on Jl. Sisingamangaraja across from the Great Mosque, you can find other bus companies heading up to Toba and beyond.

GETTING AROUND

Polonia airport is right in the city, a rarity these days, with access to hotels even possible by *becak* (pedicab) just outside the front gate, a short walk of about 300 meters—good to remember if you are traveling light. The city's road network is a maze of one-way streets. Many roads are undergoing construction as Medan is installing the first centralized sewage and water system of any large city in Indonesia. The project has been underway for years and massive holes in the road may slow you down, or cause diversions.

TAXIS. Go anywhere in Medan for under $3. There are at least 12 companies, of which 4 have new "argo" metered cabs (Metax, Karsa, Kostar and VIP). Stick with metered cabs if you are new to the area and short on Bahasa Indonesia. Otherwise state your destination and bargain hard before getting in. Metered taxis are AC and the fare is 35 cents at flagfall and 40 cents for each additional km. Since central Medan is fairly compact, use your judgment on whether your driver may be artificially extending your trip. All major hotels have their own taxis at higher, less negotiable rates. One of the best ways of seeing Medan is to rent a taxi by the hour—about $4 an hour, minimum of 2 hours.

MINIBUSES. Medan has a system of *sudako*, the local version of the *bemo*—converted pick-up trucks, open at the back, which ply fixed routes. Fares are Rp100 to Rp150 per ride depending on the destination. Try this if you have a bit of Bahasa Indonesia to keep things straight. You can get almost anywhere within the city although you may have to change. State your destination and don't feel pressured to get on the first one passing by if it's already overloaded. A newer company uses larger Toyota trucks refitted for passengers.

MOTORIZED BECAK. The other alternative is the noisy, smoking motorized *becak*, a pedicab with a tiny 2-stroke engine that is now on the wane as in other large centers in Indonesia. Rates must be negotiated before getting in. State your destination, perhaps settling on half the driver's initial offer. Generally any journey within the central part of town will cost under $1. Charters are cheap, around $2 per hour, and this is a convenient, if nerve-wracking, way to get around.

TRANSPORT OUT OF MEDAN

TAXIS. For trips to the countryside, you can hop in a shared taxi at the Olympia Theater, Jl. Haryono M.T., or on Jl. Irian Barat (for Berastagi). You pay per seat at rates determined by the distance you travel. Berastagi costs about $2.50 a person, Pematang Siantar $3, and Prapat about $5. You can also charter taxis for out-of-town trips for between $30 and $50 a day, depending on the distance. Agree on the route and the amount beforehand.

The following companies are reliable: **Bengawan**, Jl. Sisingamangaraja, tel: 327788. **Cantik**, Jl. Semarang 44, tel: 327532. **Deli**, Jl. Singosari 3C, tel:322174. **Indah**, Jl. Brigjen. Katamso 60, tel: 516615.

BUSES. Alternatively, you can take buses from the offices on Jl. Amaliun and around the corner on Jl. Sisingamangaraja, across from the Mesjid Raya (Grand Mosque). Check the Medan map for the location of various terminals.

CAR RENTALS. Only think of driving yourself if you have had experience in Indonesia, otherwise hire a driver with the car. Can be arranged at the Hotel Dharma Deli, through a recently-opened agent for National and Nippon. Medan has traffic jams at peak hours in certain areas, and parking is always a problem. Taxis can also be rented by the hour or day (see above).

CHANGING MONEY

In the airport arrival hall is a small booth where you can change enough to get you into town. Once settled into your hotel, make further exchanges at a bank to get a better rate. Change enough money in Medan for your needs up-country, as rates are much better here.

You can get cash for your Visa/Mastercard at Bank Duta and BCA; or Amex at Panin Bank.

When leaving Indonesia, Bank Kesawan specializes in changing money and therefore holds many currencies besides US dollars.

Most banks are in the center of town along Jl. A. Yani and near the town square (*alun-alun*) in front of the post office. Several new ones are going up along Jl. Arifin in Kampung Keling, humorously referred to by locals as Medan's answer to Wall Street. For good service and rates, try the following: **Bank Bali**, Jl. Zainul Arifin, tel: 511000, 513707. **Bank Central Asia**, Jl. Bukit Barisan 3, tel: 52806, 327133. **Bank Duta**, Jl. Pemuda 9, tel: 511666. **Bank Kesawan**, Jl. Jend. A. Yani 29, tel: 24108, 512160. **Bank Niaga**, Jl. Pemuda 13, tel: 321411. **Panin Bank**, Jl. Jend. A. Yani VI/6.

INFORMATION AND TOURS

All hotels give helpful information on the area. There is a tourist information booth at the airport, where the staff speak good English. The main Tourist Information Office is at Jl. A. Yani 107 (tel: 511101), right next to the Tjong A Fie mansion. Though not absolutely the last word in service, the staff do their best to answer specific questions.

Quite a number of agencies run tours in and around the city, and in fact anywhere in Sumatra. These companies have competent drivers and guides and all kinds of vehicles, from AC cars to minibuses to huge coaches, and can arrange customized tours for any size group for surprisingly little money, which saves you the hassle of arranging your own transport. They'll also get you discounts on hotels.

The following companies are recommended (call for rates): **Edelweiss**, Jl. Irian Barat 47-9, tel: 517297, 530863. Specializes in jungle treks, diving and adventure tours, including the Alas River rafting trip. **Everprompt**, Jl. Sutomo 450, tel: 23456. **King's Star**, Jl. Pemuda 24B, tel: 515111. **Pacto**, Jl. Brigjen. Katamso 35D, tel: 510081, 513669. Probably the best all-round agent. **Worta**, Jl. Brigjen. Katamso 32E, tel: 327600. **Universal**, Jl. Palang Merah 26C, tel: 515229.

ACCOMMODATION

Rates vary with season and demand. Several new luxury hotels are now opening, while the older ones are planning extensive renovations. The result is some fairly satisfying options.

Expensive ($40 and up a night)

Danau Toba International (259 rooms) Jl. Imam Bonjol 17, tel: 327000. Has its own fitness center and a great pool, with attractive floating bar. Other fine facilities include two music lounges, one hosting international bands nightly, and a poolside bar with great atmosphere. Also a coffeeshop and Chinese, Japanese and Javanese-Sundanese restaurants, all good. $44 S, $72 D.

Dharma Deli (178 rooms) Jl. Balai Kota 2, tel: 327001. An old Dutch hotel on Jl. A. Yani, right across from Medan's fine turn-of-the-century "kitsch" central post office, and next to two colonial buildings which housed the mayor's office and Bank Indonesia until recently. Hotel Dharma Deli retains a link with the past in its foyer, reception area and dining room, which are left from the old colonial Hotel DeBoer. 80 cosy secluded room in the old wing look onto a garden. Other facilities are modest but attractive, including the DeBoer Grill and Coffeeshop, Kuala Bar, a pool and poolside bar. Rooms are reasonable at $35 D up to $80 D.

Dirgha Surya (51 rooms) Jl. Imam Bonjol 6, tel: 321555. Semi-government owned and recently renovated. Under a Singapore manager, it has moved up recently in class and price. It has a first class coffee shop, probably the best in town, and is conveniently located next to the Surya Food Center (see "Dining" below). It also boasts the Xanadu disco and night club, one of the best night spots in town. $40 a night.

Garuda Plaza (154 rooms) Jl. Sisingamangaraja 18, tel: 326255. A Minang-style building around the corner from the Maimoon palace and a 15-minute walk from Jl. A. Yani. Recently renovated with a small pool, modest health club, and restaurant. From $45 up.

Polonia (178 rooms) Jl. Sudirman 14, tel: 325300. The best known place for Indonesians and old Medan hands, just outside the airport. Recently renovated, it has one of the best Chinese restaurants in town and a modest but well-appointed health club with good squash courts and a pool. Rates start at $33.

Tiara (204 rooms) Jl. Cut Mutiah, tel: 516000. The top place in town. Part of the Griya chain, located in a shady residential area between Jl. Imam Bonjol and Jl. Diponegoro, just a few minutes' walk from Jl. A. Yani. Its Clark Hatch health center has a new facility and there are two good tennis courts, several restaurants, and a bar and lounge with daily entertainment. Also has a new convention center, the best in Sumatra. $58 S to $62 D for standard rooms; executive rooms are 30 percent higher.

Intermediate ($10-40 a night)

Angkasa (52 rooms) Jl. Sutomo 1, tel: 322555. A larger gov't-owned hotel. Rooms in the main building face onto the two swimming pools. $20 for the cheapest single up to $40 for a suite. The restaurant is known for good Chinese food, though it has a raucous band.

Dhaksina (40 rooms) Jl. Sisingamangaraja 20, tel: 324561, 324531. Clean and functional, with strict house rules (no guests in rooms!). Near bus company offices, Grand Mosque and palace. Padang restaurant below and another across the street. Rates from $10 to $20.

Elbruba (48 rooms) Jl. Perintis Kemerdekaan 19, tel: 520119. Fairly good value, $20 S and $30 D, both with AC.

Pardede International (113 rooms) Jl. Juanda no. 14, tel: 521444. Has a small pool, a fairly

good restaurant, and an infamous night life. Rooms from $30, cottages for $18.

Wai Yat Jl. Asia 44, tel: 321683. A long-established hotel run by an American educated Chinese and his charming Japanese-American wife, Wai Yat is a favorite for a long list of faithful clients, and great value for your money. It houses a fine Chinese restaurant, known for its babi hong (roast pork) and dimsum on the weekends. Rooms from $9 to $19 with AC.

Wisma Benteng Jl. Raden Saleh, tel: 528426. Run by the Indonesian Army. You may not find it listed in most guides, but in fact Wisma Benteng provides good, clean AC rooms at a very reasonable price. The restaurant is one of the more populer Chinese restaurants in town, which manages the nearly impossible feat of serving really delicious seafood and other Chinese delicacies without any pork (halal). $17.50 in very pleasant garden surroundings. $2.50 more gives you hot water; VIP suites in another building are $40.

Budget (under $10)

Losmen Irama Jl. Palang Merah 112S, tel: 326416. The best and most hospitable place for the budget traveler. Especially known as a touchdown point for those en route to Nias, as it is run by a Nias family. A private room (non AC) is only $2, with extra bed for $1.75, both with coffee in the morning. The proprietors can help arrange budget travel, particularly on Nias.

Penginapan Tapiana Nabaru Jl. Hang Tuah 6. Also highly recommended; situated in a beautiful spot just next to the Vihara Gunung Timur Chinese temple by one of Medan's quiet parks.

Jacky's Traveller's Centre Jl. Kediri 96. Dorm beds at $1.75, rooms at $5, or crash on the floor of his Indian restaurant down the street for 50 cents if you are really on a shoestring.

DINING

Budget eating. The most accessible and reasonable place is the Surya Food Center, a collection of foodstalls next to an open field called Lapangan Benteng near the Hotel Dirgha Surya. Hundreds of things to choose from, and many of the stalls are open until after midnight. Similar but smaller centers are found in all the new shopping plazas. The 2nd and 3rd floors of Deli Plaza have particularly good and inexpensive places, as well as Thamrin Plaza on Jl. Thamrin. Literally hundreds of small Chinese eateries dot the city and can turn out tasty, inexpensive meals from a fairly standard menu.

Chinese. The best Chinese food, mainly Cantonese and Hokkien, can be had in hotel restaurants—the Polonia, Danau Toba (good Szechuan), Jumbo, Asia, Wisma Benteng (without pork), Evergreen, Mikado (not a Japanese restaurant) and Wai Yat. Special mention should be made of the old Tip Top Restaurant on Jl. A. Yani. Turn of the century pictures of Medan on the walls show it standing there as the premier

Dutch social spot in town. Now best for its European and Chinese food, it has the only sidewalk cafe in Medan, a pleasant place to relax in the evenings after the traffic on Jl. A. Yani dies down.

European. This is the weakest category in Medan's repertoire. If you are yearning for some Western food, however, try the coffee shop or Ambarita Grill at the Hotel Tiara. An old favorite for nostalgic Dutch travelers is the DeBoer Grill at Hotel Dharma Deli. Also highly recommended is the Cafe Labuhan coffee shop in the Dirgha Surya, which has improved immensely after recent reorganizing. Lynn's Bar and Grill, Jl. A. Yani 98 across from the old Tjong A Fie mansion, is a small quiet place which presents passable steaks and the like at equally passable prices, in a small, quiet atmosphere. Last but not least, the Tip Top Cafe next door has grills, pastries and coffee.

Fast food like Colonel Sander's and Church's can be found at several locations in the plazas for those yearning for such fare, at more or less original prices. Colonel Sander's also has Swenson's Ice Cream in tandem at all locations. There is a brand new Pizza Hut on the corner of Jl. Sudirman and Jl. Multatuli.

Indian. In spite of the large Indian population, the Indian food here is not great. Recently there has been a spate of new establishments. The best known is Kohinoor, on Jl. Hindu, which offers North Indian cuisine, and Jacky's Traveller's Centre, Jl. Kediri 30 in Kampung Keling. Jacky built up his business by first conquering the yogurt market on Samosir. After several disasters, including a run-in with the city's *becak* drivers (after he distributed fliers telling travelers to stay away from them because they were crooks—this actually made national news!), and a few changeovers of cooks after his competition stole them away, his restaurant is still in action and very reasonable. Jacky offers both North and South Indian food. There are also several smaller foodstalls around the area, on Jl. Jenggala and Jl. Cik Ditiro. For good quick Indian roadside stalls, including the well known *martabak* bread with minced mutton, egg and onions, try the stalls along Jl. Pagarruyung next to Sri Mariamman temple in Kampung Keling. Be sure to specify no chili if you wish to survive what are delicious *martabak*, as local taste favors superhot. You can also get good *martabak* in the Surya Food Center.

Japanese. Without question the best Japanese restaurant in Medan is the Yokohama at Jl. Nibung Raya 58. Owned and run by an experienced cook from the Japanese aluminum project at Inalum, the food is excellent at what are probably the most reasonable prices in the world, with a small and well-appointed atmosphere. Next choice is the Fuji in Hotel Danau Toba. Prices are still reasonable.

Javanese/Sundanese. Around town there are several Javanese and Sundanese style restaurants noted for their fresh fried *gurame* fish, *sop kambing* (mutton soup) and other delicacies. Try Ratu Kuring on Jl. Let.Jen. S. Parman 252B, and Inti Sari Kuring on Jl. Airlangga in Kampung Keling. For good Javanese food, the best is Rumah Makan Jenar, Jl. Let. Jen. S. Parman 307. Hotel Danau Toba has a newer poolside restaurant in the back called Riung Lembur, more expensive but very pleasant. Try also the wonderful fried chicken at Ayam Kalasan on Jl. Iskandar Muda next to Medan Plaza. The chickens are the so-called *ayam kampung* or farmyard chickens raised in a village eating household scraps without any hormones or special supplements. The birds are long, lean and taste fantastic compared to an obese factory broiler. They are deep fried with spices and coconut, served with rice and sambal. If you are with a small group this makes for a very delicious and economical meal.

Korean. On the 7th floor of Thamrin Plaza, right next to one Medan's busiest Karaoke bars, is the Thamira Hall—serving the closest thing to Korean food in Medan, and pretty close at that. For about $4 a person you can enjoy a self service, all-you-can-eat barbecue with built-in grills on the tables. You can also order *à la carte*.

Padang. With so many Minang migrants (they actually dominate the professional sectors), there are many good Padang restaurants in Medan. Garuda, located at Jl. Gajah Mada 8 over the bridge after Kampung Keling, and also at Jl. Pemuda 20-CD, are the best in town. Also try the Ambassador on Jl. Palang Merah for a more Malay-type cuisine. For similar fare from the Mandailing (southern) Batak area, try Restu Ibu on Jl. Multatuli around the corner from the Hotel Tiara convention hall.

Seafood. Jl. Selat Panjang in the center of town behind City Shopping Center, between Jl. Cirebon and Jl. Semarang, is the place for roadside stalls serving Chinese-style seafood. The atmosphere is a bit raucous, but the chili crab and other delicacies will take your mind right off the noise. Ask about prices in advance. Jl. Semarang nearby is a good choice for roadside meals in the evening. You can also venture out to the port of Belawan, where there is a similar array of seafood places with plenty of fresh crabs, shrimp and fish. Be sure to ask the prices first if you are on a budget, as some dishes can be quite expensive.

SHOPPING

Shopping in Medan is to some extent simplified by the fact that stores selling the same thing tend to be right next to each other, or even right on top of each other. Thus, if you're looking for baked goods, the three best bakeries in town, Royal Holland, Suan's and Tahiti, are all on Jl. Cik Ditiro in Kampung Keling. All the major antique shops are on Jl. A. Yani just doors from each other. The pattern continues with new pockets of businesses around town.

This perhaps follows the pattern in the markets, as if Medan were a mammoth marketplace following micro patterns on a huge scale. You will find that you can accomplish a great deal of shopping along Jl. A. Yani or Kesawan as it is know locally, and at Deli Plaza just a short walk past the post office. This street is within easy walking distance of most hotels. If you're short on time and don't speak Indonesian, this is the best shopping strip in town. If you're a bit adventurous, don't hesitate to try other places listed below.

Antiques. By far, Jl. Yani is the place to browse for antiques mostly from this area, with no less than seven stores along the road: Toko Bali, Marcopolo, Asli, Rufino, ABC, Selatan, Borobudur, and Toko Seni on Jl. A. Yani VII just around the corner from the London Sumatera building. Batak, Acehnese, Minang, and Javanese antiquities of all sorts, shapes and sizes are to be found in stores jam packed with goods. Be selective, don't hesitate to bargain hard, and be assured if you are traveling on to Java the Javanese items are better and of course more plentiful there. The various Batak peoples have some impressive, massive carvings for house ornaments, rice storage vessels and masks. Acehnese, Melayu and Minang items are largely various types of gold threaded material, ceremonial daggers and brass and silver work. For a smaller, more selective presentation, try Crispo's on Jl. Arifin just past the bridge on the left in Kampung Keling, especially good in the area of wooden carvings and furniture.

Books. The oldest and most convenient shop is Toko Buku Deli, Jl. A. Yani 48. The newer Gramedia at Jl. Gajah Mada 23 has a better selection. Mr. Ben at Jl. Muara Takus 48-50 has a good selection of foreign magazines and newspapers (as well as imported foods!).

Cassettes. For the best selection of Indonesian regional music, popular music, and a surprisingly wide range of international pop, Jazz and classical, try the cassette shops on the ground floors of Deli Plaza or Medan Plaza. All cassettes sold in Indonesia are now regulated under international copyright agreements.

Clothing. Monza ("Monginsidi Plaza"). Humorously referred to as Monza by local residents, the collection of roadside vendors or kaki lima as they're called offers a wide range of clothing which is mostly not appropriate for lowland tropical climates, particularly sweaters, jackets and the like. Sizes also may not be right for larger people but you can enjoy having a look at how the local people keep themselves well dressed and probably hot. Be prepared to bargain to the usual 50 to 60 percent. For all sorts of other clothing, go to any of the plazas. Everyone is fitted out here at reasonable fixed prices, though sizes may require some looking around. Quality of clothing is high, and many tourists from nearby Singapore and Malaysia dive for clothing stores here because it is so cheap. Look for large department stores like Suzuya, Yuki and Yaohan (no relation to the chain in Malaysia and Singapore). For batik—readymade clothes as well as material—Batik Keris and Batik Semar on Jl. Arifin in Kampung Keling are branches of the well-known central Javanese manufacturers, at fixed prices.

Everyday needs. By far the easiest way to buy toiletries, stationary, and virtually any other day-to-day things is to visit a supermarket in any of the shopping plazas. Most central is Deli Plaza, but all have huge stores packed with everything and anything available in Indonesia at fixed reasonable prices without bargaining.

Film supplies of an unusual nature, such as specialty films and such are difficult to find in Medan. Best selections are in several shops in Kampung Keling on Jl. Arifin.

Gold. Gold prices in Medan are probably among the best in Southeast Asia, though you must be a bit patient regarding particularly designs or quality. There several shops on Jl. Yani which are reputable, as well as several more expensive shops in the various plazas. If you have some Indonesian, try shops in Pasar Petisah.

Markets. The Medan word for market is pajak, not pasar as elsewhere in Indonesia. The largest of Medan's many markets is Pajak Sentral. Try your hand here for traditional Batak ulos cloth. Coffee, marquisa (passion fruit), and other produce items are best at Pajak Peringgan on Jl. Iskandar Muda. The durian of this area are good, though small, and can be purchased in season. Pineapples and papayas count among the most impressive, the mangoes not up to those found in Java and elsewhere. Try Pajak Ikan Lama, off Jl. Perniagaan for a large selection of contemporary textiles. Chinese medicine and foods are in abundance around the central part of Medan's "Chinatown"—the area bordered by Jl. Thamrin, Jl. Asia and Jl. Sumatra. Try Pajak Hong Kong on Jl. Thamrin near Thamrin Plaza, a predominately Chinese market, and the several Chinese apothecaries in the area.

SPORTS ACTIVITIES

Medan is, in some respects, a golfer's paradise. Where else in the world can you be 5 to 10 minutes away from two interesting 9-hole courses, with green fees of only $3.50 (caddy fees about the same), that are virtually empty most of the time? **Polonia Golf Course** is right on the other side of the airport, run by the Air Force. Though the greens are a bit uneven and the fairways occasionally a bit unkempt, it is an enjoyable, relatively easy course. **Nicotiana** is located out Jl. Karya, run by the government plantation PTP IX, and much more challenging. **Tuntungan** is an international standard 18-hole club about half an hour out on the road toward Berastagi. Green fee is $10 for non-members, about the same for caddies.

On the road to Pematang Siantar and

Prapat are several more plantation courses worth your attention. Try the "water course" at **PTP II**, in Tanjung Morawa, just past the intersection with the Belawan toll road, for more water hazards then you've probably seen in your whole life. Try the course at **PTP V**, Galang, for a few 600-m par fives with rolling fairways and truly spectacular scenery designed by an Italian. Anyone can play on these plantation courses; green and caddy fees average $10.

Major hotels have health clubs. The Clark Hatch club in Hotel Tiara and the Hotel Danau Toba club have well maintained tennis courts.

COMMUNICATIONS

The Intelsat building on Jl. Perintis Kemerdekaan is the central office for domestic and international long distance calls, telegrams and faxes. For domestic calls you can also make use of the recently-opened Warung Telekomunikasi (WarTel), found all over town in all the shopping plazas. To save time and money, you can use a number of new pay phones, recently installed in many sites around the city, which take prepaid cards for direct dialing domestically and internationally without going through the operator. Cards are available in a number of denominations up to Rp100.000 ($50) and can be purchased in many of the larger hotels and at WarTel offices in all of the plazas. The cards can be keyed for automatic dialing of frequently called numbers.

ENTERTAINMENT

Discos. Medan's night life is coming up, with several good discos. Try the Dynasty at Hotel Danau Toba or the Xanadu at Hotel Dirgha Surya nearby. The Bali Plaza Restaurant on Jl. Kumango 1A around the corner from the Panln Bank has a lively bar and club upstairs, and check out the Tropicana on Jl. Mangkubumi. Without a doubt the best bands and live music in a small high energy atmosphere are still to be found at the Music Room at the Danau Toba. Karaokes are all over and the best can be found in the major shopping plazas.
Cultural activities. Medan is ethnically rich though a bit quiet culturally, and appears to be going through a kind of cultural awakening. Most hotels in and outside the city provide various shows presenting regional dance and music. It is often possible to see good performances of music, dance and theater when it does happen. Taman Budaya, the Department of Education's cultural center on Jl. Perintis Kemerdekaan often has activities of all sorts. Universitas Sumatera Utara (USU), the large national university in Medan has an active program in regional culture and frequently hosts programs. Nommensen University has an active music department and also holds frequent concerts of music and culture from this area as well as performances of Western classical music and jazz by local performers and international guests artists. Call Jurusan Etnomusikologi at Universitas Sumatera Utara (tel: 23210), or Jurusan Musik at Nommensen University (tel: 522922) for current information.

MUSEUMS

Museum Negara, Jl. H. M. Joni, off Jl. Sisingamangaraja. The provincial government museum, housed in a neotraditional building. Guides are available at the front foyer. Has a small but interesting collection of archaeological and ethnographic materials, though exhibits are rather poorly organized and labeled. There are three 12th-century South Indian statues from Kota Cina, an early trading site near Belawan, a Tamil provincial-style buddha image dating from the late 11th or 12th centuries, a headless Visnu and the lower part of a female diety imported from the Madras area of India for the use of Tamil merchants trading in the Karo hinterland eight centuries ago. There are also remains of an Islamic *nisan* or gravestone from Kelumpang, Deli, inscribed to the memory of the Imam Sadiq ibn Abdullah, an important Islamic personage dating from 1590 (998 H). Batak and Malay artifacts, a ceramic collection and traditional *adat* dress are also on display.
Bukit Barisan Museum, Jl. Arifin. Indonesian Armed Forces museum, interesting for its particular holdings from the Sumatran theater of the Indonesian revolution in the 1940s.

HEALTH

There is quite a range of hospitals, clinics and other medical facilities in Medan. Should you require medical assistance, recommended hospitals and outpatient services can be found at St. Elizabeth's Hospital (tel: 512455) on Jl. Imam Bonjol near the airport, Herna Hospital (tel: 515397) on Jl. Mojopahit, Materna Hospital on Teuku Umar (tel: 513252) near Jl. Zainul Arifin in Kampung Keling (has well equipped radiology department with CAT scan equipment), and Melati Hospital on Jl. Timor off Jl. Perintis Kemerdekaan (tel:530039).

RAFTING AND TREKKING

Alas River trips are arranged by **Edelweiss**, Jl. Irian Barat 49 (tel: 517297). Under the supervision of an American guide from the Sobek company, you can take an exciting rafting trip of 5-7 days at $499 per person, with a minimum of 5 persons per party, a bit more for fewer people. Leave Medan on Friday, overnight in Berastagi, then enjoy 3 days of rafting and camping with spectacular scenery and sumptous food. They can also arrange jungle treks through Gunung Leuser National Park. **Jacky's Traveller's Centre** has also recently begun arranging more modest canoe trips within the Alas system and treks around Berastagi.

— Ed Van Ness

PART III

Introducing North Sumatra

North Sumatra, with its colorful and ethnically mixed population, is Indonesia's most populous province outside of Java. It now has a total of over 11 million inhabitants—more than the entire population of Kalimantan or all the islands of Nusa Tenggara. Dynamic Bataks, Malays, Javanese, Indians and Chinese have created a fascinating kaleidoscope of modern and traditional Indonesian culture. The economy, long established on the basis of plantation agriculture, now supplemented by the huge Asahan aluminum project and various service industries, is one of the strongest in the nation. Tourism, based on the scenic beauties of Lake Toba and the Karo Highlands, is next only to Bali and Yogyakarta.

There are two major ecological zones in the province—a fertile, swamp-fringed eastern plain largely given over to plantations, and a central volcanic core—the Bukit Barisan—formed 70 million years ago by tectonic movements. There is in addition a narrow coastal plain to the west, and a chain of sparsely-inhabited islands lying 125 km off the western coast, of which Nias is the best known.

The jewel of northern Sumatra, Lake Toba, was initially formed some 75,000 years ago in one of the most violent volcanic eruptions ever known—a cataclysm which created volcanic deposits over 600 m thick and hurled ash as far as the Bay of Bengal. A second series of eruptions some 30,000 years ago built up a new volcano inside the older one, and the depression formed by these convulsions now measures about 120 km long by 45 km wide. By comparsion, the much publicized eruption of Mount St. Helens in Washington State left a crater only 2 km in diameter.

The Toba explosion also resulted in the formation of a zoogeographical boundary in the Toba area. Species such as the orangutan, the white-handed gibbon, Thomas' leaf monkey and 17 types of birds are found only to the north of this region—while the tapir, tarsier, Sumatran rabbit, banded leaf monkey and 10 species of birds are found only to the south of it. It seems that the eruption created a vast, desolate region that many wildlife species were unable to cross.

The Bataklands

It is not known when the first humans came into the area but the Batak who dominate the highlands probably arrived from the Philippines and Borneo between 3,000 and 4,000 years ago. Si Raja Batak, the mythical ancestor of all Batak peoples (according to Toba legends), is said to have descended at Mt. Pusuk Buhit (1,981 m), a volcano on the western shores of Lake Toba. There are now six contiguous Batak groups, each with its own language and customs (see "The Batak").

European knowledge of the huge lake in these highlands came quite late. Marsden, who spent 8 years in Bengkulu in the late 18th century, heard rumors of its existence. Two British missionaries, Burton and Ward, entered the Silindung Valley from Sibolga in 1824, but appear to have been carefully restrained from reaching Toba, then considered sacred by the inhabitants. The first European to actually see the lake was the eccentric Dutch linguist, H. N. van der Tuuk, in 1853. Two Boston missionaries, Lyman and Munsen, were less lucky. In the early 1860s they accidentally shot and killed a Batak woman whilst out hunting and were unceremoniously eaten for their pains.

The Batak hinterland came under Dutch control only in the early years of this century, and direct European influence in this area was consequently very brief—coming to an end with the Japanese occupation in 1943. It has commonly been assumed that prior to this time the Batak were an extremely primitive and isolated people. Shocking accounts in the early literature paint them as savage

Overleaf: *The ceremonial* tortor *dance on Samosir.*
Opposite: *A Toba Batak. Photos by Kal Muller.*

headhunters, cannibals and warriors. This image is rather misleading. The Batak not only possessed their own system of writing and a highly developed culture, but seemed to have had early and prolonged trading links with each other and with the outside world.

The Dairi country just to the west of Toba around Sidikalang, for example, was once rich in benzoin—a form of incense that from time immemorial has been in great demand for ritual purposes all over the East. It has long been an important trade item and is still exported from Tarutung to Java. Rotan from the mountains was also important, and Samosir, formerly known for its weavings, also supplied markets around the lake with distinctive earthenware cooking pots known as *hudon*.

Early foreign contacts

Relatively little is known of the early history of the Batak homelands, as tangible archaeological evidence has been difficult to come by. Sherds of Song, Yuan and Ming stonewares nevertheless indicate that several Karo villages, such as Siberaya near Tiga Panah, were in contact with foreign traders by the end of the second millennium AD. Karo folktales suggest that there were well-armed Indian traders here centuries ago, and a small bronze Krisna image in Tamil style was found at Ajibuhara on the Karo Plateau in 1925.

Then there are the Dravidian connections of the Sembiring Sinyombak—Karo Batak septs who formerly set adrift the remains of their dead at the great Pe'kualuh ceremony held at Siberaya. The Sinyombak are forbidden to eat dog meat, though the reason for this is not entirely clear. According to folklore, it is because a Sinyombak ancestor was saved by his dog. There is, however, a more likely reason—an erstwhile association with Tamil traders from South India who came here seeking camphor and benzoin.

The Sinyombak Karo have an interesting group of family names—Berahmana, Culia, Depari, Keling, Meliyala, Pandya, Tekang and Mukham—which relate mainly to South Indian dynasties or castes, and probably originated from an association with a South Indian trading guild, the Ayyavole, who appeared in northern Sumatra in the 11th century AD. The Ayyavole were one of several Indian trading groups who had their own temples, priests and armies, and operated across political boundaries—supplying rulers and aristocrats with valuable textiles, incense, medicinal and ritual items. An Ayyavole inscription dating from AD 1088 has been discovered on the west coast of North Sumatra near Barus.

Other evidence of South Indian presence is reflected in Karo place names such as Lingga, Cingkem and Kubuculia. A small Batak group to the south of here, the Pardembanan, appear to have also exhibited strong Indianized traits. They lived between the Silau and Asahan rivers but have now been completely absorbed by the Simalungun Batak.

In the Padang Lawas area 200 km south of Medan, moreover, there are some impressive remains of the Hindu-Buddhist Panai culture. The most important of these is the brick *biaro* at Bahal near Gunung Tua, erected between the 10th and 14th centuries. Here too is evidence of external trade with northwest India and China—a village named Senamandala, after the ruling dynasty of Bengal, and a *marga* or clan named Daulay, after a locality in the northeast Indian district of Orissa.

Magic seems to have played an important role among the Batak in these earlier times, for there are many tales of the *orang jadi-jadian*, men who could transform themselves at will into majestic tigers—tales which fit in well with the evidence of Tantric Buddhist practices from the archaeological remains.

Conversions and migrations

Prior to Indonesian independence, the various Batak groups largely remained within their ancestral homelands. The Dutch finally annexed the Karolands at the turn of the century and built the first road into the plateau in 1908. The Karo are now largely converted to Christianity and to a lesser degree to Islam, though a number still maintain their ancient *pebegu* animistic religion.

The Toba were converted to Christianity by German and Dutch missionaries in the late 19th century, while the Mandailing and Angkola groups were largely converted to Islam by fanatical Paderis from Minangkabau during the Paderi Wars of 1816-1832. Today, however, Christians and Muslims live peaceably here in a land dotted with mosques and churches, united by the strong bonds of *adat*, strongly influenced by old kinship ties.

The breakdown of law and order at the end of the Japanese occupation occasioned a mass exodus from these uplands to the vastly more fertile and largely empty east coast plains, and many Batak have now spread all across Indonesia as teachers, civil servants and businessmen—enjoying vast new economic opportunities that were previously undreamed of.

— *E. Edwards McKinnon*

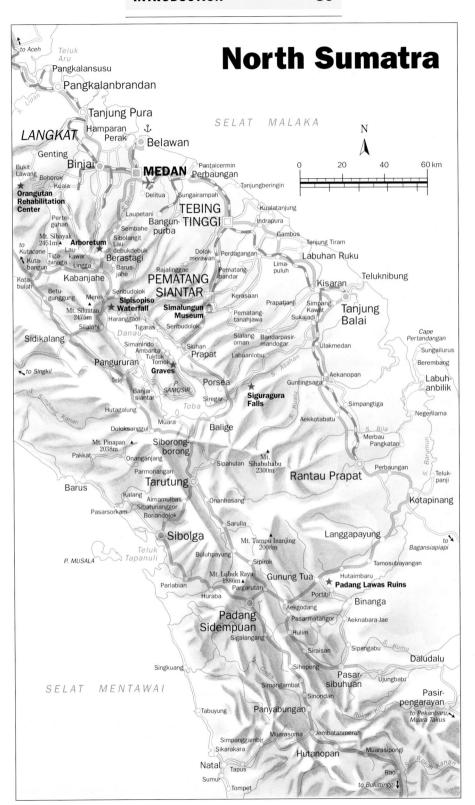

North Sumatra

to Aceh
Teluk Aru
Pangkalansusu
Pangkalanbrandan
Tanjung Pura
LANGKAT
Hamparan Perak
Genting
Binjai
Belawan
Bukit Lawang
Bohorok
Kuala
Orangutan Rehabilitation Center
Perteguhan
Mt. Sibayak 2451m
Arboretum
to Kutacane
Kuta bangun
Tigabinaga
Laukawar
Lingga
Berastagi
Barusjahe
Kabanjahe
Kotabuluh
Betunggunggung
Merek
Sipisopiso Waterfall
Mt. Siluatan 2475m
Harranggaol
Silalahi
Tigaras
Sidikalang
Danau
Simanindo
Ambarita
Tuktuk
Tomok
Panguraran
Tele
to Singkil
Banjarsiantar
P. SAMOSIR
Graves
Hutagalung
Muara
Doloksanggul
Mt. Pinapan 2038m
Pakkat
Siborong-borong
Onanganjang
Parmonangan
Tarutung
Barus
Kalang
Airnamulbas
Sibatunanggor
Bonandolok
Pasarsorkam
Sibolga
Teluk Tapanuli
P. MUSALA
Buluhpayung
Parlabian
Mt. Lubuk Raya 1886m
Huraba

MEDAN
Delitua
Pantaicermin
Perbaungan
Sungairampah
Tanjungberingin
Laupetani
Sembahe
Sibolangit
Laudebukdebuk
Bangun-purba
TEBING TINGGI
Kualatanjung
Indrapura
Gambus
Tanjung Tiram
Dolok-merawan
Perdagangan
Rajalinggae
Pematang-bandar
Labuhan Ruku
Limapuluh
PEMATANG SIANTAR
Seribudolok
Kerasaan
Prapatjanji
Kisaran
Teluknibung
Simalungun Museum
Seribudolok
Pematang-tanahjawa
Simpang Kawat
Sukajadi
Tanjung Balai
Siuhan
Sialang-oman
Bandarpasir-mandogar
Ulakmedan
Cape Pertandangan
Prapat
Labuanlobu
Sungailurus
Berembang
Porsea
Guntingsaga
Aekanopan
Labuh-anbilik
Siregar
Siguragura Falls
Toba
Simpangtiga
Negerilama
Balige
Aekkotabatu
Merbau Pangkatan
S. Bila
Sipahulan
Mt. Sihabuhabu 2300m
Rantau Prapat
Perbaungan
Teluk-panji
Onanhasang
Kotapinang
Sarulla
Langgapayung
to Bagansiapiapi
Mt. Tampu Inanjing 2008m
Sipirok
Tamosubayangan
Sigalangang
Pargarutan
Gunung Tua
Hutaimbaru
Padang Lawas Ruins
Portibi
Binanga
Aekgodang
Pasarmatangor
Aeknabara-Jae
Padang Sidempuan
Hulin
Siraisan
Sipangabu
Daludalu
Singkuang
Sihepeng
Pasar-sibuhuan
Ujungbatu
Pasar-pengarayan
to Pekanbaru
Muara Takus
Tabuyung
Simangambat
Sinondan
Panyabungan
Natal
Tapus
Simpanggambir
Sikarakara
Muarasoma
Jembatanmerah
Muarasipongi
Hutanopan
Sumur
Tompet
Rao
to Bukittinggi

SELAT MALAKA
N
0   20   40   60 km
SELAT MENTAWAI

THE BATAK

Flamboyant Peoples of the Highlands

The colorful but notoriously forthright and aggressive Batak peoples inhabit a cluster of spectacularly beautiful and fertile volcanic basins at the northern end of the Bukit Barisan range—focusing around Lake Toba, with the huge island of Samosir at its center.

The term Batak is probably an abusive nickname given to them by coastal Muslims. It seems once to have been used widely in insular Southeast Asia to vilify pagan, upland peoples; a mountain tribe in the Philippines, totally unrelated to the Sumatran group, shares the same name, and a highland people in Malaysia is called Batek. Because it connotes heathen, pig-eater, cannibal and bumpkin, some Batak eschew the appellation altogether. One Batak group, however—the Toba Batak—have reclaimed the old moniker as an ethnic badge. Batak they are, and proud of it!

Today there are about six million Batak,

Batak Groups

MEDAN

Karo

SELAT MALAKA

Sima-
lungun

Pakpak

Danau
PULAU
SAMOSIR

Toba

Toba

SELAT
MENTAWAI

Angkola

Mandai-
ling

N

0   20   40   60km

more than half of whom live in the highlands surrounding Lake Toba. They are divided into quite a number of distinct Batak societies, each with its own language, style of ceremonial dress and traditions, and these are generally grouped under six separate ethnonyms (see diagram below). The various languages fall into three distinct sub-groups—with the Toba, Angkola and Mandailing in one, the Karo and the Pakpak in another, and the Simalungun by themselves in a third.

A Toba creation myth portrays Si Raja Batak as the founding patriarch of all Batak peoples, and a mountain to the west of Lake Toba known as Pusuk Buhit ("Central Hill"), as their point of origin. The linguistic pattern does not clearly confirm this, but the Toba Batak who now live in the area around the mountain are indeed the most numerous and visible group.

Nobles, commoners and slaves

Simalungun and Toba societies were divided into three ranks: nobles, commoners and slaves. Rank was acquired from one's parents and had little to do with wealth or achievement. The Toba raja was identified by his elaborate tunic and armband made from the shell of the giant mussel *Tridacna gigas.* (The pre-Islamic Bugis of South Sulawesi and the chiefs of Nias also wore such armbands.)

In the southern Batak regions, the raja held dominion over several genealogically-related villages. Only married men had a say, though the opinions of older female shamans were greatly respected. Among the Simalungun, slaves were the absolute property of their masters and could be crippled or killed at will. In the south, slaves were protected by *adat* (customary law), and in Karo society slaves were not a significant category at all, comprising only those who had fallen into debt. Neither among the Karo nor the Pakpak was there any nobility, nor any effective political leaders above that of village chiefs.

All Batak peoples are patrilineal, and their societies are segmented into clans who can theoretically trace their ancestry to a single male through a succession of male descendants. The Simalungun have only four clans, the Karo five, but the other Batak societies have 50 or more. Batak clans are exogamous; that is, marriage is fobidden within the clan, even if no blood relation can be found. A man may have more than one wife, and in the past

Right: *The famous royal tomb at Tomok, on Samosir Island, as it looked ca. 1920.*

powerful leaders often had several.

The preferred marriage for a man is in fact with his mother's brother's daughter. The family of the bride is revered as a source of fertility and prosperity. (The Karo call them "the visible god.") A substantial brideprice has to be paid to the bride's family, which occupies an honored place at the wedding and subsequent ceremonies. Complex networks of bride-givers and bride-takers, built up over many generations, provide a sense of identity for the individual. Despite changes brought on by the spread of education and improved communication since independence, such traditional networks are still very important.

Trade and Indian influence

Despite their geographic isolation, the Batak had regular contact with the outside world. Salt, cloth and iron were brought into the highlands in exchange for gold, rice, cassia —an inferior kind of cinnamon—and valuable tree resins such as camphor and benzoin. Horses were also bred and exported. *Ulos*, woven shawls that convey fertility and blessing when presented by bride-givers at weddings, radiated out from the Toba region to the surrounding Batak areas.

Trade between the highlands and the coast was on a large scale. Marsden mentions that at the end of the 18th century, 100,000 bamboo measures of salt were being imported annually to the Tapanuli region. Along these trade routes came Indian influence. The Toba language contains about 175 words of Sanskrit origin, especially calendrical terms, and the vocabulary of magic and divination. Batak writing, chess, spinning, religious ideas and even many clan names are of Indian origin. A modified Indian script was used to produce books about magic and curing written on bark and folded accordion style.

The first clear historical reference to the Batak comes in the 13th century, when the Chinese geographer Zhau Rugua mentions the name Ba'ta, a location on the northeast coast of Sumatra. The first account of the Batak in English was by Charles Miller, the East India Company botanist at Bengkulu, who visited the Batak countries in 1772 in the company of another Englishman, Giles Holloway. He wrote: "They have no king, but live in villages absolutely independent of each other, and perpetually at war with one another: their villages they fortify very strongly with double fences of camphor plank pointed, and placed with their points projecting outward, and between their fences they put pieces of bamboo, hardened by fire and concealed by the grass, which will quickly run through a man's foot."

In his detailed account of the Batak published in 1783, William Marsden astounded his readers with the paradox of a cannibalistic people who possessed a system of writing. Warfare was endemic and hostilities were for-

ANTIQUARIAAT ACANTHUS, UTRECHT

mally declared. "The first act of defiance is firing, without ball, into the kampong of their enemies. Three days are then allowed for the party fired upon to propose terms of accommodation, and if this is not done, war is then fully declared."

Attacks took place usually around midnight. Captured enemy were put in stocks, unable to stand or to sit, some of them for years—their legs withering from lack of use. If a village was captured, its inhabitants were enslaved and (in Toba) the village was burned.

Public cannibalism

Frequently mentioned in such accounts was the Batak habit of eating people. An Arab text from the 9th century mentions that Sumatra's

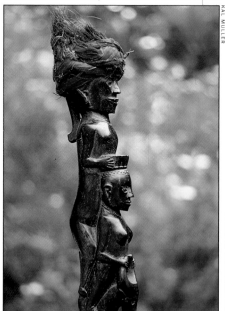

inhabitants ate human flesh. Marco Polo alluded to the same rumor, as did a series of Portuguese travelers in the 16th century, none of whom actually set foot in Batak territory. Among the Batak, public cannibalism was actually an infrequent form of capital punishment. During one and a half years spent among the Toba Batak (1840-1), the geographer Junghun witnessed only three cases. He left a vivid account of one:

"The captive is bound to a stake in an upright position. A number of fires are lighted, the musical instruments are struck. Then the chief draws his knife, steps forward and addresses the people. It is explained that the victim is an utter scoundrel, not a human being at all, but a *begu* ("ghost") in human

form, and the time has come for him to atone for his misdeeds. All draw their knives. The raja cuts off the first piece, being either a slice of the forearm or the cheek, if this be fat enough. He holds up the flesh and drinks with gusto some of the blood streaming from it. Then he hastens to the fire to roast the meat before devouring it. Now all the remaining men fall upon the bloody sacrifice, tear the flesh from the bones and roast and eat it. Some eat the meat raw, or half raw to show off their bravery. The cries of the victim do not spoil their appetites. It is usually eight or ten minutes before the wounded man becomes unconscious, and a quarter of an hour before he dies."

Cannibalism may have seemed more endemic than it actually was because of the fact that many Batak keep the bones of their illustrious ancestors, and these family treasures were often misconstrued as grisly trophies. It may have been in their interests, moreover, to cultivate this unsavory reputation. Rumors of Batak cannibalism no doubt contributed to the region's isolation, helping the Batak maintain control of trade routes into the highlands, and discouraging attempts at conquest by lowland kingdoms. Batak men often hired themselves out as mercenaries, too, and in this role blood-thirsty reputations served them well. The various Batak groups were not equally anthropophagous (the Karo deny that they ever ate human flesh), and while the custom may have persisted as late as the 20th century among the Pakpak, Toba and Simalungun, it was probably rare.

The Batak village

Prior to colonial rule, the Toba Batak lived in villages fortified with earthen and bamboo walls. The village consisted of 6 or 7 houses, at least one council house (*sopo*) and a skull house. The *sopo* surpassed even the chief's house in the splendor of its decorations, with rich leaf-and-flower designs carved on its beams. The houses faced one another across a rectangular square. Boys and widowers spent their nights in the *sopo*; in the south, unmarried girls were guarded by the village chief or slept in a separate house, where they were allowed male visitors. Karo houses were larger (holding as many as eight families), and their villages tended to be larger and more irregular in layout.

Batak houses were built on piles above the ground. The interior was open and quite barren of furniture, but at night mats were let down to provide privacy. Open hearths produced a constant fog of smoke, which in the absence of a chimney was forced to find its way out through the thatched roof.

Early Dutch visitors found these living conditions far from ideal. The scholar Neumann describes a Toba house in the mid-19th century thus: "Soot covers the walls and ceiling, the corners are full of cobwebs, the floors are covered with *sirih* chews and chicken excrement. The houses are like caves into which the openings in the walls scarcely admit a ray of light. Centipedes and scorpions wander about freely, ants build their runways, cockroaches fly unmolested, and lice lurk all over. When the houses are filled with smoke, one asks oneself how human beings can spend a night in one of them."

Like the Toraja of Sulawesi, who share the same ancient heritage, the Batak house was divided into three levels symbolizing a threefold division of the cosmos—the underworld, the earth and the upperworld. Animals were kept below the house (where they warned against attacks), people lived in the middle and sacred heirlooms were hung under the eaves. Important items were kept in the *sopo*: the skulls of slain enemy, magical writings incised on bark, and the bronze drum which summoned villagers to feast or council.

Economic life

Every Batak was, and to a large extent still is, a farmer. Rice is the most important crop, followed by maize, potatoes, taro, yams and various vegetables. Coffee, tobacco, cinnamon, coconut and sugar (and earlier indigo) are raised as cash crops. Cattle, buffalo and other livestock are also important. Irrigated land is very valuable because it may be cultivated continuously, but where thick grasses have taken over, dry fields can be worked with deep hoes between long periods of fallowing. Around the lake, women supplement their income with weaving, and throughout the Batak region men and women transport and sell the region's produce. Rural families who farm and trade, or draw a wage as teachers or bus drivers, are often the most well-to-do.

Toba villages and the surrounding lands belong to a patrilineal descent group, and women ideally move to their husband's village. In reality a man often lives in his wife's village if more land is available. Land passes to male heirs, but this legal standard often bends to accommodate women's needs. Women inherit land as widows, for example, and may receive it as gifts from parents or brothers, or be granted the lifetime use of fields.

As the population in rural areas expanded, migration became the solution to land shortages, and families increasingly invested in education. Some who move away maintain ownership of land, leaving it to be worked by relatives. The Toba regard their land as a sacred legacy from the primal ancestor or village founder; it must not be sold to outsiders.

Cosmology and magic

Traditional Batak religious beliefs were influenced by Hindu-Buddhist ideas, but as in Bali these rested on an older Austronesian substratum dating back some 5,000 years.

The Toba universe was divided into three. The upperworld, which had seven levels, was the home of gods, the middle world belonged

to humans and the underworld was the home of ghosts and demons. A high god, Mula Jadi Na Bolon—the Creator—was a remote, mythical being who had a fabulous blue chicken for a wife and did not concern himself much with human affairs. Attending more closely were the ancestral spirits, and these remain important for the Toba today.

Ancestors protect and receive honor from meat-sacrificing communities of descendants, called *bius*. Descendants of a village founder constitute a small *bius*; larger ones are made up of several villages tracing their origins to still more distant ancestors. In the past, major

Opposite: *A magical shaman's staff, or* tunggal panaluan. **Above:** *An ancestor figure.*

bius kept their ancestors' bones in hand-hewn stone sarcophagi, some with a stylized *singa* or "lion" head carved on their face. In recent years, these sarcophagi have been replaced by massive concrete structures and statuary.

Batak medical theory focuses on the condition of the soul. The soul of a healthy person is "hard" and remains firmly in place. Illness befalls someone who has been startled, causing the soul to flee the body. By ritual means, a shaman calls the wandering soul home again and thus "cures" the patient.

Karo shamans (*guru*) were both men and women, although male *guru* tended to have a higher status. Women *guru* were often spirit mediums as well as healers. The Toba shaman (*dukun*), usually male, was instrumental in communicating with spirits, both good and evil, and was second only to the village chief in importance. He was consulted before any undertaking, such as war or harvesting.

The shaman had a magic staff (*tunggal panaluan*) carved with ancestral figures and used to produce rain and to protect the village against enemies. This staff possessed a "warrior" spirit, the *pangulubalang*, which was obtained by kidnapping a child from a hostile village. After extracting an oath from the victim, boiling lead was poured down his throat and he died a quick but painful death, thus securing his ghost as an obedient ally. A magical substance made from his entrails was placed in a hole in the center of the staff.

Muslims and Christians

Starting in the early 19th century, the southern Batak began to face increasing pressure from the neighboring Minangkabau areas to convert to Islam. This culminated with the Paderi War (1816-33), when southern Batak succumbed to the burning and looting of West Sumatran Muslims who aimed to spread their faith and control the gold trade.

The war pushed as far north as the Toba region, but not many Toba converted to Islam. All of the Mandailing did, however, and most of the Angkola, and these southern groups began to renounce the name Batak and to dispense with their traditional clan names. Karo who moved to the East Coast similarly converted to Islam and began to consider themselves Malays. In the past, Batak and Muslim were exclusive categories, although today Batak Muslims are better able to reconcile their religious and ethnic identities.

The Batak were an early and obvious target for Christianizing European missions (see "Missionaries") and today the Toba church is the largest in Indonesia. Benefitting early from mission schools, the Toba moved rapidly to fill positions as teachers, medical technicians and office clerks in the post-colonial order. As a result they remain disproportionately represented in government and in careers requiring education.

— *Rita Smith Kipp*

KAL MULLER

MISSIONARIES

19th Century Protestant Conversions

Christian traders had visited Sumatran ports as early as the 10th century, and Franciscan monks ministered to the foreign community of Aceh in the late 17th century, but the only real prospects for Sumatran converts during the colonial period were among the more isolated peoples who had firmly resisted Islam —particularly the Batak of the highlands and the Niha (of the western island of Nias).

In the 19th century, several missionaries undertook the dangerous journey into Batak territory. Some were unlucky. In 1824 two members of the English Baptist Mission Society, Burton and Ward, translated some of the Bible into Batak and spent a week in the Silindung Valley, but were discouraged from continuing by Britain's surrender of its Sumatran possessions to the Dutch at this time. The French Catholic mission in Penang attempted to extend its work to Nias in 1832, but the first two priests sent, Vallon and Berard, died within weeks of reaching Gunungsitoli.

Two American protestants, Lyman and Munson, also visited Nias briefly and then traveled from Sibolga into the Silindung Valley, where they were attacked and killed in 1834. A few Dutch missionaries worked in the Dutch-controlled southern Batakland in the 1850s, but since these areas were largely now Islamic, their progress was minimal.

The great Dutch linguist van der Tuuk (himself part Indonesian) was the first European to see Lake Toba. Though employed as a Bible translator, the eccentric scholar had little interest in promoting Christianity, and instead spent his time compiling a dictionary and grammar of the Toba Batak language.

Conversions really got underway with the decision of the German Rhenisch Mission Society (RMG) to work here in 1861, and the arrival the following year of Ludwig Nommensen, who set off for the Bataklands armed only with a Bible and a violin. He was far-sighted enough to distance himself from colonial authorities and helped the Toba Batak as a doctor, mediator and teacher. Beginning in the Silindung Valley, his work spread north to the shores of the lake and beyond, and bore fruit in conversions of whole communities in the 1880s. By 1900 the Toba Batak were predominantly Protestants, and Christianity had begun to seem a part of Batak identity.

Out of the shock of this transition, nevertheless, were born a number of movements attempting to blend Christian, Muslim and traditional beliefs with the messianic figure of Sisingamangaraja. The Parmalim movement flourished at the end of the 19th century to the south and east of Lake Toba, while the militant Parhudamdam movement threatened European plantations during the WW I years.

There were growing pressures against what some saw as the paternalistic control of European missionaries, leading in 1927 to a breakaway independent church, the Huria Kristen Indonesia (HKI). In response, the Rhenisch Mission was reconstituted in 1930 as a self-governing Batak church (HKPB). This helped meld the Toba into a self-conscious group as they began their expansion into commercial and teaching roles all over Indonesia.

In contrast to the somewhat marginal place of Christians in many parts of Asia, the 3 million Toba Batak Christians are aggressive and unapologetic about their status as Indonesian nationalists who played their part in the revolution and now have a significant role in the Republic's army and government.

Christianity made much slower progress among the Karo and Simalungun, partly because it was associated first with Dutch and later with Toba Batak domination. There were only 5,000 Karo converts by 1940. The removal of Dutch missionaries by the Japanese proved a stimulus to the growth of the Karo church, and with the suppression of communism in 1965 there was finally a mass movement of Karo to Christianity, spurred on by the government's distrust of anyone who "did not have a [universal] religion."

In Nias, systematic missionary work began with the Dutch conquest of the island in 1890. By 1915 there were 20,000 Niha Christians and by 1940 a majority of the islanders, some 135,000 people, were converts. Catholics were excluded from evangelizing in the Bataklands until the 1930s by a colonial partition agreement, but thereafter made rapid gains. Today Catholics represent over 10 percent of the total Batak population.

— *Anthony Reid*

Opposite: *Toba Batak dancers at Ambarita.*

BATAK HOUSES

Traditional Communal Dwellings

Highways leading into the Batak highlands mostly date from the Dutch period, and the settlements seen along the roadside here are not traditional ones. Batak villages were formerly sited far from the main roads for reasons of security. In the Karo highlands, for example, they perched high atop ridges surrounded by deep ravines, which made them more easily defensible. To see traditional Batak houses you thus have to venture off the main roads into more remote areas.

There are a great many regional architectural styles, but most Batak houses have certain features in common. All are essentially rectangular wooden structures on piles, with high pointed roofs. The internal space is open and unfurnished, and was traditionally inhabited by several families. Two families normally shared a common hearth. There is often a balcony or verandah at the front for storage and for guests, and domestic animals such as pigs and buffalo live underneath the floor.

All old houses were traditionally thatched with the fibers of the arenga palm, which also provides palm sugar and wine. The walls and pillars were often ornately carved and painted in symbolic motifs. The *boraspati ni tano* or lizard was a favorite—a good luck and fertility symbol of the earth deity, combined in the Toba area in panels with two or four female breasts. The all-important *sopo* or rice barn stood directly in front of the house.

Today much has changed. Modern single-family brick or cement houses built on the ground are the norm, while corrugated metal sheets often replace *ijuk* thatch on the older houses. In most Batak areas in fact the traditional houses have all but disappeared. Here and there, nonetheless, especially in more isolated areas, one can still find fine examples of traditional Batak architecture.

Karo and Simalungun houses

Traditional Karo houses were massive affairs —constructed and occupied by eight related families. Each family had a living space of about five square meters organized around four hearths. Many older houses are still in use, although the residents are not usually related to one another, as the original owners have often now rented out the "apartments."

Old Karo houses can be seen in villages around Kabanjahe. In the village of **Lingga**, for example, often visited now by tourists, the old houses stand grouped in rows one behind the other. Most date from the 1930s, as no new ones have been built since independence, and each year their number dwindles as one or two collapse through disuse and neglect.

An unusual characteristic of Karo houses is their lack of a distinctive front or back, as they have identical entrances on opposite sides with access by means of bamboo platforms. In some very old houses a deep wooden gutter runs down the center of the floor, dividing the house in half. Debris was swept into this gutter and it served an important ritual function during ceremonies.

The only decoration on many old Karo houses is a large triangular top piece made of braided bamboo, with the inauguration date of the house inscribed on it. Other houses have a decoration that is not immediately recognizable—a lizard pattern braided into palm fibers binding the ribs of the walls together. The broad, round house beams are also sometimes decorated with plant motifs, and the house corners may be adorned with interlocking geometric patterns designed to prevent bad influences from entering.

Traditional houses always had a rice barn, but these are no longer in use today, as rice is now kept in plastic bales inside the house. In some rice barns there was an extra sleeping room for the young men of the village, who were not permitted to sleep in the multi-family dwelling after puberty. Nowadays, adolescent boys sleep in empty houses and the rice barns are used to play chess and chat, especially in the warmer western Karo areas.

Old Simalungun Batak houses are very simple, except for a few belonging to the former rajas. These are built like Karo houses— the raja's living quarters are in front, entered via a wooden staircase, and his wives lived at the back, with their own rooms but sharing a collective entrance. Only two authentic Simalungun royal houses remain—one in **Hutaraja**, the other in **Purbatongga**. A third one in nearby Pematang Purba was actually built during the 1930s as a new home for the

Right: *Toba houses at Tomok, on Samosir Island.*

Hutaraja chief. In Hutaraja, particularly, many of the old houses are still intact and a visit to this village—located about 5 km northeast of Pematang Purba along a small track—gives a good impression of Simalungun villages in the days before the plantation boom.

Toba and Mandailing houses

Toba villages are the most traditional of all Batak settlements. They are normally quite small—consisting of 8 to 10 houses facing each other in rows. A broad central avenue between them is used to dry rice and other produce, and is filled with people during annual village festivals, which mostly take place in June and July. Compared with the enormous Karo houses, those of the Toba Batak are modest. Four families formerly lived in one, which is scarcely imagineable today given their small size. Nowadays one family lives in a house that is often furnished with tables and chairs—even a stereo set.

Toba houses have a distinctive front verandah with a wooden staircase. Very old houses had a trapdoor that could be quickly closed in case of hostilities. At the front of the house the roof protrudes further than the back, and underneath it is an open balcony. During festivals the orchestra sits here and plays to accompany ceremonies taking place below.

The houses are often beautifully decorated with elaborate painted carvings—geometric or cosmological motifs like the "tree of life" which supposedly reaches to heaven. Oracle animals are also depicted, as is a striking, stylized face or *singa* (which literally means "lion" but is not really a lion at all). Like the *gaja dompak* or elephant figure, the latter is probably influenced by the Hindu-Buddhist *makara* or elephant-like sea monster that adorns ancient temple portals.

The placement of a *singa* on the ends of the house was formerly accompanied by special ceremonies and feasting, as if to signify that this was the moment the house was brought to life. Human heads are said to have been suspended in grass bundles from the *singa* at this time, imparting their potent life force to the newly-consecrated house.

Typical Mandailing Batak houses are still found in the remote villages of Simpang Banyak Jae and Simpang Banyak Julu around **Kuta Nopan**, at the southern end of the province. These houses resemble Karo Batak ones, but each houses only a single family. Metallic decorations are attached to the top of the roofs like charm bracelets, and through the influence of neighboring Minangkabau houses, some have a gallery attached.

Opposite the village chief's house one can find an assembly building where nine drums used during festivals are suspended. A raised floor serves as a seat for the village chief on special occasions, and the corners of the floor are marked by four lovely wooden statues.

— *Periplus Editions*

GOTTFRIED ROELCKE

BATAK TEXTILES

Professional Weavers from the Toba Area

Woven fabrics (Toba *ulos*, Karo *uis*) play an important role in traditional Batak society. They are used not only as clothing, but as important gifts presented on ritual occasions to symbolize and reinforce the bonds existing between related groups of people. The need to exchange traditional fabrics at ceremonies such as weddings, births and funerals is indeed the main reason such cloths continue to be produced today, though one can also see them being worn by village women as shawls or head coverings.

In many areas, villagers no longer weave their own traditional fabrics but instead purchase reproductions that are machine-made in the larger towns, for example in Pematang Siantar and Balige. Remaining village weaving centers are mostly located in the Toba Batak region, where the main source of livelihood is still rice agriculture and the soils are relatively poor. When not working in the fields, village women here try to earn a bit of extra money by weaving.

Weaving for a living

In some areas, weaving has long been a full-time occupation practiced by village woman who accept commissions from traders and merchants in the towns (themselves also women). One area where such commercial weaving continues to be practiced is along the northwestern shores of Lake Toba, in the so-called *sitelu huta* ("three villages")—namely Tongging, Paropo and Silalahi. These villages were formerly accessible only by boat, and this form of transport still plays a major role here—especially on market days, when boats converge on the market village in the morning and return late in the evening.

Although the women of the *sitelu huta* are themselves Toba Bataks, they do not normally produce traditional Toba textiles. For generations they have instead produced fabrics for Karo Batak clients to the north, who—thanks to more fertile soils and export crops such as citrus and vegetables—had more money to spend on their traditional fabrics and jewelry than the Toba.

To ensure the accurate reproduction of their traditional motifs, Karo women formerly dyed their own yarns and then had them delivered by intermediaries to the *sitelu huta* villages for weaving. This practice continues

KAL MULLER

today, though one now finds other types of fabrics being woven here alongside the Karo cloths. Some are modern creations employing synthetic dyes; others are traditional Toba patterns produced in quantity for the tourist trade and sold in souvenir shops in Prapat and around Tomok on Samosir.

Earlier in this century, as the trade with the Karo flourished, many Toba weavers from the *sitelu huta* moved to the Karo area so as to have better access to their market. During the 1920s, when Kabanjahe was still a small, prosperous village, the village chief set aside a special area for these Toba weavers. As the village grew into a regional market center, more and more weavers moved here, and one now finds a whole enclave of Toba Batak weavers and dyers living in Kabanjahe.

Weavers here order their dyed yarns from Toba dyers who also live in the town. These dyers plant indigo in their backyard gardens, but this is often insufficient to meet their needs. Once a week additional supplies of concentrated indigo are brought in from one of the three Toba villages in exchange for locally-dyed yarns, and in this way a connection with the area of origin is maintained.

The patterns woven for the Karo depend on orders, but also on the individual preferences of the weaver. Some older weavers refuse to work with synthetically-dyed yarns. Toba weavers in Kabanjahe tend to be older than their counterparts in the homeland vil-lages around the lake, and they tend to produce more traditional patterns. This is encouraged by their clients, as the Karo themselves are quite conservative.

Today, however, many of the fabrics produced here employ non-traditional dark red colors—a style of coloring emanating from the Simalungun area. These colors have been popular among the Karo for some time now, and younger Karo often do not even know that their own traditional fabrics were once exclusively dyed with indigo blue.

The Toba women in Kabanjahe also weave their own traditional *sitelu huta* village patterns. Some of these they sell, others are kept aside for their own use, to be distributed among family members after their death.

The traditional weaving and dyeing industry is severely threatened today by manufactured goods that look similar but are cheaper and also much thinner—produced with synthetic dyes and yarns. Unfortunately, these fabrics are catching on to the point where the younger generation buys them almost exclusively. There is even an increasing demand for machine-woven fabrics that reproduce traditional Karo motifs using gold and silver threads instead of the traditional dyed colors of indigo and red.

— *Beatriz van der Goes*

Opposite: *A young Toba weaver at work.*
Below: *An example of the Toba* ragi idup *cloth.*

ERIC OEY

SIMALUNGUN AREA

Through the Plantation Belt to Toba

The Simalungun or Timur ("Eastern") Batak occupy the highlands between Lake Toba and the east coast—today a key plantation region with huge estates producing palm oil, rubber, cacao and tea. The area is traversed by a 100-km stretch of the Trans-Sumatra Highway leading up to Prapat via Pematang Siantar.

The name comes from an earlier period in the region's history and means "desolate land" though it is in fact quite fertile. The Simalungun area borders the Karo highlands to the north and the Toba Bataklands to the south. On the west it is bounded by a thin string of Toba settlements, such as Tigaras along the eastern shore of Lake Toba, and in the south by the Asahan River which drains Lake Toba.

The land slopes generally south and east down from the Karo Plateau and the Toba rim to low-lying coastal plains, and is cut by deep ravines and several sizable rivers—the

largest of which is the restless and unpredictable Bah Bolon ("Great River") which flows through the market town of Perdagangan to the sea at Kuala Tanjung, the new port built for the Asahan aluminium project.

The country was formerly divided into a number of small and sparsely-populated independent states: Silimakuta, Purba, Raya, Pane, Dolok, Siantar, Tanah Jawa and Bandar—each under its own raja, who held considerable power in his domain. Somewhere in this area was also the ancient kingdom of Nagur.

The Simalungun and the Karo have much in common—Indianizing traits in their dialect, religious practices and script, as well as the presence of village federations known as *urung*. The Simalungun were, however, reputedly cannibals, whereas the Karo were not.

The major Simalungun *marga* or clans are distinct from those in the other Batak areas—namely Damanik, Sinaga, Saragih and Purba. Islamic influence is strong in areas adjoining the coastal Malay settlements. By the early years of this century, the rajas of Purba and Raya invited Rhenish missionaries into their territories. In 1907, the rajas signed the Korte Verklaring of submission to the Dutch, and in 1908 a colonial adminstration was established in Pematang Siantar.

Soon after the arrival of the Dutch, Toba migrants began moving into then unoccupied areas, creating vast expanses of irrigated rice fields, a technique quite alien to the Simalung-

JILL GOCHER

un, who practiced only swidden agriculture. More Toba migrants poured in after Independence, and today the Toba comprise a large proportion of the area's population.

Unlike in other Batak areas, Simalungun lands were held not only by the dominant clans but also by the rajas. After the establishment of Dutch rule, this allowed them to dispose of vast tracts of uncultivated land for plantations, which of course afforded them considerable benefits. Consequently much of Pane, Siantar and Tanah Jawa became cov-

ered in large plantations worked by Javanese labor. This is the only Batak homeland area in which plantations were established, and few old Simalungun villages remain.

Medan to Tebing Tinggi

The highway east of Medan through the Deli-Serdang coastal area is broad and fast, passing through endless groves of rubber trees and oil palms. Those wishing to tour the estates can make arrangements at the Tourist Information Office on Jl. A. Yani in Medan.

A turnoff at Perbaungan leads north to **Pantai Cermin** ("Mirror Beach"), a favorite local holiday and weekend picnic spot, 45 km from Medan. Here are casuarina-lined beaches for swimming and fishing, though incomparable to those along the west coast.

About 76 km from Medan you enter the large town of **Tebing Tinggi**, the east coast rail junction where lines link Pematang Siantar with Medan and Rantau Prapat further to the south. In the rail yard here you can watch old steam locomotives being serviced, some of them dating from the turn of the century.

The main road to Pematang Siantar and Toba turns off here and enters the Simalungan area just south of Tebing Tinggi, passing through the enormous government-owned oil palm and cacao estate of Pabatu. Further along the road is the American-owned Dolok Merangir rubber estate, one of the few plantation enterprises still owned by foreign capi-

tal. The famous American botanist and ethnographer, Harley Harris Barlett—author of *The Labors of the Datoe*—worked here in 1918 and again in 1927.

Pematang Siantar

Pematang Siantar, North Sumatra's second largest city, is the administrative and commercial hub of the Simalungun plantation area, founded by the Dutch early in this century. Colonial houses can be seen amidst the urban clutter, and at 400 m above sea level the climate is notably cooler than on the coast.

The pre-war Siantar Hotel on Jl. W.R. Supratman was used as a headquarters by a small contingent of Dutch troops, and was attacked and burnt by revolutionary forces in 1945. It has now been restored and appears to have changed little since colonial times.

The **Simalungun Museum** on Jl. Ahmad Yani has an interesting collection of *pustaha laklak*—the bark books in Indic Batak script used by *datuk* magicians to record their sacred formulae. It also has notable examples of stone *pangulubalang* or Simalungun guardian images collected during the 1930s. The Siantar Zoo offers an interesting collection of Sumatran wildlife, and a wide variety of seasonal fruits such as durian, mangoes, mangosteens, *rambutan* and *salak* are offered for sale in Siantar's market.

From Pematang Siantar the road ascends steadily through palm plantations and a vast patchquilt of irrigated *sawah*. A few traditional houses and tombs appear by the roadside in the broken country around the Toba rim. The first glimpse of the lake is always breathtaking—a shimmering sheet of blue with the verdant cliffs of Samosir rising steeply from it in the distance.

— *E. Edwards McKinnon*

Opposite: *A rubber plantation.* **Above, left:** *The Simalungun Museum in Pematang Siantar.* **Above, right:** *Siantar's distinctive motorized becaks.*

A Verdant Highland Plateau

Taneh Karo or Karoland—the homeland of the Karo Batak people—is an exceptionally fertile plateau set in the midst of the volcanic Bukit Barisan highlands south of Medan. Its northern edge rises sharply from densely-forested foothills some 50 to 60 km from the coast, while the southern edge just touches the shores of beautiful Lake Toba. With an area of about 5,000 sq km, the plateau is like a gigantic bowl surrounded on all sides by jagged mountain peaks—looking almost as if it has been scooped right out of them.

For some time now this verdant plateau has served as northern Sumatra's green-grocer. With the construction of a road up from the coast in 1908, European crops such as cabbage, corn, carrots and potatoes were introduced, and Karo farmers began to culti-vate market gardens to supply a rapidly-grow-ing urban population in the lowlands—for a

time even supplying vegetables across the straits to West Malaysia and Singapore. Dutch-engineered irrigation works have been main-tained and expanded since independence, and few agricultural regions of Sumatra are as productive as these highlands. The *mar-quisa* (passion fruit) juice produced here is particularly famous throughout Indonesia.

The plateau's elevation ranges from 700 to 1,400 m—assuring a delightfully cool climate throughout the year, with temperatures of between 10 and 28 degrees C. The soil is deep and of rich volcanic origin, the whole region being overshadowed by two active volcanoes —Sibayak (2,170 m) to the north, near Beras-tagi, and Sinabung (2,451 m) to the west, visi-ble from Kabanjahe—both of which continu-ally emit plumes of steam. Although the rug-ged escarpment separating the plateau from the coasts formerly served as a formidable barrier to travel, the area has nevertheless been a crossroads for the transinsular trade in salt and tree resins since very early times.

The 'first arrivals'

The Karo people, known among themselves as the *merga silima*—the "five clans"—are a distinct cultural entity with their own lan-guage, history and traditions. According to their own legends, they were the earliest inhabitants of these highlands; their name in fact means "first arrivals."

Despite the assertions of some early Euro-

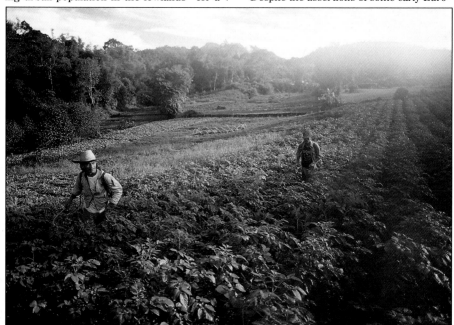

JILL GOCHER

pean explorers, the Karo were never cannibals, though they may have had some rather unconventional habits by European standards. The filing and blackening of teeth, which died out only in the early years of this century, combined with the red-stained lips obtained from chewing *sirih* or betelnut, undoubtedly gave them a somewhat bizarre and fearsome appearance.

About 300,000 Karo today inhabit the plateau, but at least as many live in the coastal lowlands to the east, where they have been for centuries. Since the 1950s many Karo have migrated further afield to Medan, Jakarta and other urban centers.

Highland Karo villages are larger than those of the lowlands (larger also than most Toba Batak villages), owing to the greater fertility of the plateau's volcanic soils. Early European travelers reported villages with as many as 3,000 inhabitants, linked through marriage and descent into loose federations known as *urung*. Intervillage skirmishes were common—even between villages within the same federation—and most were sited high up on the edges of ravines and surrounded by ramparts of earth and hedges of thorny bamboo for defensive purposes.

Each highland village was autonomous, with its own hereditary chief. In the 19th century, some lowland Karo lived under the authority of coastal Malay sultans, but the highlanders bowed to no central authority until the area was finally conquered by the Dutch in 1904. Aceh had earlier attempted to exert control here and to convert the Karo to Islam, but with little success.

Distinctive adat houses

Traditional Karo *adat* houses—with their open floorplan in which eight related families live together under a single upswept or rectangular roof of *ijuk* thatch—are a microcosm of traditional Karo society. The most common floorplan has four hearths, each shared by two families. A central walkway runs through the center of the house leading to doors at either end, with two hearths on either side of the walkway. In these large, partitionless spaces domestic life is carried on in full view of one's neighbors. Though related, each family works, cooks and eats as a separate unit, and life is somewhat inevitably shared with dogs, cats, chickens and other livestock.

The distinctive, oversized roofs decorated with triangular dormers and topped with buffalo horns have no clear purpose, but allow space under the eaves for smoke to pool in the absence of chimneys, and also for rats, bats, lizards and a host of insects to collect. Blackened heirlooms, tools and other objects are hung above the hearths and in the rafters.

Smaller structures with the same roof

Opposite: *The Karo plateau is Medan's greengrocer.* **Below:** *The Berastagi fruit market.*

KAL MULLER

design serve as granaries or contain the bones of distinguished ancestors. In the past, each village had a men's house where men gambled, smoked and rested during the day, and where adolescent boys slept at night. Today, most villages also have a *los*—a shelter for ceremonial events.

Unfortunately, few of these traditional houses remain. During the revolution, the Karo burned all villages along the main roads rather than leave anything for the Dutch, and in the post-war period, single-family dwellings have become the fashion. Traditional houses do still exist in more remote villages off the main roads, but are increasingly rare today and falling into decay.

Wife-givers and wife-receivers

Like other Batak peoples, the Karo reckon descent patrilineally, though neither the village nor the multi-family house is the domain of a single descent line. Each person belongs to one of five Karo clans (*merga silima*) from birth. Marriage between persons within the clan is forbidden, even if there is no traceable blood tie between them.

A family's marriage relations are as important as clan relations by descent, and as with other Batak groups, a distinction is made between wife-receivers (*anakberu*, families into which one's daughters marry), and wife-givers (*kalimbubu*, families whose daughters marry into one's own family). The former are one's social inferiors while the latter are one's superiors. Wife-receivers can be called on to assist at ceremonial events, while wife-givers are honored as a protective, supernatural "visible gods" affecting one's fertility, health and prosperity. In order to be complete, a village or traditional household had to be formed of all three kinds of families—the founder, as well as both types of relatives by marriage. The clan composition of Karo villages and houses is therefore very mixed.

The Karo conceive of their society as a community of kinsmen linked by marriage as well as descent. Meeting for the first time, two Karo inevitably ask each other a series of standard questions in order to construct a metaphorical kinship relation. Whether strangers or neighbors, all Karo address one another with kin terms; first names are seldom used except with children—unless intended as an insult! Recognizing no kings and giving deference only to their kinsmen, the Karo are egalitarian and competitive in their social interaction. The subservience and flowery

etiquette of many other Indonesian peoples thus grate on Karo sensibilities.

Religious pluralism

The first Dutch Reformed missionary arrived in Medan in 1890, at the behest of European planters who hoped the Karo could be Christianized. At first, the mission was confined to the foothills around Sibolangit, but with the Dutch annexation of the highlands, it moved to Kabanjahe. The mission was never very successful in either locale, apparently because Christianity was too closely associated with the hated colonial regime; only a handful of Karo had converted by the time of the Japanese occupation. After the Dutch left, however, an independent ethnic church developed and the Karo began to convert in large numbers.

Today, Karo society is religiously plural. About 60 to 70 percent belong to one of several Christian denominations, while as many as half of the remainder are Muslims; the rest still practice the traditional Karo religion. The latter focuses on ancestral spirits residing in unusual natural formations such as volcanoes or hot springs, and on a host of spirits that either protect or bring illness, death and crop failure. After a funeral, at seances lasting

Above, left and right: *Karo inhabitants of the old village of Lingga near Kabanjahe, now a tourist sight.* **Right:** *Traditional female Karo headdress.*

until dawn, female mediums work in consort with their spirit familiars to retrieve the souls of the deceased. At this ceremony, called *erpangir* (literally: "hair-washing"), even ordinary people become possessed, dance ecstatically and demand special foods.

The ancient Karo *pebegu* or spirit religion demanded special respect for the souls and remains of the dead. After initial interment in an earthen grave, the bones of revered ancestors were dug up after a suitable period of time, washed, and ritually placed in *geriten* or skull houses outside the house of the living.

Most ceremonies in Karoland today have a decidedly secular character, however. The religious portions of a funeral, whether Christian, Muslim or traditional, generally occur at the beginning and end—leaving the hours in between for meals, discussions of inheritance and dancing. Weddings follow a similar pattern. A Christian couple may have a church wedding in the morning and in the afternoon host a traditional feast with dancing.

Dancing at such events involves two large groups of men and women facing one another—the sponsors on one side, their kin on the other. Bending their knees and dipping to the beat of a giant gong, the dancers move their arms and hands slowly. At funeral dances, kin groups carry items of clothing that belonged to the deceased to enhance the grief of the survivors—Karo funeral dancers are expected to weep openly. During the dances, stylized forms of sung poetry are used to address the deceased and express one's sorrow.

Weddings and funerals remain important arenas for celebrating kinship and community relations. They reflect a family's wealth, renown and social network, and may be delayed for years so as to marshal the sufficient funds. Until a proper wedding or funeral is held, a family feels itself in debt to the community. A couple may marry in a simple church or civil ceremony—but years later, often with two or three of their own children present, they will sponsor a lavish wedding feast. Similarly, a family may bury a parent in a simple grave, but after some years will retrieve the bones, lovingly clean and reinter them in a splendid cement edifice while sponsoring an elaborate feast and dance.

Since the 1950s, the Karo have placed great emphasis on education. There are today over 2,000 university graduates in a society of no more than 800,000 people, surely one of highest educational levels achieved by any Indonesian ethnic group. Young Karo attend universities throughout the archipelago, then settle in the cities as engineers, nurses, bureaucrats, businessmen and academics. They return to the homeland periodically for funerals and weddings, and provide money to construct the imposing concrete tombs shaped like house or churches that increasingly dot the Karo homeland.

— *Rita Smith Kipp / E. Edwards McKinnon*

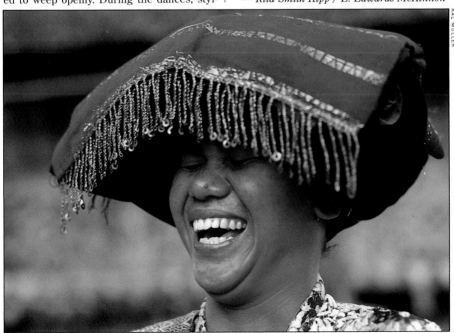

KAL MULLER

BERASTAGI

Scenic Hill Station on the Karo Plateau

The delightfully cool and picturesque town of Berastagi nestles at the northern edge of the Karo Plateau, 68 km south of Medan (about 2 hours away by car). At 1,330 m elevation, the climate is deliciously mild during the day and bracing at night. The town arose during the 1920s as a Dutch hill station, complete with 9-hole golf course and spacious European villas —even a Dutch school. Today it is a popular weekend resort for Medan residents, and it also makes a convenient stopover point on the way up to Lake Toba. There is a large market selling wonderfully fresh fruits, flowers and vegetables, and this is the perfect base for an exploration of the volcanic Karo highlands—with their thick pine forests, soothing hot springs and traditional villages.

The road up from Medan

About 20 km from Medan, the urban heat and traffic are soon left behind as you begin the climb into the forested foothills of the Bukit Barisan. Sharp S-turns provide panoramic views back across the verdant plains to the city. About 40 km from Medan, history buffs may be interested to stop at the town of **Sembahe**, where a pathway behind the shops next to the main bridge leads half a km or so upstream to a rubber estate where the first "Hoabinhian Sumatralith" neolithic stone tool was discovered in 1926. Nearby is the so-called Rumah Umang—a stone burial chamber with rough relief carvings that is several centuries old. In season, good durians may be purchased in Sembahe and along the road up to Sibolangit.

Several km further on, the **Sibolangit Botanical Garden** lies on an escarpment overlooking Sembahe and the lowlands. This pleasant patch of undisturbed rainforest is worth a stop to wander the pathways amidst giant ferns and moss-covered trees. Botanists will find an interesting variety of native flora, while birders will have a field day. Leeches and mosquitoes are a problem in the wet season, however, so bring along your repellant!

Ten km before Berastagi on the right is the turnoff to Daulu and Semangat Gunung —two villages at the base of active Mt. Sibayak (2,094 m). Also here is **Lau Debuk Debuk** ("Bubbling Water"), a hot sulphur spring regarded as the home of friendly forest spirits (notice the offerings of *kretek* cigarettes

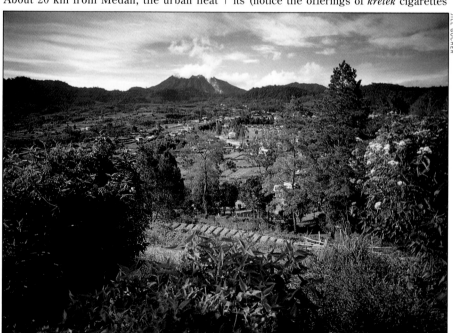

JILL GOCHER

left in lengths of split bamboo or palm stems by the edge of the pools), and also a favorite haunt of friendly locals, who like to enjoy a communal bath after sunset, when the cold air contrasts deliciously with the piping-hot, sulphur-laden water. Sip a cold beer or a hot tea while gazing up at the steaming volcano. A traditional masseuse is on hand to iron out tired muscles. Those wishing to climb Mt. Sibayak may continue along the same road to Semangat Gunung.

Seven km before Berastagi, at **Tongkoh**,

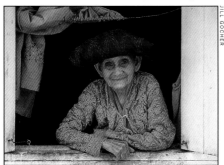

is an arboretum originally established in 1916 that has now been renamed "Great Bukit Barisan Forest Park." A project of the local district head (*bupati*), the park has a zoo, modern cabins for weekenders and elephant rides for the children. Unfortunately, a lot of concrete has been used to formalise the park and "enhance" its beauty.

Visiting Berastagi

Berastagi is a center for vegetable, flower and fruit farming—exporting truckloads of produce everyday to Medan. One of the area's most popular products is enormous yellow passion fruits, made into a refreshing cordial to mix with soda or water. The broad main street is lined with souvenir shops, restaurants and hotels, and the central market attracts farmers from the surrounding area. Here you can watch Karo village women in traditional costume grappling with the produce they have come to sell.

Berastagi is dominated immediately to the north by smoking Mt. Sibayak, while further to the west is higher Mt. Sinabung (2,451 m). Each of these volcanoes can be climbed in a day, though you need to be reasonably fit (see "Practicalities"). On the western edge of town, Gundaling Hill (1,496 m) rises some 110 m above the surrounding plateau, and a park at the top provides good views of the volcanoes. This was the former Dutch resort area, and crumbling old bungalows are found

scattered amongst new concrete hotels. It is close enough to walk up and around in an hour or so. At the northern edge of town is the delightful Bukit Kubu Hotel, a relic from the colonial era set amidst a manicured 9-hole golf course.

Traditional Karo villages

There are many old villages around Berastagi, ranging from very good to "not interesting." Visit a few to compare. The better known are Pecaren, Lingga, Cinkes, Dokan, Barusjahe and Juhar. Many are only accessible via hilly tracks or by changing *bemos* several times, so hire a guide at your hotel.

Right on the northern outskirts of Berastagi, the village of **Peceren** has a number of traditional houses interspersed with more modern ones. It is easily accessible; a guide will show you one of the houses where a small shop has been set up. The family sells crude wooden Karo and Minang figures, and the father serenades you with his *kecapi* lute as traditionally-clad grandmothers look on.

The most popular Karo tourist village is **Lingga**—16 kms southwest of Berastagi and about 5 km northwest of Kabanjahe. Situated near the source of the Lau Garut at an altitude of 1200 m, Lingga has a number of *rumah adat*—some reputed to be 250 years old—but is becoming dilapidated as it is more difficult now to build new *adat* houses due to the rising cost of timber and manpower. Guides will happily show you about and explain various facets of Karo life, including the "birthing seat" on a wooden step by the chief's house where some women still give birth, attended by the village *dukun* (medicine man), gripping two handles high above her head. It is possible to stay in the village and if you care to pay, traditional dances will be performed.

— *E. Edwards McKinnon and Jill Gocher*

Opposite: *View of Mt. Sibayak from Berastagi.*
Above, left and right: *The village of Lingga.*

Berastagi Practicalities

Most prices in US dollars. AC = air-conditioning. Telephone code is 0628.

The highland town of Berastagi is often overlooked in the rush to Lake Toba, but its refreshing weather, incomparable scenery and many activities make it a worthwhile stopover. Luscious *marquisa* (passion fruit), tomatoes, avocadoes, oranges and other goodies are grown locally and can be purchased in the market.

Berastagi has two main areas for tourists: Jl. Veteran, the main street, and the Bukit Gundaling Hill area to the west overlooking the town. While backpackers stay in the cheap *losmens* and homestays around Jl. Veteran, well-heeled Dutch groups head for the bright new hotels on Gundaling Hill, with their fabulous views of Mt. Sibayak.

GETTING THERE

From Medan, you can catch buses to Berastagi from the depot on Jl. Iskandar Muda. One leaves about every 15 minutes and costs about 60 cents. For extra comfort and a better view, ask for the front seat, even if it means waiting for the next bus. Taxis can also be chartered for the trip for around $25 from Indah Taxi or Bengawan Taxi on Jl. Sisingamangaraja near the Grand Mosque, or from one of the hotels (see "Medan Practicalities").

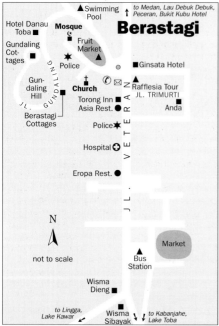

ACCOMMODATION
Expensive (above $30)

Many new hotels have recently opened in Berastagi, mostly around Gundaling Hill.

Danau Toba (34 rooms and cottages) Jl. Gundaling, tel: 20946/7. In a landscaped garden. Facilities include swimming pool, billiards, TV and video, taxi service and 24-hr room service. $38 to $45 weekdays; $30 to $37 weekends.

Gundaling Cottages, tel: 20946. $34 and up.

International Sibayak (101 rooms) Jl. Merdeka, tel: 20928. Newest and biggest in Berastagi. Facilities include TV (7 channels), pool, gym, disco, tennis courts. $55-$115 incl. breakfast.

Moderate ($10 to $30)

Berastagi Cottages (70 rooms) Jl. Gundaling. Spacious rooms with hot water, bath and sitting room in open, landscaped grounds, with a good view of both volcanoes. $20 to $33.

Bere Karona Jl. Pendidikan, tel: 208888. New, with bar, restaurant and conference facilities. $14 standard, $32 for 2-room bungalows.

Bukit Kubu (40 rooms) Jl. Sempurna 2, tel: 20832. Charming old colonial hotel at the northern end of town, set amidst a 9-hole golf course, with tennis courts and a great view of Mt. Sibayak. Rooms in the old wing have polished wood floors, spacious sitting areas, hot water. Service is friendly. $14 economy, $24 standard, up to $48 for a bungalow. Book in Medan at Jl. Sudirman 24, tel: (061) 519636.

Kolam Renang, Jl. Kolam Renang, next to the public swimming pool. Has a big garden and a good restaurant. $10-$13.

Rose Garden (89 rooms) Jl. Picaran, tel: 20099, 20399. Most facilities, including hot water. $25 up to $55 for a suite.

Rudang (43 rooms) Jl. Sempurna 16. $19 to $29; includes breakfast. Near the Bukit Kubu; popular with tour groups.

Budget (under $10)

Scattered along Jl. Veteran and down the side-streets are numerous small, cheap hotels in the $1-$3 range. Try the **Ginsata**—friendly, with a restaurant downstairs (Jl. Veteran 79, tel: 20901, right where the Berastagi bus stops). The newly-built **Anda** (Jl. Trimurti 76-79) is a bit cleaner—down a sidestreet off Veteran. The **Torong Inn** on Jl. Veteran (tel: 20828) is also clean, with a great Padang restaurant; try their fried chicken! **Wisma Sibayak** at the southern end of Jl. Veteran (Jl. Udara 1) is the most popular of all budget hotels, but a bit ratty these days. Rooms are $3; dorm beds $1.

For a bit more money, you can get a room with a view. **Wisma Ikut** is in an old colonial villa on the way up Gundaling Hill, with clean rooms, a big garden and a great view ($4). Several other places along Jl. Pendidikan offer rooms for the same price: the **Karo Hill** and the **BIB**. The **Miranda**, also on Jl. Pendidikan, has bungalows at $8. **Kaliaga Bungalow** on Jl Gundaling offers rooms with a hot shower for $9.

DINING

In spite of the wealth of fresh vegetables and fruits available in Berastagi, dining here is not an uplifting experience. The local specialities are roast pig (*babi panggang*) and stewed dog. Many *rumah makan* also serve spicy Padang food, but a steady diet of this for 3 or 4 days begins to pall even for the Padang enthusiast. Chinese food is also available; the best is in the big **Asia Restaurant** on Jl. Veteran, where a reasonable Chinese banquet can be ordered up. Smaller restaurants around Jl. Veteran serve the usual *mee goreng* and *nasi goreng*. **Eropa** on the west side of the street has huge servings at very cheap prices. Restaurants in the hotels are also quite enjoyable. The **Bukit Kubu** dining room serves European fare with white colonial tablecloths and friendly service. Also try the **Berastagi Cottages**, **International Sibayak** and the **Kolam Renang**.

CHANGING MONEY

Best place is in Medan. Once into the country, you are at the mercy of low rates. Most hotels will change money at a low rate. Nearest bank is BNI at Jl. Upah Tendin 41 in Kabanjahe, but the rates are no better.

INFORMATION AND TOURS

Head for **Rafflesia Tour and Infomation Center** (tel: 149) in the middle of town on Jl. Veteran, opposite the Post Office. Purnama Purba will help you plan your stay. He speaks good English, has lots of information and can hire a guide or book onward travel tickets. The guide can lead you around on public transport, or you can also hire a car here for $40 a day (not bad if split 4-ways). He can also arrange a climb up the volcanoes, a river rafting expedition on the Alas River and a jungle trek to Bukit Lawang. Some of the guesthouses in Berastagi can also assist with guides, car rentals and information. Try Pak Pelawi at Wisma Sibayak.

SHOPPING

Most antique and souvenir shops are along Jl. Veteran, the main drag. Look for **Christo Antiques**, which has a nice collection of genuine antiques and art. You will find some new Karo artifacts made by the "old men" in **Lingga** village, also **Peceren** on the outskirts of town.

PERFORMANCES

The museum at Lingga holds performances of Karo Batak dancing on Sun, Wed and Fri from 2-5pm. Lingga villagers will dance for guests who want to pay from $5-$10. The Rafflesia people put up notices advertising local cultural events. For a fee of $5 to $8 (depending on the distance) they will take you to a Batak wedding or some other village ceremony, complete with transport and interpreter.

CLIMBING MT. SIBAYAK

For the energetic who wish to climb Mt. Sibayak, a trail runs from behind Gundaling Hill. A longer trail leads up from the Medan road north of Berastagi near Lau Petani Waterfall. Ask at your hotel for directions, and hire a guide for a few dollars. Leave early in the morning.

The trail from Berastagi leads over a saddle in the east-west ridge past Mt. Singkut (1,680 m) and down the wall of the former caldera into the Daulu Valley to the village of **Semangat Gunung**, then up the cone of the volcano itself —which consists of two main peaks, Mt. Sibayak (2,094 m) and Mt. Pintu (2,212 m).

The trail passes through thick jungle and up some very steep slopes, and is quite wet and slippery in places. Make sure you have good shoes and a jacket or sweater, as it gets cold at the top. Buy snacks and drinks in Semangat Gunung to take along. It takes around 3.5 hours from Berastagi to reach the summit, but you can shorten the hike considerably by catching local transport to Semangat Gunung via **Daulu**.

Get to the top before 10 am, when it is still clear. There is a blue-green sulphurous lake at the bottom of the crater, bubbling menacingly. Beware of the fumes emitting from the fumeroles. Locals say you should be very respectful to the spirit of the mountain, presenting offerings of cigarettes and *sirih* (betel).

On the return, it's definitely best to hop on a *bemo* in Semangat Gunung and get off at the **Lau Debuk Debuk** hot springs to enjoy a well-earned soak in the steaming mineral waters, before catching transport back to town.

VISITING KARO VILLAGES

More than 270 Karo Batak villages dot the hills around Berastagi. Some are the ancient residences of the five important clan chiefs, others simple farming villages. Many require a trek along dirt tracks, however a number are also accessible by road. Get a group of people together and hire a car or a *bemo* for the day, as many hours will otherwise be wasted waiting for buses and *bemos* while you could be seeing something. If you do want to go by public transport to save money, hire a "guide" (a young boy who speaks some English and knows the area) from your hotel in Berastagi for about $5 a day.

The village of **Lingga**, 16 km from Berastagi, can be reached by first taking a bus to Kabanjahe, then a *bemo* to the 3-way intersection at Surbakti, from where you catch another bus to Lingga. The trip to **Cinkes** similarly involves 3 or 4 changes. **Barusjahe** can be reached by bus from Kabanjahe in about half an hour.

— *Jill Gocher*

LAKE TOBA

Jewel of the Sumatran Highlands

Lake Toba, with the mystical island of Samosir at its center, forms the very heart of the beautiful but often harsh Toba Bataklands—a huge volcanic depression set high in the treeless mountains of northern Sumatra. The lake was formed some 75,000 years ago as the result of an enormous volcanic explosion—probably the greatest the world has ever known. This is the largest lake in Southeast Asia—measuring 100 km long, north to south, and 31 km across—with a surface area of about 1,145 sq km. The island of Samosir alone, inside the lake, is 530 sq km—about the size of Singapore. This is also the world's deepest lake, over 450 m deep, though accurate surveys of the lake floor have yet to be made.

Remarkably, no important rivers flow into Toba from the sides of the lake. All drainage from the surrounding areas flows down to the coasts, as the thick mantle of tuff from the Toba explosion has formed a steep "collar" around the lake, blocking earlier drainage channels. The lake's surface lies 906 m above sea level, but may once have been 150 m higher. Thousands of years ago, the collecting water overflowed the caldera to the southeast and eroded the soft tuff, cutting its way out through spectacular, steep-walled ravines via the Siguragura, Harimo and Tangga falls to form the Asahan River. The water level has begun to mysteriously subside again in recent years, and no adequate explanation for this has yet been given.

The Toba Batak homeland of which Lake Toba forms the central part actually comprises five regions. The first is the island of Samosir within the lake itself. The second is the Uluan ("Headwaters")—a fertile region along the southeastern lakeshore between Prapat and Porsea, where the Asahan River drains the lake. The third is Habinsaran ("The East" from Toba *binsar* meaning "sunrise")—an extremely broken, mountainous region which lies further to the southeast, at the headwaters of the Kualu River. The fourth is the Silindung Valley to the southwest, and the fifth is the Hombung region west of the lake.

Dotting the countryside throughout the region, wherever there is adequate water, are Toba villages with houses, churches, tombs and verdant rice fields. The volcanic soils are exceptionally fertile and the Toba area has been inhabited for many centuries.

Berastagi to Prapat

The main route up to Toba from Medan passes through Pematang Siantar and the Simalungun Batak areas and has already been described above (see "Simalungun"). Increasingly popular with tour buses and independent travelers, however, is the scenic backroad across the Karo Plateau from Berastagi that skirts the northeastern edge of the Toba caldera. This is a longer but far more exciting route visually, with many interesting stops.

The first town you pass after leaving Berastagi is the district capital of **Kabanjahe** ("Ginger Garden"), 14 km to the south—a bustling town surrounded by rice fields and market gardens in the very heart of Karoland. This is a crossroads where the highway from Aceh's Alas Valley meets the Medan highway (see "Western Aceh").

Twenty-four km south of Kabanjahe, the road touches the northern rim of the Toba basin at Merek, and a sideroad from here winds down to the lakeshore past a spectacular waterfall known as **Sipisopiso** ("Like a Knife"), which shoots out of a cave at the edge of the plateau and plunges 120 meters straight down to a small, gushing stream below. A gazebo provides panoramic views over the village of **Tongging** at the lake's edge.

From Merek, the road to Prapat hugs the high rim of the ancient caldera, skirting the lake and brushing the bare slopes of Mt. Singgalang (1,865 m) just north of the village of **Seribudolok** ("Thousand Peaks"). A turnoff to the left here leads down an old Karo trail to Bangunpurba, in the East Coast plantation belt. Some 15 km down this road, at Tinggi Raja, are a series of terraces and hot springs with sparse but interesting flora.

Back on the Prapat road, some 4 km past Seribudolok, a sideroad to the right winds 10 km down to the lakeshore at **Haranggaol**, a picturesque market village known for its garlic and shallots. A ferry crosses over to Samosir from here on Mondays and Thursdays, and there are small hotels, canoes and speedboats with fishing equipment to while away the time as you wait.

You are now in Simalungun Batak territory, and at **Pematang Purba**, 8 km past Seribudolok, is the wooden palace of the former Simalungun ruler. Built in the style of a traditional *adat* house, it is said to be 200 years old and has been restored as a museum—

Overleaf: *Tuktuk Peninsula, dotted with hotels.*
Left: *Tongging, at the northern end of the lake.*

Toba's Formation

Neogene Marine Deposits	Welded Rhyolite Tuffs and Breccias
Pre-tertiary Basement Complex	Acid Tuffs
Basic-intermediary Magmas and Eruption Products	Granitic Batholith

Toba Lake

to Berastagi,
Kabanjahe

to
Bangunpurba

Rakutbosi

Siganantang

Mt. Singgalang
1865m

S. Turitun

Hutaraja

Merek

Seribudolok

**Simalungun
Palace**

Mt. Melas
1941m

Mt. Siluatan
2457m

Pematang Purba

Mt. Penataran
1558m

**Sipisopiso
Waterfall**

Bangunseribu

Tigarunggu

Tongging

Sibaulangit

Haranggaol

Purbatongga

Mt. Wakantenembu
1529m

Mt. Pankuruhan
1718m

Paropo

Ferry

Sima

to Aceh

Mt. Sibartong
2051m

Bukit
Siantar

Danau Toba

Maras
Silalahi

Silancang

*PULAU
MALAU*

*PULAU
TAO*

Fe

Harangmalau

Simanindo

Gunungbenua

Mt. Sulusuhi
1555m

Parbaba

**Batak
Museum**

Sidikalang

Suhisuhi

Binagaara

Hutaraja

S. Rangkan

S. Sigilang

Hutabangun

Sigalingging

Mt. Batumartindi
1781m

Buhit

Partangkoan

Mt. Penjeraton
1309m

Kasingahan

to
Singki

Boltokhuta

Simanampang

Sigaol

Pangururan

*Danau
Sidihoni*

Kerajaan

Mt. Kapur
1047m

Sihotang

**Hot
Spring**

Simbolon

Hutabatu

Parbakalan

Situmorang

Pusuk Buhit
1981m

Siantar

N

Tele

Mt. Hutabatu
1373m

Hitetano

0   5   10   15 km

0   2   4   6   8 mi

**Panoramic
View**

Palipi

Turpuksihotung

Simanampang

Banjarsiantar

Mt. Uludarat
2157m

Lumbannahon

Lumbar

Tuktuk Peninsula

Danau Toba

Toledo Inn

Judita

Hariara
Rest.

Nelson
Abadi
Tony's
Rusly's
Laster Jony's
Murni
Antonius

Endy's

Kennedy's

N

Lekjon

0   100   200   300 m

Bernard's
Matahari's
Rosita's Batak House
Silintong Hotel

to Ambarita

Church

Romlan
Marraon

footpath

Horas

OPS Travel
Service

Lesley
Smiley's

Linda's
Sahatma
Dumasari

Pepy's Rest.

Carolina

to Tomok

Mt. Sompean
1623m

S. Ahirra

S. Sulpi

Hutapaung

Pollung

Lumbanganjang

Sosordolokdol

S. Simonggo

Marade

Huta

Lagubati

S. Sisira

Matiti

Parhebangan

Baturaja

Siboronboron

Sosortombak

Sosortolong

to Barus

Dol

freshly-painted in the traditional colors of red, black and white. Although the original earthen and bamboo defenses are now gone, the old entrance tunnel can still be seen. The main complex formerly housed the raja and his 12 wives; its dark interior contains royal memorabilia and is well worth a visit. There is an ancient path from here leading down to the lake, and if you have more time, the nearby Perkebunan Marjanji tea estate operates guided tours of their facilities.

At Tigarunggu, 5 km past Pematang Purba, a right-hand turn leads to Prapat via a rough but scenic road that follows a forested ridge overlooking the lake. At a tiny crossroads at Simarjarunjung is a restaurant with a magnificent view. At Sipintuangin, 3 km further on, there is a sideroad to the right leading down to **Tigaras**, another market town on the lakeshore with a ferry service over to Samosir. The main road continues high above the lake through Huta, and rejoins the main Pematang Siantar-Prapat highway near Siuhan. From here, a hard right takes you down through a tunnel and above a sheer cliff at Sibagunding, and after rounding a corner you enter the resort of Prapat.

Prapat

Prapat occupies a small, rocky peninsula jutting into the lake, and has recently expanded southward over a ridge into the adjacent village of Ajibata. A resort since before WW II,

the town has boomed in recent years with the opening of many new hotels. The old Prapat Hotel overlooking the harbor was famous throughout the Indies in the colonial period. Indonesia's first president, Soekarno, was imprisoned in Prapat for several months by the Dutch in early 1949, together with Haji Agus Salim and Sutan Syahrir.

Good waterskiing, speedboat trips, paddlecraft and tennis are all available. Bougainvilleas, poinsettias, honeysuckle and other flowers bloom year round in the equable climate. Shops sell an array of Batak textiles, woodcarvings, ceramics and other goods mixed with the occasional genuine antiques, offered by traders who are aggressive and persistent. Fruits and vegetables are to be found in the market. The local mango, known as *kueini*, has an interesting flavor but is not as good as East Java's *harum manis*.

In the immediate vicinity of Prapat are some interesting geological exposures of granite, fossiliferous sediments, limestone and sandstone. Just to the south, in the Naborsahon River valley, are beautiful terraces indicating the previously much higher levels of the lake.

Samosir Island

Samosir, the huge, arid "Island of the Dead" in the middle of Lake Toba, is a stark remnant of a second powerful explosion that rocked this volcanic cauldron some 30,000

KAL MULLER

years ago. At this time a subsidiary peak formed but then subsequently split and slumped back into the earlier crater (see diagram). The eastern part now forms the Prapat peninsula and the Uluan shore down to Porsea; the western edge forms Samosir. The island measures 45 km by 20 km, and in fact was originally a peninsula. It became an island only after the arrival of the Dutch in 1906, who dug a canal through the narrow, 200-m isthmus connecting it to the mainland at Pangururan. This action, it is said, caused some considerable consternation among the local inhabitants, as they feared the island would slip into the lake and disappear.

The eastern side of the island rises very steeply up from a narrow strip along the lakeshore to a central plateau towering some 780 m above it. The plateau slopes gently back to the southern and western shores of the island and is dotted with tiny villages that cling precariously to clifftops pierced by deep ravines.

The Samosir plateau is largely barren—with scattered forests, marshes and a small lake. A road of sorts runs all around the edge of the island, but is very rough in places, with some dilapidated and dangerous bridges in the southwest. From Pangururan—the *kecamatan* administrative center on the western side of the island—a road links Samosir to the mainland, climbing up a steep escarpment to dramatic 1,800-m heights at Tele that offer a spendid panorama of the lake, with

Samosir Island spread out down below.

During the northeast monsoon, which blows from September or October through to January, a strong wind known as *alogo bolong*, the "great wind," often springs up at midday from the heights, creating waves of over a meter in height and making it difficult and sometimes dangerous for boats on the lake. Local ferries, often overloaded with people and produce, are occasionally lost in such storms. Formerly, the Batak used enormous dugout canoes known as *solu* cut from a single forest tree, to cross the lake. Today only very small dugouts are seen.

F.M. Schnitger, author of *Forgotten Kingdoms in Sumatra*, visited Samosir in the 1930s and recorded *adat* houses, stone tombs and burial cists in no less than 26 different villages. It seems, however, that since that time many villages have been abandoned, names of others have changed, and some of the enormous stone sarcophagi for which the island is known have been moved from their original resting places so they are not always easy to find. Off the beaten track, time and patience is required to seek out the ancient tombs. But then for many people, a visit to Samosir simply involves an easy ferry ride over to the village of Tomok, where the most famous of all Toba Batak sarcophagi lies just a few minutes' walk from the pier.

Gateway to Samosir

Samosir is accessible by regular ferry from the resort of Prapat, a journey of under an hour—but also by less frequent ferries from Haranggaol and Tigaras on the Simalungun shore to the north. The two main landing points on Samosir are Tomok—a traditional village with beautiful stone tombs and houses—and Tuktuk, where the island's many

Opposite: *The ferry to Samosir.* **Left:** *The famous sarcophagus of the Sidarbuta chief in Tomok.* **Above:** *The chief's wife atop the tomb.*

hotels and restaurants are concentrated. Speedboats can also be rented in Prapat to make a trip around Samosir in 2 to 3 hours.

At **Tomok**, famous for years now as the "gateway to Samosir," the visitor is greeted by a row of stalls selling a bewildering array of Batak handicrafts—traditional *ulos* cloths, carvings, Batak calendars and musical instruments (including the traditional two-string violin, the *harwab*, and the guitar or *hasapi*). Small hotels and restaurants are nearby.

Directly inland, hidden in a bamboo thicket under an ancient banyan tree, is the most famous of the giant Toba sarcophagi. Carved from a single block of stone, the tomb dates from the early 19th century and belongs to a chief of the Sidarbuta clan. In front is an enormous, carved *singa* face—a mythical part buffalo, part elephant-like creature. The saddle-shaped lid is surmounted by the carving of a woman holding a cup or bowl, probably a *paranggiran* used in sacrificial rites. She is said to represent the wife of the dead chief.

There are other modern tombs and stones here, including lichen-covered stone ancestor seats dating from 1950, and a modern sarcophagus made as recently as 1979. The *adat* houses stand in a row opposite, facing away from the lake, with their all-important rice barns in front. They are carved with foliate designs painted in the holy Batak colors of black, white and red—their traditional *ijuk* palm fiber thatched roofs now replaced by

corrugated zinc.

Just to the north of Tomok is the small peninsula of **Tuktuk Ni Asu** ("Dog Peninsula") with its sandy beaches and scores of hotels offering budget accommodation, now a booming resort that is Samosir's answer to Bali's Kuta Beach. Offshore is the tiny island of Pulau Pasir, site of an ancient burial cist.

Four km to the north of Tuktuk along a narrow, paved road is **Ambarita**, an attractive village with ancient stone walls that were once topped with a thick *pagar* or fence of thorny bamboo. Inside are stone seats and modern statuary, the work of a certain Siallagan some 40 years ago. The villagers invent endless stories to explain these attractions to the tourists, for like villagers everywhere they enjoy spinning a good yarn.

Some 19 km further north is **Simanindo**, where the elaborately decorated house of Raja Sidauruk has been declared a museum. Visitors can witness a traditional *tortor* dance and *sigalegale* puppet performance here for a fee, complete with a lively *gondang sabangunan* ensemble. The *sigalegale* traditionally served as a receptacle for the soul of the deceased in Batak funerary rites, though the custom may have originated only about 100 years ago in the Balige area. Just opposite Simanindo is a rocky islet called **Pulau Tao**, with a shallow bay and a small hotel.

About 2 km past Simanindo is **Harangmalau**, the northernmost point on Samosir. At nearby Situngkir and Sialangoan are unusual tombs belonging to the chiefs of Sihaloho. One has a cist decorated with a bull or buffalo head in relief and a lid that is carved into three points. The end above the bull relief is decorated with a *boraspati ni tano*, the sacred lizard that is thought to bring good luck.

Several km further on, past Parbaba, is

Left: *House decoration* (singa) *with foliate designs.*
Above and right: *The* tortor *ceremonial dance and* sigalegale *puppet performance at Simanindo.*

Suhisuhi—site of an ancient sarcophagus and a number of modern cement tombs. To the south at **Hutaraja** are five old sarcophogi of the Simarmata clan, including that of Raja Ompu Bontor within the village itself. In front of the chief's house is a miniature dolmen-like monument said to be the spot where a young girl was sacrificed when the house was built. Human sacrifice was apparently once quite common in Toba, used to magically capture and convert the spirit of an unwitting victim into a powerful spirit protector.

A further 5 km on is **Pangururan**, the sub-district administrative center, where a bridge connects Samosir to the mainland. Just over the bridge, a small road to the right leads up to a popular hot spring on the slopes of Mt. Pusuk Buhit (1,981 m), sacred mountain of origin for all Batak peoples. This is where the first ruler—Si Raja Batak—is said to have descended from the heavens. The main road from the bridge winds up to **Tele**, 900 m above the lake, offering panoramic views back across Samosir.

South of Pangururan the road hugs the lakeshore past Simbolon to Nainggolan and Sungkean. Just north of Simbolon, at **Pansur Duggal** (probably the Pancur of Schnitger), is a group of three modern sarcophagi and a number of ancient burial urns. On the rise above Simbolon is the sarcophagus of Raja Ompu Silo Simbolon with an unusual carving of a female figure with raised arms below the *singa*. At Huta Godang, near Nainggolan, is the ancient sarcophagus of the Parhusip clan. There are more important sarcophagi at Huta na Bolon and Sipinggan.

South from Tomok

Back on the eastern side of the island, a tiny road leaves the shore just south of Tomok and winds up steeply onto the Samosir plateau (1,689 m), offering wonderful views of the lake. It then follows the crest of the plateau southward. About halfway to the south coast, at the tiny village of **Parmonangan**, a rebuilt replica of the original Situmorang clan house can be seen. On one end it has unusual relief carvings featuring four protruding female breasts and a woman with her arms upraised. The road continues from here down to the south coast at Onan Runggu.

If one has the inclination, however, one can more profitably follow Jean-Paul Barbier, curator of the Barbier-Müller Museum in Geneva, and explore the coasts south of Tomok by boat, putting into shore at will. Along the way you pass lovely coves with white sand beaches and picturesque villages. Around **Panjomuran** and **Pagar Batu**, 8 and 9 km south of Tomok, rows of low stone columns on the shore once supported boathouses storing the huge Situmorang war canoes (*solu*) used to raid neighboring villages. From Pagar Batu, a path leads up to a terrace on the plateau where a village once stood. All that remains now are a number of tombs and a *lesung batu* or stone mortar. Near the southeastern tip of the island at Sitamiang are elaborate concrete tombs built in the form of miniature Toba-style houses.

Prapat to Porsea

Having explored Samosir, you may want to return to Prapat and travel south to the Uluan region to view a number of fascinating tombs and villages. From Prapat, take the smaller backroad through Ajibata, which winds steeply up a mountain face behind the resort and affords rewarding views back across the lake. Small villages with superbly decorated *adat* houses are set back off the road in clumps of bamboo; unfortunately, most have been pillaged of all removable decorations for the "antique" trade.

To the left of the road, 22 km from Prapat, is the village of **Hutagaol** belonging to the Manurung clan, built in 1935 above an earlier village of the same name. Several km further on is the hamlet of **Lumban Binanga II**, with fine examples of modern Toba house decoration. About 8 km further south, a group of villages on the left—Lumban Na Bolak, Lumban Tabu, Lumban Sibinbin and Lumban Simariasonak—have some of the best examples of traditional *adat* buildings in the Uluan style, with animistic and anthropomorphic carvings and friezes. These villages belong to the Sitorus clan; **Luban Tabu** has been declared a

cultural monument under the protection of the Ministry of Education and Culture.

The area south of here around **Porsea** is where the 60-m-wide Asahan River drains Toba to the east. The river is quickly joined by tributaries from the north (Aek Mandosi) and the south (Aek Bolon), and the alluvial plain formed by these rivers is extremely fertile, dotted with properous villages. The road down into the Asahan Valley turns off to the left some 3 km before the town of Porsea. About 1 km along this road on the right is a group of lovely villages, including Lumban Kuala—where there is a fine example of a carved sarcophagus lid belonging to Raja Pabalubis of the Manurung clan.

From here the road descends steeply eastward into the **Asahan Valley**, where the river enters a narrow ravine with vertical walls 250 m high cut from the soft volcanic tuff. This is the site of the Inalum hydroelectric plant—a Japanese-built complex of 3 dams completed in 1975 at a cost of US$2 billion. The largest such plant in Indonesia, it generates 500 Mw of power annually, enabling the plant at Kuala Tanjung on the coast to electrolyze 225,000 tons of aluminium. Access to the road and the falls beyond requires a special permit, obtainable from the Inalum office.

Beyond the plant at **Siguragura** the ravine narrows to a mere cleft in the rocks and the river plunges over a spectacular 200-m falls into another cleft further down known as

KAL MULLER

Sampuran Harimo ("Tiger Falls"), whence it plunges once again into the vale of Tangga, through yet another falls. Formerly, on the south face of the latter, ascent was by means of a series of ladders, hence the name *tangga*—meaning "ladder." From here the road zigzags down into the Asahan plantation belt by the coast, rejoining the north-south Medan road at Bandar Pulo.

The southern lakeshore

Bordering the lake south and west of Porsea

are more fertile *sawah* dotted with villages. **Laguboti**, on the Aek Simare between Porsea and Balige, is known for its woodcarving and statues. At Sigumpar just west of here is the grave of I. L. Nommensen, the German missionary who almost single-handedly converted the entire Toba Batak population to Christianity at the end of the 19th century.

South of Laguboti, a rough trail leads to **Huta Ginjang** and the extensive remains of long-abandoned fortified villages at an altitude of 1,650 m, with earthen walls and tunnel approaches, which to this day are very poorly documented. When the weather is clear, the view from these heights is incomparable, but at this altitude it is often cold and misty.

Balige is an important market town at the southern end of the lake, 65 km from Prapat. The town has a large *pasar* built in the traditional Tapanuli style, and is known for its textile production. There is a monument here to the last Batak priest-king, Sisingamangaraja XII (see below), and to General D. I. Panjaitan, who was murdered in Jakarta in the communist coup of 1965. Two museums are also found here—the Balige Museum and the Sisingamangaraja XII Museum. The latter houses a collection of artifacts relating to this national hero, who is buried at Soposurung.

Various Batak festivals in which local youths engage in traditional sports are now held in Balige. These include the Pesta Horas and Pesta Pantai Lumban Silintong, which in-

cludes a fishing competition. Five km west of Balige a turnoff to the left leads up to the hilltop guesthouse at Adian Nalambok near **Gurgur** offering panoramic views of the road south to Tarutung. At Jonggi ni Huta, just off the main road to the south, is a burial mound and equestrian statue of the Raja Pangalitan of the Nababan clan.

From the town of Siborongborong, about 20 km past Balige, a small road leads north to the southwestern shore of the lake at **Muara**, a small settlement of Malay-type houses dominated by the twin eminences of Dolok Sikke (1,092 m) and Dolok Sitoruna (1,153 m). The town, whose name literally means "estuary," overlooks a bay of the same name and a large island called Pulau Sibandang. Just before entering Muara, at Sosorugan, is an interesting modern tomb in the shape of a traditional house. Just to the south, in the square at Huta na Godang, is the famous equestrian statue, now painted, of the Siregar clan founder, with his wife seated nearby. A number of small fetish shrines are to be seen at other villages in the vicinity, such as Balaian ni Guru and Lumban Tikkatikka.

Past Muara, on an isolated bay encircled by steep hills at the southwestern corner of the lake, is **Bakkara**—the former seat of the mystical Batak priest-kings, the Sisingamangaraja. Around the village are stone walls and other relics of their martial past. The last ruler, Sisingamangaraja XII, was killed in a skirmish with Dutch forces in 1907 following 30 years of guerilla warfare in which he established a god-like reputation among the populace. The Dutch entered the area in 1878, and in the ensuing struggle burned scores of villages, causing the inhabitants to flee.

— *E. Edwards McKinnon*

Opposite: *Steep escarpments line Samosir's eastern edge.* **Above, left:** *Touring the lake by boat.* **Above, right:** *Modern concrete Toba Batak tombs combine traditional and Christian themes.*

Lake Toba Practicalities

Covers Prapat and Samosir Island. All prices in US dollars. S = single, D = double.

Lake Toba is one of the awesome natural wonders of the world—a crater lake of such size that there is an island in the middle of it the size of Singapore. There is still no definitive data on how deep the lake actually is, though 450 m is the usual estimate given. At 900 m above sea level, the climate is refreshingly cool at night and tolerably warm during the day.

For many travelers, Prapat and Samosir are a welcome relief, while for others they have perhaps too little (or too much) action to be interesting for very long. It wholly depends on your personal interests and state of mind. The opportunities for hiking, swimming and boating are endless, and the highland lake climate and environment are exhilarating. The absence of a highly developed "resort" infrastructure, now just beginning, may not suit everyone's taste, but the low cost of accommodation and food and the magnificent scenic beauty of the place make it unforgettable.

The Toba Batak are a curious mix of rural, tribal personalities with an often surprising degree of cosmopolitanism. It is not unusual on Samosir, for example, to find people who outwardly appear to be local villagers speaking fluent German or English, due to their contacts with missionaries and tourists, or even to study abroad. The Toba Batak are well known for their forthright openness, and don't be surprised if you are asked questions which might seem impertinent coming from strangers. Don't be surprised also at the decibel level of normal conversation. For the Toba Batak, the volume settings are permanently on full blast and this is apparently not related to any particular change in mood. A normal conversation differs from an argument in content, not necessarily in tone.

In both Prapat and Samosir, hotels in all classes are remarkably good value. All the big hotels are in Prapat, which is slightly more expensive generally, but most of the sights are on Samosir, which has only small hotels and homestays that are restful and rustic. Be sure to book ahead if you want to stay at any of the better places on Samosir. At certain times of the year—around big Indonesian holidays—the hotels are overrun with domestic visitors from Medan. Toba is also increasingly popular with visitors from Malaysia and Singapore, who can get 5-day package tours for as little as $300 including airfare, hotels and transport (check the *Straits Times* classifieds). All good establishments in Tuktuk now have phones as well as booking offices in Medan, which can save you expensive long distance calls. Be sure to inquire if they will pick you up in Prapat and ferry you across to Samosir.

GETTING THERE

Toba is only accessible overland, either from the south via Bukittinggi and Tarutung, or from Medan. There are two ways to get here from Medan, either directly along the Trans-Sumatra Highway via the Simalungun Batak areas, or across the Karo Plateau via Berastagi. The more direct Simalungun route through Pematang Siantar takes about 3.5 hrs without stops. The Berastagi route takes much longer, about 6 hrs, but is vastly more scenic and a stopover in Berastagi is to be highly recommended (see "Berastagi Practicalities" for travel details on this route). Yet another way to get to Samosir is from the west via Sidikalang, across a bridge connecting the island to the "mainland." This is strictly for the adventurous, however, since road conditions can leave much to be desired.

By car. Private cars arranged through major hotels in Medan will cost about $20 per person. Taxis arranged by phone with companies such as Indah (tel: 516615) or Cantik (tel: 327532) will pick you up and charge about $6 per person (see also "Medan Practicalities").

By bus. Buses are much cheaper, about $1 to $1.50, and run all day to Prapat from Medan, taking 4-6 hrs. Be sure to get on an express bus, however, to avoid doubling your travel time. Go to the offices on Jl. Sisingamangaraja (opposite the Grand Mosque) and have a look at the bus or a photo of it before buying a ticket. The biggest bus company is ALS, with offices at Jl. Amuliun 2A in Medan (tel: 061-22014). They have a depot in Prapat and an office near the ferry terminal in Tiga Raja, and they operate to all cities in Sumatra.

MONEY

Change all the money you will need before leaving Medan, since rates are extremely poor in the Toba area. Check the recommended banks in "Medan Practicalities."

Prapat

Telephone code is 0625 for Prapat.

Vestiges of traditional Toba culture are best tracked down in Samosir, just across the water, and there is actually little reason to base yourself in Prapat unless you really must have luxury accommodations. Nevertheless the place is absolutely filled with hotels of all classes, some clinging to cliffs overlooking the lake, others spread out with lovely gardens and manicured lawns. The main downtown market is busy and crowded. The ferry terminal forms the center of activity, however, as groups of foreigners and locals converge to crossover to Samosir.

Everything in Prapat is basically within walking distance, and *bemos* run along a circular route connecting the bus terminal, ferry, shops and telephone office. Fare is Rp200.

TOURIST INFORMATION

There are several agencies in Prapat advertising tourist information and tours around the area, but in fact you don't really need their help. Hotels in the area will provide you with all the information you need and you can usually hire a young "guide" or member of the family who speaks some English to escort you around for $3-$5 per day.

ACCOMMODATION
Expensive (over $25 a night)
Danau Toba International Cottages (91 cottages) Jl. Nelson Purba, tel: 41172, 41641, 41683. New, individual cottages on a sandy beach by the lake. Waterskiing, sailing, windsurfing. $37 up to $50. Medan booking office: Hotel Danau Toba Medan, Jl. Imam Bonjol 17, tel: (061) 327000, fax: 530553.
Danau Toba International Hotel (82 rooms) Jl. Talun Sungkit 19, tel: 41583, 41119, 41630. Up the road on the end of the same peninsula with Hotel Prapat, on a hillside facing the lake. $37 to $43. Medan booking office: Jl. Imam Bonjol 17, tel: (061) 327000, fax: 530553.
Niagara (145 rooms) Jl. Pembangunan 1, tel: 41028, 41068, fax: 41233. A brand new hotel high atop a hill overlooking the lake, on the next peninsula behind Prapat, past the market at Tiga Raja and visible from the ferry slip. 24-hr coffeeshop, enormous pool, tennis courts, 9-hole golf course. $40 up to $130. Medan booking office: Jl. Guru Patimpuo 1, tel: (061)

521128, 525982, fax: 529680.
Patra Jasa (36 rooms) tel: 41796 or in Medan 323535. Owned by Pertamina, the state oil company, and located on a peninsula about 3 km before you enter Prapat on the right. Commands a magnificent view of the lake, has soft spring beds and an icey swimming pool with lovely grounds. Ask for a room up in the main building. $30 to $45 S/D for superior rooms and $280 for the presidential suite.
Prapat (85 rooms) Jl. Marihat 1, tel: 41012, 41018. Right on the water in Prapat, with its own private beach, the oldest hotel in the area, opened in 1911. $44 standard, $52 deluxe, $65 for a suite.
Tara Bunga Sibigo (42 rooms) Jl. Sibigo 1, tel: 41089, 41700. Next door to the Prapat, also with rooms right on the water. $22 S, $25 D.

Intermediate and Budget (under $25)

For intermediate and budget places you are better off over in Samosir (see below), however Jl. Haranggoal does have several small hotels. **Pago Pago Inn** is the best known, though there are others. If you are catching an early bus to Bukittinggi or elsewhere, stay right at the bus terminal. **Andilo Nancy Travel** has clean and quiet rooms behind their office for $2.50 a night (tel: 41548, 41276). **Baringin Tua** next to the ferry terminal, also with a busy travel desk, has 5 rooms for $4 each a night (tel: 41534).

DINING

Most people head for the **Asia Restaurant**, located just beyond the entrance to Prapat on the left as you come in, serving mediocre Chinese food in a big, barn-like room. **Hotel**

Prapat has a gracious old dining room overlooking a garden facing the lake. Other more modest Chinese restaurants are on Jl. Haranggaol: **Singgalang**, **Hong Kong** and **Bali**.

SHOPPING

For souvenirs, there is a collection of stalls on the corner of Jl. Haranggaol leading down to Tiga Raja, the local market and boat slip. Take your time, bargain hard and keep in mind that you will probably find more of a selection over on Samosir.

Samosir Island

Telephone code is 0645.

In spite of being a tourist spot for many years, Samosir is still very natural. Five minutes out of Tuktuk or Tomok and you are in the country; churches and strange tombs dot the hills.

Tomok will normally be your first port of call on the island, unless you have arranged transport directly to a hotel at Tuktuk. Right in front of the main boat slips, and about 100 m up from the ferry landing, is a road leading inland, lined with souvenir shops. Take your time and look around. Don't hesitate to offer a small fraction of what the vendors are asking. If they accept your offer, however, you have to buy. As you walk up the road you will see a small enclave of traditional houses on the right. Still inhabited, these give you an immediate idea of what a typical Batak *huta* or nuclear village is like—two rows of houses facing each other. Here, you can also see one of the island's most famous sights—the 200-year-old, boat-shaped sarcophagus of King Sidarbuta, surrounded by those of his descendants. Magnificent old banyan trees dominate the area; one recently collapsed, having become top-heavy with age, but miraculously no one was hurt even though a number of shops were decimated.

Tuktuk is where everyone stays on Samosir, a tiny peninsula jutting out from the island, which continues to sprout small hotels, restaurants and souvenir shops at a very rapid rate. Prices are remarkably low, and it's a very scenic spot.

Ambarita has an archaeologically important meeting place for the king of the Siallagan *marga* or tribe that supposedly served as a kind of hall of justice. In an adjacent clearing, those condemned were executed. There are also some large, impressive stone chairs and a number of traditional houses, souvenir shops and a good trail leading up to the plateau and across the island.

Simanindo is up at the northern end of the island, site of some of the best traditional Toba Batak houses, particularly that of King Sidaruruk, which is now a small museum. As you enter, people somehow magically appear at nearly any time of day to present the intriguing *sigalegale* puppet dance and *tortor* communal dance normally performed at important festive occa-

sions. The boat-building on the waterfront in Simanindo is also well worth seeing.

Pulau Tao is a tiny island just off Simanindo, with a hotel and a small museum.

Pangururan is a town located just at the bridge connecting Samosir to the mainland on the Dairi or western side. There is a hot spring nearby on the slopes of Mt. Pusuk Buhit, and the town has several small hotels.

GETTING THERE

Getting over to Samosir is possible by several means, at wildly variable prices. The easiest and cheapest way is to hop on any one of a number of double-decker, flat-bottom boats which ply back and forth from Prapat to Tomok or Tuktuk for about 40 cents a person. Be sure to specify your destination, whether Tomok or Tuktuk. Many of the larger hotels on Samosir have their own boats, so if you have booked in advance, keep your eye out for them.

You can also hire a speedboat at negotiable but always rather expensive rates, usually $10 per boat, seating up to 4 people.

If you've come by car or motorcycle, you can take your vehicle across on a ferry up past Tiga Raja. After coming into Prapat from Medan, continue along the one-way road past the market and up the hill; the turnoff to the ferry is about 100 m up on the left. The ferry runs every 3 hours back and forth; cost is about $6 for a full car, about $1 for a motorbike.

When arranging boat transport, keep in mind that conditions on Lake Toba can be extreme, with large waves and strong winds coming up during squalls, particularly in the months of the northeast monsoon, Sept to Jan. If it is raining heavily, have a look around Prapat until it passes. The peculiar geography around the lake makes most storms short-lived.

GETTING AROUND

On Samosir, there is no good public transport as yet. Minibuses do travel around the island, but they have no schedules and transport is generally unreliable for motor vehicles due to bridges being frequently out, though recently there have been many improvements in road conditions around the main tourist areas of Tomok and Tuktuk. The best way to see the sights on the east coast of the island is to walk, though it does get rather hot in the middle of the day if the sun is out.

The better hotels provide vehicles for touring, mostly minibuses at rather high rates, but these are convenient for many visitors, for whom it is too tiring and too hot to walk.

An even better solution for trips around the island, however, is to hop aboard one of the boats which ply around the coast throughout the day (though be aware that nearly everything stops at dusk). Stand on any dock or projection into the lake and sooner or later one will come along and pick you up. Be sure to state your destination and fix the fare in advance to avoid unpleasant surprises. You may think you are traveling and paying as a normal passenger; the boat man may insist you are chartering the whole craft!

You can also rent bicycles for $2.50 and motorcycles for $8-$10 a day. Samosir is ideal for both: straight roads, no traffic and short-to-medium distances. Inquire at your hotel or at Pepy's Restaurant in Tuktuk, in front of Carolina. Also available in Tomok and Ambarita. If you have a mountain bike, bring it along! These can be perfect for going up across the island and off the main roads.

If you are driving on Samosir, be sure to fill up at the gas station in Prapat (just beyond the Asia Restaurant), as there are no stations on the island and petrol is expensive.

ACCOMMODATION

Most hotels are located on Tuktuk Peninsula, and this is the perfect place to base youself—comfortable and convenient, halfway between Tomok and Ambarita, the two big tourist attractions. A big new hotel called Ambaroba is being built and will provide the island's first luxury accommodations, but for the moment most hotels are in the moderate and budget ranges. Below are some of the most popular places that should be booked well in advance. There are others; walk around Tuktuk and check them out before you decide.

Expensive (above $25 a night)

Pulau Tao Cottages (20 cottages) on Tao Island, just across from Simanindo. Bookings can be made by writing to PO Box 4, Pematang Siantar. Or just take a chance and head there by boat from Prapat (about 1.5 hours), or from Simanindo (just 5 min). $30 a night.

Toba Beach (96 rooms) Located about 2 km south of Tomok in the village of Parambatan (turn left coming out of the boat slips in Tomok as opposed to right to Tuktuk), tel: 41275. Stands on the lakeshore more or less by itself; the lakeside restaurant is one of the most pleasant on the island. $44 S/D.

Moderate ($10-$25 a night)

Carolina (tel: 41520). Everyone's favorite in Tuktuk. You just can't beat the facilities: the restaurant is definitely the best on the island, with a newly constructed open-air pavilion in the style of a Javanese *pendopo* providing dazzling views of the lake and the surrounding mountains. Great food and the most attentive and pleasant service anywhere. Several types of rooms are available, includng a number of traditional Toba Batak houses, ranging in price from $4 to $18. The more expensive rooms have hot water. Medan office: (061) 326207.

Silintong (51 rooms), tel: 41345. Interesting rock formations jut out into the lake in front of the hotel and a grove of tall pines offers pleas-ant shade and a meditative place to sit by the lake. Has a small but good restaurant. $17.50 S, $21 D. Medan booking office: (061) 529265, 511497.

Toledo Inn (tel: 41181). The oldest hotel on the island, sited just where the Tuktuk peninsula meets the main island. Has one of the better swimming beaches on Samosir, and a large pleasant restaurant. Popular with large groups from abroad: it's wise to book ahead. $21 a night. Medan office: (061) 513561.

Budget (under $10)

For the budget traveler there are any number of *losmen*-type accommodations around Tuktuk, mostly traditional Toba Batak houses on pilings. **Carolina** has rooms within this range, probably the best in their class. Also try **Romdan**, **Tuktuk Timbul**, **Abadi**, **Sibayak**, **Romlan** and others around the peninsula and just to the north of it. Still others can be found in Tomok, Ambarita, up on the central plateau at Partungkoan—a 3-hr trek from Ambarita—and scattered about elsewhere.

All are quite similar—Batak-style houses with several rooms, many facing right onto the lake. Prices are quite standard at about $1 a night for a bed in a dorm room up to $4 a night for a private room, with several gradations in between, depending on facilities and locations. Take your time and walk around the peninsula. Tuktuk is a great place for anyone on a budget —Sumatra's answer to Kuta Beach!

DINING

All the larger hotels have decent restaurants. **Carolina** rates as the best for food, price and setting, but try virtually any of the larger hotels for a similar, if perhaps somewhat more varied and pricey menu. No restaurant in Tuktuk is very expensive, however.

Generally speaking, the restaurants serve a fairly typical menu consisting of several Chinese-style dishes, some Malay curries and a few Western/Dutch staples. The small hotels serve the typical travelers' fare: fruit juices, yoghurt, toast, jaffles, fried chicken, fried noodles, *gado-gado* and fried rice for under $1 a meal.

Toba Batak food is hardly distinguished, but there is a kind of local golden carp, *ikan mas*, which is cooked in delicious spices. The most distinctive local dish is of course *saksan* or roast pig, served with a spicy sauce heavy with ginger that includes the blood of the animal and goes right together with the mountain air and the vigorous Batak character. If you are interested in trying this, inquire at your hotel.

CULTURAL PERFORMANCES

Lake Toba and Samosir form the cultural center of the Toba Batak, one of the six great Batak groups in North Sumatra. Unfortunately most of the music and dancing of these people is performed only in the context of important life cycle rituals, not as recreational events for audiences to observe. If you are lucky you may happen upon a ritual celebration, or *pesta* as it is called, almost anywhere on the island. If you wish to observe from close proximity, you are usually welcome as long as you observe due propriety in dress and manners.

There are two kinds of musical ensembles. The larger ritual ensemble, known as *gondang sabangunan*, is used in major outdoor ceremonies and features a unique combination of five tuned drums and a large double reed instrument played with circular, continuous breathing. The speed and dynamic, rhythmic energy of this music are breathtaking. Participate in dances only if you are invited to do so since the *tortor* ritual dance is not a social activity but rather a kind of choreographed enactment of relationships between the various groups present at the event.

Gondang sabangunan and *tortor* dancing can be seen in daily performances between 10:30 and 12:30 in Simanindo, 23 km north of Tuktuk. Cost is $2. Bike, walk or boat there and make a day of it.

The smaller chamber version of this ensemble, the *gondang hasapi*, has a wider array of smaller, less penetrating instruments, and is used indoors or in less formal situations. The music consists of a repertory of songs sung with tremendous gusto in the Batak language, usually self-accompanied on guitars. *Lagu Batak*, as these are called, are akin to the Spanish flamenco and Portuguese *fado* traditions, from which they have developed.

Groups can be found in all major hotels, either in regularly-scheduled performances, or on request. Carolina puts on a show every Sat night, with audience participation in the form of dancing. You'll also encounter spontaneous music-making on the streets at night, as the Bataks are very fond of singing and many professional buskers now make a living from the tourist trade. You will also find that the plucked stringed instrument which forms the core of the group, the *hasapi*, makes a nice souvenir and is sold in many shops around the island.

The Toba Batak are fervent Christians due to the work of German Lutheran missionaries in the latter decades of the 19th century, and the countryside is dotted with churches. The musical side of Lutheranism found exceptional resonance among the singing Batak, and over half of a church can often be seen singing Lutheran hymns with Batak lyrics in old unison style and impressive, improvised 4-part harmony. Some of the melodies still sung here have long ago disappeared in Europe!

Each church may have as many as 10 choirs —children, elderly, mixed, all sorts—which will periodically stand up from their pews and belt out a number. You may certainly feel free to enter any church on Sunday morning, if properly attired. All services are normally in the Batak language, but even if you can't understand what is being said, attendance will certainly provide you with some unique insights into the local culture.

FISHING

Freshwater fishing is good in Lake Toba, though limited to a number of relatively small rock bass type fish called *mujair* and *nilam*, which feed on earth worms and freshwater shrimp easily retrieved from the rock beds around the lake. Fishing tackle is available at some hotels, and you can also rent small boats or canoes.

TREKKING ON SAMOSIR

The Lake Toba region offers many hikes, none very difficult. A bit of physical exertion gets you up into the hills and reveals incredible panoramas that the slothful sybarites who stick by the lakeshore never see. Most of the hiking is along good trails. You will often meet Bataks along the way who are not "trekking"—just walking to get where they have to go, as they have most of their lives.

It is only on the cross-Samosir trek that you see the best of nature unspoiled by man. With the timber industry cutting tracks across the plateau to truck out logs from the interior, many places can now be visited in the comfort of a public minibus (cheap but without schedules) or a rented car (expensive). There are still many paths, however, which can only be covered by hiking. This is the best way to see the scenery, traditional houses, elaborate graves and to maximize your contacts with the friendly Bataks at your own pace.

Hiking boots make it easier on your feet, but tennis shoes are OK. Things can get muddy. Bring along some raingear, a hat, a light sleeping-bag or blanket, drinking water, a sweater or jacket for cool mornings. Insect repellant is useful in the late afternoon. Unless already well-tanned, take a long-sleeved shirt, long pants and sunscreen. Bring plenty of *kretek* cigarettes to offer to Bataks you meet along the way, and lots of small denomination bills to pay for food, coffee or whatever. Don't expect locals to change Rp10.000 notes!

Treks from Tomok

For a short trek, the walk from Tomok to Silakhosa hamlet on the top of the cliff offers wonderful views. The path is not *quite* as steep as it looks from the bottom and takes only 1.5 hours for those in reasonable shape. (The kids from Silakhosa go back and forth to school in Tomok every day along this trail.)

Start from the once-paved road next to the Raja's tomb in Tomok, straight past all the souvenir stands; bear right around the first group of houses and keep going through a couple of front yards, ignoring the yelping dogs. (They had better bark: useless watch dogs are eaten!) Soon you are winding up the cliff with great views of the terraced rice fields, Prapat and Tuktuk. You reach the pine trees in about 45 minutes, and the going gets a bit steeper. The lake is then partially hidden until you get to the top.

You can get a good, strong cup of coffee in one of the homes in Silakhosa. Coffee is the main cash crop in this area, carried down for sale in Tomok. The descent can be slippery when wet, so good soles are recommended.

There are a couple of other easy half or full-day treks out of Tomok. A 9-km road follows the shore of Lake Toba south as far as **Luntung**, and you can then catch a minibus back. Or you can take the paved road up into the plateau all the way to **Oran Runggu**, 34 km away on the island's southernmost tip. This newly-paved road leaves the shore just south of Tomok and rises gently to give a view of irrigated rice fields terraced in semicircular patterns. Large lumber trucks rumble past you from time to time, but otherwise it's delightfully peaceful.

If you want to keep going in this direction, **Parmonangan** village lies 2 or 3 hours up the road. You could spend the night here or follow a track westward from Parmonangan across the plateau to Palipi on the southwest coast. You can also keep on going straight down to Oran Runggu for your overnight. An hour or so beyond this village to the west along the coast, there is a small *losmen* at **Nainggolan**.

Across the Island

The most popular trek on Samosir, taken by some 200 hearty foreigners in 1990, cuts right across the island between Ambarita or Tomok on the east coast and Pangururan on the west coast. There are two big advantages to starting from Pangururan and walking back. One is that the gradual climb up from the west coast is much easier and you go down instead of up the spectacular drop on the east coast, with the fantastic scenery spreading out in front of you (instead of behind your back!). The second reason is that you avoid the problem of having to arrange transport back to Tuktuk once you arrive in Pangururan, exhausted, at the end of your trek. Instead, you can hike or hop a *bemo* back to Tuktuk and relax, have a bath or a swim and a nice cool drink.

If you get an early enough start, you can actually make the whole trip in a single day—getting up early and driving around to Pangururan, then hiking back across the island in a hurry, which takes 8-9 hours. It's much better to plan to spend the night somewhere along the way, however, so you have more time to stop and talk to people, enjoy the views, etc. At **Pangururan**, most trekkers stay overnight at the 10-room Barat Guesthouse ($1.50 to $3 per person). More upmarket accommodation is also available at the 43-room Hotel Wisata ($3.50 to $14). The owner of the Barat can find a guide for you ($8 a day), who will carry your gear and do some interpreting. However,

the main trail to Tomok is not difficult to follow.

You start from Pangururan along the main coastal road south heading past the Roman Catholic church, then turn left before the market. Three hours' walk brings you past scenic Lake Sidihoni to **Ronggurnihuta** village (16 km from Pangururan). People there are used to foreigners, and will put you up for the night (mattress, pillow) and feed you for $2.

From Ronggurnihuta, it's another 5 to 6 hrs to Tomok or Ambarita, down a steep cliff with spectacular views. You definitely don't want to do it at night! Of the two, the trail to Tomok is much better, with better panoramas. It's easy to get lost on the Ambarita trail unless you have a guide.

There are several other paths leading across the island from Ronggurnihuta. One goes north to **Partungkoan** village in the middle of the plateau, where you can stay at Jhon's Accommodation, then continue on to Simanindo or Ambarita. Another goes in a southeastwardly direction to Parmonangan. From here, paths lead down to villages along the south and west coasts.

— *Edward Van Ness/Kal Muller/Jill Gocher*

TAPANULI

The Rugged Southern Bataklands

North, Central and South Tapanuli districts occupy roughly the southern third of the province, bordering Lake Toba to the north and Riau and West Sumatra to the south. North Tapanuli is inhabited by Toba Bataks, while the areas to the south are home to the Angkola and Mandailing Batak, many of whom converted to Islam under intense pressure from Minang Paderi warriors in the 19th century. For the most part this is a rugged but picturesque country, with longitudinal valleys running north-south in the Bukit Barisan and a broadening coastal plain to the southeast.

Three main roads pass through the area. East of the mountains, the Trans-Sumatra Highway traverses the plantation belt south of Tebing Tinggi to Rantau Prapat and Kota Pinang. It then cuts inland across the arid and undulating Padang Lawas plain past Gunung Tua to Padang Sidempuan—the main market town and administrative center of South Tapanuli, known for its *salak* palm fruits, grown on the slopes of Mt. Lubukraya (1,886 m).

Two roads also lead to Padang Sidempuan from the Toba Highlands via Tarutung. One follows the Batang Toru Valley past Pearaja and Sipirok, joining the east coast route at Pagarutan. Another, more attractive route, drops down to the west coast at Sibolga.

The east coast route

Fifty km east of Tebing Tinggi, an interesting detour from the main highway leads north to the coast at **Tanjung Tiram** ("Oyster Cape"). This village, with its fish market and sandy beach, lies on the river mouth beyond Labuhan Ruku and is the site of an early 19th-century Malay port known as Bogak. For the adventurous, it is possible to hire a boat from here to visit **Pulau Berhala**, a small island 3 hours offshore reputed for its fishing.

Just south of Labuan Ruku at **Limau Laras** is a small, recently-restored palace—seat of the former Malay ruler. In the early 19th century this was an important center for gold-and-silver *songket* weaving, a tradition that continues in one or two isolated villages.

Much further to the south, at Kota Pinang, the highway meets the Barumun River and heads inland across the vast **Padang Lawas** ("Great Plain") region. At the upper reaches of the Barumun lie the mysterious Tantric remains of the ancient Panai Kingdom—made famous by F.M. Schnitger's romantic explorations in the 1930s. This region was an important ancient crossroads, providing access to valuable forest resins in the Bukit Barisan as well as to alluvial gold deposits in the south. Panai, "with water in its bathing ghats," is mentioned in the South Indian Tanjore inscription as having been conquered during the Tamil Chola raid of AD 1018.

Most of the visible remains are concentrated around **Gunung Tua** in a dry rain-shadow area that has a distinctive savannah-like flora. The most impressive remains are three brick *candi* or *biaro* (from the Buddhist term *vihara* meaning monastery) located at Bahal near Portibi, east of Gunung Tua high above the banks of the Barumun River. These *candi* with their eastern Indian and Tantric Buddhist associations are thought to date from between the 10th and 13th centuries. Unfortunately, their sculptors used a soft volcanic tuff, and their work has weathered badly over the centuries. Bahal I, with its sculptured brick panels, has been badly restored in recent years. Other sites are little more than heaps of bricks, though the settings of these remains —associated with orgiastic rites and human sacrifices—are dramatic, especially at sunset.

The Toba Highlands route

South of Siborongborong, **Tarutung** is the administrative center of North Tapanuli district. In the village of Pagaran just to the south lies the unusual sarcophagus of Datu Ompu Panonson Lumban Tobing. According to Barbier, this cist has been moved at least 3 times as it was thought to bring its owners bad luck.

The inland route from Tarutung south to Padang Sidempuan leads past **Sipirok**—a village in the shadow of active Mt. Sibualbuali (1,820 m) known for its weaving and ceramic production. At nearby Padang Matinggi are Dutch redoubts built as a defence against the Paderis in the 1830s. A side road from Sipirok runs northeast to Sipogu past an exposed carbonized forest buried by an eruption of Mt. Sibualbuali. Also in the vicinity, at Tor Sibohi, is a forest reserve with sulphur hot

Right: *Sunset over Sibolga, on the west coast.*

springs reputed for their medicinal properties. A new hotel has been established here.

The west coast

The west coast of North Sumatra, with its narrow plain, steep hills and deepwater bays, is one of the most scenic parts of Sumatra. The 66-km road down to Sibolga from Tarutung follows the sinuous Silindung Valley through deep ravines and dense forests across steep fern-covered slopes—rounding 1,200 hairpin bends that afford magnificent views of Tapanuli Bay as you approach the coast.

The town of **Sibolga** is the administrative center for Central Tapanuli and a major port for steamers and ferries bound for Nias. This is the western gateway to the Batak highlands, overlooking striking Tapanuli Bay, which derives its name from *tapian nauli* meaning "beautiful beach." The town is noted for its seafood, and the bay is dotted with islands—the largest of which is Pulau Mursala, known for its clear waters and bountiful marine life. The British maintained a trading post on Pulau Puncung Kecil, closer to shore, from 1756 to 1824. It was from here that the first Europeans entered the Bataklands in the 1820s.

Good beaches with shady coconut palms await you 11 km south of Sibolga at **Pantai Pandan**, a traditional fishing village where fish are barbecued fresh from the sea. Stalls also sell seashells, coral and gemstones.

Barus, 65 km north of Sibolga, is the site of an ancient port known to the Arabs as Fansur or Pancur since at least the 6th century. Barus had an international reputation as a source of high quality camphor (*kapur barus*) and benzoin brought down from the Dairi region. Numerous Islamic graves dating from about the 14th century also indicate that it was a center of Islamic learning. Earlier there may even have been a Nestorian Christian church here. The Dutch established a trading post in 1668 and there is a well-preserved 19th-century colonial fort, now occupied by the local police.

A Tamil stele dating to AD 1088 was found at the mouth of the Batang Garigis River at **Lobu Tuo** ("Old Village"), north of Barus. The inscription, written in the Tamil Grantha script (often referred to as "Pallawa" in Indonesia), commemorates the activities of a certain Tamil merchant guild known as "the 1500 (swamis of Ayyavole)." It now lies in the National Museum in Jakarta. Remains of a second Tamil inscription, as yet undeciphered, have also been recovered here.

A road climbs up steeply up from Barus to the Dairi (Pakpak) highlands via Pakkat and Dolok Sanggul. Just off this road at **Sijungkang**, overlooking the Sigomot River, is an abandoned village with Islamic Batak grave-markers painted black, white and red and an unusual carved image of a woman mounted on an elephant.

— E. Edwards McKinnon

NIAS ISLAND

Archaic Island of Megaliths

Nias is a small island, 130 km long and 45 km wide (slightly smaller than Bali), lying just 125 km off Sumatra's west coast—close enough that the latter's volcanic peaks can be seen on a clear day. Like the other western islands off Sumatra, however, Nias stands quite apart— the island's rugged terrain, malarial climate and warlike population having served to isolate it from the mainstream of Sumatran culture for many centuries. By contrast, Sumatra was always a fertile land of riches, and early traders and travelers seemed to have preferred it to the hostile environment on Nias.

As a result, Nias never experienced the dramatic influx of Indian, Islamic and European cultural influences to the degree these were felt in other areas. The island's inhabitants have instead followed their own line of development, building on an earlier Austronesian sub-strata of culture which they hold in common with other Indonesian peoples. Today they are best known for their spectacular tribal art and architecture—a unique style that has fascinated generations of scholars and collectors.

Ancient 'megalithic' traditions

Little is known about the island's prehistory, which is a pity since—as any visitor can see— the inhabitants have been working in durable stone and bronze for a very long time. Gold and imported ceramic artifacts form a part of nearly all aristocratic households, and Nias nobles moreover keep meticulous genealogies, some going back 50 generations, noting not only the names of the ancestors but the locations of their villages.

Despite the absence of hard archaeological data, the island's prehistory has nonetheless been the subject of much speculation— much of it intended to portray Nias as a kind of museum for prehistoric Indonesian civilizations. The most prominent theory, put forth by Robert Heine-Geldern in the 1930s, was that the island was populated during the first millenium BC by hill tribes from Assam or Burma, who brought with them a "megalithic" culture characterized by large stone monuments erected during communal feasts to enhance the status of the aristocracy.

This story has been repeated in nearly every account of the island published since the 1930s, yet there is good reason to ques-

COEN PEPPLINKHUIZEN

tion its validity. Recent archaeological evidence from the rest of Indonesia has yet to demonstrate such early dates for "megalithic" cultures elsewhere, and local genealogies seem to indicate that Nias culture acquired many of its distinctive traits no earlier than about AD 750, or around the time that Indian influence was arriving in the archipelago. A more probable line of development is that aristocratic Nias culture developed locally out of a simpler society perhaps akin to that of the Mentawai Islands to the south.

In any event, indigenous oral histories agree on one point—that Nias culture originated in the Gomo River area in the central part of the island. Here the gods descended and begat the human race, and the Nias people today refer to themselves as *ono niha* or "children of the people"—an explicit reference to these founding ancestors. From Central Nias the culture spread north and south, developing local variations but always maintaining explicit symbolic reference to the ritual and artistic homeland in the Gomo area.

Slaves and gold

The association of western Sumatra with the gold trade probably spurred on early explorations of Nias. In the 15th century, Chinese navigators gave the name "Gold Island" to one of the Batu Islands south of Nias. A century later, perhaps dissatisfied with the meager quantities of gold they found in Sumatra, the Portuguese explored Nias, and their presence is still very much alive in local oral histories. Arab traders also arrived at a very early date, but records of their contacts are sketchy. Two identical accounts describe a large patrilineal village in which head-hunting formed part of the marriage ritual; the earliest is dated 851.

In later times, Nias became known as a popular and plentiful source of slaves. From Acehnese sources we learn that there was a European post here in 1626, probably Portuguese, which the Acehnese attacked in order to monopolize the slave trade. The Dutch arrived in 1665, also to buy slaves, and in 1693 signed contracts with the island's district chiefs. In the 1820s, Raffles became intensely interested in the island as a place to buy rice and pigs that were reportedly free of tuberculosis. Between 1819 and 1825, English missions were sent to negotiate an end to the slave trade, and from these contacts we have the first detailed accounts of the island.

The Dutch assumed control of Nias in 1825, at first continuing the slave trade but later outlawing it and enforcing their will through force. Using the slave trade as a pretext, they deposed the independent chiefs of South Nias. In the 1840s they constructed a fort in Lagundri Bay (now a favorite surfing spot with young foreigners), which was later destroyed by an earthquake and tidal wave. In the 1860s, the Dutch launched military invasions that resulted in much suffering and the ravaged several villages. They are still despised for this in parts of South Nias.

Early attempts were made in the 1830s to Christianize the island, with little success. But the arrival in 1865 of German Rhenish missionaries from Barmen marked the beginning of a major change in Nias society. Within a few years the entire northern part of the island had been converted. Central and South Nias later succumbed not to the Bible but to a combination of epidemics and brutal policing. Beginning in 1909, religious art was destroyed or confiscated in large quantities in South Nias.

The island's population today numbers about 500,000 and despite a century of contact and conflict with the outside world, Nias culture remains remarkably intact. The language is a distinctive member of the huge Austronesian language family, and closely related dialects are spoken on the nearby Batu Islands and Simeulue, yet it is surpris-

KAL MULLER

Overleaf: *A war dance.* **Opposite:** *A North Nias wedding.* **Right:** *A village chief in traditional garb.*

ingly different from all other Indonesian languages, more closely resembling a Polynesian tongue in many ways.

Nias society is strictly hieratic. The nobility (*si'ulu* or *salawa*: "that which is high") do not intermarry with commoners (the *sato* or *sihönö*, literally "the thousands") and have certain special privileges. Slaves (*sawuyu* or *harakana*) were formerly important as servants and as trade items. They were not considered to be human and therefore had to live outside the village areas.

Throughout Nias, two types of traditional dwellings directly expressed the rank and wealth of the inhabitants by the size and complexity of their construction. The traditional *omo hada* could be inhabited by any village citizen, while aristocrats who can afford enormous feasts and sacrifices built special houses called *omo sebua*, or "big houses." Such houses are no longer constructed, due partly to the diminished wealth and influence of the chiefs, but also to the fact that they require the capture and display of human heads for their consecration. While such heads are no longer displayed, they are still under the main pillars of some *omo sebua*.

The island's three culture areas—North, Central and South Nias—now display great differences in language, art and custom. But from a Nias point of view the distinctions are much greater than this, as each region is subdivided into numerous village groups according to their lineages. To the *ono niha*, culture is thus defined on a village level and each village has its own variations in art and custom.

Visiting Nias

The main point of entry to Nias is **Gunungsitoli**, the former Dutch administrative center and base for early German missionaries. It remains the district capital, and aside from a few local architectural embellishments in the town square, looks much like any other Indonesian port town. One notices almost

immediately, however, that nearly all living things seem to be smaller here. The *ono niha* are diminutive people with features quite distinct from their neighbors in Sumatra. Local cats and dogs are small, and one may even be astonished to find chicken eggs the size one would expect of quail eggs.

To see something of the culture one must venture out of the town. In nearby **Hiliana'a** is a fine, rare example of a traditional chief's house, distinguished—like other North Nias houses—by its oval floorplan. In the western

part of North Nias, the village of **Hiligowe** has large village protector figures in stone (*gowe*) that are remarkably intact, though the genitalia have been removed. The nearby village of **Onolimbu** has similar statues in a more blocky style.

Central Nias is extremely inaccessible, yet has some of the island's greatest art treasures. The houses here are rectangular and ornamented with bold geometric sculptures. Villages along the Gomo and Tae rivers are particularly important; **Orahili Idanö Gomo**, **Lahusa Idanö Tae** and **Tundrumbaho** are known for their striking plazas with vertical (*behu*) and horizontal (*harefa*) megaliths. Also found here are round, mushroom-shaped stones called *ni'ogazi* used by women to dance upon—their slapping feet producing musical tones as they imitate the motions of various animals. The so-called *osa'osa* are stone seats of honor with one or three carved monster heads, formerly used by the nobility during large ritual feasts. The village of **Holi** has a unique old *omo sebua* with pyramidal skull tombs in the square in front of it memorializing the great chiefs of old.

The island's most spectacular area, however, is the South—reached by boat from Sibolga or Gunungsitoli. The most important

Above, left: *Spirit mask used in ritual war dance.*
Above, right: *The famous "stone jumping" ritual.*
Right: *The lovely palm-finged beach at Lagundri.*

village here is **Bawömataluo**, with a massive flight of stairs at the main entrance. It was built in 1888 following the Dutch attacks of 1863; below it stands the newer village of Orahili on the site of the former village destroyed by the Dutch and their allies.

The largest and oldest *omo sebua* in Nias is in this village, still inhabited and owned by the royal family, but run now as a museum (make a small donation at the back). Although the inhabitants claim it is 400 years old, the house actually dates from the founding of the village 100 years ago. Some of the pillars are more than a meter thick and the house is 20 m high. It has exquisite wall carvings that commemorate great ritual feasts held for the smithing of golden head ornaments.

Brackets at the front of the house originally held old Dutch and Chinese plates used by the rulers during feasts. Two small chairs carved in relief inside once held images of the village founders (*adu zatua* or *adu nuwu*). Opposite them is a whimsical relief carving of a steam-powered warship with uniformed Dutch officers aboard. This probably represents a steamer used in the 1863 invasion, but has now become a symbol of man's harnessing of nature, as indicated by the scene of a crocodile being captured below it.

A similar symbolism is displayed by massive megaliths in front of the house. The larger, horizontal stone represents a ship and commemorates the founder of the village, a certain Laowo. On its bow, humans and monkeys capture a shark. A horizontal stone opposite it commemorates the last ruler to hold official titles, a local hero named Saonigeho. The towering vertical stones commemorate feasts to raise the status of the living, while horizontal stones are ships to transport the spirits of the dead.

Bawömataluo literally means "sun-mountain" and in front of the *omo sebua* is a circular flagstone known as the *fusö newali* or "village navel;" close examination reveals a worn circular pattern on it representing the sun.

Smaller but still impressive *omo sebua* can be found in the villages of Onohondro, Hilinawalö and Hilinawalö Mazingö. The first two are not far from Bawömataluo but the third is quite some distance; none should be attempted unless you are in good physical shape.

Onohondro and **Hilinawalö** both played an important role in an ancient renewal ceremony in which a figure of a giant tiger representing the ruler was carried on a high platform and then thrown into the Gomo River. This river, named after the one in Central Nias, is near Onohondro and links the inhabitants to their roots in Central Nias. Afterward, the ruler carried on as usual until the next such ceremony was held, 7 to 14 years later. The ceremony was outlawed by missionaries in 1913, but has recently been revived to celebrate Indonesia's independence day.

— *Jerome Feldman*

KAL MULLER

PART IV

Introducing Aceh

Aceh province occupies the northernmost end of Sumatra, its long coastline guarding the entrance to Asia's most important sea lane—the Strait of Malacca. Almost all maritime traffic between East and West passes through these straits, and Aceh was for many centuries the first landfall for Arab and Indian mariners who came to Indonesia in search of spices.

By the end of the 13th century, trading posts and petty kingdoms along Aceh's east coast had developed into Indonesia's first Islamic states. Marco Polo visited Aceh in 1292 on his way back to Venice from China, and wrote of Muslim kingdoms called Ferlac and Samudra. (The name Sumatra probably derives from the latter.) He also claimed to have seen a unicorn, which was probably a Sumatran rhinoceros.

For the next 600 years, foreign merchants and Indonesian traders mingled in Aceh's ports. During a "Golden Age" at the beginning of the 17th century, in the reign of powerful Sultan Iskandar Muda, Aceh became one of Asia's greatest trading emporiums, and in its main port of Kuta Raja (now Banda Aceh) a dozen languages could be heard.

Since the 17th century, Aceh has enjoyed a reputation as the most staunchly Islamic area in Southeast Asia. It has also been proudly independent, resisting domination by a succession of Asian and European powers. Aceh was finally brought under Dutch rule only after a long and bitter struggle against Dutch colonial forces from 1873 to 1903. But the independent spirit of the Acehnese was never completely broken. In 1953, just 3 years after Indonesia's independence was secured, a 10-year rebellion against central government control broke out. As a result, Aceh was declared a *daerah istimewa* or "special region," and granted a degree of autonomy in matters of religion, customary law and education. Only the sultanate of Yogyakarta in central Java has a similar status.

Today, Aceh's economy is booming, despite a population of just 3 million. Following the discovery of huge natural gas fields on the east coast around Lhokseumawe and Lhoksukon, economic growth has been rapid. Most of the gas is exported to Japan in the form of LNG; Aceh also has sizeable reserves of oil, gold, silver, copper and coal. Since 1980, Aceh has contributed between $2 and $3 billion annually to Indonesia's foreign exchange earnings. The province's per capita gross domestic product is one of the highest in the nation.

Despite periodic unrest and the constraints this has placed on the building of roads, schools and hospitals, Aceh's rural economy remains buoyant. For several centuries, Aceh's narrow but fertile coastal strip has produced an annual surplus of rice and cash crops, notably pepper. (In the 17th century, and again in the early 19th, Aceh produced over half of the world's pepper.) Modern fertilizers have boosted rice yields, and the coastal population is well-off by Indonesian standards.

Over half of the province's population live in its coastal region, though there are no large towns. Even the capital, Banda Aceh, has only 80,000 inhabitants. The next largest town is Sabang, on Weh Island, with 25,000 inhabitants. Smaller towns and villages dot the 600 km coastline between Banda Aceh and Medan, connected by an excellent trunk road.

The rugged and isolated interior of Aceh provides a sharp contrast to the fertile coastal plain. Huge mountains rise along both sides of a central valley. This thickly-forested and sparsely-populated region is the home of the Gayo people—an ethnic group who practice syncretic Islam mixed with traces of animism.

Aceh is perfect for travelers who want to avoid the beaten track. A basic knowledge of Indonesian is a must, and a healthy respect for Acehnese religious sensibilities is advised.

— *Kal Muller and Eric Oey*

Overleaf: *The Great Mosque of Banda Aceh.*
Opposite: *An Acehnese couple in traditional costume. Photos by Kal Muller.*

COASTAL TOWNS

Old Islamic Harbors of the North

The northeastern coast of Aceh was the site of Indonesia's earliest Islamic kingdoms. A number of short, fast-flowing rivers descend from the Bukit Barisan mountains to meet the shore here, and for centuries these estuaries provided sheltered anchorages, water and provisions for ships before and after the long voyage across the Indian Ocean. Ports like Samudra-Pasai (Lhokseumawe), Tamiang (Langsa), Peureulak, Samalanga and Pidië (Sigli) developed to service this trade. All of them converted to Islam during the 13th and 14th centuries, then came under the sway of the powerful sultanate based at Banda Aceh (Kotaraja) in the 16th century.

These ancient ports are now somnolent coastal towns connected by a fast asphalt highway running 600 km from Medan up to Banda Aceh. The economy of the region was formerly based on rice, pepper and plantation (rubber and oil palm) agriculture, but is now developing rapidly as the result of an oil and natural gas boom. Oil was discovered here in the 1890s and first developed by the Bataviaasch Petroleum Maatschappij, later to become Royal Dutch Shell. In 1971, some of the richest concentrations of natural gas in the whole of Indonesia were discovered here.

Medan to Banda Aceh

The road from Medan to Banda Aceh follows the old narrow gauge Aceh tram railway, built to help pacify the region during the Aceh War in the latter part of the 19th century. The Aceh tram itself has long fallen into disuse, but the track can still be seen along the route northward, crisscrossing the main road from Pangkalan Brandan to Langsa. Old rubber and oil palm plantations line either side of the highway, interrupted by low-roofed traditional houses on high posts.

At **Kuala Simpang**, about 140 km and 3 hours from Medan, the road crosses the Tamiang River. From here onwards, distinctive Chinese Red and Indian Brahman cattle are a common sight along the roadside. Reaching **Peureulak**, the site of a 13th century Islamic state (the Ferlac of Marco Polo), the road crosses the Peureulak River and some distance later passes Kuala Berkah Beach before crossing into North Aceh regency at Pantonlabu, on the Jambuaye River.

Past Lhoksukon a road branches inland to

the village of **Minye Tujoh**, Matangkuli, where an unusual early Islamic gravestone or *nisan* is carved in the Majapahit style of 14th century Java and is inscribed in two languages —Arabic and Old Javanese. Such tombstones are a notable feature of the Acehnese landscape and mark the sites of former villages. Indeed, "Aceh stones" (*batu Aceh*), as they are called, were a major export from the 15th to the late 19th centuries, and have been found as far afield as the Malay Peninsula, Brunei, Kalimantan (Banjarmasin) and Java (Banten).

At nearby **Blangme** (*blang* means "cultivated rice field"), some 18 km southeast of Lhokseumawe, are extensive Islamic grave complexes marking the site of the twin cities of Pasai and Samudra, the latter being the port which gave its name to the whole island of Sumatra. In the early 15th century, Samudra-Pasai was a strong rival of Malacca. Formerly sited on both banks of the Krueng Pasai River, it was reputedly the first polity in Sumatra to convert to Islam and was a major entrepôt frequented by all peoples of the east. En route from China to Europe, Marco Polo spent 5 months here waiting for the monsoon to change prior to taking a ship to India in 1292. Both Samudra and Pidië, to the north, were engaged in the lucrative pepper trade.

One of the graves at Blangme is that of Malikul Saleh, first sultan of Pasai, who died in 1297. Here also are tombs of other Pasai royalty made of reworked marble taken from the Hindu temples of Gujerat and decorated with Arabic calligraphy. Best known of these is the grave of Sultanah Bahiyah, who died in 1428. Access to the grave complexes at Blangme is by a track which leaves the main road just east of the bridge at Geudong and leads northeast toward the coast.

The site of the former palace of the sultans is said to be on a high sandy hill named Cot Istana, meaning "palace hill," adjacent to the site of the Royal Mosque at Kota Krueng. This is also near Blangme, reached via a track through the rice fields to the village of Kota Krueng. The story of the founding of Pasai and how Cot Istana was chosen as the palace site was recorded in the *Hikayat Raja-Raja Pasai* or "Chronicle of the Pasai Kings."

Lhokseumawe is the site of several large development projects centering round the oil and gas fields. P.T. Arun is an enormous LNG plant, with a capacity of some 18.8 million metric tons per annum, most of which is exported to Japan. Other large-scale projects in the area are the Asean Aceh Fertilizer plant (capitalized at over US$141 million), a kraft paper factory at Krueng Geukeuh and an LNG plant at Blang Lancang. The town of Lhokseumawe itself is the administrative center for the regency of Aceh Utara (North Aceh), which is also an important rice-grow-

Below: *The tiny, somnolent harbor at Sigli.*

KAL MULLER

ing area. This, like the other smaller east coast towns has benefitted to some degree from the development of the LNG industry and has a well developed business center and ample accommodations.

The next major town after Lhokseumawe is **Bireuen**, where locally-grown coffee, cinnamon, cloves and tobacco are marketed. A side road forks to the left here and climbs up through thickly-forested hills and coffee plantations into the northern Gayo Highlands—centering around the town of Takengon and scenic Lake Tawar (see "Gayo Highlands").

At **Samalanga**, 35 km past Bireuen, is an elaborately carved *rumah adat* or traditional Acehnese house which belonged to the late Major-General Teuku Hamzah. Ten km on, at **Babah Awe** near Meureudu, are the remains of Kuta Bateë, an Acehnese fortification.

At **Sigli** (Pidië), between the estuaries of the Krueng Baro and the Krueng Tuka, can be seen the remains of another old Acehnese fort—Benteng Kuta Asan—visible to the left of the road. In the 16th century, gold was brought over the hills from Meulaboh on the west coast to the east coast at Pidië, where it was traded to foreign merchants.

Just to the north of here, in the limestone hills above Pidië Point, reached via a side-road from Sigli, is the **Guha Tujoh** or "seven caves" complex, accessible from Menasah Cot via Kayeëkuniet. At **Klibeuet**, 6 kilometers from Sigli, is the grave complex known as

Teungku di Kandang, the tomb of Sultan Ma'arif Syah—the last sultan of Pidië, who died in 1511. A scenic road to the south of Sigli leads up into the highlands to the traditional village of **Tangse**, 52 km away.

Past Sigli, the main highway swings away from the coast and rises up over a pass to the south of Mt. Seulawah (1,806 m), with its twin peaks of Agam (male) and and Inong (female), to meet the Krueng Aceh River at Seulimeum. The road continues down the river 18 km to **Indrapuri**, site of one of the three main mosques of the former kingdom of Aceh Besar (Greater Aceh). The mosque at Indrapuri is said to have been established on the foundations of an earlier Hindu-Buddhist temple. It is set amidst coconut palms on a small hill overlooking the right bank of the river, and can be reached by road via a bridge which crosses the Krueng Aceh just below it. After Indrapuri, the road follows the valley of the Krueng Aceh, past well-irrigated rice fields into Banda Aceh.

Sights of Banda Aceh

This former capital of the fiercely independent sultanate of Aceh is steeped in history. After its conquest by the Dutch it was known as Kutaraja or "king's town" but was renamed Banda Aceh after independence.

The site of the former *dalem* or palace of the Acehnese sultan is marked by the former Dutch Residency, built in 1880 after the

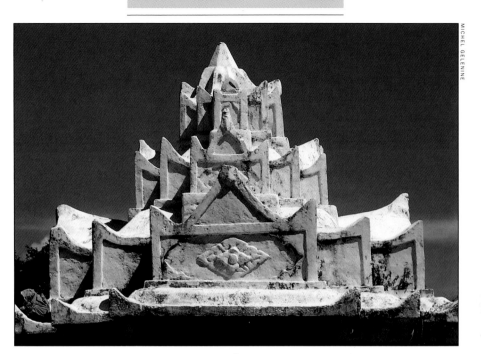

MICHEL GELENINE

palace had been raised by invading Dutch forces. It is now the **Governor's House** (Pendopo Gubernur). The graves of the former sultans, including the great Iskandar Muda, are just to the northeast on the opposite bank of the river, with their gigantic *nisan* or gravestones and other interesting remains.

The **Museum Negeri Aceh** (Aceh State Museum) nearby holds an interesting collection of historical and ethnographic materials. A large bronze bell, the Cakradonia, hangs in front of the museum. It was reputedly presented to the Sultan of Pasai by the Chinese imperial eunuch Zheng He in 1414. It is said to have been seized by Sultan Ali Mughayat Syah (1514–1530), founder of the state of Aceh, when he conquered Pasai in 1524. Another story, however, indicates that it was cast in 1469. In the same complex is a traditional Acehnese house.

Upstream from the palace area, a short distance to the southwest, is the enigmatic stone and plaster *gunongan*—possibly a symbol of authority deriving from the pre-Islamic *meru* or sacred mountain, once part of the **Taman Sari** royal pleasure garden within the palace grounds. It was connected to the palace by a lovely gateway, the *pintu khob* or *pintu aceh* which became a symbol of the kingdom and was used to decorate jewelry and coins. This entire complex was reputedly built by Sultan Iskandar Muda (r. 1607-1636) during Aceh's "Golden Age." Nearby is Kandang XII, the

burial place of Sultan Iskandar Thani (r. 1636-1641), where remains of a gold ornamented coffin were excavated some years ago.

The neatly-kept **Kerkhof** or Dutch churchyard to the west of Taman Sari contains some 2,000 graves of Dutch KNIL army soldiers who died during the 19th century wars with Aceh. Many were actually Javanese, Menadonese and Ambonese enlisted men, and more actually died from disease than on the battlefield.

The grand **Baiturrahman Mosque** at the center of Banda Aceh was designed, surprisingly, by an Italian architect and built by the Dutch between 1879-81 to replace the mosque destroyed by their troops during the Aceh wars. The design is Moghul Indian, not traditional Acehnese (as a visit to the older mosque in nearby Indrapuri clearly shows). The market to the north side of the mosque has numerous shops selling Acehnese gold and silver filigree jewelry, among which the *pintu aceh* ("Aceh door") broach design is rightly famous. Other handicrafts, such as the *rencong* or slightly curved traditional dagger worn by both Acehnese men and women, and woven pandan mats and bags, are found.

Sidetrips from Banda Aceh

The beach at **Ujung Bateë**, 17 km northeast of Banda Aceh, and the new harbor with the

Opposite: *An* ojek *or* pedicab *in Banda Aceh.*
Above: *The enigmatic* gunongan *in Taman Sari.*

The northeastern coast of Aceh was the site of Indonesia's earliest Islamic kingdoms. A number of short, fast-flowing rivers descend from the Bukit Barisan mountains to meet the shore here, and for centuries these estuaries provided sheltered anchorages, water and provisions for ships before and after the long voyage across the Indian Ocean. Ports like Samudra-Pasai (Lhokseumawe), Tamiang (Langsa), Peureulak, Samalanga and Pidië (Sigli) developed to service this trade. All of them converted to Islam during the 13th and 14th centuries, then came under the sway of the powerful sultanate based at Banda Aceh (Kotaraja) in the 16th century.

These ancient ports are now somnolent coastal towns connected by a fast asphalt highway running 600 km from Medan up to Banda Aceh. The economy of the region was formerly based on rice, pepper and plantation (rubber and oil palm) agriculture, but is now developing rapidly as the result of an oil and natural gas boom. Oil was discovered here in the 1890s and first developed by the Bataviaasch Petroleum Maatschappij, later to become Royal Dutch Shell. In 1971, some of the richest concentrations of natural gas in the whole of Indonesia were discovered here.

Medan to Banda Aceh

The road from Medan to Banda Aceh follows the old narrow gauge Aceh tram railway, built to help pacify the region during the Aceh War in the latter part of the 19th century. The Aceh tram itself has long fallen into disuse, but the track can still be seen along the route northward, crisscrossing the main road from Pangkalan Brandan to Langsa. Old rubber and oil palm plantations line either side of the highway, interrupted by low-roofed traditional houses on high posts.

At **Kuala Simpang**, about 140 km and 3 hours from Medan, the road crosses the Tamiang River. From here onwards, distinctive Chinese Red and Indian Brahman cattle are a common sight along the roadside. Reaching **Peureulak**, the site of a 13th century Islamic state (the Ferlac of Marco Polo), the road crosses the Peureulak River and some distance later passes Kuala Berkah Beach before crossing into North Aceh regency at Pantonlabu, on the Jambuaye River.

Past Lhoksukon a road branches inland to the village of **Minye Tujoh**, Matangkuli, where an unusual early Islamic gravestone or *nisan* is carved in the Majapahit style of 14th century Java and is inscribed in two languages —Arabic and Old Javanese. Such tombstones

are a notable feature of the Acehnese landscape and mark the sites of former villages. Indeed, "Aceh stones" (*batu Aceh*), as they are called, were a major export from the 15th to the late 19th centuries, and have been found as far afield as the Malay Peninsula, Brunei, Kalimantan (Banjarmasin) and Java (Banten).

At nearby **Blangme** (*blang* means "cultivated rice field"), some 18 km southeast of Lhokseumawe, are extensive Islamic grave complexes marking the site of the twin cities of Pasai and Samudra, the latter being the port which gave its name to the whole island of Sumatra. In the early 15th century, Samudra-Pasai was a strong rival of Malacca. Formerly sited on both banks of the Krueng Pasai River, it was reputedly the first polity in Sumatra to convert to Islam and was a major entrepôt frequented by all peoples of the east. En route from China to Europe, Marco Polo spent 5 months here waiting for the monsoon to change prior to taking a ship to India in 1292. Both Samudra and Pidië, to the north, were engaged in the lucrative pepper trade.

One of the graves at Blangme is that of Malikul Saleh, first sultan of Pasai, who died in 1297. Here also are tombs of other Pasai royalty made of reworked marble taken from the Hindu temples of Gujerat and decorated with Arabic calligraphy. Best known of these is the grave of Sultanah Bahiyah, who died in 1428. Access to the grave complexes at

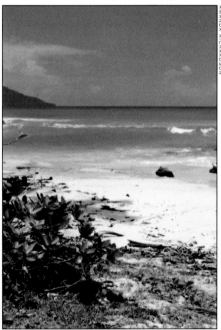

WEH ISLAND

Sabang's Easy Life Evokes the Past

At dusk, as the sun dips behind the western arm of Weh Island just to the north of Banda Aceh, the dominant sounds are the lapping of seawater against the rusting cast-iron legs of a pier, and the chatter of fishermen and strollers. Despite a magnificent deep-water harbor and a strategic location at the entrance to the Strait of Malacca—one of the busiest sea lanes in the world—Sabang, the main town on the island, has sunk into somnolent obscurity.

It wasn't always this way. Thin Phin Sun, portly and genial propietor of a restaurant not far from the waterfront, arrived from China in 1923 with his parents. They had emigrated to join a relative who established a successful business supplying tropical hardwood from the island's forests. "There was much more business then than now," he recalled as customers waited for an order of sweet-and-sour fish, steamed prawns, noodles and mixed vegetables. Pinned to the wall near the table where he does his nightly accounts is a fading black and white panorama of the harbor in 1914. It shows more than a dozen ocean-going passenger liners and freighters anchored offshore or tied to the pier.

As steamers replaced sailing ships in the late 19th century, the Dutch decided to develop Sabang, then a tiny fishing village. They brought coal from mines in Sumatra and stored it in row after row of tin-roofed warehouses that still line the waterfront. A dry-dock for repairing ships and an oil storage depot were built. Fresh water was piped from a lake in the mountains to supply the ships and the Dutch offices, bungalows, clubs and other facilities in the new town. At one point in the early decades of the 20th century, Sabang was a more important port than Singapore. But the transition from steam to diesel power at sea ensured that this ascendency was shortlived.

Japanese military forces quickly entrenched themselves on Weh after overrunning Singapore in 1942. They were only dislodged when Japan surrendered three and a half years later. Visitors to some of the island's beaches swim and sunbathe in the shadow of derelict concrete bunkers and gun emplacements dug into the sides of cliffs and rocky headlands.

War and foreign occupation seem far removed from the tranquil and unhurried life of Weh today. Fishing, coconut and clove plantations provide a subsistence livelihood for many of the 20,000 people who live on the 150 sq km island. In the late March and early April, just after the harvest, the sides of the narrow roads are lined with pungent cloves drying in the sun.

"Life is easy here," said Ismet Harun, who sailed around the world as a merchant seaman for 10 years before coming home to Weh. He has his own small motorised fishing boat. "I can earn enough money working as a tourist guide or as a fisherman," he said.

Weh experienced a second promising burst of business activity after 1970, when the Indonesian government gave Sabang tax-exempt status as a free port. Shipping and trade flourished. Jobs were easy to get and relatively well paid. But in 1986, alarmed at the growth of smuggling to and from the island and anxious to develop Batam, near Singapore, as Indonesia's premier free trade zone, the central government withdrew Sabang's special status. Since then, the population on Weh has declined as people moved to other parts of Indonesia in search of work.

Fishing, a newly established rattan cooperative and tourism seem to offer the best hope of future employment on the island. The crystal clear waters and coral reefs teeming with colorful fish are a natural magnet for tourists. A trickle of tourists, mainly backpackers content to stay with villagers or in several guesthouses in Sabang arrives on the daily ferry from Sumatra. There is no hotel. The nearest thing to nightlife, apart from Mr. Thin's restaurant, are a couple of cinemas.

Sadly, illegal dynamite fishing is slowly destroying some of the best coral, including sections of the splendid undersea garden off Rubiah Island not far from Sabang. Villagers and officials blame unscrupulous fishermen from Sumatra. They say the destruction is difficult to stop because the dynamiters operate at night and use fast boats to carry the loads of stunned fish away.

— *Michael Richardson/Int'l Herald Tribune*

Opposite: *One of Weh's irresistible beaches.*

GAYO HIGHLANDS

Proud People and a Lovely Highland Lake

The Gayo Highlands occupy the mountainous central portion of Aceh—an isolated area cut off from the surrounding coastal plains by the rugged peaks of the Bukit Barisan range. This is the homeland of about 250,000 Gayo people who speak their own language and are known for their dynamism, for the vitality of their traditional arts, and for their high levels of education.

There are four main Gayo regions, each centering around a a lake or river valley bordered by high forested ridges. The Lake Tawar region to the north is the most populous, especially the area around the town of Takengon. A good road links Takengon to the north coast at Bireuen, 100 km away. South of Takengon and separated from it by a mountain range is the Isak region, where a number of villages stretch out along the Jambuaye or Isak River.

The road south from Isak winds over a high mountain pass to the southern Gayo region and its main town of Blangkejeren. It is gradually being improved to allow year-round traffic, and from Blangkejeren it is possible to continue southward to Kabanjahe in the Karo Batak area. East of the Isak valley is the Serbejadi region (centered on the village of Lukup), known for its production of *gambir*, the leaf which is distilled into a hard plug and combined with betel, *sirih* and lime for chewing.

Conquest and resistance

In the 17th century these highlands formed part of the Acehnese kingdom ruled by Sultan Iskandar Muda, Aceh's greatest ruler. It was during this period of Acehnese dominance that most of the Gayo converted to Islam.

The Gayo were virtually unknown to Westerners before this century. In 1904, Dutch troops entered the highlands to force the submission of local rulers. The troops met strong resistance along the way and in the Blangkejeren area wiped out several villages that refused to capitulate. The massacres caused a public outcry in the Netherlands.

During the subsequent period of Dutch rule, government and private companies set up coffee, tea and dammar resin-processing enterprises in the Takengon area. The Gayo at this time quickly began growing cash crops, mainly vegetables and coffee, to supplement their staple rice crop.

By the early 1930s, the Gayo began to establish schools to teach secular and religious subjects. Gayo students sought further education outside the region and were quick to obtain advanced degrees in Java. Gayo poets produced religious poetry that taught the essentials of Islam; their poems were written in Gayo using the Arabic script, and one book was even published in Cairo in 1938.

The Gayo strongly supported the Indonesian nationalist cause and fought hard during the revolution, but many Gayo also participated in the Darul Islam rebellion against the central government in the 1950s. As elsewhere in Indonesia, the massacres of 1965 left a deep emotional scar in the highlands.

Gayo pride themselves on their strong kin ties, their attention to traditional social values and the vitality of their poetry and storytelling. They also value their capacity to adapt to the modern world. Unlike in many other

Left: *A Gayo man from the Takengon area.*
Right: *Lake Tawar in the late afternoon mists.*

remote areas in Indonesia, the Gayo place great emphasis on schooling, on mastery of the Indonesian language, and on promotion of Islamic values and scholarship.

Rivalries exist between villages and between the two former political domains of Bukit and Ciq near Takengon. These emerge in colorful contests of sung poetry (*didong*) between clubs from different villages. *Didong* contests are team events and last from about nine in the evening until dawn. On these occasions, feelings of resentment and hostility between villages can legitimately be given palpable expression in versified taunts and challenges exchanged by the two teams.

The Takengon area

The Takengon area boasts a cool, dry climate, dense forests and the scenic beauty of Lake Tawar. In 1900 the journey to Takengon from the north coast town of Bireuen had to be made on foot and took up to a week. Today, barring a mudslide or mechanical failure, the bus trip takes about three hours.

The road climbs and winds through pine forests and small stands of coffee. One passes the village of Lampahan, where for many years a plant processed dammar pine sap into resins and turpentine. Since 1989 a logging project has begun to change the face of the landscape, though the hills are still heavily forested. The road finally reaches a high cliff overlooking the smooth surface of Lake Tawar, and then descends into the valley.

Takengon sits at an altitude of 1,200 m on the edge of Lake Tawar, in a caldera formed by the implosion of an ancient volcano. The lake is the headwaters of the Peusangan River which flows northward to the Straits of Malacca. The town was constructed during colonial times, and consists of a central commercial area with rows of shops and a two-story market building, a cluster of government buildings, several schools, a silver-domed mosque built in the 1970s, and several residential neighborhoods. Much of the recent government architecture incorporates the vividly-colored whorls and arabesques of traditional Gayo house designs.

Acehnese, Javanese, Chinese and Minangkabau as well as Gayo live in the town. The Acehnese, mostly bachelors, come here to engage in small-scale trade. Many send money back to their home villages, where they expect to return to marry. Some of the Javanese living in or near the town were brought to Takengon in the 1920s and '30s by the Dutch as laborers on the dammar pine estates. Most live in separate villages where their children learn Javanese and Indonesian. The Chinese remain distinct from the Gayo because of their religious (Buddhist and Christian) and economic ties to Medan and overseas.

A walking tour of Takengon

First climb to the top of **Buntul Kubu**, the

large hill overlooking the town, for a splendid overview of the area. The building on top of the hill was constructed by the Dutch and is now the district office for cultural affairs. Ask here about forthcoming cultural events in the area. Then descend the hill back to the town and visit the "Padang prayer house" (*mersah padang*) next to the river near the new 2-story market building. This prayer house was built by Minang settlers in the late 1920s as a place for their modernist style of worship.

Next to the prayer house a road leads down to the river and a footbridge. From the middle of the bridge, a view of the river and the older houses lining its banks may be enjoyed. On the left bank is the community of **Bale**, with its own reformist prayer house; on the right, further downstream, is the community of **Asir-Asir**, whose prayer house was built by traditionalist Muslims to preserve the older style of congregational worship. All three prayer houses once served as mosques but Friday worship is now only held in the large, silver-domed government mosque. Continue across the river to Bale to visit the new Buddhist temple (a center for Sumatra-wide Buddhist celebrations) and the Catholic church. Caretakers of each are happy to tell the history of the Chinese in the area.

A rich Muslim ritual life characterizes the town, and the Gayo welcome questions from visitors about their religion. Friday is the day of worship at the mosque in town. Men and women then come to town from surrounding villages to shop before and after the noon service. You may be fortunate enough to arrive during the celebration of the *idul adha* feast of sacrifice during the pilgrimage month, or the *idul fitri* feast following Ramadan. Families and entire communities then prepare lavish meals, engage in joyous worship, and visit each other's houses for snacks and to ask forgiveness from each other for any mistakes committed the previous year.

Around Lake Tawar

Lake Tawar is a vital source of livelihood and recreation for the people of Takengon. On three sides of the lake the land rises steeply to peaks of 2,400 to 2,800 m. Several trails lead from the town up these slopes and afford splendid views of the lake.

The village of **Kebayakan** lies by the lake just north of Takengon. The main road to the village takes you through rice fields past the intricately-carved house of the last ruler of the area, Kejurun Zainuddin. Just outside of Kebayakan, and worth a brief stop, is an older style wooden prayer house, once a mosque, with a ball-shaped ornament on the dome. This village is a mosaic of *kampungs*.

A good road also leads south from Takengon across the Peusangan River around the lake's southern shore. Ask at the Hotel Renggali, just outside of town, for a boat and a guide to explore the calm lake from the water. Farther along are small villages, rice terraces and fishing platforms. Inhabitants of these villages use nets suspended from fishing platforms to catch the carp and minnow-like *depek* fish which abound in the lake.

Local Gayo folktales often tell of a particular spot—here is the shore where the Green Princess threw herself into its waters, there the ledge where Syiah Utama rested on his journey to bring Islam to the villagers, and that rock formation is actually a bride who turned to stone as she gazed back on her beloved village as she was leaving.

Hot springs and coffee gardens

A day trip to the north of town should include a visit to the hot springs at Simpangbaleg, a look at the coffee gardens, and a stop at a handicraft shop in the village of Bebesen.

Go first to **Baleatu**, about one km to the north of Takengon, to see the area's open-air morning market (*pasar pagi*). Since the 1930s the highlands have been a center for

Takengon Area

Lampahan

to Bireuen

Simpang Beliq   Baleatu

SIMPANGTIGA
REDELONG

Bukit
Payatumpi   Kebayakan
Bebesen
Tan Saril   Hotel Renggali
Remesan   Takengon   Danau   Kalasegi
Laut Tawar
Simpang
Uning   Toweren
S. Peusangan   Suku
SIMPANG   N
KELAPING
Kung   0   2.5   5   7.5 km

Isak   to Blangkejeran
S. Jambuaye

Right: *Traditional Gayo* kerawang *embroidery.*

fruit and vegetable growing, and for trade in tobacco and coffee. Gayo handicrafts are sold in the market, including large and small ceremonial mats and baskets plaited from dyed reeds. Nested basket sets are used by Gayo women to carry ingredients for betel chewing. Men and women also embroider intricate *kerawang* designs onto cloth.

Next stop is **Simpang Beliq**, 20 km north of Takengon on the main Bireuen road (at km 80), which has a hot spring that is open all year round. The town is also a market center for the coffee grown in this northern Gayo region, whose high altitudes are ideal for producing export-quality Arabica beans. Stop at one of the coffee gardens that line the road to see the trees, and sample the local brew at one of the many small roadside coffee shops.

On the way back to Takengon, stop in **Payatumpi** (km 97) to see one of the distilleries that produces aromatic oils from the patchouli and citronela plants. This is a growing industry here, and the distillery is open to interested visitors. Finally stop at the village of **Bebesen**, just north of Takengon, to visit a *kerawang* cloth embroidery shop.

South to Isak

From the western end of the lake, the Peusangan River flows through broad plains cultivated with rice on its way to the north coast. The main road leading south from Takengon to **Isak** first passes westward for about 10 km through this scenic Peusangan Valley, winding through rice-growing villages with coffee gardens perched on steep slopes to either side. The view from the village of **Tan Saril**, just outside Takengon, is especially beautiful.

These villages along the Isak road afford fascinating glimpses of everyday life in the highlands. Most villagers spend a good deal of the year in their rice fields—preparing the ground for planting (either with horse-drawn ploughs or by driving water buffalo over the earth to loosen it), transplanting seedlings, weeding, harvesting, threshing (usually with the feet) and milling.

The Gayo once lived in multifamily longhouses, but today nearly all families live in smaller dwellings. (A surviving longhouse in **Kung** village, visible from the Isak road, has walls attractively carved in Gayo motifs.) Each village consists of several distinct kin groups. Most members of each group trace their kin ties (through men or women) to each other, and work together to prepare feasts, mourn the dead and hold weddings.

The paved road continues up over the Bur Lintang pass, climbing to 1,800 m before descending into the lush, forested Isak River valley. After lunching at Isak, continue downstream for several kilometers and stop along the river for a dip in its fast-flowing waters. The trip out here and back to Takengon takes a full day.

— *John Bowen*

WESTERN ACEH

Crashing Surf and a Raging River

The coasts and highlands of western Aceh contain some of Indonesia's most spectacular scenery. Until recently the area was virtually inaccessible, but recent improvements in road conditions have made travel considerably easier, and it is now possible to go down the west coast from Banda Aceh to Tapaktuan thence to Medan or Lake Toba via the town of Sidikalang (or the opposite way, of course). By public bus the entire journey takes about 20 hours.

An incredibly scenic detour leads up the Alas Valley into the huge Gunung Leuser National Park around Kutacane. If arrangements are made beforehand in Medan, you can then raft down the Alas through exciting rapids amidst beautiful mountain scenery.

The west coast

Good beaches and dramatic vistas line Aceh's west coast. Powerful waves crash against the shore, and great caution should be exercised when swimming. Small hotels are found in Meulaboh and Tapaktuan, which make convenient stopover points. Depending on the weather and the time of year, magnificent sunsets blaze out across the Indian Ocean.

Leaving Banda Aceh heading south, the road passes the Andalas cement works by the beach at **Lhoknga**. It then climbs through broken country planted with clove trees, past tiny fishing villages and bays lined with brightly-colored *perahu*. Between Lhong and Seudeu it edges along a precipice, affording spectacular views of the Indian Ocean below and the offshore islands of Pulau Breueh and Pulau Peunasu. The road then descends past a waterfall at Mt. Geureutee to **Lamno**—a small and nondescript market town, some of whose inhabitants are said to have inherited blue eyes from the crew of a Portuguese ship the was wrecked nearby in the 16th century.

Further south, the road hugs the shoreline and one is continually reminded of the wildness of the ocean by the foaming surf and seaspray. Four major rivers here have only been bridged in the past several years. In season, large, juicy pomelos (*jeruk bali*) can be obtained.

Just north of **Calang**, the road turns inland around a sheltered, picturesque bay before heading south past a rocky headland, swamps and sandy beaches to Keudepasi, where it again briefly skirts inland over a new bridge across the Krueng Woila. The road then races past beachside coconut palms and casuarinas to **Meulaboh**, the harbor and administrative center for West Aceh. There is a ferry from here to Simeulue, a remote offshore island known for its clove production.

On the beach just north of town is a monument to Teuku Umar, hero of the Aceh wars who was ambushed and killed by the Dutch in 1899. Also near Meulaboh is a large Indonesian/Belgian oil palm estate and an airstrip. The mountainous hinterland of the region has long been known for its gold production.

South of Meulaboh, the road continues on through Peukankuala and Pantai Seunagan to Kutanibong, where it turns inland, skirting a vast swamp before returning to the coast at Blangpidië. Sixty km further south is **Tapaktuan**, another small port and the administrative center for South Aceh. From Tapaktuan the road again turns inland through mountainous, sparsely-populated country to the North Sumatra border, and the coffee-growing area of the Dairi Batak around Sidikalang.

Rafting the Alas River

The Alas is the longest river on Sumatra's west coast. It starts high up in the central Aceh highlands and flows southward through Gunung Leuser National Park, which boasts the most extensive wildlife of any park in Indonesia—including 520 species of birds, 194 reptiles and 62 kinds of amphibians.

Sobek, the American white water specialists, organize trips down the Alas with experienced guides. The river offers just enough of a challenge for most people—the rapids are classified as class III, halfway between leisurely and impassable. These 4 to 6 day jaunts offer a thrilling combination of white water, unspoiled rainforests and sightings of rare wildlife. Catered comforts includes coolers of beer and meals that border on the gastronomic. And there's always the tantalizing possibility of rounding a bend and startling a herd of elephants, or sneaking up on a red orangutan.

Right: *Rafting the Alas River rapids.*

Most people join the trips in Medan, leaving early in the morning for the 8-hour ride up through Berastagi and Kabanjahe and into the Alas Valley. All gear and passengers are carried in an old Mercedes bus. The first night is spent camping on the banks of the Alas above Kutacane. The guides cook dinner, inflate the boats, and teach everyone to pitch their tents. Tired by these exertions, the crew quickly falls asleep, lulled by the rushing water and a chorus of crickets.

The next morning, after a bright and early breakfast and a quick wash, everyone dons life jackets and piles into two bright yellow inflatable boats. The guides take their positions in the middle, grasping their long oars, and push off from the bank.

Soon you are spinning in the first of the rapids, caught in the embrace of the foaming Alas. The river rushes past majestic trees draped with vines, leaves mingling to form a solid wall of vegetation. Occasionally, you see monkeys swinging through the branches.

By late morning, however, you are drifting through the cultivated Kutacane plain, and the guides have to row hard to keep things moving. The scorching sun beats down mercilessly, and bemused villagers stare as you float past. Friendly waves, shouts of "Da-Da" (hello and goodbye) and the occasional "Hallo Mister" greet you as drift downstream.

At late afternoon, you pitch camp again. This is sometimes in populated areas and attracts the attention of villagers who stand or squat, staring silently; to them it's like watching TV. With the fall of darkness they disappear and the mosquitoes come out; everyone soon heads for the protective tents, quite exhausted by the day's events.

Early the next morning you begin the best part of the trip—three easy days of unspoiled gorges through an astonishing, ever-changing panorama. Vegetation-clad cliffs rise from the swift waters. River and jungle sounds mingle in a natural symphony of the rushing water, the flapping of hornbill wings, the six-note ascending scale of a cuckoo, and the cacophony of cries from siamang gibbons in the treetops.

At the end of the fourth day you camp at the confluence of a cascading tributary. Just upstream, a low branch overhangs the water. Swinging hand over hand along the branch you can hang over the rapids, legs dangling in the rushing water, then let go and be carried into calmer waters below.

On the sixth day, you traverse the river's lower reaches towed by an old river boat. The bus picks you up for the six-hour ride back to Medan, stopping in the afternoon for a coffee and a fresh cob of corn overlooking the northern end of Lake Toba. If you like, however, you can also leave the group here and head up to Banda Aceh, traveling the west coast route described above in reverse.

— *E. Edwards McKinnon and Kal Muller*

KAL MULLER

Aceh Practicalities

Includes Weh Island (Sabang) and Takengon (Gayo Highlands). All prices in US dollars. S=single; D=double; AC=airconditioning.

Aceh has a reputation as the most Islamic province in Indonesia. The government has declared this a "special region" (*daerah istimewa*) with virtual autonomy in matters of religion, customary law and education. Nevertheless, provided you are sensitive to Islamic traditions and culture, and dress neatly and conservatively (no shorts or sleeveless T-shirts), you will find the Acehnese hospitable and friendly.

Banda Aceh

Telephone code for Banda Aceh is 0651.

GETTING THERE

By air. From Jakarta via Medan, Merpati flies daily to Banda Aceh, with 4 extra weekly flights. From Jakarta, the fare is $185; from Medan $54. The taxi ride from the airport to town costs $5.50 and takes about 15 minutes.
By bus. The most popular way of getting to Banda Aceh from Medan, a distance of 600 km, is by bus. The journey takes 12-15 hours, fare is about $8. Most bus company offices in Banda Aceh are on Jl. Mohammed Jam. The best are Atra, tel: 23631 and Kurnia, tel: 21002. Others include Melati, tel: 23520; ARS, tel: 22949; Flamboyan, tel: 22949; ATS, tel: 23545; and Wiruri, tel: 23399. (The ALS office is on Jln Merduati, tel: 22949.) If you are traveling straight to Banda Aceh, it is worth taking a "direct" or "nonstop" bus.

GETTING AROUND

Most places are within walking distance, or you can take little minibuses called *labi-labi*, Rp200 for any distance. There are also motorcycles with sidecart (called *becak mesin*) big enough for two, Rp500 (bargaining required), or *becak* for highly negotiable prices. There are now metered taxis from the Cempala company, tel: 22963. There is good bus service on all paved roads around the town, just flag one down; they are crowded but cheap.

ACCOMMODATION

Banda Aceh has a wide range of hotels, from the comfortable to the bare and basic. You get good value for money in all categories.

Expensive ($20 and up)

Kuala Tripa (40 rooms) Jl. Mesjid Raya 24, tel: 21455, 21879. $22.50 up to $75 for a suite. The best in Banda Aceh; the restaurant serves Chinese and European food. Bar and disco (the only one in town), swimming pool and billiards. Next to a large park, near the central mosque, but some distance from shops and restaurants.
Paviliun Seulawah (22 rooms) Jl. Masjid Ibrahim II/3, tel: 22788, 22872. $18-$27, restaurant with set meals—breakfast $2, lunch and dinner $3 each. Not well located, but quiet (at one end of a huge playing field on which stands the remains of Indonesia's first airforce plane).
Rasa Sayang Ayu (40 rooms) Jl. Teuku Umar 439, tel: 21983, 21379. $18-$30, bar and restaurant, souvenir shop, travel service. On the edge of town near the bus station.
Seulawah (22 rooms) Jl. Nyak Adam Kamil 1, tel: 21749, 22610. Fairly close to most of the town's attractions.
Sultan (60 rooms) Jl. Panglima Polim, tel: 22581, 23663, and 23582. $18-35. On a quiet street. Restaurant has European, Chinese, Japanese and Indonesian dishes; bar and coffee shop. There is a shopping complex nearby. The hotel organizes one-day speedboat tours to Sabang on Weh Island for guests.

Moderate and Budget (under $20)

Aceh (29 rooms) Jl. Mohammed Jam 1, tel: 21354. An old Dutch guesthouse built in 1906, now decayed but fairly clean and without "modern" touches to spoil things. The cheaper rooms at $2.50 are spartan and not very nice, but the ones for $7 are airy with AC and verandah. Opposite the beautiful central mosque.
Lading (80 rooms) Jl. Cut Mutia 9, tel: 23160. $3.25-$7.50. All rooms have toilet/bath.
Lamprit (8 rooms) Jl. T. Nyak Arief 125, tel: 23995. Non AC $5.50, AC $8.50, breakfast included. All rooms with bath. Close to the tourism office but far from the downtown area.
Medan (60 rooms) Jl. A. Yani 15A, tel: 21501, 22636. $5-$20. Restaurant and coffee shop, money changer with rates almost the same as banks, peaceful patio at the back around a pond. The $5 rooms have squat toilets.
Palembang (13 rooms) Jl. Chairil Anwar 51, tel: 22040. $3 for outside facilities, $5 for private bath. If the communal TV is too loud at night, ask to have the volume turned down.
Prapat (43 rooms) Jl. A. Yani 17, tel: 22159. $5.50 for fan, $14 for AC and TV. Very clean, Chinese-owned. From the top floor there is a view of the river and the domes of the central mosque. Several restaurants nearby.
Raya (14 rooms) Jl. Mesjid Raya 30 (near the Kuala Tripa Hotel), tel: 21427. $3-$5.50.
Sari (27 rooms) Jl. Merduati 12, tel: 22919. $3-$6.50. The better rooms have private bath; located away from the town center.
Sri Budaya (20 rooms) Jl. Masjid Ibrahim III/5E, tel: 21751. A colonial house, fairly clean. $3.25 to $8.50 with bath and AC.
Yusri (16 rooms) Jl. Mohammed Jam, tel: 23160. $4-$11. All rooms with attached bath but none with AC. The best have spring mat-

Banda Aceh

JL. GABUS

JL. SISINGAMANGARAJA

JL. SECH. M. YAMIN   JL. POCUT BAREN

JL. PERDAMAIAN

JL. SUPRATMAN

Aroma

JL. SYIAH KUALA

JL. TAMAN SISWA

Sari Hotel

International Hotel

Prapat Hotel

Aceh Barat Hotel

Palembang Hotel

JL. CH. ANWAR

Medan Hotel

Sultan Hotel

Krueng Wayla

Lamprit Hotel

Police

Tourism Office

Immigration Office

Telecoms Office

Bank Indonesia

JL. MERDUATI

JL. CUT MEUTIA

JL. CUT NYAK DHIEN

JL. KARTINI

JL. PANGLIMA POLIM

JL. DARMA

JL. T. NYAK ARIEF

JL. SYEH ABDUL RAUF

JL. LAMPASEH

Lading Hotel

Bank BNI 46

JL. DIPONEGORO

JL. PERDAGANGAN

Tropicana

JL. A. YANI

JL. S.R. SAFIATUDDIN

JL. PANTE PIRAK

JL. KESEHATAN

JL. T ABDUL HAMID

JL. T ANGKASAH

Post Office

N

not to scale

JL. KHA DAHLAN

Yusri Hotel

Taxi Station

JL. MOHD. JAM

Market

✤ **Baiturrahman Mosque**

Krueng Aceh

JL. IMAM BONJOL

Sri Budaya Hotel

Aceh Hotel

Paviliun Seulawah Hotel

JL. A. MAJID IBRAHIM II

JL. A. MAJID IBRAHIM III

JL. MESJID RAYA

JL. BALAI KOTA

JL. SULTAN ALAUDDIN MAHMUDSYAH

JL. CIK DITIRO

→ to Medan

Aceh Information Center

RI 001 Seulawah
(Indonesia's first airplane)

Kuala Tripa Hotel

JL. A. MAJID IBRAHIM I

Raya Hotel

← to Uleelheu

JL. SULTAN ISKANDAR MUDA

Grave of Sultan Iskandar Thani

★ **Aceh State Museum**

★ **Grave of Sultan Iskandar Muda**

★ **Heroes' Cemetery**

JL. TAMAN MAKAM PAHLAWAN

★ **Pintu Khop**

★ **Pendopo Gubernur**
(Governor's House)

JL. TEUKU UMAR

★ **Gunongan**

JL. NYAK ADAM KAMIL II

JL. PEMBINA

Kerkhof ★

JL. NYAK ADAM KAMIL III

JL. NYAK ADAM KAMIL IV

JL. MANSURSYAH

★ **Art Center**

JL. NYAK ADAM KAMIL II

JL. NYAK ADAM KAMIL I

Seulawah Hotel

Bus Station

JL. SEULAWAH

← to Meulaboh

Rasa Sayang Ayu Hotel

tresses, a sitting room and two baths.

FOOD

There are many reasonably priced restaurants along Jl. Ahmad Yani. Most serve Padang food. The **Tropicana** serves good *rendang* (spicey beef) and *dendeng* (sun-dried strips of beef with fiery red chilis). Reasonable Chinese and European dishes can be found at the **Aroma** on Jl. Cut Nyak Dhien. The **Minang Surya** on Jl. Safiatuddin offers good Padang cooking. There are also several reasonable eating places on Jl. Panglima Polim. For breakfast, try the sweet rolls and coffee at **Satyva Modern Bakery** on Jl. Chairil Anwar. The bustling **night market** at the corner of Jl. Ahmad Yani and Jl. Chairil Anwar is a good place to sample cheap Indonesian and Chinese dishes, such as *bakso* (meatball soup), *mie goreng* (fried noodles), *martabak* (Indian omelette) and *pisang goreng* (fried bananas). **Rumah Makan Ujong Batee**, Jl. Krueng Raya, 17 km east of Banda Aceh towards the port, serves an incredible spread of seafood and Acehnese dishes, served Padang style—lots on the table, you pay for what you eat. Delicious food, especially the huge crabs. $4-$6 per person to eat your fill. The view of Weh Island compensates for the abandoned road works camp next door, full of empty asphalt drums and rusting vehicles.

TRAVEL SERVICES

The main **Garuda/Merpati** office is in Hotel Rasa Sayang Ayu, tel: 22846. No **PELNI** boats call at Banda Aceh, but their office on Jl. A. Yani 49 (tel: 23976) can make reservations and sell tickets for boats calling at other Sumatran ports.

The best and the longest established travel agency is **Krueng Wayla** on Jl. Sri Ratu Safiatuddin 26, tel: 22066, 22150. They have a 3-day, 2-night tour of Banda Aceh and vicinity. This includes the weaving at Siem village, the Acehnese fort at Indrapatra, and Lhoknga beach. Cost is $99 to $118 per person including hotel, depending on the size of the group, with a $30 surcharge for a single room. A longer tour adds Mt. Gerutee with its fine views and tropical jungle, and Seuhom waterfall, $135 to $182 per person. Their 3-day, 2-night tour of Weh Island runs from $117 to $183. They also offer an Aceh to Medan tour via Lake Tawar, 4 days and 3 nights, $218 to $387. Krueng Wayla has two branch offices in Medan, at Jl. Nibung Raya 74, tel: (061) 526226 and Jl. Panglima Nyak Makam 28, tel: 528937.

Tours can also be arranged by the Hotel Sultan and the Kuala Tripa Hotel, as well as by the Tourism Office, Jl. T. Nyak Arief 92, tel: 22697, 23692 and the Tourist Guides Association, Jl. Merduadi 125, tel: 23811.

SHOPPING

The **Pusat Promosi Kerajinan Aceh** is a government-run crafts shop at Jl. Sri Ratu Safiatuddin 54, open 8 am to 4.30 pm. Here you can buy ornate umbrellas, woven silk sarongs, baroque fans, embroidered dresses and fancy shoes.

Goldsmith shops cluster at the beginning of **Jl. Perdagangan**, near the mosque. You can have new jewelry made to your own design, or pick up old traditional pieces.

For antique weapons, clothing and porcelain, try **Daud's**, tel: 22794. Their antique kris daggers (some with gold sheaths), swords and cutlasses cost from $150 up to $2,000. Their special pieces for the serious collector can be viewed by appointment.

Markets in Banda Aceh sell an amazing variety of fresh fruits and vegetables from the Gayo highlands. The sprawling **Pasar Aceh** market is a good place to browse for small household craft items, such as wooden spoons, knives made from scrap metal, straw hats and local basket wares.

Weh Island (Sabang)

Weh (more often referred to by the name of its main city, Sabang) is a small island (154 sq km) off the coast of Aceh. The island has fine beaches, caves with birds and bats, marvelous snorkeling, hot springs at **Senekai**, and a 1,300 ha tropical game reserve.

Most of Sabang's attractions are concentrated at the northwest of the island, around **Iboih village**. The Iboih Nature Reserve has monkeys, reptiles, birds (including the rare Nicobar pigeon), wild pigs, flying foxes and a dirt road which ends on top of a cliff lookout over the Indian Ocean. In the clear waters of **Rubiah Island**, a small island near Iboih, sea gardens contain giant clams, lionfish, octopuses, barracuda, stingrays, colorful reef fish and a wide variety of corals. Scuba diving facilities are in the works.

GETTING THERE AND AROUND

By air. SMAC has a daily flight from Banda Aceh to Weh for $20. The aircraft is a small 8-seater and offers marvelous views of deserted beaches, coral reefs and clear seas.

By boat. To reach Weh by boat, charter a *bemo* to Uleelheue, 9 km west of Banda Aceh, or Krueng Raya, 33 km east of Banda Aceh for about $1. The ferry then takes 2.5 hours. Economy class is $2.50. All ferries dock at Balohan, 12 km south of Sabang. From here, it's an 11 km, $4 by taxi into Sabang town.

Bemos are fairly frequent during the early morning and late afternoon. There are also **taxis** for hire, along with **motorcycles** and **boats**, including a glass bottom boat.

ACCOMMODATION

In Sabang, the **Sabang Hotel** has a good view of the bay but is out of town. There are four *losmen*, all centrally located—**Pulau Jaya** (47 rooms) Jl. Teuku Umar 17, tel: 21344, $2-$7.50. **Holiday** (30 rooms) Jl. Perdagangan Belakang 1, tel: 21131, $4-$11. **Irma** (15 rooms) Jl. Seulawah 3, tel: 21235, $3-$5; and **Sabang-Merauke** (9 rooms) Jl. Seulawah 1, tel: 21139, $2-$3.50. At Iboih village there are several homestays with prices from $2-$4.

BEACHES

Pantai Kasih is the nearest beach, 2 km along the peninsula. The white sand **Gapang Beach** near Iboih is popular with locals on weekends. **Sumur Tiga Beach** is said to have fine sand and good swimming and snorkeling, while **Ujong Kareung Beach** offers lots of coral, reeffish and starfish.

Takengon (Gayo Highlands)

A busy, dirty town on Lake Tawar with many redeeming qualities—beautiful scenery, friendly Gayo people who are helpful with foreigners.

GETTING THERE

Early morning and evening buses from Banda Aceh (8 hrs, $3.50). There are also daily direct buses from Medan (12 hrs, $5). If you cannot get a direct bus, get off at Bireuen, on the main highway, and take a local bus up for $1.10, about 3 hrs. Things can get crowded but you can buy two seats if you need extra room. During the dry season, you can come the "long way" from Medan via Kabanjahe up the long Alas Valley to Blangkejeren, then over the Gayo mountain range to Takengon. Allow 2 to 3 days for the journey. During the rains, the Takengon-Blangkejeren road can be cut for weeks at a time, but only over an 8 km trekkable stretch.

GETTING AROUND

With some bargaining, a small **minibus** seating 8-10 can be hired for about $20 for the 48-odd-km tour around Lake Tawar. The motel **taxis** cost $2 an hour. A **speedboat** with a 40HP outboard rents for about $20 for a one-hour tour encircling the lake. A smaller boat with a 15HP outboard motor offers a more leisurely 3-hour round trip for the same price.

ACCOMMODATION
Moderate ($10 to $30)

Renggali (27 rooms) a couple of km south of Takengon. Best place around, with all rooms facing the lake. Tel: (0643) 21144, 21630, 21352. $19-28 S, $22-$30 D. Indonesian or continental breakfast $4, American breakfast $5, lunch $6, dinner $7. (All prices include 21% tax and service.) Coffeeshop, drugstore, tennis court, fishing, water cycling, water skiing, powerboat for 4-6 persons $30 per hour. Credit cards accepted. Bookings can be made through through Griyawisata Corp., Jl. Melawai VI/2A, Kebayoran, Jakarta 12001, tel: (021) 7397417, 711484, 712769.

Triarga (16 rooms) Jl. Pasar Inpres, tel: 21073. $5.50-$23; near the bus terminal. Overpriced. Taxi for rent at $2.75 an hour.

Budget (under $10)

Batang Ruang, Jl. Mahkama 5, tel: 21524. The owner, Pak Ade, speaks some English and he and his family are helpful and friendly. Clean double rooms with bath: $3.50. Warmly recommended. Special Gayo dance performances with 15 dancers can be arranged for $40-$50. Pak Ade can arrange minivans and boat hire.
Danau Tawar, Jl. Lebe Kader 35, tel: 21066, near the police station, lean and good value, $6.50-$10 for single or double.
Libra Indah (11 rooms) Jl. Yos Sudarso 267, tel: 21011, next to the racefield on the Isak road. $4 without private toilet, $7-$8 with, but only the VIP room at $9.75 has a sit-down john.
Mesrah Indah (8 rooms) Jl. Lembaga Pemasyarakatan 46, tel: 21644. $7.50 with attached toilet/bath. Without bath $4.50. Near the prison, just past the racetrack on the road to Isak. No eating facilities nearby.
Parawisata (10 rooms) Jl. Terminal 263, just at the edge of downtown, tel: 21322. $3.25-$7. The better rooms have squat toilets, TV, soap and towels.

FOOD

Of the hotels, only the Reggali has a restaurant but there are many Padang style restaurants in town. The centrally located **Sinar Minang** is recommended. The **Mitra**, which is 4 km out of town, serves Javanese dishes.

SHOPPING

Unfortunately, there's very little traditional Gayo embroidery produced these days. Most is now done by machine, with new motifs replacing the traditional ones. It is still possible to pick up old clothes, cushion covers, shoulder bags and Muslim hats embroidered with traditional motifs.

Try the market, the Hotel Renggali, the Motel Triarga, or the Losmen Batang Ruang. A well embroidered *sarung* can cost around $30-$50 and blouse $10-$15. Colorful mats called *kertan* are made here while *berdemjike* mats are made around Isak. Engraved pottery, called *keramik* can sometimes be bought at the above places. With a little bit of luck, you could see some made at the village of Kebayakan, not far from Takengon. For embroidery, try the nearby village of Babasan.

— Kal Muller

PART V

Introducing West Sumatra

After Lake Toba, the fertile valleys and scenic lakes of the West Sumatran highlands are undoubtedly the most memorable—and also the most often visited sights on the island. This is the traditional homeland of the dynamic Minangkabau people who have scattered and settled throughout Indonesia—and who are known far and wide for their canny business sense, their ubiquitous, spicy-hot cuisine and their old matriarchal ways.

West Sumatra is actually composed of three distinct regions—a volcanic highland, a long coastal plain which is swampy in places and cultivated in others, and a string of jungle-clad islands lying about 100 km offshore. The province is dominated by the Bukit Barisan—two parallel ranges of mountain peaks interspersed with broad valleys and several highland lakes. Most of these mountains are still covered in a blanket of pristine montane forest, broken in places by jagged peaks which thrust above the tree line.

The highest peak in West Sumatra is Mt. Kerinci, a dormant volcano standing 3,800 m high (the highest in Indonesia outside of Irian Jaya). A number of others rise above 2,000 m, notable smouldering Mt. Marapi (2,831 m) just to the southeast of Bukittinggi.

The largest and most spectacular lake is Maninjau—17 km long and 8 km across—which snuggles inside an ancient, steep-walled crater just to the west of Bukittinggi. Another crater lake, Singkarak, is similar in size and lies just to the southeast of here. Both are easy to reach, and have accommodations and facilities like waterskiing.

The central and northern highlands of the province contain several valleys which have been intensively cultivated for hundreds, perhaps thousands of years, forming an ancient cultural heartland for the region. Three of these, the *luak nan tigo* ("three valleys"), with a combined area of some 250 square km, are the homeland of the Minangkabau—or, more simply "Minang" people—who have spread from these beautiful mountain valleys throughout the whole of Sumatra to Java and even to the Malay peninsula. This is partly the result of a Minangkabau tradition known as *merantau* (going abroad to seek one's fortune). Minang or Padang restaurants, as they are know, are a familiar sight throughout much of the archipelago, and are even found today in many European and American cities.

The mountainous southeastern portion of the province is still wild—largely covered in jungle and inhabited by elephants, tigers, leopards, tapirs, bears and rhinos. Much of it is included in the huge Kerinci-Seblat National Park, which spills into three neighboring provinces and encompasses several stunning crater lakes—the most spectacular being the one atop Mt. Tujuh). Access to these wildlife areas is not as difficult as one might think, and a number of trekking and wildlife tours are now available in Padang and Bukittinggi.

One hundred km off the coast of West Sumatra lie the Mentawai Islands, which were uplifted when the Indian continental plate collided with the Sunda shelf some 80 million years ago. The island chain consists of four large inhabited islands—Siberut, Sipora, North and South Pagi, and numerous smaller ones. Most are still covered in tropical rainforest, and are fringed by unspoilt coral reefs teeming with marine life.

The large island of Siberut is noted for its exceptionally archaic culture. Until very recently the inhabitants practiced many Stone Age traditions, and even today one can find traditional *uma* or longhouses where tattooing and elaborate rituals designed to please the souls of the community are held.

—*John Miksic and Eric Oey*

Overleaf: *Shimmering West Sumatran rice fields.*
Opposite: *A Minangkabau bride. Minang women are known for their strong character and considerable commercial talents. Photos by Kal Muller.*

THE MINANGKABAU

A Unique Matrilineal Society

West Sumatra is home to about 4 million Minangkabau (often simply called Minang)—an energetic people known throughout Indonesia for their matrilineal kinship, their finely-honed commercial instincts, their fiery cuisine and their strong faith in Islam. They are also famous travelers and migrants, due to the traditional practice of *merantau* (young males going abroad to seek their fortune), and indeed more Minang probably now live outside of West Sumatra than remain. All of them nevertheless consider these beautiful highlands—the *darek*—to be their homeland.

The Minang are among the warmest and friendliest people in Indonesia, and take great pleasure in discussing their unique culture with foreigners. Visitors who make even the slightest attempt to become acquainted with Minangkabau customs and traditions are quickly treated almost as members of the clan rather than aliens from a distant land.

Adat and Islam

The Minangkabau have fascinated generations of anthropologists on account of their unusual combination of a matrilineal family system with a firm adherence to Islam. They are in fact one of the few peoples in the world to have maintained a system of matrilineal kinship into modern times—one in which descent and inheritance are traced through women rather than men. Every Minang thus belongs to his or her mother's descent group, and family houses (*rumah gadang*), as well as paddy fields, are the property of women.

Traditionally the wife remained with her maternal relatives after marriage, and men did not live with their wives but in a special men's house called the *surau*. They also spent a great deal of time in their mother's house, and were more responsible for their sister's children than for their own. This old system has broken down during the 20th century, but in many villages the houses are still arranged in clusters belonging to sisters or otherwise related groups of women.

The Minangkabau are organized into matrilineal clan groups—called *suku*—and in each village a number of *suku* are represented. According to tradition, there were originally only four clans, but they became divided in the course of time and there are now approximately 25, each with its own name.

KAL MULLER

The *suku* are in turn divided into lineages or *paruik* (lit: "womb"), which consist of all descendants of a single grandmother or great-grandmother. These *suku* and lineages were normally exogamous—which means that members were not permitted to marry someone in their own clan or lineage. This kinship structure is no longer very relevant to young Minang, especially those who have moved to Padang or or other parts of Indonesia, and is now in the process of dying out.

Land, houses and certain valuable goods are owned in common by a lineage, and these possessions may not be sold except under a few conditions. (Nowadays the selling of land is not so rare as it once was, however.) Male representatives of the lineage, such as the *penghulu* or "headman," are responsible for the management of communal property, but it is the women who have the right to use and bequeath it to their offspring. The oldest woman of each household has a plot that she passes on to her daughters after her death, or when she is too old to farm it. Thus the economic position of women is very strong. On the other hand, land no longer has the same value it used to, as population pressures and economic changes have encouraged people to seek alternative sources of income.

Despite the fact that they are devout Muslims, few Minangkabau question the compatibility of such matrilineal traditions with those of Islam. "*Adat* (custom) is based on *syarak* (Islamic law), and *syarak* is based on the Holy Book (the Koran)," they say. Minang intellectuals and religious leaders, however, have frequently criticized the traditional matrilineal pattern of inheritance as running counter to Islamic law, which states that sons are entitled to two-thirds of their parents' estate, and daughters only to one-third. The outcome of such debates is usually a compromise—that old ancestral property should be divided according to matrilineal custom, while earned property should be inherited according to Islamic law. But this has so far not been put into general practice and houses are still inherited by daughters rather than sons.

Patterns of leadership

One of the most famous Minang legends concerns the struggle between two heroes, Datuk Ketumanggungan and Datuk Pepatih Nan Sebatang, over the proper form of government. In the end, neither won. Some families followed Ketumanggungan, and supported an aristocratic system—they became known as *laras* Koto Piliang and the village of Sungai Tarab in Tanahdatar was their stronghold. Houses of families belonging to this *laras* can be identified by their stepped ends, denoting various levels of superiority. Follow-

Opposite: *A Minang wedding marks the entrance of the husband into the wife's clan.* **Below:** *Silver crafts produced in Koto Gadang, near Bukittinggi.*

ALAIN COMPOST

ers of Pepatih Nan Sebatang supported an egalitarian form of rule and formed the *laras* Bodi Caniago. Their stronghold was Lima Kaum and extended to cover much of Agam. Their houses have flat floors. Perhaps this legend has a historical basis; it may relate to a cleavage created by the introduction of new concepts by the half-Javanese prince Aditya-varman in the 14th century.

In any case, the system of village government of the two was essentially the same. Although women controlled property, men conducted village affairs (at least in public). There was a council composed of the headmen (*penghulu*) of all lineages in the village (i.e. those with a common female ancestor), and the eldest brothers of the eldest women from each house (*mamak*). Every *suku* in the village also had its own head. Thus the system was rather complicated, with diffused authority and a need for frequent discussion, in conformity with the pan-Indonesian preference for consultation and consensus. The council house or *balai* was an important structure in the village, and many old *balai* are fine examples of traditional Minang architecture.

Life in the longhouse

In former times, each household consisted of three to four generations descended from a single great-grandmother living under one roof. Households had a corporate character; members worked the rice fields together and shared in their yield. The house was the center of social life for the women; the bedrooms were occupied by young married women of the family and their children. On the day of her wedding, a daughter was given the best bedroom at the back of the house, while the older sister or cousin who previously occupied it would have to move to another room. Women past child-bearing age did not have a bedroom of their own; they usually slept near the fireplace. Little children slept with their mothers, and young girls could sleep in the

large open space at the front, which also served as the living area and guest room.

In all respects the house was more of a women's than a men's place. The men spent much of their time outdoors. Young boys spent the night in the *surau*—the Islamic prayer house where they received a religious education. Old men often slept there as well. A married man in the prime of life moved between his mother's and his wife's houses—going at night to his wife's house, then arising to return to his mother's house before

dawn. They were therefore referred to as "visiting husbands."

This association of women with the house and of men with public life was combined with restrictions between the sexes. Men and women—particularly unmarried girls—who did not belong to the same household or kin group were not to meet and interact freely. A father could not caress his own daughter, and parents-in-laws were not allowed to sit on the same mat or bench with their children-in-law, or eat from the same banana leaf, lest their fingers touch one another's.

Within the *rumah gadang* there was a complex division of authority. The oldest woman was considered the head of the household with regard to internal affairs. When she became too old, the woman next in seniority was appointed in her stead. She was assisted and advised by a senior male member of the family—the *mamak*, usually translated as "mother's brother"—who was responsible for the well-being and upbringing of his sisters' children, over whom he exercised final authority. External matters were thus firmly in the hands of men.

A man's family role was thus primarily directed towards his mother, his sisters and his sisters' children, and his role as a husband and father was marginal. A man had little authority over his wife and children, and had few obligations towards them. As a result, the conjugal tie was weak, and polygamy and divorce were frequent.

The practice of merantau

The Minangkabau are best known within Indonesia for their exceptional mobility, coupled with a very strong entrepreneurial spirit. Everywhere in Indonesia (now in many foreign cities as well), for example, one can find restaurants serving spicy Minang food—usually referred to as "Padang food."

The mobility of Minang men probably had its roots in the fact that before marriage they slept outside the family longhouse and had few familial obligations. Economic factors also played a role. Because of the matrilineal inheritance system, men had few material interests in the village, as land and inherited wealth were in the hands of women. Trade with harbors on both coasts of the island has been carried on since ancient times—lowland areas referred to by the term *rantau* (which now refers to any place outside the highlands)—and Minang men are particularly known for their trading abilities.

Even prior to the 19th century, it was customary for a young man to leave the village for one or more years to gain experience and seek material wealth in the outside world. When he returned he was prepared to marry, and his worldly ways and possessions made him a much more desirable husband than those who had stayed behind. In former times, migration was thus largely restricted

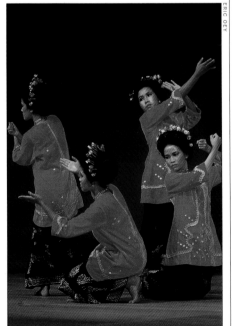

to men, and was temporary.

During the last century, as the population increased and arable land became scarce, this custom became a more general and permanent feature of Minang society. Men in their productive years, whether married or not, moved away to find better jobs. Many took their wives and children with them, and did not return to their village except for short visits. Today some single women are even known to migrate on their own.

This out-migration has had a considerable impact on Minang village life. One thing which invariably strikes the visitor is the large proportion of adult women as compared to men in many rural areas. These days women can join their husbands in the *rantau* if they want to, but then "who will look after the house and the fields?" as many of them say. As a result, many Minang women run households by themselves while the husbands and sons live elsewhere, some of them returning home at regular intervals, others very seldom.

In general, when the men go away to make money, the women tend to see this as profitable arrangement—but it is crucial of course that they keep in touch and send some money back! If there is no news from the husband for a long time, the wife may ask for a divorce. Yet even while very far away from home, most Minang retain a great fondness for their village. As a Minang proverb says: "It may rain gold in the *rantau* and stones in our village, but my love goes to the village."

Successful migrants often contribute to the physical development of their home village, and in villages where the level of migration is high, one sees roads, prayer houses, mosques and elaborate ceremonies that have been financed by wealthy fellow villagers who now live far away.

The performing arts

The Minang have developed a number of unique art forms, including their own *pencak silat*—the combination of dance and martial arts common throughout Indonesia. Traditional dramas called Nalam Sijobang, Randai Simarantang and Bakaba once existed, but are now seldom performed. Graceful women's dances with descriptive names like *tari piring* ("plate dance"), *saputangan* ("kerchief dance"), *kerbau jalang* ("wild buffalo dance") and *tari gelombang* ("wave dance") are similar to those found in other areas of Sumatra.

Opposite: *Traditional crafts in Koto Gadang, near Bukittinggi.* **Left:** *A* tari piring *dance performance.*

The Minang are also very fond of versifying in a traditional form known as the *pantun*. Like other Sumatrans, they were skilled in spontaneously composing these rhymed quatrains, especially during courtship—when the ability to create extemporaneous *pantun* was crucial to winning over one's sweetheart.

Into the modern world

The Minangkabau family has undergone significant changes during the past century as a result of demographic, economic and ideological factors. A rapidly growing population has led to a land shortage, and a growing market and money economy now plays an important role in daily life. An increasing number of people, especially men, work outside the agrarian sector. This has meant an ever-increasing exodus of Minangkabau men and their families to towns and cities throughout Indonesia. The strengthening of Islamic values, and the modern ideal of the nuclear family, have also had a considerable impact.

According to Islam and the modern family model, it is the husband, not the uncle or the mother, who is the head of the family. As a result, the *rumah gadang* has lost its function as the center for an extended family, and the modern household has become much smaller. Even in rural areas, many families now consist of just a father, a mother and their children. In such families the father is the head of the household, with authority over (and economic responsibility for) his wife and and his own children. Minang men are no longer "visiting husbands."

Nowadays men tend to become permanent residents in their wife's house, unless they leave their village as migrants. Divorce rates and polygamous unions have decreased sharply. Women have also gained much more access to the public world as a result of new educational and employment opportunities. The worlds of men and women are no longer as separate as they once were.

These changes do not imply that matrilineal kinship is no longer important. Most Minangkabau are proud of their cultural heritage, and traces of the old family structure are still clearly visible. Inheritance still has pronounced matrilineal features, and the matrilineal descent group still plays an important role in people's lives. Closely-related women such as sisters, mothers, daughters and cousins still reside close together. The role of the *mamak* may have been partly replaced by the husband/father, but men still feel responsible for their sisters and their sisters' children. And although men often now reside in their wife's house in rural areas, their place in that house is still rather marginal. The new, one-family dwellings one sees throughout the highlands today do not mean that the matrilineal family system has completely disappeared.

—Joke van Reenen and John Miksic

ALAIN COMPOST

RUMAH GADANG

Distinctive Minangkabau 'Big Houses'

Much of the uniqueness of the Minangkabau is exemplified in their architecture. To understand their houses is also to understand the way the family is run. The Minang themselves explicitly make this connection.

Traditional Minang houses are called *rumah gadang*, literally "big house." They are elongated rectangular structures with gables which rise to peaks at either end. The house normally has only one doorway, in the middle of the longer side, but some older examples have the doorway at the end.

The peaked roofs are often said by the Minangkabau to represent buffalo horns. This is related to a Minang myth and folk etymology regarding a contest between a Javanese buffalo and a Minang calf, which the calf won (see following section, "History").

The Minangkabau house was traditionally constructed with a technique called a stressed ridge beam. The long roof peak was made from a straight piece of wood, upon which the rafters were laid. After a time the middle inevitably began to sag and the ends were pushed upward, thus producing the distinctive saddle shape. The Toraja of Sulawesi have similarly shaped roofs, which they explain as representative of their ancestors' boats. The origin of the technique probably dates back to prehistoric times, for similar houses are depicted on bronze drums found in Vietnam and southwest China. They once existed in Java as well.

The houses are divided into a number of apartments, each occupied by women related to the matriarch of the household. Thus the basic family unit consisted of a grandmother and her children and grandchildren. According to tradition, the number of apartments should always be uneven. One of the largest such houses still in existence, at Sulit Air, is 64 meters long and is divided into 22 dwelling areas (thus an exception to the rule). The largest concentration of traditional houses is in the Payakumbuh area, where almost 2,000 still stand, comprising about 25 percent of all houses in the area.

Although the general shape of the *rumah gadang* is standard, specific types are associated with the three main Minang valleys, and with the division between the Bodi Caniago and Koto Piliang alliances. The Koto Piliang houses (associated with an aristocratic form of government) have a raised floor area called an *anjuang* at either end, whereas the (egalitarian) Bodi Caniago floors are flat.

Traditional houses are decorated by carvings which are often painted. The system of carving is not left to chance, but organized according to a fixed scheme. Certain patterns may be used on window sills, others on the *anjuang*, in the attic, on the rafters, etc. The patterns derive from plant and animal motifs and carry symbolic meanings. For example the pattern called *tangguak lamah* symbolizes humility and courtesy; *jalo taserak* recalls the difference between good and evil; and *jarek takambang* reminds the viewer of the importance of social mores. Thus Minang woodcarvings, like the traditional costumes, are a way of constantly reminding people of the proper way to behave in society, and the house is an advertisement for morality as well as a symbol of Minang social structure.

—*John Miksic*

Left: *Minang girl in traditional costume.* **Right:** *An old* rumah gadang, *now the Bukittinggi museum.*

GOTTFRIED ROELCKE

HISTORY

Fertile Land of Rice, Gold and Pepper

The fertile Minang highlands were settled by Austronesian-speaking peoples several thousand years ago, and this was the first area in Sumatra to develop a culture based on irrigated rice cultivation. Early European visitors like Raffles were astounded by the density of population which they found here.

Very little is known of the history of West Sumatra before AD 1400, though mines in the highlands were probably exporting gold from quite early times—lending the island of Sumatra as a whole the ancient name of Svarnadvipa ("Island of Gold"). The west coast is studded with treacherous reefs, however, and trade goods were formerly carried down the course of the Indragiri River to ports along the eastern coast of the island.

A small bronze Buddha head has been found at Indrapura, in the southern part of the province, and now lies in the Padang museum, but few other antiquities have been discovered. We must presume, therefore, that during the first millennium AD these highlands remained on the fringe of the great east coast civilizations, Srivijaya and Malayu, which derived their wealth from maritime trade.

Seaborne settlers

Minang legends dating from Islamic times trace the ancestry of West Sumatra's inhabitants back to Sri Maharajo Dirajo ("The Glorious King of Kings"), a descendant of Alexander the Great whose ship sailed to Sumatra and lodged atop Mt. Marapi—the volcano southeast of Bukittinggi whose summit was then the only land protruding above the sea. As the waters receded, he and his followers settled at Pariangan ("Abode of the Ancestors"), a village in the Tanahdatar Valley on the volcano's southern slopes. From here they spread to the nearby valleys of Agam and Limapuluh Kota ("Fifty Fortresses").

Another popular story tells of a threatened attack by a huge army from Java. Greatly outnumbered, the Minang proposed a contest between two buffaloes in lieu of a bloody armed conflict. The Javanese agreed, and produced an enormous beast from Java. To their great surprise, the Minang brought forth a tiny calf. What the Javanese did not realize was that the calf had not been fed for days, and had a knife tied to its snout. The calf nuzzled the belly of the startled war buffalo, goring and killing it. The Javanese withdrew, and the Minangkabau have ever since claimed that their name derives from *minang* ("victorious") and *kabau* ("buffalo").

There may be a kernel of historical truth in the story. The Javanese did launch several attacks against Sumatra in the late 13th and 14th centuries, and ancient earthen ramparts with names like Kota Jawa ("Javanese Fort") testify to a Javanese presence. But it seems likely that the story of the buffalo calf is apocryphal, and the name Minangkabau probably derives instead from *pinang kabhu*—an archaic expression meaning "original home."

Conversion to Islam

West Sumatra first appears in the historical record in the 14th century, when a Javanese-Sumatran ruler named Adityavarman issued stone inscriptions in and around Tanahdatar. His rule seems to have had little impact upon the agrarian society of the highlands, however, and after his death (his last dated inscription is 1374) we hear little of his successors.

The momentous conversion to Islam which began around this time seems to have come about as a result of increasing trade with India and influence from Aceh. In the 16th century, large quantities of gold were exported from West Sumatra. Portuguese sources mention that Muslim traders from Gujerat in northwest India called at Pariaman on the west coast to exchange their valuable cloth for gold. In the late 16th century, the sultanate of Aceh claimed sovereignty over Pariaman, and for the next 60 years kept foreign traders out of the Minang areas—channeling West Sumatran products through her port at Banda Aceh.

During the 16th and 17th centuries, West Sumatra became one of the world's premier pepper-growing areas, attracting traders from India, China and Portugal (later also Holland and England). The Dutch ultimately gained control of Padang, in 1663, and established a fortified trading post on the banks of the Batang Arau River, where the West Sumatra

Right: *The mausoleum of Imam Bonjol, the Paderi leader captured by the Dutch in 1837.*

governor's office now stands.

A Portuguese envoy to the Minang court brought back the first description of the highlands in 1683. A triumvirate of rulers apparently controlled each of the three Minang valleys at this time, and their prestige (if not their power) extended to neighboring Batak and Rejang areas, where legends speak of founding rulers sent from the chief Minang court at Pagarruyung in Tanahdatar.

In the late 18th century, the coast came under British rule twice—first during the Anglo-Dutch war of 1781-84. Though Padang was later returned to the Dutch, the British continued to buy pepper and gold at Pariaman. This had the effect of making Bukittinggi and the surrounding Agam area more prosperous than the court center at Tanahdatar. Agam also suffered in one respect—one of the main British imports was opium.

Padang again came under British control between 1795-1819, during the Napoleonic Wars, when Holland's eastern possessions were entrusted to Britain for safekeeping. It was during this period that Thomas Stamford Raffles, lieutenant-governor of Java and later founder of Singapore, visited the Minang area and brought back this glowing report: "As far as the eye could distinctly trace was one continued scene of cultivation, interspersed with innumerable towns and villages, shaded by the coconut and other fruit trees. I may safely say that this view equalled any-thing I ever saw in Java. The scenery is more majestic and grand, the population equally dense, and the cultivation equally rich."

The Paderi wars

Centralized Minang authority lasted up until the late 18th century. Power rested on royal control of the mines, but by the 1780s the gold was depleted. New sources of income developed—coffee, salt, gambir and textiles —but these were under the control of Muslim traders, whose commercial activity gave rise to an emerging Islamic reform movement.

The reformers were led by the Paderis, puritanical teachers who denounced the lax observance of Islamic law and the matriarchal Minang *adat* which favored female inheritance. Death was the usual penalty for opposing them; most secular leaders, including the royal family, were slaughtered for refusing to accept Paderi dictates.

In 1803, violence broke out in the village of Pandai Sikat in Agam (today a peaceful center for traditional weaving and woodcarving) when a Paderi reformer, frustrated in his attempts to abolish cockfighting, gambling, opium smoking and the drinking of palm toddy, torched the new village council house. Paderi ideas soon took root in poorer villages on the sides of the valleys, where food was scarce, and by 1821 the hills around Agam were mostly under Paderi control. The Limapuluh Kota area also converted, seemingly

KAL MULLER

without much violence, but there was fierce fighting in Tanahdatar, with no side gaining the upper hand. By the time Raffles visited in 1818, the court at Pagarruyung had been razed three times. The Paderis' religious zeal even extended to the territory of the Tapanuli or southern Batak, who accepted Islam at the point of a sword.

Following the conclusion of the Napoleonic wars, the Dutch returned to Padang to find trade in the highlands badly disrupted by the upheavals. Fearful that the Paderis might challenge their own position, the Dutch made a treaty in 1821 with a nephew of the Raja Alam of Pagarruyung, who had fled the fighting and was living in Padang. He promptly granted them the Tanahdatar valley, and they proceeded to build a fort there and at what is now Bukittinggi (formerly Fort de Kock).

Assisted by local residents, the Dutch used this fort to expand their control over much of Tanahdatar and south Agam, including Pandai Sikat. However, the Paderis put up stiff resistence, halting their advance in 1823. As the war dragged on, the Dutch cut off all trade and applied increasing military pressure. In 1831, new fighting broke out and this time the Dutch were more successful. The war ended in 1837 when the town of Bonjol, home of the most powerful Paderi leader, Imam Bonjol, was finally stormed. By 1832, Paderi power was broken and the Minang highlands were firmly under Dutch control.

The struggle for independence

Throughout the 19th century, debates regarding the proper form of Islam and the permissible degree of accommodation with traditional Minang culture continued. West Sumatrans also played a prominent role in the modernist Muslim movement of the early 20th century, especially in the call for educational reforms, including schools for women. By the 1920s, many educated young Minang become frustrated by a lack of suitable jobs, and in 1926 an armed insurrection broke out, incited by communists. Many who joined it were captured and sent to the dreaded Dutch prison camp at Boven Digul in New Guinea.

After WW II, Padang was the scene of clashes between British forces and young Indonesian revolutionaries. And during the revolution, Bukittinggi was even for a short time the capital of Indonesia. On July 27, 1947 the Dutch launched a "Police Action" on Java and arrested several nationalist leaders. Shortly before his arrest, Soekarno, the first president of the republic, cabled his minister of finance in Bukittinggi and appointed him head of an emergency government. International pressures eventually forced the Dutch to free the republican leaders, and on January 1st, 1950, West Sumatra became a province in the newly independent Republic of Indonesia.

—*John Miksic*

ANTIQUARIAAT ACANTHUS, UTRECHT

MINANG TEXTILES

Sumptuous Threads of Tradition

Traditional Minangkabau textiles, ornately brocaded with gold and silver threads, play an important role in birth, circumcision, marriage and funeral ceremonies. These shimmering and intricately patterned fabrics, dubbed "gold cloths" by early Western travelers, are material expressions of Minang *adat*—the customary laws which guide one through life from cradle to grave. In the words of a local proverb, "textiles are the skins of *adat*."

Women weave these sumptuous textiles on a base of silk or cotton, onto which a raised pattern of gold or silver threads is added—a process known as *songket*. The most prized threads were thinly coated with gold or silver leaf. More common threads were of fine copper or bronze wire plated in precious metal. Until the beginning of this century, *songket* textiles were woven at four places in the Minang region—Koto Gadang, Padang Panjang, Paya-kumbuh and Silungkang. Since 1900, however, the ceremonial cloths have been woven only in a few villages and weaving of the famed *kain balapak* has largely been confined to Pandai Sikat, a tiny village 12 km south of Bukittinggi. Today, silk weaving is a thriving cottage indus-try, and traditional textiles are in great demand both with tourists and with the Jakarta elite.

In the past, the finest silk, gold and silver threads were imported from China, and dyes were obtained from flowers or by grinding rocks. More than a hundred traditional motifs were known, employing plant and animal fig-ures as well as geometric patterns. Unfortun-ately, after the conversion of the Minangkabau to Islam in the 15th century, the original mean-ings of most textile motifs were lost.

The most distinctive part of a Minang wom-an's ceremonial costume is the two-pronged headdress, called a *tanduk* or *tilakuang*. Dis-playing one's wealth in a spectacular fashion, the *tanduk* indicates the wearer's village by the manner in which it is folded. The headdress is also said to reflect social values; a large, flat tri-angle of cloth crowning the two-horned red, black and gold headdresses of the village of Tanjung Sungayung, for example, reminds the wearer to treat people from all social classes without preference or prejudice.

—*Kunang Helmi Picard*

Opposite: *Payakumbuh ca. 1910.* **Below:** *Weaving in the village of Pandai Sikat, south of Bukittinggi.*

DANA IRFAN

PADANG

A Colonial Port and Its Waterfront

Padang is the provincial capital of West Sumatra and the principal gateway to the Minang highlands. The city, which has a population approaching 500,000, has grown at the rate of more than 10 percent a year over the past ten years, and Padang's port, which is 6 km south of the city, is the largest on Sumatra's west coast. Ships call here to load rubber, cinnamon, coffee, tea, nutmeg, plywood, rattan, cement and coal mined at Ombilin in the highlands.

The main attraction in downtown Padang is the **Provincial Museum** (Museum Negeri Adhityawarman) at Jl. Pangeran Diponegoro 10, next to the Hotel Minang. The museum stands in a park and is built in the traditional Minang style known as Gajah Maharam. Collections include prehistoric artifacts, stamps, imported ceramics, manuscripts, modern art, and ethnographic displays of the Minang and

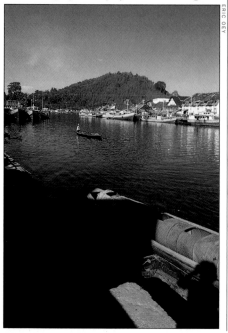

the peoples of the Mentawai Islands, which lies to the west off Padang's coast.

One gallery is devoted to artifacts connected with Minang ceremonies such as weddings, funerals and the investiture of village leaders; another displays implements used in agriculture, crafts, Islamic worship and other daily activities. The **Taman Budaya** cultural center, which is right next door to the museum, holds periodic art and cultural exhibitions.

Historic Padang

It is pleasant just to wander through the older parts of Padang, especially the area around **Kampung Cina** (Chinatown), south of the central business and hotel district, where turn-of-the-century houses line the streets. Start from Jl. Hiligoo and continue south along Jl. Pondok and Jl. Niaga. On these streets, you can find Chinese herbalists and coffee shops with distinctive inlaid tiles, hardwood floors and teak furnishings that serve cool drinks during the heat of the day.

At the southern end of Jl. Niaga, turn right (west) along the river through the **Muara district** (meaning "estuary"), past the old colonial waterfront where small cargo vessels still dock. Stroll by century-old warehouses loaded with fragrant cinnamon and other spices awaiting shipment to Jakarta and Singapore. This wharf saw its glory days in the 1920s, when coffee production reached a peak in the Minang Highlands.

Hand-paddled ferries cross the sluggish Batang Arau River from here, which is full of small boats and a sight in itself. On the other side you can follow a footpath to the Chinese cemetery up on the hillside, where you have a splendid late-afternoon view of the waterfront and the city. The hill, called **Bukit Monyet** ("Monkey Hill") used to be a favorite subject of 19th-century Dutch artists.

To the west of here, standing guard at the mouth of the Batang Arau and overlooking the sea, is a perfectly-formed hill known as **Gunung Padang**. A path leads up to Siti Nurbaya Park at the top (named after the heroine of an early Indonesian novel), where you can find the remains of an old bunker and the Dutch trigonometrical point for all early surveys of West Sumatra. Near the base of the hill is a WW II cannon which still points across the harbor entrance.

Left: *The mouth of the Batang Arau with Gunung Padang in the background.* **Right:** *The facade of a modern bank reflects the roof of the Provincial Museum, built in traditional Minangkabau style.*

Beaches and coral islands

From Padang Hill a path leads south about 4 km and an hour's walk along the coast to the area's most popular beach, **Air Manis** ("Sweet Waters"). The beach can also be reached by direct minibus from the downtown terminal, but avoid it on Sundays, when it is usually crowded. At low tide, wade across to a little islet just offshore. On the beach, Bapak Chili offers basic accommodation and food. A better restaurant has recently opened at the southern end of the beach, and also offers rooms at moderate prices.

The beach borders a fishing village, and is associated with a popular legend about a young man, Malin Kundang, who rose from humble origins to become a rich merchant overseas. When his mother heard that he had come back with his ship, she prepared his favorite food, and wearing her best clothes went to his ship to meet him. However, Malin Kudang felt ashamed of his mother, who was old and toothless by this time, and whose best attire consisted of nothing but a few rags. He pretended not to know her, and ordered his crew to cast her away. His mother's heart broke and she cursed him. As the ship went off, thunder flashed and lightning roared, and the ship sank. Everyone aboard perished, and were turned to stone—a coral outcropping at the beach is said to be their remains.

GOTTFRIED ROELCKE

Bungus is another small village 25 km south of Padang—some 45 minutes by *bemo*. It is situated on a lovely bay with calm water and a good beach, a section of which has been made into a resort. It suffers somewhat from its proximity to a plywood factory, and lack of shade. A small admission is charged.

From Bungus you can hire a small outrigger to visit the coral islands which lie an hour offshore. All the islands have some shade, but at high tide there is often just a narrow fringe of sand left between the water and the rocks. **Sirindah Island**, farthest out to the west, has little shade but is the only one without a rocky core so that you can walk across it. All the islands are ringed by wonderful white sand beaches, sometimes interrupted by rocky outcrops or huge boulders, and all are encircled by colorful coral reefs. The reefs teem with small fish, ranging from 2 to 30 cm in length and displaying an incredible variety of colors ranging from bright blue and green to combinations of yellow, tan, turquoise, pink and brown. The reefs are gradually being destroyed by coral hunters, but the islands are still a minor paradise. Bring snorkeling gear, food and drinks.

Another good beach is **Pasir Jambak**, which lies north of Padang past the airport. To get there, take a direct *bemo*, or watch for the signboard saying "Pasir Jambak" about 2 km past the airport, where you take a left. You will have to walk the last km from the entry gate to the beach, and a small entrance fee is charged.

Cruising

Many of the boats at anchor in Padang harbor are cargo vessels which ply the waters between here and the Mentawai Islands to the west. Because of a lack of regular transport, few travelers ever reach the Mentawais, although cargo boats leave the harbor almost daily for a four- to ten-day swing through the islands, delivering 20th-century goods such as IndoMie (instant noodles) and canned sardines, in exchange for local products and tribal handicrafts.

For those willing to disregard the conventional wisdom about the boatmen, who are widely reputed to be lawless scoundrels, this is a real Indonesian adventure—sleep under the star-filled firmament while afloat on the Indian Ocean, and call on unexplored islands inhabited by fascinating, primitive peoples. Take along some food and leave behind your inhibitions (see "Siberut").

—*J. Miksic, G. Roelcke and J. Goodfriend*

Padang Practicalities

Most prices in US dollars. AC = air-conditioning. Telephone code is 0751.

For most travelers, Padang serves as a stepping stone on the way to the Minang Highlands. But Padang itself is a surprisingly clean and pleasant town with good hotels, decent restaurants and competent travel agencies. Many government buildings are constructed in neo-traditional Minang style with saddle-back roofs sweeping outward to form symmetrical peaks, sometimes as many as 12 in number.

GETTING THERE

Padang is half-way up Sumatra's west coast and is served by a good network of land, air and sea routes.

BY AIR. Flight frequencies and fares are as follows: **From Singapore** Garuda flies in every Tues, Thurs and Sat ($120). **From Kuala Lumpur** Sempati flies on Mon and Sat ($125); **From Batam** Garuda flies on Thurs and Sun ($55); Sempati on Sat and Mon ($50). **From Jakarta** Merpati flies 3 times daily ($95); and Mandala is also daily ($80). **From Medan** daily Merpati flights ($60). **From Palembang** Merpati flies daily ($40). **From Pekanbaru** Merpati departs on Wed, Fri and Sun ($25).

Padang's Tabing international airport is 15 minutes north of the city on the road to Bukittinggi. The 6-km taxi ride costs $3-$5, depending on your destination. Arrange your cab at the airport service counter to avoid unnecessary hassles with "free-lance" drivers. A cheaper way of getting to Padang is to walk 200 m out to the main road and hop a *bemo* into town for 15 cents, or a bus to Bukittinggi for $1.

BY BOAT. Pelni's KM Kerinci leaves Jakarta's Tanjung Priok harbor every other Friday morning for the 36-hour trip to Padang, arriving Saturday evening in Padang's Teluk Bayur harbor, about 7 km south of town. Fares range from $50 for first class to $22 for fourth class. The "no-class" tickets are even cheaper ($16) but that kind of travel is only advisable if you are very short of money.

BY BUS. For information on bus travel, see "Leaving Padang" below, and the Travel Advisory at the back of the book.

GETTING AROUND

Most things in Padang are within walking distance. If you don't feel like walking, there are metered taxis—but a more romantic, though slower method is to take a *bendi*, a horse-pulled cart which can be hired for $1 for 3-4 km. Bemos and buses ply fixed routes for Rp100 and up, depending on distance.

ACCOMMODATION

First class ($30 and up)

The best and most expensive hotel in Padang is the new **Pangeran Beach** at Jl. Juanda 79, on the northern edge of town on the way to the airport, with rooms from $55. Swimming pool, beautiful beachfront, pleasant bar, and good restaurant, especially for Western food. Tel: 31333, 21753, 22085. Visa, Mastercard.

Hotel Pangeran, Jl. Dobi 3, tel: 31233, is the best in the downtown area, with rooms from $20-$45. The most popular medium class hotel, it has a good bar which serves draft Bintang and is frequented by Padang's expatriate community. Visa and Mastercard.

In the same range are **Hotel Natour Muara** at Jl. Gereja 34 (tel: 25600, 25078), $28 single to $42 double; and **Hotel Mariani** at Jl. Bundo Kanduang 35 (tel: 25466), $16 for a simple single up to $38 for a good double. Both are just around the corner from the Pangeran Hotel.

Intermediate ($15 to $30)

Wisma Mayang Sari, Jl. Sudirman 19, is on the road into town from the airport. Rooms from $15 to $28 for a double with AC, Western breakfast included. This is a good place for transit passengers who want a clean, convenient and reasonable place to stay. Tel: 22647, 23555. Visa and Mastercard.

Equally pleasant is the **Femina Hotel**, in town at Jl. Bagindo Aziz Chan 15, close to several banks, the Garuda office, the Post Office and the central market (tel: 21950, 22670). Rooms from $7 (single with fan) up to $27 (AC double). This and the Pangeran are the best in their respective classes.

In a similar price range but less well-kept are **Wisma Anggerek** at Jl. Sudirman (tel: 21477), the **Bougainville** (tel: 32423) and the **Padang** (tel: 22563), all on Jl. Bagindo Aziz Chan.

Dymen's Hotel International, Jl. Prof. Dr. Hamka 141 (tel: 22611, 26822), has reasonable rooms, all at $24. It is located on the northern end of town directly opposite the airport but far away from everything else. Visa and Mastercard.

Budget (under $15)

Hotel Machudum, Jl. Hiligoo 43, near the central market, is an old place built during colonial times. Its faded glory is compensated for by its courteous staff and quiet rooms. Rates start at $8 for a fan and bathroom; a few dollars more buys you AC and carpeting. Tel: 22333, 27732.

Most budget travelers stay in one of the simple hotels on Jl. Pemuda, directly across from the terminal. They provide basic-to-medi-

Padang

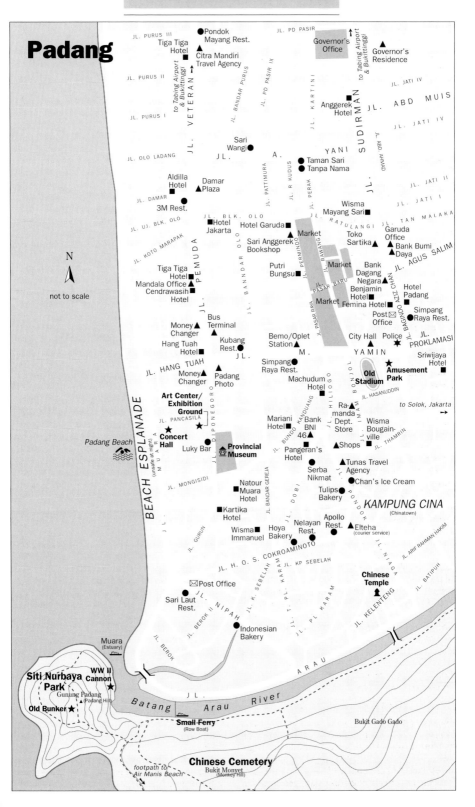

JL. PURUS III

JL. PD PASIR

●Pondok
Mayang Rest.

Governor's
Office

▲Governor's
Residence

Tiga Tiga
Hotel■

▲Citra Mandiri
Travel Agency

JL. BANDAR PURUS

JL. PD PASIR IX

to Tabing Airport
& Bukittinggi

to Tabing Airport
& Bukittinggi

JL. PURUS II

JL. VETERAN

JL. KARTINI

JL. SUDIRMAN

JL. JATI IV

JL. ABD MUIS

■Anggerek
Hotel

JL. PURUS I

JL. OLO LADANG

Sari
Wangi●

JL.   A.

JL. PATTIMURA

JL. R KUDUS

JL. PERAK

Y A N I

JL. ABD AHMAD

JL. JATI IV

●Taman Sari
●Tanpa Nama

JL. JATI II

JL. JATI I

Aldilla
Hotel■

▲Damar
Plaza

JL. DAMAR
3M Rest.●

N
↑
not to scale

JL. UJ. BLK. OLO

JL. KOTO MARAPAK

JL. BLK. OLO

■Hotel
Jakarta

■Hotel Garuda

■Sari Anggerek
Bookshop

JL. BANDAR OLO

JL. PEMUDA

JL. PERMINDO

JL. RATULANGI

JL. RAWANG

JL. PASAR BARU

▲Market

Market

Market

JL. TAN MALAKA

Wisma
Mayang Sari■

Toko
Sartika■

Bank
Dagang
Negara■

Benjamin
Hotel●

Femina Hotel■

Garuda
Office■

▲Bank Bumi
Daya

JL. AGUS SALIM

Hotel
Padang■

Tiga Tiga
Hotel■

Mandala Office▲
Cendrawasih
Hotel

Putri
Bungsu●

▲Simpang
Raya Rest.

JL. PROKLAMASI

Money▲
Changer

Bus
Terminal■

Hang Tuah
Hotel■

Kubang
Rest.●

JL.

Post ⊠
Office

City Hall▲

Police★

Sriwijaya
Hotel★

JL. HANG TUAH

Money▲
Changer

▲Padang
Photo

JL. DIPONEGORO

Simpang●
Raya Rest.

M.   Y A M I N

Amusement
Park★

■

Art Center/
Exhibition
Ground

JL. PANCASILA

Machudum●
Hotel

JL. BANDAR GEREJA

JL. BONJOL

JL. HILIGOO

Old
Stadium

★

JL. HASANUDDIN

to Solok, Jakarta →

Padang Beach
(unsafe at night)
≈

BEACH ESPLANADE

JL. MUARA

★Concert
Hall

Luky Bar●

🏛Provincial
Museum

JL. MONGISIDI

JL. GURUN

Mariani
Hotel■

JL. BUNDO KANDUANG

■Bank
BNI
46▲

Pangeran's
Hotel●

Ra-
manda
Dept.
Store

▲Shops

Wisma
Bougain-
ville●

JL. THAMRIN

Serba■
Nikmat

Tulips●
Bakery

▲Tunas Travel
Agency

●Chan's Ice Cream

KAMPUNG CINA
(Chinatown)

Natour■
Muara
Hotel

■Kartika
Hotel

Wisma■
Immanuel

Hoya■
Bakery

Nelayan●
Rest.

Apollo●
Rest.

▲Elteha
(courier service)

JL. PONDOK

JL. NIAGA

JL. ARIF RAHMAN HAKIM

JL. H.O.S. COKROAMINOTO

JL. K. SEBELAH

JL. T. PL. KARAM

JL. KP SEBELAH

JL. DOBI

JL. PL KARAM

Chinese
Temple
⛩

JL. KELENTENG

JL. BATIPUH

⊠Post Office

Sari Laut
Rest.

JL. BEROK II NIPAH

JL.

●Indonesian
Bakery

JL. BEROK

Muara
(Estuary)

Siti Nurbaya
Park

WW II
Cannon★

Gunung Padang
▲(Padang Hill)

Old Bunker★

ARAU

Batang   Arau   River

JL.

Bukit Gado Gado

Small Ferry
(Row Boat)

footpath to
Air Manis Beach

Chinese Cemetery
Bukit Monyet
(Monkey Hill)

um rooms with fan or AC. Best bets in this price bracket include the **Tiga-Tiga** (tel: 22633, $7-$14) and **Hang Tuah** (tel: 26556, $5-10).

Hotel Cendrawasih is next to these two, and a little further north is **Hotel Aldilla** at Jl. Damar I (off Jl. Pemuda); both in the same price range but a little less clean. Further out, at Jl. Veteran 33, there is the popular new **Tiga-Tiga**, rates $8-12, tel: 22173.

The **Wisma Immanuel** offers good rooms from $10 and a quiet location at Jl. Tanah Beroyo 1 (off Jl. Bandar Gereja), tel: 23917. (This hotel could be a little difficult to find.) Other hotels are conveniently located near the central market.

Hotel Garuda, Jl. Permindo 4, tel: 31696, 27232, has rooms from $4 (fan) to $15 (AC). **Putri Bungsu** at Jl. Permindo 40 (tel: 22230, 23922) offers rooms from $7-$22. Closer to the bus terminal is the **Jakarta** at Jl. Belakang Olo 57 (tel: 23331) with rooms from $5 to $9.

FOOD

Padang is naturally THE place to sample the famous, spicy *nasi padang* food that has now found its way throughout Indonesia and the world. Chicken and fish, prepared in coconut curry, fried or with *sambal* chili paste, are served with raw cabbage, *rendang* (spiced beef with shredded coconut), *dendeng* (black, sun-dried strips of beef served with fiery red chillies) and curried eggs. The waiter will bring as many as 20 plates of food to your table, but you only pay for what you eat. It is entertaining to watch the waiter assessing the damage and toting up the bill. Be warned that most restaurants close before 10 pm.

The best place for Padang's spicy specialties is probably **Simpang Raya**, with a main branch on Jl. Bagindo Aziz Chan, opposite the Post Office, and a smaller one on Jl. Bundo Kanduang. Many other restaurants too numerous to mention also serve *nasi padang*. Some worth trying are **Tanpa Nama** ("No-name") on Jl. Rohana Kudus (ask for the yellow chicken curry!) and **Bahagia** at Jl. Ujung Gurun 91. The hottest food (*pedas*, not *panas*!) is served at **Putri Balqis** on Jl. Khatib Sulaiman.

For Javanese style food (not so spicy, but rather sweet), try **Taman Sari** on Jl. A. Yani (the *kueh teow goreng* fried rice noodles are recommended) or **Purnama** opposite City Hall. Highly recommended also is **Pondok Mayang** at Jl. Veteran 52, a little way out of the city center, which has a casual, open-air setting. It serves good Javanese food and delicious grilled fish, where you may view swimming in tanks in its "pre-grilled" state in front of the restaurant.

Indonesian style fast food—meat balls and noodles in soup—is served at **Mieso Raya** on Jl. Imam Bonjol. A string of small Chinese coffee shops lining Jl. Niaga in Kampung Cina (Chinatown) also serve *kueh teow* noodles with pork or *bakso* (beefball soup) in the evenings.

The **Apollo** at Jl. Hos Cokroaminoto 36 serves the best Chinese food in Padang. A popular restaurant with an extensive menu. The food is "expensive" here by local standards (but still cheap by Western standards). Expect to pay $5-$10 a person. Even the classic *mie goreng* (fried noodles) are quite delicious.

For seafood, try **Nelayan** at Jl. HOS Cokroaminoto 34 or **Sari Laut** at Jl. Nipah 3 (it is cheaper to eat downstairs at Sari Laut). The new Restaurant Sari at Jl. Thamrin 79 (just across the bridge on the way to Teluk Bayur and Bengkulu) boasts Sundanese grilled fish and prawns in addition to the usual steamed and fried crabs, fish and prawns. Prices at all of the above places are quite reasonable.

Western food is best at the two **Pangeran** hotels. If you want something cheaper, try the **3M Restaurant** at Jl. Damar 69, opposite the Damar Plaza shopping complex a little north of the bus terminal. Modeled on Bukittinggi's famous Coffee Shop, it offers reasonably-priced sandwiches and omelettes for breakfast, and French onion soup, wiener schnitzel or spaghetti for lunch and dinner, complemented by a range of fruit juices.

Good bakeries are the **Indonesian Bakery** (Jl. Nipah), **Tulips** (Jl. Pondok) and **Hoya** (Jl. HOS Cokroaminoto).

A charming cafeteria with a lovely vista of Padang city is found on the top floor of the Damar Plaza shopping center, not far from the bus terminal and the Hang Tuah and Tiga-Tiga hotels. It serves *gado-gado* and noodle soup, ice cream and drinks.

For a romantic drink in the late afternoon, go to the **beach esplanade** on Jl. Samudra, where food stalls provide a pleasant view of the surf rolling in. At night, however, the esplanade tends to be somewhat unsafe.

NIGHTLIFE

There is little respectable nightlife in Padang. You could try **Luky Bar** by the museum, or go for an ice cream and the thickest *kretek* smoke you can imagine at **Chan's** in Jl. Pondok. This is the only place in Padang with good live music. The notorious **Seamen's Bar** in Teluk Bayur is no place for a respectable woman!

SHOPPING

Batak, Minangkabau, Acehnese and Lampung handicrafts are sold in Padang, though better examples and lower prices can be found in Bukittinggi. A few shops on Jl. Imam Bonjol sell *kain songket* (woven cloth brocaded with gold or silver thread), silverwork, ironwood carvings, Chinese ceramics and Dutch antiques.

Toko Silungkang on Jl. Imam Bonjol 6 is named after the village in the Padang highlands where *songket* cloths are woven.

Songket Silungkang on the same street sells inexpensive silver and rattan souvenirs and postcards. They also have a new branch on

Jl. Juanda, convenient for those staying at the new Pangeran Beach Hotel.

Batik Semar on Jl. Hiligoo near the Hotel Machudum has souvenir-type handicrafts.

Toko Sartika on Jl. Sudirman, opposite the Garuda office, sells textiles from the Padang Highlands and Lampung, and can arrange to ship goods to your home country.

Toko Saudara (Jl. Pondok), **Wijaya Baru**, and **Ramanda Deptartment Store** (the last two on Jl. Imam Bonjol) cater for Western tastes in food, and sell cheese and ham. Toko Saudara also stocks some of the less common Western cigarette brands.

Padang's best bookshop is **Sari Anggerek** on Jl. Permindo, north of the central market.

SERVICES

The **Tourism Office** on Jl. Khatib Sulaiman is inconveniently located halfway between Padang and the airport at Tabing. Go early or phone beforehand (tel: 22118). Maps and brochures are available. **Dinas Pariwisata Sumatra Barat** is the provincial tourist office, at Jl. Sudirman 3, but it is easier to wait until Bukittinggi as the information is the same and the office is more conveniently located.

Bank Negara Indonesia 1946, Jl. Dobi 1, gives good rates and the service is quick. **Bank Bumi Daya**, **Bank Rakyat Indonesia** and **Bank Dagang Negara** on Jl. Bagindo Aziz Chan are just as good. There are two money changers near the bus terminal and one at the airport.

The **General Post Office** is at Jl. Aziz Chan 7, open Mon-Thurs 8-12 and 13:30-16:00, Fri and Sat 8-11:30. Another post office is on Jl. Khatib Sulaiman opposite the ANS bus company office, yet another is on the corner of Jl. Nipah and Jl. H. Cokroaminoto.

International calls can be made at the **Perumtel telephone and telegraph office** on Jl. Veteran 47, open 24 hours, 7 days a week.

LEAVING PADANG

BY AIR. Air travel arrangements can be made at the offices of **Garuda/Merpati** (Jl. Sudirman 2, tel: 23431, or 23471 for the airport office) and **Mandala** (Jl. Pemuda 29, tel: 22350). **Sempati** is handled by Kota Piring travel agency at Jl. Veteran 65, tel: 24155 (just north of the telecoms office). Good travel agents are: **Tunas** at Jl. Pondok 86 (tel: 21313, 28806), **Natrabu** at Jl. Pemuda 29 (tel: 25366), and **Citra Mandiri** at Jl. Veteran 36 C (tel: 21851).

Buses and bemos to the airport leave from the central bus station on Jl. Pemuda, across from the Tiga-Tiga Hotel; fare Rp250. Taxis to the airport cost $3-$4; they can be found outside the major hotels or flagged down anywhere in town. There is no duty free shop at Tabing airport.

Flight frequencies are as follows: Sempati flies **to Kuala Lumpur** on Tues and Sat ($125). Garuda flies **to Singapore** on Wed, Fri and Sun

($120). Merpati flies **to Palembang** daily ($40); **to Pekanbaru** on Tues, Thurs and Sat ($25); **to Medan** daily ($60); **to Batam** on Thurs and Sun ($55); **to Jakarta** thrice daily ($95). Mandala also flies daily **to Jakarta** ($81), as does Sempati every day except Tues. Sempati also flies **to Batam** on Sat and Mon ($50) and **to Medan** daily. For the latest schedules, check the Padang daily newspapers or with a travel agent.

BY BUS. Buses depart from Padang's bus terminal for most major Sumatran towns once or twice a day, more frequently to Bukittinggi, Solok, Batusangkar and Payakumbuh, and the schedules are published every day in the Padang newspapers. The 2-3 day trip to Jakarta costs $13-$22, depending on class; the 16-hour journey to Medan costs $7-$12. Bukittinggi can be reached in 3 hours for less than a dollar. Other destinations include Tanjung Karang (28 hours, $16), Pekanbaru (6 hours, $5), Bengkulu (14 hours, $7).

Bus tickets for shorter trips can be bought at the bus terminal. For short-haul trips, take the NPM buses because they are newer and less prone to breakdowns. The long-haul services, notably ANS (which offer on-board facilities like toilets), also have offices in town. The ANS office is on Jl. Khatib Sulaiman (tel: 26689), with a branch near the terminal (tel: 26214).

BY SEA. The KM Kerinci sails to Jakarta every other Sunday evening: arrange your tickets well in advance at the Pelni office at Teluk Bayur. KM Kerinci does not only go to Jakarta but then on to Surabaya, Ujung Pandang and Kalimantan. On the preceding Saturdays, you can leave in the evening for an overnight trip to Sibolga, from where you can catch a boat to Nias. For tickets you have no other choice but to go (or send someone) to Teluk Bayur harbor, 7 km south of town. Tel: 22109. Book early as demand for space is always high!

TREKKING AND CRUISING

The **Department of Forestry** on Jl. Raden Saleh 8 will arrange a *surat jalan* (visitor's permit) for Siberut, the Mentawai Islands and the Kerinci-Seblat National Park. They sometimes also help arrange trekking itineraries and may be able to tell you where the *Rafflesia* is flowering (but better check with a travel agency).

For trips to Siberut from Padang's Muara harbor, see "Siberut Practicalities."

—Gottfried Roelcke and Jay Goodfriend

BUKITTINGGI

Delightful Hill Town With Scenic Vistas

The town of Bukittinggi (lit: "High Hill") lies at the center of the Agam valley—one of three valleys which together form the Minang heartland. While Padang is the modern commercial, educational and administrative center of the province, Bukittinggi is the cultural capital of the Minang realm.

The largest city in the highlands, Bukittinggi grew up around a Dutch post, Fort de Kock, built in 1825 during the Paderi conflict. This attractive, bustling town was the birthplace of many Indonesian intellectuals, cabinet ministers and diplomats—including Mohammed Hatta, the nation's first vice-president.

Although less than a degree south of the equator, Bukittinggi has a cool climate due to its elevation—900 meters above sea level. It rains frequently, but many tourists nevertheless find this to be the most hospitable city in Sumatra—everything is within walking distance, food and lodgings are good, there is lots to see and the residents are very friendly.

A walking tour

Bukittinggi's principal landmark is the **Jam Gadang** ("Great Clock")—a clock tower with a miniature Minang house on top overlooking the main square. Visible from many parts of town, it is a good starting point for an exploration on foot. On Saturdays and Sundays, the lively **Pasar Atas** central market next door spills out into the streets. All kinds of fruits, vegetables, spices and meats (except pork) are sold in open-air stands run by assertive Minang ladies. There are sections for everything—brightly colored plastic wares seem to be the main attraction. Bargaining is a popular social activity here rather than a test of wills or an attempt to cheat the unwary traveler. Keep your sense of humor, and bargain hard if you are buying!

From here, walk up Bukittinggi's "mainstreet," **Jalan Ahmad Yani**, which is lined with antique and souvenir shops, restaurants and offices. Two unique stair-streets lead down from here to the right, to Jl. Cinduamato, and are lined with more souvenir shops.

To get a good view of the town and the surrounding area, climb up Jl. Cinduamato to **Taman Bundo Kanduang** park at the top of the hill, where a zoo and a museum are located. The name of the park refers to the legendary "Great Mother" symbolic of the matrilineal Minang. The zoo is crowded on Sundays, when it is the principal place in town to see and be seen, but the animals are kept in rather miserable conditions.

The museum in the park is housed in a traditional Minang *rumah gadang* complete with thatched roof and flanking granaries. Inside are examples of wedding costumes and *tanduk* headdresses in the shape of buffalo horns. A small fortune in fine gold jewelry is on display; for several centuries this area was the archipelago's leading producer of the precious metal. The museum also displays old matchlock rifles used against the Dutch, as well as musical instruments.

Breathtaking panoramas

Bukittinggi was formerly called **Fort de Kock**, after the Dutch fortification erected at the edge of a steep-sided ridge here in 1825. Stone ruins and a few cannon are all that is left of the fort, known locally as the *benteng*, but there is a lookout tower that is an excellent spot to watch sunsets and take in a view of Mt. Marapi ("Fire Mountain"), which occasionally vents puffs of smoke. The view alone is worth the walk—to get here, take a path up from Jl. T. Umar, near the corner of Jl. A. Yani.

Another breathtaking panorama is available on the southwestern edge of Bukittinggi, which skirts the lovely **Ngarai Sianok Canyon**. Part of a tectonic rift valley running the entire length of the island, this canyon has sheer walls and a flat bottom, and offers a haunting early-morning spectacle—as dawn caresses the peak of Mt. Singgalang in the background, blankets of mist drift around the canyon's 100-meter cliffs. A river meanders through rice fields below, disappearing in the hazy distance beyond.

A lookout point known as **Panorama Park** overlooks the canyon and is a popular spot with locals who come to stroll in the afternoon air. A path leads down into the canyon, past Japanese-built tunnels under the park. One can explore these tunnels, but a flashlight and guide are essential.

Hike to Kota Gadang

Kota Gadang is a village of silversmiths a few km from Bukittinggi across the Sianok Canyon. Walk one km down into the canyon, turn left and cross a small bridge over the river, and follow the trail up a long flight of steps. From here the village is ten minutes' walk: ask for directions along the way. The speciality here is delicate silver filigree. You can buy pins in the form of ornate flowers, tiny earrings in the shape of Minang houses, and a plethora of exquisite miniature objects. Larger items include model sailing ships, traditional Minang houses and the clock tower.

— *John Miksic*

Opposite: *Bukittinggi's landmark, the Jam Gadang.*
Below: *Ngarai Sianok Canyon and Mt. Singgalang.*

COEN PEPPLINKHUIZEN

THE MINANG HIGHLANDS

Exploring the Ancestral Homeland

The ancient homeland of the Minangkabau —the *luak nan tigo* or "three valleys" of western central Sumatra—is an incredibly beautiful highland region of lush rice fields, towering volcanoes and spectacular crater lakes. These three valleys roughly define the corners of a triangle centering about sacred Mt. Marapi (2,891 meters), the highest and most active volcano in the area and the spot where, according to local legend, the first Minang ancestors are thought to have settled.

To the south and east of the volcano is the valley known as **Tanahdatar** ("Level Land"), with its focus around the small town of Batusangkar. This is where the royal Minang court was located from the 14th to the 19th centuries. Ancient tombs, inscriptions, palace sites, megalithic stones and other remains dot the area. Tanahdatar was renowned for its gold and iron mines in former times.

The **Agam** valley lies to the north and west of Marapi, centering around the town of Bukittinggi. As we have seen, this area developed rapidly during the last two centuries as a result of contacts with Europeans on the west coast at Pariaman and Padang.

The third and most fertile of the valleys is known as **Limapuluh Kota**; it lies to the east around the large town of Payakumbuh. Megalithic remains abound here, and it is thought that this may in fact have been the earliest of the valleys to have been settled. Access to the east coast is provided by the courses of the mighty Kampar and Indragiri rivers.

Framing these valleys is a tightly-packed cluster of volcanic peaks and two enormous crater lakes, Maninjau and Singkarak. As in the Toba area, these volcanoes have contributed to the fertility of the soils, and as a result the Minang highlands have been relatively densely populated for many centuries.

Although the culture and language in all three valleys is the same, each is unique from the standpoint both of history and of scenic beauty. What follows, therefore, is a series of itineraries using Bukittinggi as a starting point, and working outwards in various directions—first west, then south and then east. While these areas can be visited in a series of day-trips; more time can of course profitably be spent making longer journeys along the scenic backroads that loop around the two lovely crater lakes and over dramatic passes separating the volcanoes, overnighting in small towns and villages where the facilities may be primitive, but where one experiences a true taste of the justly renowned Minangkabau hospitality.

West to Lake Maninjau

West Sumatra's most famous sight is undoubtedly Lake Maninjau (meaning: "To Look Out Across")—a lake set inside of an ancient crater that is 17 km long and 8 km wide, surrounded on all sides by steep, 600-m jungle-clad walls. Maninjau's spectacular scenery rivals that of Toba, though on a smaller scale.

The lake shimmers on windless days and its transparent waters teem with fish, which swim to the surface at the drop of a crumb. This is the ideal place to relax and enjoy the tranquility of nature. The swimming is good, there are pleasant walks through picturesque villages and dense forests, with adequate facilities that include several hotels, restaurants, boats and even water skiing.

The 2-hour journey to the lake is a wonderful experience in itself. Take the main road south from Bukittinggi for 5 km then turn right (west) at a clearly-marked crossing. This road skirts the foot of Bukit Kapanasan, passes the small town of Matur, then crosses a lush valley before climbing up the crater's rim to **Embun Pagi** ("Morning Dew"). The view from here is breathtaking (elev: 1,097 m) and it is worth asking the bus driver to stop so you can take photos. There is even a small cottage hotel where you may spend the night. In the early morning, clouds drift below as small children swarm about selling brightly-colored straw handicrafts. From Embun Pagi, the road winds down through 44 hairpin turns to Maninjau village (470 m) at the edge of the lake.

Puncak Lawang is another, higher lookout point north of Embun Pagi. From here you can hike down the crater wall to the lake at Bayur, a village 4 km north of Maninjau. To get there, take the turn-off to the north (right) at Matur to the village of Lawang, a distance of about 5 km; a signboard points the way down to the lake (to the left), just near the toll gate. But before descending, walk another 30 min (or persuade the *bemo* driver to take you) up to Puncak Lawang—the highest point on the crater rim, with TV relay station and a panoramic view down to the lake and back to Mt. Singgalang.

The steeply descending track down from Lawang passes through forests, coffee plantations and village gardens before meeting the lakeshore road. Allow 2 to 3 hours for the descent. It is an easy walk from here back to Maninjau village.

Small boats leave from Maninjau, ferrying

Opposite: *The Minang Highlands contain some of Sumatra's most fertile and productive rice lands.*
Below: *Spectacularly scenic Lake Maninjau.*

KAL MULLER

Bukit Karang
386m
Padangkubu

to Lubuksikaping,
Padangsidempuan

Simaung

Paninja

Bukit
Kayupayung
1129m

Lakung

Binjai

Malayu

Bukit
115

Muarotantang

Bukittalang

G. Sirabungan
▲ 1726m

Bukit Kambing
1461m

B. Air Sinamar

Airkijang

Sungaimangkirai

Kurai

Balimbing

Balai

to
Airbangis
Timadang

Sipisang
Tangah

Sungaiguntung

Mudikliki

Kotatinggi

Anggemudik

Dalam

Bukit
Batunandua
1340m ▲

Bukit Batukapur
1198m

Simpangtigo

Kotoalam

Belai

Pasir

Gumarang

Tantaman

Sikumbang

Tarok

Palembaian

**Rafflesia
★ Sanctuary**

Batukambing

Simpangkarun

AGAM

G. Gadang
1595m

Puncak Lawang
★ (panoramic view)

Lawang

B. Stanok

Kotobaru

Kotokecil

Rangas

Matur

Gadut

G. Silayang
1724m

Bayur

AGAM

Fort de Kock

Hot Spring ★

Embun
Pagi

Bukittinggi

Mukomuko

Maninjau

Lubuksao

Bukit Panarahan
1526m

Bukit Kapanasan
398 m

Lubukbasung

*Danau
Maninjau*

Nagari

Pahambatan

Kotogadang

to
Tiku

Padanglaring

Sigitan

Kubu

Bukit Pauh
1430m

Padangluar

Sungairangas

*Cape
Sitapung*

Pondok

Kototuo

Sarik

Kampungpinang

Murmalintang

AGAM

Kotobaru

Kapalagasan

Bukit Tanjung Balit
1292m

Bukit Pandan
1534m

G. Singgalang
2877m

Pandaisikat

Sungaigenangging

**Weaving
Village** ★

**Traditional Hou
Royal T**

Balai
(cou

Padangpanjang

Surau
(men's house)

Alahanpanjang

Padangolo

Gunun

to
Tiku

Bukit Tinjaulaut
1441m

Pada

Sungailimau

Sosok

Ganting

Kayutanam
Pasarlimau

Logan

Kudu

Bukit Barangin
428m

Bukit Parhantianlum
1225m

Bayur

Ambungkapu

Sicincin

Naras

Sinambang

Sungaisarik

Koto-
mambang

Sungaisarik

Manggung

Sikapak

Barangan

Sikilir

Cibadakair

Tobahtinggal

G. Gadang
1625m

Pariaman

Sampan

Belahair

Padangkandang

Paritmalintang

Sikabu

Padangbunga

Sungai-
Jaban

Pondok

Pauhduku

Pauhambar

Teluk

Pinang

Sinur

Tanjung-
medan

Sigimba

Sintuk

Parupuh

Lubukalung

to Padang

Ulakan

to Padang

SELAT MENTAWAI

Minang Highlands

to Mahat

Sipinggal

ang

Kotaacik

G. Bongsu
1254m

Telaga

Council House,
Menhirs

Guguk

Pagang

Parumpang

Parambahan

LIMAPULUH
KOTA

Payakumbuh

Kotatengah

Piladang

Padangbusuh

Tigatanjung

Tabatpatah

View

Salimpaung
Raorao

Situmbuk

LIMAPULUH
KOTA

Sawahgombang

Sungayang

TANAH
DATAR

riangan

Tabek

Simabur

Dusun
Tuo

Limo
Kaum

Batusangkar

Rumah Gadang
(traditional houses)

Sumpur

tutabal

Balimbing

Umbilin

Bukitkandung

Danau
Singkarak

Ampang

Telagalawas

G. Tungku
820m

anair

Parakgadang

Kudang
Karang

Airhilang

Muarapinggai

nggahan

Parapahan

Apa

Berok

Saningbakar

Sumani

Singkarak
to Solok

to Bangkinang, Pekanbaru

Bukit Sikat
865m

Harau Canyon

Lamaksari

Tanjung Pati

Nankadok

Taram

Padangalai

Limbukan

Padangambacang

Tanjungkalin

Pakanarbaa

G. Malintang
2262m

G. Sago

Ladanglawas

Kawai

Padang Seminyak

Padang Magek

Pagarruyung

Pierced Stone

Limo

Palace

Malayu

Fort
van der Capellen

Saruaso

Jajaknabi

Telagagunung

Sawahgalung

Bukit Rotan
513m

Lurahdalam

Bukit Sibumbunjantan
990 m

Rumah Gadang
(traditional house)

Rawang

Sulitair

Tanjung-
alai

Batu-
galas

G. Papan
957m

Kabangtiga

Kapalabandar

LIMAPULUH
KOTA

Sungaipuh

Labuhgunung

Lingkungan

Mangunaitinggi

Tanjung Gadang

Alangawas

Batangarang

Tapiseto

Bukit Padanglawas
940m

TANAH
DATAR

Panglan

Patamas

Guguksari

Kotoalam

Kotoalam

Kumbayau

Dataralai
Sungaiancing

Talawi

Kototuo

Kolok

Mandahiling

Telagogunung

Sigapung

N

0   3   6   9 km

S. Sibayang

Bukit Kubanganlado
1022m

Bukit Gabus
1187m

Bukit Sapan
779m

G. Mandiangin
1274m

Tanjungangsat

S. Pakis

S. Pigago

S. Tampo

S. Bulus

Tigojangko

G. Gedang
747m

Sibiluru

Piliang

Sawahpauh

Bundung

Bukit Ngalautiris
536m

Bukit Kudobarkatuk
633m

Padanglawas

Tanjung Ampalu

Palaluar

Batugadang

Datar

Koto-
tujuh

to
Muarabungo

Pamuatan

Bukit Kayugadang
309m

Sawahlunto

S. Umbilin

to Sijunjung

to Solok

villagers around the shores of the lake. This is the best way to sightsee, stopping at various villages along the way. A small road also skirts the northern lakeshore via the villages of Bayur and Kotokecil to **Mukomuko**, on the opposite (western) shore. A river cuts west through the crater wall here and drains the lake; there is a hydroelectric project and a hotspring nearby.

A rough track also leads from Maninjau to Mukomuko around the lake's southern perimeter. From here, the main road continues west down to the Indian Ocean at **Tiku**, whence it is possible to travel down the coast to Pariaman and Padang. For a round-trip, with a full day at the lake, allow 3-4 days.

South to Pandai Sikat

The renowned weaving village of Pandai Sikat (or "Sikek"—the name literally means "weavers") lies just 12 km (about 20 minutes) south of Bukittinggi, at the southern tip of the Agam valley in the saddle between Mts. Singgalang and Marapi. Weaving has been a major occupation in the Agam area since at least the 1780s. Cotton was planted in the western lowlands to supply the industry, but proved insufficient and more thread had to be imported from Surat in India. Today weaving still forms one of the principal sources of livelihood in Pandai Sikat, along with woodcarving, blacksmithing and coppersmithing.

To get there from Bukittinggi, turn off the main road to the right (west) at Kotobaru and follow a small sideroad for 1 km. Young men sit by the side of the street carving decorative murals and furniture, while girls weave the traditional gold-and-silk *songket* on large shuttle looms to supplement the family income. If you have found *songket* cloths expensive in Bukittinggi, take some time out to watch the girls at work—a full day's labor lengthens the fabric by a mere 10 cm or so!

An added bonus for visitors to Pandai Sikat is the exquisitely carved and painted vil-

lage meeting house where marriages are held, the Koran is read and community business is discussed. The village mosque is nearly surrounded by a large artificial pool, whose water is used for bathing and washing clothes. This may reflect the continuation of a pre-Islamic custom of placing religious sanctuaries on man-made islands.

The dormant cone of **Mount Singgalang** (2,877 m) towers to the west of Pandai Sikat. It is an easy 4-hour climb to the top along a well-trodden trail from a TV relay station that

is visible from the village. On a plateau near the summit is a small lake. Get an early start, in order to get to the top while it is (hopefully) still clear. Descend along the same path, or via a track leading north to Kototua, on the Maninjau road. (This takes about twice as long, however.) It is also possible to climb **Mount Marapi** from here (register first at the police station in Kotobaru), however the ascent is treacherous and is better attempted from the southeastern flank (see "Highland Practicalities").

Valley of the ancestors

The **Tanahdatar** plain to the south and east of Mt. Marapi is blanketed by majestic rice terraces and dotted with traditional houses. This is where the ancient Minangkabau kingdom was located for some 500 years before being wiped out by Paderi rebels in the early 1800s (see "History). Most of the main sights may be visited in a single day by walking and hopping on and off local *bemos*.

From Bukittinggi, travel south to Padangpanjang, then turn east (left). The road passes villages with fine examples of traditional architecture. Don't miss the large wooden *surau* or men's house at **Batipuh**, construct-

Above, left and right: *The crafts of woodcarving and crocheting, as well as weaving, are practiced in the village of Pandai Sikat.* **Right:** *The mosque at Kotobaru, near Pandai Sikat.*

ed in the aristocratic Koto Piliang style.

Just after Batipuh, turn off to the left (northeast) in the direction of Batusangkar. The road here skirts the southern flanks of Mt. Marapi, and after about 5 km a small track to the left (north) scrambles up the steep volcanic slopes to the traditional village of **Pariangan**, 850 meters above sea level.

Pariangan is set in a picturesque valley with stairways leading to traditional houses, large ponds and a royal tomb. The people here are extremely friendly. Around 4 pm, villagers drift back to their homes from the rice fields as the afternoon sun slowly recedes, casting a warm glow onto the tranquil, green-and-gold landscape. The traditional *surau* or men's house is one of the last of its kind still in use; there is a hot spring outside.

The name Pariangan derives from *para hyangan* meaning "place of the ancestors," and legend has it that this was the first village established by the Minang ancestors who descended from Marapi's peak. Numerous pieces of evidence support the claim that this is indeed one of the oldest villages in West Sumatra. A 14th-century inscription by Adityavarman can be found on a boulder overlooking the hot spring and *surau*. And the local name for this spring is "Raja's Hot Water."

Other important locations in the village include the Medan Nan Bapane ("Hot Field") —an open council ground with stone seats. In the same plot is an artificial mound called a *munggoh*, and an enormous grave over 20 meters long said to be the burial place of Tun Tejo Gerhano, the architect who designed the old council house in Tabek (see below).

A km further up from Pariangan is a field called *sawah gadang setampang baniah*—the "great paddy of the seeds." According to tradition, this was the first cultivated field in West Sumatra, and all rice grown in the area is said to have come from a single sheaf of seedlings. Across the path from here is a hill known as Bukit Seguntang, the same name used for the sacred hill in Palembang where that first Malay ancestors are said to have settled. Nothing remains, but according to tradition a stone structure once stood on the hill, subsequently destroyed by a flood.

On the way back, just before reaching the main road, stop in the village of **Tabek** to see several examples of old Minang architecture. The council hall (Balairung Sari) is believed to be the oldest building in West Sumatra.

Seven km further east you enter the village of **Dusun Tuo** ("Old Village"). Here, on the north (left) side of the road in an enclosure, is the ancient *batu batikam*—a "pierced stone" on an altar-like structure surrounded by stone ancestor seats. According to legend, the stone was pierced in a battle between two powerful Minang chiefs, Datu Ketumanggungan and Datuk Perpatih Nan Sabatang. The site has been faithfully restored. Some anthropologists have suggested that the

KAL MULLER

ALAIN COMPOST

house of the former district chief, now the residence of the *bupati*, across the road from the council hall. In front of the *bupati's* house is a collection of bits and pieces from the past. These include another 14th-century inscription, a spout from a fountain in the form of a woman, now headless, holding her breasts from which water once poured. (Similar spouts have been found at ancient royal bathing places in East Java and Bali.) There is also a curious statue assembled from two broken figures cemented together at the

pierced stone is a female symbol, and might have been used in religious ceremonies. Nearby are traces of terraces, suggesting that the site once contained more structures.

A further km east is the village of **Limo Kaum** ("Five Clans"). In a low shed here are three large standing stones and several other stone objects—including a mortar and an inscription—collectively known as the Kubu Rajo. The large stones were probably back rests for stone seats. The number three is significant, for it may be connected with the ruling triumvirate of the ancient Minangkabau kingdom, and these may have been thrones for the three kings to use during audiences or ceremonies. The name Kubu Rajo may be interpreted as "Raja's Fort" or "Raja's Grave." The former is probably the correct meaning.

Another section of the site contains a number of stones set up on small terraces. One of them once bore an inscription issued by the 14th-century ruler Adityavarman, in which he compared himself to a heavenly wish-granting tree or *kalpataru*—a motif often sculpted on ancient temples in Java.

Limo Kaum also contains good examples of Minang architecture, all within walking distance. The mosque is especially famous, built in the early Sumatran-Islamic style with a five-storied roof supported by 121 huge wooden pillars, with a large pool beside.

The old royal capital

From Limo Kaum, proceed another 6 km east to **Batusangkar**, the largest town in the Tanahdatar area and the site of an early Dutch fortification, Fort van der Capellen, built in 1821 during the Paderi Wars. The council hall (*balai adat*) at the southeastern corner of the town square is built in traditional Minang style, ornately carved with designs found in local textiles. It was built in 1967.

Little can be seen of the old Dutch fort (now the town's police station), and the most vivid reminder of the colonial presence is the

KAL MULLER

waist: the lower portion probably belonged to a female deity, while the upper part was male.

Beyond Batusangkar, visitors may make a small circuit of several important historic sites east of the town. Proceeding in a clockwise direction, thus leaving Batusangkar by the northeast, one arrives first at **Pagarruyung** —a small village 3 km away which may be reached on foot, *bemo* or horse-drawn *bendi* ($2 for the return journey). This was the site of the palace of the last Raja Alam of the Minangkabau, Sultan Arifin Muning Alam Syah. In 1815 the extremist Paderi movement attacked the royal family and massacred all but the sultan and one of this grandchildren.

No trace of the palace remains, but visitors may see several 14th-century inscriptions and other stones collected here.The inscriptions are probably from Bukit Gombak, further to the south, where other 14th-century inscriptions have also been found at a place called Batu Basurat (literally "Inscribed Stone").

Following the road south along the banks of the Selo River, the next important village is **Gudam**. A Muslim graveyard here contains unique tombstones with designs featuring a kris in a belt and other more characteristic Minangkabau shapes. According to tradition, the stones mark the burial places of Pagar-ruyung nobles. In nearby **Padang Magek**, however, similar stones with ornate decoration are said to have marked out a course for traditional horse racing ceremonies. Such races were still held in recent times, and probably date back to the pre-Islamic period. It is quite common for ancient stones to have been incorporated into later Islamic graves.

Further along, at **Padang Seminyak** is the famous Balai Janggo—the recently reconstructed palace of the Minangkabau ruler. A fire destroyed the old palace in 1976, but six years of construction have restored its former magnificence. This enormous rectangular building resembles a traditional *rumah gadang* but on a much larger scale. A long, wooden-pillared central hall, heavily decorated with textiles, greets the visitor. Opposite the entrance is a row of rooms. And at either end of the hall, stairways lead to upper floors where historical objects and Minang handicrafts are displayed. The guard will allow you to climb to the upper floors and can be persuaded to show you the ceramics that were salvaged after the fire. The uppermost floor provides an excellent view of the surrounding countryside.

In front of the palace stand two rice storage barns (*rankiang*). Behind is the royal bathing pool and a path that leads to the royal hunting grounds. The restoration is pleasantly devoid of gaudy coloring, imitation regalia or government propaganda, and the grounds are impeccably well kept. A small admission fee is charged. To avoid the tour groups from Bukittinggi, visit the palace in the morning or late afternoon.

From here the road crosses the Selo River, skirts the foot of Gombak Hill and returns to Batusangkar—thus completing the basic Tanahdatar tour. Rather than retracing the same route back to Bukittinggi, however, follow a scenic backroad over a pass between Mts. Marapi and Malintang, through the traditional villages of **Raorao** and **Tabatpatah**. From atop a ridge after Tabatpatah, on the other side of the pass, one has a sweeping panorama of the entire Limapuluh Kota area on a clear day—including Payakumbuh and the Harau Canyon, with shimmering rice fields and hazy mountains in the distance.

Lake Singkarak

Those with more time to spend will want to go south from Tanahdatar to Lake Singkarak —a crater lake similar in size and scenic beauty to Maninjau. From Batusangkar, a sideroad serviced by *bemos* climbs up over the low crater wall and down to the lake, passing through the charming hilltop village of **Balimbing** (the name means "starfruit") —a traditional place with several *rumah gadang*, some said to be 300 years old and built without a single nail. The dark wood of the houses lends them an air of antiquity— inside the ceilings have been blackened by countless kitchen fires.

The road meets the shores of the lake at the town of **Umbilin**, where hotels and restaurants provide a convenient stopping-over point. It is not as peaceful as Maninjau, due to the traffic, but boats can be rented and it is still a good place for swimming, hiking and just lazing about.

A highway skirts the lakeshore leading south from Umbilin to the town of Singkarak at the lake's southern tip. Just before Singkarak a turn-off to the left (east) leads up a steep and winding road offering excellent vistas back across the lake (*bemos* go up here several times a day from Umbilin).

The road leads to a remote hilltop village known as **Sulitair**, ("Scarce Water"), where there is a huge, 64-meter *rumah gadang* containing 20 individual apartments, occupied now by just 4 families. Reminiscent of a Dayak longhouse, it is considered by local residents to represent the last material vestige of their ancestral *adat*. Young men returning home from the *rantau* must re-acquaint themselves with local custom by living in the *rumah*

Above, left: *Carved stones at Limo Kaum.* **Above, right:** *The restored Balai Janggo palace at Padang Seminyak.* **Right:** *The palace's ornate interior.*

gadang prior to marrying one of the village's pretty maidens. The building is reputed to be 100 years old, and is erected on the site of an older house destroyed by fire.

East to Limapuluh Kota

The broad and fertile valley known as Limapuluh Kota (the "Fifty Fortified Villages") spreads out at the northern foot of Mt. Malintang (2,262 m). The largest town here is **Payakumbuh**, an administrative and market center 33 km east of Bukittinggi. The entire valley is intensively cultivated, and is scattered with scores of large megalithic stones that were mysteriously arranged and carved by an unknown prehistoric people. These remains suggest that Limapuluh Kota may have been where the first ancestors of the Minang lived.

More than 20 of these megalithic sites are found within a 20-km radius of Payakumbuh, mainly along the banks of the Sinamar River northwest of the town. A small sideroad follows the river, arriving after 13 km at the village of **Guguk**. On the right side of the road here is the old village council house or *balai adat*, and in an adjacent open space stand a number of megaliths—the tallest measuring 2.75 m. Most are typical West Sumatran menhir—upright stones with a curving top portion said to resemble the hilt of a *keris* or the head of a bird. The precise meaning of this form is unknown; several of the stones are decorated with vine-like spirals, the symbolism of which is likewise mysterious. One menhir has an elaborate incised design that seems to be a stylized depiction of a vagina. There are 9 vertical stones, as well as 8 flat ones that may have been used as seats.

In addition to the council house site, many more stones are found scattered throughout the village. These include 26 menhirs, an unusual enclosure made of river boulders and 4 stone objects usually referred to as mortars (*lumpang batu*). Similar stones were used in more recent times to pound rice flour. These mortars represent a domestic artifact of great importance, associated with the powerful female sex (since women did the pounding), and have been incorporated into Minang folklore. Legends describe uses other than rice pounding, such as house pillar supports or stepping stones used to mount horses. The wide variety of shapes and sizes of the mortars, and the range of their decoration, indicates that they probably had still other uses.

Many more menhirs and stone objects can be found to the south of Guguk around Kuranji and Sungai Talang, as well as to the northwest in the villages of Balubus (15 km from Payakumbuh), Limbanang (20 km) and Suliki (26 km). The latter three lie along the same road and can be visited in a few hours.

From Limbanang, a track to the right leads up into a remote, bowl-shaped valley known as **Mahat**. The valley is about 5 km in diame-

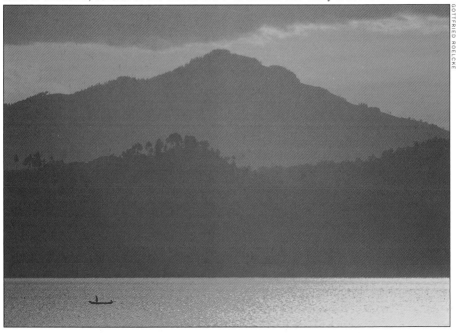

ter and is ringed by steep-walled mountains where hundreds—if not thousands—of fascinating megaliths are found, including some of the most interesting carved menhirs in West Sumatra. During the colonial period, the Dutch were drawn by the valley's natural beauty and historic interest and built a government rest house here.

Why were these megaliths erected? The valley provides at least a partial clue: archaeologists have discovered skeletons beneath several of them, indicating that the stones were in some cases used as grave markers. But excavations at other sites have produced no evidence of burials. Local stories ascribe to them a role in communal feasts, or even in predicting the weather. Only the most intrepid travelers will want to make the journey to this isolated valley, as it has no accommodations and is only accessible by foot, horseback or jeep during the rainy season.

The road to Riau

Limapuluh Kota's most famous attraction lies 14 km northeast of Payakumbuh, just off the main highway leading to Pekanbaru in neighboring Riau Province. This is the stunning **Harau Canyon**—a broad geological cleft whose 100-m granite walls enclose a lush 315-ha nature reserve where one can trek through dense rainforests, splash around in a delightfully cool waterfall, and spot monkeys, butterflies and birds. The reserve is inhabit-

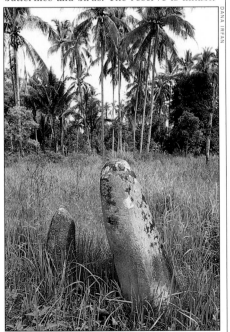

ed also by tigers, leopards, panthers, tapirs, deer and honey bears—but the most you are likely to see of the latter is a few tracks. There is a museum, however, displaying the animals stuffed, as well as an observation point and trails leading up into the canyon.

To get there, take the main highway from Payakumbuh 11 km north to the village of Lamaksari and turn left; the reserve is 3 km in. Snacks and drinks are sold at stalls, but bring your own food if you want something substantial. There is a small admission fee.

On your way back, detour a further 3 km north on the main road to **Kotobaru**, where excellent Minangkabau *songket* is woven. From here, one can also continue north on a much longer detour (4 hours each way) across the border with Riau to the ancient remains of **Muara Takus**. Here, in a clearing in the jungle, stands the largest ancient brick building in Sumatra—a tall stupa flanked by the ruins of several other brick sanctuaries.

The stupa has the unusual form of a tower rather than the squat bell-shape normally associated with Buddhist architecture. This brick and sandstone stupa, known as Candi Mahligai, was restored in the 1980s and the new exterior completely encases the earlier building. On the west side near the ground, an exposed part shows the visitor what the surface of the older building looked like.

Several other foundations can be seen nearby. To the west is Candi Bungsu, a platform on which stood two more stupas, and to the north is Candi Tua—originally the largest structure of all, with two stairways leading up to yet another stupa. The temples are surrounded by brick walls 74 m long on each side. An earthen rampart more than 2 km long surrounds the complex, but only three sides are distinguishable.

This mysterious site lies in a remote area, yet it must have been important—for the elaborateness of the ruins indicate that a sizeable population once lived here. There is no record of any kingdom in this area, but short inscriptions found among the ruins point to a date in the 11th or 12th century AD. A legend describes the site as the burial place of a Hindu ruler who was turned into an elephant, and wild elephants are said to return to the site on the night of every full moon to dance in homage to their departed lord.

— *John Miksic and Jay Goodfriend*

Opposite: *Lovely Lake Singkarak at sunset.*
Left: *Hundreds of mysterious megaliths lie scattered about the Payakumbuh area.*

KERINCI-SEBLAT

Sumatra's Largest National Park

Kerinci-Seblat is Sumatra's largest National Park, encompassing a 345-km long strip of mountainous uplands in the Bukit Barisan Range, parallel to the west coast of Sumatra. The scenery is among the most spectacular on the island, dominated by volcanic cones that include Mt. Kerinci—at 3,800 meters the highest mountain in western Indonesia.

Altogether the park covers an area of almost 15,000 sq km spread across four provinces: West Sumatra, Jambi, Bengkulu and South Sumatra. It was set up to preserve the unique habitats to the south of Lake Toba, in the same way that Gunung Leuser Park preserves a representative portion of habitats north of the lake. The massive volcanic eruption which formed Lake Toba about 100,000 years ago laid waste to such a vast area in between that a biological barrier was created separating populations in the northern and southern parts of the island. Today there are significant differences between the wildlife of the two areas: the white-handed gibbon, for instance, only occurs north of Lake Toba, while the dark-handed gibbon is found only to the south. The same applies to many birds: 17 species live only to the north, while 10 are found only south of Toba.

Apart from orangutans, which are only found north of the divide, Kerinci-Seblat is home to most of the larger Sumatran mammals—including rhinos, tigers, elephants, sun bears and tapirs, which only live in the south. It also has several endemic mammals, including the Giant Sumatran rat and the Sumatran rabbit. The agile serow, a black mountain goat, lives on forested, inaccessible limestone hills in the park, sometimes quite close to cultivated areas. Persistent stories of short, hairy people known as *orang pendek* exist among local people; it is possible that these tales arose from sightings of sun bears in the poor forest light, or from a folk memory of *orangutans,* which once lived in southern Sumatra.

Visiting the park

Kerinci-Seblat has few facilities for visitors, and should therefore be tackled only by people with plenty of time to spare. The best way is to travel south from Padang to Sungaipenuh (see "Highland Practicalities"), where there is a Conservation Department office. It

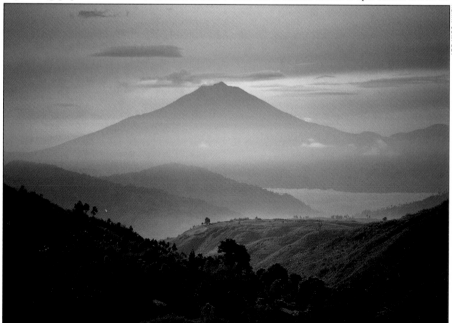

is also possible to approach the park via a mountainous road leading down from the Trans-Sumatran Highway at Bangko, to the east, and there are twice-weekly flights to Sungaipenuh from Jambi.

Sungaipenuh lies at the center of a fertile valley watered by the Kerinci River. Paddy fields, tea, clove and coffee plantations are surrounded by the park's forested mountains. Maintaining the boundaries of protected areas is difficult here because of the burgeoning human population around them.

In Kerinci-Seblat there are two additional factors which exacerbate the problem: the fact that its territory is administered by four different provinces, and the dense population of the Kerinci Valley within the park itself. This area gives an excellent demonstration of the conflict between the needs of wildlife and human populations, a conflict which is by no means of recent origin. There is evidence that the forests around Kerinci were disturbed by man 7,500 years ago, probably to make it easier to hunt game and also to plant crops. Bronze or Iron Age kettledrums have been found near Lake Kerinci, and standing stones, or megaliths, have been found in Jambi. Living remnants of ancient cultures survive in the Kubu people, hunter-gatherers who still live their traditional existence in forested areas of Kerinci-Seblat and other parts of southern Sumatra (see "The Kubu").

An especially beautiful spot is the lake-filled crater atop Mt. Tujuh, northeast of Sungaipenuh. **Lake Kerinci** is more easily accessible by public transport, however. These lakes, and the forest immediately around them, offer the best places to see the park's rich avifauna, which includes hornbills and jungle fowl; maroon, black and yellow-banded broadbills with their turquoise bills; grey wagtails and chestnut-crowned forktails of the rivers; and the racket-tailed drongos— easily recognized by the illusion they give of a bird being chased by two black butterflies.

Montane forest

Because of the varying altitudes of terrain in Kerinci-Seblat, it contains a great range of habitats, including lowland forests, alpine vegetation and the highest freshwater swamp forests in the western part of the Indonesian archipelago. This type of forest can be seen at Lake Bento, south of Mt. Tujuh, and northwest of Lake Kerinci, where the turbulent action of waves in the lake has prevented the formation of peat.

A climb up Mt. Kerinci or one of the other mountains shows a dramatic change in vegetation from the tall, varied trees of the lower elevations to the stunted, moss-draped montane forests and the sub-alpine heaths and bogs near the summit. A striking plant of Kerinci's upper elevations is the Javan edelweiss *Anaphalis javanica*, which only occurs on volcanoes. It generally grows to about 4 meters high and appears whitish-green all over because of its covering of fine, white hairs. The flowers appear white too, except for a central yellow disc. The volcanic cone itself is bare of vegetation, reflecting its recent activity: it last erupted in 1934. The largest flowers in the world grow in Kerinci-Seblat too, the parasitic *Rafflesia arnoldi* with its monstrous flesh-pink blooms, and the 2-meter high spikes of *Amorphophallus titanum*.

Local guides can be hired for trips into the park in Sungaipenuh (check at the Conservation Office), although because there are few visitors to Kerinci-Seblat they are unlikely to be experienced. As well as agreeing on a fee in advance, it is best to specify the exact duration of walk you wish to make and, if possible, precisely where you want to go.

—Janet Cochrane

Opposite: *At 3,800 m, Mt. Kerinci is the highest peak in western Indonesia.* **Above, left:** *The rich valley around Lake Kerinci has been settled for centuries.* **Above, right:** *Rainforest on Mt. Kerinci.*

Highland Practicalities

Includes Bukittinggi, Lake Maninjau, Batu-sangkar, Lake Singkarak, Payakumbuh, Solok and Kerinci-Seblat Reserve. Prices in US$ unless stated otherwise. AC=Air-conditioning.

Most visitors to the Minangkabau Highlands base themselves at Bukittinggi as it is centrally located and offers by far the widest variety of accommodations, restaurants and other facilities. Although much smaller, Batusangkar is an alternative base if you are interested primarily in seeing the antiquities and traditional villages of the Tanahdatar region. If swimming, hiking, relaxing and scenic beauty are what you are looking for, however, then stay at Lake Singkarak or, better still, Lake Maninjau.

Bukittinggi

Telephone code for Bukittingi is 0752

Bukittinggi, the most important town in the Minang highlands, lies 108 km from Padang. The journey takes you through the lush, tropical vegetation of the Anai Valley to the Agam plateau. Bukittinggi is a pleasant town—clean and cool at 930 meters elevation.

GETTING THERE

From Padang the bus takes 3 hours and costs 70 cents. Many hotels in Padang offer taxi service to Bukittinggi for around $25 (for 4-5 persons); or just flag down a taxi in town or at the airport and bargain with the driver. As you drive through the Anai Valley, waterfalls and rapids cascade alongside the highway. The railway from Padang to the coal mines at Umbilin, on the shores of Lake Singkarak, runs alongside the road. This is one of the world's most magnificent rack-and-pinion rails, with tunnels and bridges, and was constructed early this century by the Dutch under supervision of a German engineer. Unfortunately, passenger service to Bukittinggi ceased some 10 years ago.
From Medan, the Trans-Sumatra Highway traverses some spectacular countryside, but the bus trip is grueling, taking about 12 hours ($9) straight through. Only for masochists. **From Prapat** (Lake Toba) is 9 hours ($8). A faster and more comfortable alternative to the bus is to share a chartered minivan with 5-6 other people. Negotiate with the driver beforehand (around $100), then sit back and enjoy the ride, stopping at will en route.
From Pekanbaru (Riau) to Bukittinggi is $4 by bus or $25 by chartered taxi. The journey takes about 4 hours.

Buses drop you at Aur Kuning bus terminal, 3 km southeast of Bukittinggi. To get into town, walk out of the terminal to the street and flag a passing *bemo*. Travelers intending to stay in the Jl. A. Yani area should ask to go to the Pasar Atas market, and then walk one block to your hotel. For hotels on top of the hill by Fort de Kock at Jl. Benteng, you may have to pay a bit extra because they are off the usual *bemo* routes. Otherwise, take a *bemo* to Pasar Atas and hire a *bendi* the rest of the way. If you are coming from from Padang you can ask to be dropped in Jambu Air, 3 km north of town. From there get a *bemo* into town.

GETTING AROUND

Walking is the best and easiest way of getting around town, as Bukittinggi's one-way streets make *bemo* routes circuitous and confusing.
Bendis (horse-drawn carriages) are also a pleasant way to get about. The horses are sleek and pampered and trot along proudly with bright red tassels on their heads. They can be found around Pasar Bawah and the clock tower. A *bendi* to Panorama Park costs under $1; walking takes 15 minutes. Bargain hard before getting in.
Metered taxis have just made their appearance in Bukittinggi and can be found around the clock tower or on Jl. A. Yani.
Minibuses can be chartered for trips around town or to Lake Maninjau or Batusangkar for approximately $30 a day. If you split the cost among 6 or 7 people, this is an excellent way to cover a lot of ground quickly and in comfort and not having to hassle about transportation all the time. Ask the owner of your hotel, the tourist office, a travel agent, or one of the restaurants on Jl. A. Yani to arrange this.

TOURS

As most places of interest are some distance from town, and finding transport can be time consuming, day tours from Bukittinggi are a convenient way of getting around. **Parindo-mulya Sentratour**, Jl. A. Yani 99, or **Batours**, Jl. A. Yani 105 offers a variety of tours. These range from afternoon trips to nearby villages or full-day excursions to Maninjau and Batu-sangkar, to week-long hiking trips. Expect to pay about $10 per person per day.

ACCOMMODATION
Expensive (above $25)

Denai's Hotel, just off Jl. A. Yani at Jl. A. Rivai 26 (tel: 21460, 21511). The best of Bukit-tinggi's better establishments. Rooms from $25; little chalets from $40, all with TV, carpeting and hot water. Well-kept, with restaurant and bar. Often fully booked by tour groups.
Dymen's International, Jl. Nawawi 3, has "luxury" rooms with AC, TV, carpeting and hot water. $30 to $70. Credit cards accepted. At the southern end of town.
Minang Hotel, Jl. Panorama 20 (tel: 21120), is

Bukittinggi

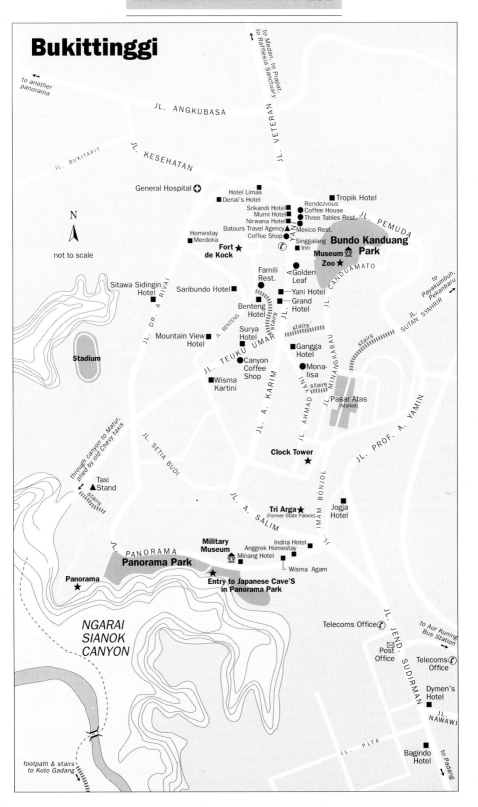

to another
panorama

JL. ANGKUBASA

JL. KESEHATAN

JL. BUKITAPIT

to Medan, to Prapat,
to Rafflesia Sanctuary

JL. VETERAN

General Hospital ✚

N
not to scale

Hotel Limas ■
Denai's Hotel ■
Srikandi Hotel ■
Murni Hotel ■
Nirwana Hotel ■
Batours Travel Agency ■
Coffee Shop

Homestay
Merdeka ■

Tropik Hotel ■
Rendezvous ■
Coffee House ●
Three Tables Rest. ●
Mexico Rest. ▲
Singgalang ●
Inn ■

**Bundo Kanduang
Park**

Museum 🏛
Zoo ★

JL. PEMUDA

JL. CANDUAMATO

to
Payakumbuh,
Pekanbaru

JL. SUTAN SYAHRIR

**Fort
de Kock** ★

Sitawa Sidingin
Hotel ■

Saribundo Hotel ■

Famili
Rest. ■

Golden
Leaf ●

Yani Hotel ■
Grand
Hotel ■

Mountain View
Hotel ■

Benteng
Hotel ■

Surya
Hotel ■

JL. BENTENG

JL. TEUKU UMAR

stairs

stairs

JL. DR. A. RIVAI

Stadium

Canyon
Coffee
Shop ●

Wisma
Kartini ■

JL. A. KARIM

Gangga
Hotel ■

Mona-
lisa ●

JL. AHMAD YANI

stairs

JL. MINANGKABAU

stairs

Pasar Atas
(Market)

JL. PROF. A. YAMIN

JL. SETIA BUDI

through canyon to Matur,
plied by old Chevy taxis

stairs

Taxi
▲ Stand

Clock Tower
★

Tri Arga ★
(Former State Palace)

IMAM BONJOL

Jogja
Hotel ■

JL. A. SALIM

**Military
Museum** 🏛

Indria Hotel ■
Anggrek Homestay
Minang Hotel ■

Wisma Agam ■

Panorama Park

P A N O R A M A

Panorama
★

**Entry to Japanese Cave'S
in Panorama Park** ★

*NGARAI
SIANOK
CANYON*

Telecoms Office ☎

to Aur Kuning
Bus Station

Post
Office ✉

Telecoms
Office ☎

JL. JEND. SUDIRMAN

Dymen's
Hotel ■

JL.
NAWAWI

footpath & stairs
to Koto Gadang

JL. PLTA

Bagindo
Hotel ■

to Padang

right across from Panorama Park and next to the Military Museum. Excellent view overlooking Ngarai Sianok Canyon and Mt. Singgalang. Over-priced at $25-$45. No restaurant or bar. **Wisma Saribundo**, just below Jl. Benteng, is over-priced at $30 for small rooms with carpeting, TV and hot water (tel: 22953).

Moderate ($8 to $25)

Hotel Bagindo, 1 km south of town on the road to Padang. Rooms from $15; well-maintained and clean (tel: 21286).

Hotel Benteng, Jl Benteng 1 (tel: 22596, 21115). Modern hotel overlooking the town and Mt. Marapi, on a quiet street. TV, telephone and bath, $15-$30; restaurant and bar.

Bukittinggi View Hotel, 7 km north of town (tel: 22444 or 22273). A great for peace and quiet, but not easily reached by public transport. All rooms $20. The restaurant and bar are usually deserted.

Hotel Limas, near the northern end of Jl. A. Yani at Jl. Kesehatan 34 (tel: 22763, 22641). Highly recommended. $12 to $25.

Merdeka Homestay on Jl. Dr. A. Rivai is a beautiful old Dutch house.

Mountain View, Jl. Benteng 3 (tel: 21621). A friendly guesthouse with a great view and a quiet atmosphere. Rooms for $8. Often full.

Suwarni's Guest House, across the street from the Mountain View, has rooms for $8, or a *tikar* (mattress) in the dorm for under $1.

Budget (under $8)

Cheaper accommodations can be found along Jl. A. Yani, all tolerable and with rooms from $2 to $5. Try the **Murni** (no phone) or the **Srikandi** (tel: 22984) at the northern end of the street, or the **Gangga** (tel: 22967). They are all popular and often full. Alternatives on Jl. A. Yani in a similar price range are the **Singgalang Inn** (tel: 21576), the **Yani** (tel: 22740), the **Nirwana** (tel: 21292), and the **Grand** (tel: 21133).

Close to Jl. A. Yani, a little up the hill on Jl. T. Umar, are the **Surya** (tel: 22587) with rooms around $8, and the somewhat cheaper **Wisma Kartini**. Not far from the northern end of Jl. A. Yani is the new and very clean **Tropik**.

EATING

Bukittinggi's most popular eating places are all concentrated along Jl. A. Yani. The **Coffee Shop** at no. 105 has a vast menu catering to the tastes of Western travelers. The toast and pancakes are popular for breakfast, but it's the dinners that bring in the crowds. You haven't been to Bukittinggi until you've eaten at the Coffee Shop! There is also a branch called the **Canyon Coffee Shop** further up the hill on Jl. Teuku Umar, with a similar choice of dishes.

The **Three Tables** and the **Mexico**, also on Jl. A. Yani, are restaurants with a convivial atmosphere. Both serve beer and steaks, but the food is better at the Mexico.

There are two Chinese restaurants on Jl. A. Yani, the **Golden Leaf** with good food and a neon-lit charm, and the **Monalisa**—a crowded but cosy place worth trying.

A new cafe with good Western pop music, the **Rendezvous**, has recently opened at the northern end of Jl. A. Yani.

The Indonesian restaurant most frequented by foreigners is the **Famili**, next to the Benteng Hotel on the hilltop. A pleasant view, refreshing evening breezes and an excellent menu make dining here a memorable experience. Students hang around in the evening hoping to practice their English on foreigners.

Opposite the clock tower is a branch of the **Simpang Raya** restaurant chain, offering the usual *nasi padang* and excellent views of the square and Mt. Singgalang. Other Simpang Raya branches are by the zoo and opposite the Bagindo Hotel. Another *nasi padang* restaurant to try is **Rumah Makan Selamat**, Jl. A. Yani 19.

Foods of all kinds can also be found in Bukittinggi's colorful market. Divided into upper and lower sections, connected by stairs, the market is full of tiny stalls serving fresh fruit, *sate ayam* (chicken satay), *nasi padang*, coffee and *es campur* (iced drinks).

SHOPPING

An unbelievable amount of antique and not-so-antique woodcarvings flow into Bukittinggi from the surrounding regions of Jambi, Riau and Palembang. The buying power of the tourist has tempted many Minang families into parting with cherished family heirlooms, or into crafting very good fakes. *Kain songket* and filigree jewelry are not cheap, but traditional village handicrafts, such as baskets and woodcarvings, are reasonably priced.

One way to buy is to hang out at a shop as the stuff comes in (villagers stop in almost every day to sell their wares). You may be able to pick up a beautiful piece of ceramic or other *objet d'art* if the shopkeeper declines to buy it. Old Dutch door knobs and light fittings, Chinese porcelains, "antique" Batak carvings and gold and silver jewelry, Sumban *hinggi*, Irian necklaces and beadware, and Dayak basketry from Kalimantan vie for attention.

Most of the action is on Jl. Minangkabau. Try the **Crystal Art Shop** for woodcarvings, old Dutch books and textiles. **Minang Art Antique and Souvenir** sells local crafts and Batak carvings. VISA and Mastercard accepted. The **Aladin Art and Antique Shop** at Jl. A. Yani 14 sells ceramics, antique textiles, as well as local handicrafts.

SERVICES

The **Tourist Office** is located in a Minang-style building on the square by the clock tower. The staff is friendly and maps are sometimes available. A notice board near the entrance gives information on local weddings, cultural performances and bull fights.

The **Post Office** is a 5-minute walk from the clock tower, on the road to Padang. Open Mon through Thurs 8-12 and 1:30-4 pm, on Fri and Sat 8-11:30.

International calls can be made from the **Perumtel** telephone and telegraph office south of the town center at Jl. Stasiun 14A (now Jl. M. Syafei). Open 24 hours, tel: 22744, 21922.

The **Garuda/Merpati Office** is in the courtyard of Dymen's International Hotel. Immediate reservations can be made for Garuda and Merpati flights. Ticket purchases require 2 days, as a courier must deliver the tickets from Padang. The other ticketing office is next to the Tourist Information Center.

RAFFLESIA SANCTUARY

There is a Rafflesia Sanctuary 10 km north of Bukittinggi in the 3,120-hectare **Rimba Panti Nature Reserve**, near the village of Batang Palupuh. Ask at the Coffee Shop on Jl. A. Yani or the Bukittinggi Tourist Information office whether the flower is in bloom (most often in Sept and Oct). Local youths will take you there by motorbike for 50 cents; a distance of 16 km. Pay another $1 to the reserve's warden, and walk in for 15 minutes. To actually see the rafflesia in bloom is an experience, as the huge, foul-smelling flowers are rare and short-lived. The Indonesian name for the flower is *bunga bankai* ("corpse flower"), so-called on account of the stench.

LEAVING BUKITTINGGI

If you came up to Bukittinggi by the usual road through Padangpanjang, the best way to return would be through Batusangkar and Solok, a scenic but much longer drive. Along the way, you are treated to unbroken views of the fertile agricultural lands in the plains below. Everywhere you see Minang farmers working in the fields—ploughing with water buffalo, replanting young rice seedlings, or harvesting the golden sheafs of grain. There are still many traditional villages here—clusters of wooden houses with typical saddle-shaped roofs, marred only by the widespread use of corrugated tin sheeting instead of thatch.

Early morning buses to Padang leave from the clock tower before 7 am. All other long-distance buses leave from the Aur Kuning bus terminal, where there is a Rp50 entrance fee. Fares to most destinations within West Sumatra are below $1. The trip to Padang costs 70 cents (more with AC) and takes about 3 hours. Fares to Batusangkar, Payakumbuh, and Maninjau are below 50 cents. Medan can be reached from Bukittinggi in 12 hours for $9; Pekanbaru in 4 hours for $4; Jambi in 24 hours for $7, and Lubuklinggau in 16 hours for $7.

The bus station is quite large; tell the security guard at the entrance your intended destination and he will direct you. Many of the town ne'er-do-wells hang out at the station, hoping to earn commissions from bus drivers for finding passengers; if you tell them where you're going they'll help you find a bus and their commission is not reflected in your fare. Buy a ticket on a crowded bus if you want to leave fast.

Lake Maninjau

Lake Maninjau is a sublime place where you can go swimming, boating and even water-skiing. The area around the lake is good terrain for hiking. There is a wider choice of accommodations and eateries than at Lake Singkarak, where there is only one good hotel and the scenery is less spectacular. To see the lake at its best, take an early bus from Bukittinggi; the journey takes about 2 hours. Tours of Lake Maninjau can be arranged through the big hotels such as the Benteng, Dymen's and Minang, which includes 7 or 8 stops en route. The Tourist Information Center in Bukittinggi also offers this tour.

ACCOMMODATION

There are two hotels and several smaller places at Maninjau village on the lakeshore. **Hotel Maninjau Indah** is centrally located in the village and has a lovely terrace and swimming pool. Rooms range from $13 for a fan-cooled room with car park view to $26 for a standard room with AC, TV and hot water, up to $65 for a VIP suite. The food is disappointing, however. **Hotel Pasir Panjang Permai**, 1 km north of the village center, has rooms from $15-$25. There is no pool, but the hotel is right on the edge of the lake. The food here is slightly better, but you have to order your meals an hour in advance. The hotel has a tennis court. **Family**, a small bungalow, is right next door. A double room is $12, or rent the whole bungalow with its 3 rooms and hallway for $30.

A number of *losmen* near the village center also offer accommodation from $2 up.

It is also possible to stay at Embun Pagi, on the crater rim above Lake Maninjau, to watch the early morning mists rise from the lake. **Embun Pagi Cottages** has pleasant rooms from $25-$50, breakfast included. Meals can also be arranged.

EATING

The best place to eat in Maninjau is the **Maninjau Coffee Shop**, on the central square. The food is good, prices are reasonable and there is a Western menu. Small warungs off the square also offer the usual *gado-gado* or *mie goreng*. Oddly enough, there is no *nasi Padang* restaurant in Maninjau village. You will find one on the other side of the lake, about half an hour's drive away, at Tanjung Alai. The delicious fish dishes alone are worth the ride.

SERVICES

The telephone office is on the main square. There is no travel agent and no facilities for changing money. The nearest banks are in Bukittinggi. The Maninjau Indah Hotel has a small shopping arcade. Both hotels have speed boats for hire for water skiing. If they are running, they cost about $22 an hour.

Batusangkar

Batusangkar is a lively and scenic town surrounded by majestic rice terraces, 50 km southeast of Bukittinggi. The local countryside is dotted with *rumah adat* and historic remains, and if you are interested in the ancient megalithic culture of West Sumatra, or simply want to get away from it all, Batusangkar is a perfect base.

GETTING THERE

From Bukittinggi, take a bus to Padangpanjang, where local buses depart about every hour for Batusangkar. The entire trip takes 1-2 hours. If you arrive from Bukittinggi or Payakumbuh (that is from the north or west), ask to be dropped off at in town rather than at the bus terminal, which is 2 km on the other side (east) of town. Coming from the east (Sawahlunto and Solok) you have no choice. The *bemo* ride into town from the bus terminal costs Rp200.

Bemos to villages in the immediate vicinity of Batusangkar (Pagarruyung, Pariangan, Balimbing and Ombilin) depart from the terminal in town at Jl. Malano Ponco, near the main market. Fares are betweem Rp150-Rp300, depending on the distance.

ACCOMMODATION

Few travelers stay in Batusangkar, and the town's small hotels usually have vacancies.
Wisma Yoherma, Jl. Parak Juar 15, tel: 130, has clean rooms with baths. The staff is pleasant and the price of the room includes tea or coffee. $4-$12.
Hotel Pagarruyung, across the street from the Yoherma is of a similar standard but slightly cheaper at $3-$10 (tel: 107 or 115).
Parma Hotel, on the same street, with rooms from $2.50 to $8, is not recommended.

EATING

Roda Baru on Jl. A. Yani, just past the sports field on the way into town, serves basic Padang food. The place is crowded at lunchtime and there is a juice bar in the rear. Another Padang place, the **Simpang Raya**, is opposite and less spicy **Soto Madura** is served next door.
Hotel Pagarruyung also has a Padang restaurant, and next door to it is the **Kubang Restaurant** which serves *nasi goreng* (fried rice), *mie goreng* (fried noodles), *martabak* (Indian omelette), and fresh tomato and avocado juice, though the *es jeruk asam* (lemonade) is better.

The **central market** is filled with restaurants which operate as coffee houses during the day. These dingy, poorly-lit establishments are venues for public debating and information. Impromptu cockfights, pig hunts and other events are conceived and advertised here.

Food stalls appear on the city's streets at night, offering inexpensive, greasy food to teenagers seeking each other's company away from their parents' constant scrutiny.

LEAVING BATUSANGKAR

Long-distance buses to Bukittinggi, Pekanbaru, Solok, Payakumbuh, Padang, etc., depart from the bus terminal (some 2 km east of town) up until about 3 pm. For long hauls to Medan or Jakarta, you have to change first at Bukittinggi or Solok.

CLIMBING MOUNT MARAPI

Mount Marapi is a live volcano spitting out sulphur fumes (including poisonous hydrogen sulphide), big dust clouds and the occasional rock barrage. The volcano is officially off-limits, and should you run into trouble you are on your own! It is a dangerous climb and you are strongly advised to take a guide. The starting point for the climb is the village of Sungai Puar, on the southeast slope, and there is a motorcycle track which continues up for some way. The walk to the top takes 6 or 7 hours; the crater is a little west of the true summit, and lower. The surrounding area is like a moonscape—a wide, rolling field of ashes strewn with stones which have blasted little craters into the layer of ash. There is no vegetation, no birds, and the place has an eerie feeling. Do not go near the crater, as it consists of fresh, loose scree. Just walk around it, keeping a safe distance. A stone thrown into the crater takes 6 seconds to land, with a splash, in a body of water 180 m down.

Lake Singkarak

Lake Singkarak, an hour from Batusangkar, is a 20-km long highland lake where you can swim and relax. It is not as peaceful as Maninjau, however. The road running along the northeastern shore of the lake connects Bukittinggi with Solok and is actually part of the Trans-Sumatran highway. Freight trains from the coal mining area around Umbilin also run past the lake loaded with black coal and screaming children.

The new **Hotel Sumpur** on the northern shore of the lake is the best place around here, with rooms from $22 (with fan), $30 (AC, TV and hot water). This hotel offers good facilities, including a pool, tennis court and water sports facilities. The restaurant serves Western food and and the fish is fresh from the lake. Visa and Mastercard accepted. Book through their office in Padangpanjang at Jl. A. Yani 91 (tel: 82529, 82533). To get there by public transport take a bus from Padangpanjang to Malalo and ask to be dropped off.

Other places to stay along the lake include the **Hotel Minang** on the northern tip, with rooms from $6-$12, and the **Hotel Jayakarta** on the eastern shore by the main road, with rooms from $8-$13. Neither is good value for money and neither serves breakfast or any other meals.

Payakumbuh

Telephone code is 0759

If you approach West Sumatra by road from Riau (Pekanbaru) this is the first major West Sumatran town you reach. It is larger than Bukittinggi, but not as charming. There are 3 or 4 small hotels; best value is the **Bougainville** with rooms from $8-$15. The rooms in the **Flamboyan** are slightly cheaper, at $7-$12, but not as nice. There are several restaurants on Jl. Sudirman; all serve *nasi padang*, but the best is **Salero** on the road to Bukittinggi, about 3 km out of town.

Solok

Telephone code is 0755

The town of Solok sits at a major junction on the Trans-Sumatra Highway, and has a surprising number of traditional houses with thatched roofs and brightly painted carved pillars. If you need to stay overnight, the **Hotel Caredek** on Jl. Perpatih Nan Sebatang (tel: 20931) is the best; rooms from $5 (no bath) up to $22 (with hot water, AC, TV, breakfast).
Hotel Ully in Jl. Syeikh Kukut (tel: 20095), has rooms from $3-$8.
Hotel Sinar Timbulun is the cheapest at $2.
Of the few restaurants, Simpang Raya and Pagi Sore are the best.

On Jl. Sudirman are a couple of banks and the telephone office. The steep descent back to Padang offers fantastic panoramas, if the air is not too hazy.

Kerinci-Seblat Reserve

Most people travel south along the main Trans-Sumatran Highway east from Solok to Muarabungo, but an alternative route takes you south on backroads down a cleft in the mountains to Sungaipenuh, through the lovely Kerinci-Seblat National Park. The scenery this way is far better, but the journey takes longer. Direct buses leave Padang for Sungaipenuh daily at about 11 am, fare is $2.50.

You leave the main Padang-Solok road at Lubukselasih and travel up the flank of Mt. Talang through a tea plantation, passing roadside stalls selling passion fruit (*markisa*)—the specialty of the area. After less than an hour you reach the twin highland lakes of **Danau Diatas** ("Lake Above") and **Danau Dibawah** ("Lake Below"), separated from each other by only a few hundred meters. A vantage point dominates both bodies of water. If you have your own transport, make a stopover.

Past Danau Diatas, it is a long and winding road down to Muaralabuh, then on through the plantations around Liki. The road makes a big detour up to a pass east of Mt. Kerinci, and down again into the province of Jambi. On the other side you pass through one of Indonesia's largest tea plantations before reaching **Sungaipenuh**, where you can stay in one of a handful of lower-middle class hotels, such as the Hotel Yani. The town is in Jambi but culturally it is still Minangkabau.

Attractions in the surrounding area include **Lake Kerinci**, a number of hot or even boiling springs converted to outdoor or indoor bathing pools, and, above all, Mt. Kerinci.

CLIMBING MOUNT KERINCI

For the climb up Kerinci, get a permit first either at the forestry office in Padang (see "Padang Practicalities") or in Sungaipenuh. Guides and porters can be hired in the village of **Kersiktua**, near the Kayu Aru tea plantation on the Padang-Sungaipenuh road, about a 45-min drive north from Sungaipenuh. You begin the climb from a ranger station at the foot of the volcano, right in the middle of the tea estate. Here, you are already at an elevation of 1,500 m and the air is pleasantly cool.

For about the first hour, a rocky track rises gently up through foothills blanketed by tea. The path then enters the forest and the climb begins in earnest. It is good, broad path that is easy to follow, but it seems to ascend almost vertically. Drinking water is not a problem, as sparkling streams run down the mountain. After about 6 hours you reach the tree line and a meadow campsite at 3,200 m, unfortunately littered with the debris of previous campers. Spend the night, and make the final assault on the summit in the morning, scrambling over loose volcanic scree for about two hours. It is important to remember that the temperature drops dramatically as you climb, and frost can occur at the higher elevations during the night.

—*Gottfried Roelcke and Jay Goodfirend*

MENTAWAI ISLANDS

Moile Moile: Be Good to Your Soul!

The Mentawai archipelago forms part of a chain of non-volcanic islands running parallel to Sumatra about 100 km off the west coast. There are four large inhabited islands in the group: Siberut (4,480 sq km), Sipora (845 sq km) and North and South Pagi (together 1,675 sq km). They are covered in dense, tropical rainforest with isolated farming settlements scattered along the river valleys.

Until quite recently, the people who live here retained many Stone Age traditions that were exceptionally archaic but nevertheless remarkably complex. Nowadays most Mentawaians are Christians. Communities which practice the old religion do still exist on Siberut, but the short-term visitor should not expect to get much more than a glimpse of the older culture, especially if he travels only to the main coastal villages on Siberut.

An archaic island culture

The inhabitants of the Mentawai Islands are descended from some of the earliest groups of peoples to have migrated to Indonesia several thousand years ago. They have preserved a neolithic Austronesian culture with some Bronze Age elements, which was virtually unaffected by subsequent Hindu, Buddhist and Islamic cultural influences. Old stone axes are still occasionally found here today (though none is still in use), and nowhere else in Indonesia has this archaic heritage been preserved so well.

The Mentawai people have neither chiefs nor slaves; instead their society is organized into clan groups consisting of about ten families living in large communal houses, called *uma*, built at irregular intervals along the rivers. The inhabitants live off the land, cultivating sago, yams, tubers and bananas. They also raise chickens and pigs and the men go hunting and the women fishing. There is no economic specialization: every man is a canoe builder, a pig farmer, a bow and arrow maker and a vegetable gardener.

The islands' remoteness meant that only at the beginning of this century did external influences begin to seep in. But when they did so, their impact was significant. Under the direction of European missionaries and colonial administrators, head-hunting and traditional religious ceremonies were forbidden.

The pace of change speeded up after Indonesian independence, when the indigenous religion was banned altogether and everyone had to embrace either Islam or Christianity. Punishment for the practice of the old religion was severe, and ritual objects were burned. The government further insisted that communal houses be constructed around a village church and school. Men were forbidden from wearing glass bead decorations and loin cloths, and teeth filing and tattooing were prohibited.

The majority of the Mentawai people became Christians at this time, learned German or Italian church melodies, built simple single-family dwellings, dressed in the modern style, and complemented their subsistence economy with products for trade. But under this veneer of conformity the old beliefs lived on, for example in secluded healing ceremonies, such as the *pangurei* "wedding celebration," in which a sick man is dressed up as a bridegroom to attract his soul back to him.

The harmonious cosmos

Traditional Mentawai beliefs hold that cre-

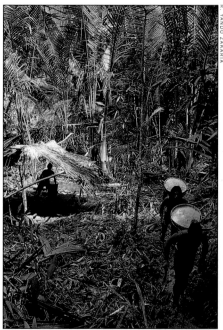

ation is a harmonious whole. There are spirits everywhere, and objects like trees and rocks have souls. Because they are invisible, man's activities can unwittingly disturb them —for example, a tree that is cut might fall on a forest spirit's dwelling. Before beginning any major activity, therefore, ceremonies are held to entertain and placate the spirits.

Everything—man and beast, plant and rock—has not just a soul, but also a personality. The few implements that the Mentawaians possess are made with special care to match

external form with inner essence. Compatibility is important: a man may possess an excellent hunting bow, but unless it "gets on" with him, he may frequently miss his target. Religious practices are directed at restoring harmony between man and the environment in which he lives.

Siberut Island

The island of Siberut is the largest in the group—an elongated rectangle measuring about 110 by 50 km. Dense tropical rainforest covers more than 90 percent of the island, which is quite hilly—the highest elevation being 384 m. These hills are interrupted by wide valleys, and the eastern slopes facing Sumatra drop gently to the sea. Along the coast, white coral beaches alternate with mangrove swamps, interrupted by muddy rivers. The island's two main administrative centers are here: **Sikabaluan** in the north and **Muara Siberut** in the south. The western shore forms the extreme edge of the Asian continental shelf—dropping steeply beneath a giant surf which rolls across from Africa.

Previously, the inhabitants of Siberut did not live in villages, but in longhouses or *uma* housing 5-10 families related to each other through the male line. Each family had its own section of the *uma*, as well as a field house some distance away where they raised pigs and chickens, cultivated tubers and bananas, gathered sago and fished. Today

only a few of these large communal dwellings remain; most were abandoned as a result of the policy of bringing islanders into the 20th century. In some areas in the south, however, people have built *uma* in new villages; these convey some idea of their former state.

A traditional *uma* is a village under one roof. Floor plan and usage reflect a strong community spirit. A notched trunk serves as a stairway to the front verandah. Skulls of pigs and game (monkeys, deer and wild boars), some of them carved and decorated, hang from the rafters. This verandah is a living room during the day, but at night it becomes a sleeping place for men and guests. The first inner room has a communal hearth used for ceremonial events; here dances are held. Women and children sleep in a second room, which serves in the daytime as a kitchen. To the right of the door on the entry wall of this room, there hangs the main fetish of the community, a bundle of holy plants. Each family has another, smaller field house (*sapou*) for daily activities. People often stay there for weeks to work or just to enjoy some privacy.

Life in the uma

Work is divided evenly between men and women. The men pound the marrow of the sago palm to obtain flour; taro and bananas are cultivated by women, and families own coconut trees planted along the rivers. Coconuts, rattan and other forest products are bartered for axes, bush knives, and material for mosquito nets and loin cloths. The basic diet of sago is supplemented by fish and the occasional pig or chicken. For big feasts, the men hunt game in the forest.

In the traditional *uma*, children grow up freely without constraints or formal educa-

Overleaf: *On Siberut, bodily adornments are considered pleasing to one's soul. Photo by R. Yando Zakaria.* **Opposite:** *Harvesting sago.* **Above, left:** *An* uma *longhouse.* **Above, right:** *Tattooing.*

tion. Boys and girls imitate the activities of adults in their play. Toward the end of puberty, adolescents are tattooed and their incisors chiseled to a point; then the boys start to acquire property of their own. The girls help their mothers, but only when married do they acquire responsibility and possessions.

On Siberut it is forbidden to marry within one's own kingroup. Wives are sought from a neighboring *uma*, and after the wedding the wife moves to the *uma* of her husband. These exogamous marriages are a means of establishing and maintaining relationships with other *umas*. Despite this, rivalries exist, manifesting themselves during religious feasts, when each group strives to outdo its neighbors. In former times, such rivalries often developed into open hostilities.

Help and support for the individual comes from the whole *uma*, and everyone participates equally in celebrations. However, differences do occur. As the group has no chieftain and all have equal rights, only open discussion can sort out problems. If a common solution cannot be found, one faction moves out and establishes another *uma*. This, say the elders, is how Siberut was settled.

A fragile equilibrium

The low population density of Siberut is attributable to an unhealthy climate. However, the people themselves view illness as the result of a person being in disharmony with his or her surroundings. It is their belief that everything has a soul; everything lives. One must be aware of these souls, so as not to disturb the existing equilibrium.

Things are not objects to be used at will; they allow themselves to be used. To obtain their approval one has to communicate, present offerings and adjust to their presence by modifying one's own behavior. If someone brings home a new gong, for example, he must not split coconuts—for otherwise the gong, too, would soon crack. In the house, the soul of the gong will be summoned to familiarize itself with its new home. Joint offerings are made to the gong and its companion objects. This ceremony serves to introduce the new object and placate the souls of the others, lest they feel jealous. Otherwise the souls of the things would turn against their owner and make him sick.

The aim of healing ceremonies is thus to placate and reconcile displeased souls. That is the task of the *kerei*—men skilled in a discourse with souls. The souls of men, the islanders believe, are perpetually in danger.

Souls can detach themselves from the body and wander about freely. Their adventures are the cause of dreams, and during their journeys a soul may encounter unpleasant adventures and flee to seek refuge with the ancestors. Then of course the person dies.

To counter this, the islanders say that a man should lead a life that so pleases his soul that it does not stray. The soul does not like to be hurried. The Mentawai people constantly remind each other of this with the words: *moile, moile!* ("slowly, slowly!"). By the same token, the soul does not like to be intimidated. Children are rarely scolded or forced to do something. The body that houses the soul should also be attractive, and this is one of the main reasons why the Mentawai people are fond of adornments and tattoos.

The great festival

The great *puliajiat* rituals of the *uma* stretch for weeks and are held periodically to reunite the souls of individuals with their bodies, and to purify the *uma* from danger. The house is decorated, and a feast is prepared; there is singing and dancing for several nights. At the climax of the celebrations the *kerei* sits on the front verandah and summons, in long songs, the souls of all the group's members. To entice them hither, carved birds are hung above the entrance to the house. Mentawai people call these *umat simagere*, "toys of the souls."

— Reimar Schefold

REIMAR SCHEFOLD

MENTAWAI WILDLIFE

Beautiful Song of the Bilou

Quite a number of animal species found on the Mentawai Islands are endemic, and many are also relatively archaic. This curious fact reflects an unusual geological history. About 500,000 years ago the islands were connected to Sumatra by a land bridge (via Nias and the Banyak Islands), but since that time they have been separated from the mainland by a 100-km strait of generally calm seas overlaying a 2,000-m deep submarine trench.

Both the contact and the long isolation are significant. The ancient land bridge allowed a considerable in-migration of plant and animal species, while the subsequent isolation has promoted a high degree of evolutionary divergence. By contrast, the other west Sumatran islands have either—like Simeulue—had no land bridges for at least the past 2 million years, and consequently have a very impoverished wildlife, or—like Nias—had much more recent contact so that their wildlife is quite similar to that of Sumatra.

The Mentawai Islands are thus biologically unique. Among the endemic species found here are monkeys, tree squirrels, flying squirrels, civets, frogs and reptiles, as well as an owl and other birds. Best known among them are the four species of primates. In no other part of the world are so many endemic primates found in such a small area.

Endemic primates

The most often seen (or heard) of the primates is the beautiful black gibbon *Hylobates klossii*, known in most areas of Mentawai as the *bilou*. The song of the female *bilou* has been described as "the most beautiful sound made by any land mammal," and is a thrill to hear in the forest on clear mornings. If you are very lucky, you may glimpse a female gibbon and her family hurling themselves

through the branches during the climax of the song. Another endemic, the Mentawai macaque, is superficially similar to the pig-tailed macaque found over much of Southeast Asia. It roams the forests in groups of up to 30 individuals, barking frequently to maintain contact with other individuals foraging on the ground.

The two other endemic monkeys are exceptional in their form of social organization. They are the only monkeys in the Old World to live in monogamous groups (as do gibbons and humans). The long-tailed *joja* (*Presbytis potenziani*), with its shiny black back and tail, white face-ring and throat, and dark brown belly, lives exclusively in such groups and can most often be found by following the sound of its *bagok* alarm calls, which are duets between the male and female—another unique feature.

The pig-tailed langur or *simakobu* (*Simias concolor*) generally lives in monogamous groups, but appears to form normal monkey troops of 7-15 members in the north of Siberut. The *simakobu* can be either a beautiful golden color or a slate grey, and the ratio of the two varies around the island. The species is particularly notable because it is judged to belong to a genus not known elsewhere, although it may be related to the wierd proboscis monkey that inhabits the mangrove swamps of Borneo.

—*Tony Whitten*

Left: *The great* puliajiat *ritual on Siberut, held to reunite the souls of individuals with their bodies.*
Right: *A baby* bilou. *Photo by Tony Whitten.*

Siberut Practicalities

There are two ways of tackling a trip to Siberut —you can go on your own, which requires time and organization, or you can join a 7- or 10-day trekking tour with English-speaking guides from Bukittinggi or Padang. Independent travelers need to speak reasonable Indonesian in order to hire local porters/guides on Siberut. They must also organize their own travel permits with the police (see "Independent Trekking").

There are 2 main coastal towns on Siberut: **Muara Siberut** on the southeast coast and **Sikabaluan** in the northeast. Muara Siberut is the larger of the two and is the major point of entry of tour groups from the mainland; it has a simple *losmen* and restaurant. Sikabaluan is a pleasant place with long, unspoilt beaches, but does not yet have a hotel. It is possible, however, to stay with local people, who are mainly transmigrasi settlers and fishermen from Sumatra. There are plenty of foodstalls in the market selling Sumatran delicacies, a welcome relief after days of campfire cooking on the trail.

The point of visiting the island, however, is to trek inland to some of the Mentawai villages. **Rokdok**, a government village 4-5 hours upriver from Muara Siberut by motorized longboat, and **Madobat** a further 2 hours upriver, are the two places from which to begin a trek. One particularly good village to visit is **Siatanusa**, a hard 5-hour walk from Rokdok. The chief and his wife,

Baukere Terese, are hospitable and enjoy company. Ask to see the sago stands and offer to help them process the sago.

The Mentawai do not expect cash payment for staying in the *uma*, or family house, but a gift of tobacco will be gratefully accepted. Bring along your own food. Tobacco is still a form of currency among the Mentawai and they greatly appreciate cigarettes. Bring several cartons for the trip—you will feel like a vending machine! Torches, batteries, cheap pen-knives and earrings also make welcome gifts. Many Mentawai have tropical sores, so administering strong antiseptic cream is appreciated.

People do not mind being photographed but it is polite to ask before you shoot. Mentawaians are very photogenic, so bring plenty of film. The damp conditions are a major problem. Bring a watertight container.

The hiking is quite tough. Sturdy trekking shoes are vital. The terrain in the jungle is rough and very muddy. There are slippery logs and rivers to cross. Leeches and mosquitoes are a constant nuisance. So be warned! This is not one for the faint-hearted.

It gets very wet in the jungle, so the rule is to wear one set of clothes while trekking, which quickly get damp and muddy, and to keep a change of dry clothes for the *uma*. Bring a small pack and be sure it is lined with a plastic bag to keep out the water. A flashlight is essential. It gets cold at night, so bring warm clothing.

Because Mentawai life is organized around the great jungle rivers, it is important to observe certain customs. You can wash and bathe in the rivers, but do not strip off. The Mentawai would find this insulting. A sarong or swimsuit will suffice. However toilet matters are strictly for the bush.

GETTING THERE AND BACK

No scheduled flights are available at present, but it may be possible to fly on charter planes from Padang's Tabing Airport to Rokot on Sipora. Check with Merpati in Padang, Jl. Pemuda 45, tel: 27908. From Sipora you can catch a motor boat to Muara Siberut. Chartering boats in the islands is expensive.

Most visitors head by boat from Padang to Muara Siberut. The best way of getting there is on a small passenger ferry, the venerable KM Rezeki, from Padang's Muara harbor. The ferry departs twice a week from Padang, Mon and Thurs at 8 pm (more or less, *jam karet*). Fare is $6 a person. The boat gets crowded so book well in advance either with travel agents in Padang or at the port itself. The better agents, Pacto and Nitour, are on Jl. Pemuda in Padang. They normally tack on a 10 percent commission for their services. The trip takes 10-12 hours, and if you want some sleep, book a berth in one of the few simple cabins on board. The cabins have four bunks and no bedding, but they allow you to stretch out for a couple of

Siberut Island

SELAT SIBERUT
Muara Sigep
SELAT MENTAWAI
G. Lomajang 280m
G. Simabebe 230m
G. Simapitpit 340m
Kagologolo
Muara Sikabaluan
Sikabaluan
S. Sikabaluan
Silogui
Siberut Reserve
G. Sinolop 280m
Muara Saibi
Muara Simatalu
Saudainu
SAMUDRA INDONESIA
Sakubo
G. Taitaitaibe 280m
Rokdok
Muara Siberut
Sabulubbek
Poarat
G. Katkatet 300m
Simansih
G. Posuk 310m
Semangkat
N
Sabatti
P. MASOKUT
P. KARANGMAJAT
0   10   20   30 km

hours; otherwise it's push and shove with the crowd below deck. Bring your own food and drink as there are no meals served on board. Report to the police station on arrival; you'll be accosted by "guides" at the boat pier who will show you how to get around.

For the return to Padang, the boat departs Muara Siberut on Tues and Fri at 8 am, stopping for a couple of hours at Sikabaluan to pick up passengers. You can disembark here, have a meal and take a stroll along the picturesque beach. Small motor boats shuttle people to and from the ferry for $1 round trip. The beach is a 10-minute walk from the harbor.

ACCOMMODATION

There is only one basic guesthouse in Muara Siberut. Cost is $1 per person in shared rooms. There is a small restaurant nearby serving simple Indonesian fare. In the villages, you sleep on the floor of the covered veranda in the *uma*, with the sweet smell of pigs wafting through the boards! An inflatable mattress and a mosquito net are highly recommmended (pick up the latter in any general goods store in Padang for about $4). Payment is up to you. Normally cigarettes or other gifts are sufficient.

TOURS

If you don't want to spend lots of time in Padang and Siberut arranging your own trip, then a tour is ideal. The guide will organize travel permits, ferry tickets, inland transport, porters and provisions for the trip, leaving you to savor this unique experience. Be prepared, nevertheless, for some long, hard walks on muddy, slippery paths and some pretty basic accommodations and food. If the idea of leeches turns you off, then better stay away!

Bukittinggi, 2 hours from Padang, is the best place to book a tour at reasonable prices. When tourists are in short supply, you frequently get hassled here, as every restaurant and hotel is eager to offer its own services. This presents a problem of choice. Be aware that the guides themselves are little more than young adventurers out to make a fast buck. Sadly, few of them know anything about the Mentawai, let alone the rainforests.

The best way is to put together a small group yourself, meet a few guides and choose one you like and trust, rather than joining up with whatever group happens to be leaving. More often than not it is simply a case of being able to get on with the guide and the others in the group. Go with a small group; more than 6 people is pushing it. In any event, insist that you meet everyone in the group before you leave Bukittinggi. Personality clashes on a trip as tough as this can ruin it.

Tours start at $100 per person for 10 days with a group of more than 6 people, rising to $135 per person if the group is smaller. For a 7-day trip expect to pay $70. A 7-day trip is not recommended as it takes 3 days to get into the interior and back from Padang, and that leaves a limited amount of time for enjoying the Mentawai hospitality.

More luxurious tours are also available in Padang. A travel agent specializing in cruises to the Mentawai islands is **PT Nusa Mentawai**, which have offices at Jl. Batang Arau 88 Blok B/9, tel: 24776, 23363. They offer well-organized up-market tours of 5 to 10 days which can be tailored to suit your interests. They have a ferry with 12 beds (maximum 25 passengers) and provide good service throughout. For a group of 3 to 6 persons they charge $440 per head for 5 days and $635 for 10 days.

INDEPENDENT TREKKING

If you decide to travel to Siberut independently you should plan to spend at least $125 on basic expenses. You will need to pay for the ferry, for accommodations in Muara Siberut and for the hire of a longboat and porters to the interior. You also need to buy provisions for the trip in Padang or Bukittinggi. This involves quite a bit of hassle and running around. However, the advantage is that you have the freedom to go even further off the beaten track, and to spend as much time as you want in each place. A survival knowledge of Indonesian is essential.

First go to the police station on Jl. Prof. M. Yamin in Padang and enquire about a *surat jalan* (permit). These are issued free of charge. You will need 2 small photos and photocopies of your passport. Then try the tourist office on Jl. Khatib Sulaiman for more information on the latest regulations governing independent visits to the islands.

Purchase all your supplies before leaving Sumatra. There are great markets in both Bukittinggi and Padang. Bring your own cooking and eating utensils, as well as plenty of cigarettes and other gifts.

Longboats can be hired from the owner of the *losmen* in Muara Siberut for the trip upriver to Rokdok, $75 round trip. Arrange a time for the boat to come back and collect you. If you are on your own, you can also try to negotiate for a place on a longboat chartered by a tour group going upriver. You can hire Mentawai porters to take you into the jungle from Rokdok for $2-3 a day. Most of the younger Mentawai speak Bahasa Indonesia.

WEATHER

There are no real seasons. Expect it to rain and most days you won't be disappointed. Just like an English summer! However the sun makes frequent guest appearances. There is plenty of thick mud all year round, so prepare to wallow.

— *Richard Davidson and Nicola Robertson*

PART VI

Introducing Riau

The name "Riau" once applied only to the chain of islands guarding the entrance to the Malacca Strait south and west of Singapore. In 1958, however, the unwieldy province of "Central Sumatra" which had been created during the Indonesian revolution (comprising what are now Jambi, West Sumatra and Riau) was subdivided, and a new Riau Province was created that included not only the neighboring Lingga Archipelago, but also a huge chunk of the Sumatran mainland and a few hundred remote islands lying in the South China Sea to the north of Borneo (the Natuna, Anambas, Serasan and Tambelan groups).

As a province Riau is thus an artificial creation composed of many disparate parts. Its land mass is huge (94,561 sq km—about the size of Hungary) and it comprises not only 3,214 islands and four of Sumatra's largest rivers, but the greatest expanse of tropical rainforest on the island, hundreds of vital sea lanes teeming with fish, and thousands of kilometers of sparsely-inhabited coastline. To top it off, Riau contains the most productive oil fields in Indonesia—pumping half the nation's crude, some 650,000 barrels a day.

The Riau mainland is a densely-jungled lowland formed over many millennia by alluvial deposits brought by the Rokan, Siak, Kampar and Inderagiri rivers—all of which begin high in the western Bukit Barisan range and meander some 300 to 550 km eastward to the coast. The lowlands are poorly drained, however, and are not particularly suitable for agriculture. Only about 2 million people—Malays and migrants from Java and Kalimantan—inhabit small settlements along the rivers. For the traveler this is not a particularly exciting area, as the sights are few and far between and facilities are primitive.

The Riau Islands, on the other hand, are one of Indonesia's best kept travel secrets.

Easy to reach from Singapore on fast and comfortable hydrofoils, the islands of Batam and Bintan have good facilities and beaches. They are jumping-off points, moreover, for romantic excursions by slow passenger ferry, chartered fishing boat or private yacht to a thousand tropical idylls that have changed little since the days of Joseph Conrad. This is the realm of the *orang laut* or "sea people"—former pirates and traders who have settled in villages perched on stilts above the shore.

Change is coming rapidly to some areas. Batam and Bintan are currently the scene of a multi-billion-dollar investment fever that will undoubtedly spill over to nearby islands. One has the feeling, nevertheless, that within this seemingly endless archipelago there will always be more than a few islands that manage to give the modern world the slip.

— *Eric Oey*

Island Riau

Overleaf: *Trikora Beach on Bintan Island.* **Left:** *A Malay woman on Singkep. Photos by Jill Gocher.*

BATAM

Singapore's Neighbor and 'Twin'

Batam is the Indonesian island just opposite Singapore—an island nation and former British colony that has blossomed in recent years to become Southeast Asia's most dynamic and prosperous economy. Batam is so close in fact—just 20 km to the southeast across a narrow strait—that the tips of Singapore's gleaming skyscrapers are visible on the horizon, and the latter's bright lights illuminate the sky at night like some futuristic film set.

Batam is only slightly smaller than Singapore, and would in fact seem to share many of the latter's geographical features—yet this sleepy, half-forgotten island was until recently considered to be of little or no value. Like so many islands in the Riau Archipelago, its porous red-clay soils were covered in thick jungle and ringed with inhospitable mangrove swamps, and its few inhabitants lived in scattered fishing villages around the coast. Many

were descended from fierce *orang laut* sea nomads and pirates who centuries ago served as sailors and fighting men in the navies of Malay kingdoms like Srivijaya and Malacca.

Batam suddenly began to take on a much greater significance in the late 1960s, however, when the head of Indonesia's oil monopoly, Pertamina, decided to develop the island as a base for its massive exploration and supply activities. The advantages of this were clear —Batam's cheap land and labor would reduce costs, while its proximity to Singapore would ensure quick access to the latter's efficient facilities and technical know-how. Following this lead, and watching with considerable envy as Singapore made rapid economic strides during the early 1970s, the Indonesian government at this time decided that Batam should in fact be developed as "another Singapore"—a regional center for industry, shipping and communications that might one day even rival the latter.

The 'Growth Triangle'

For a number of reasons, Batam's development was very slow in getting off the ground. A lack of basic infrastructure meant for many years that most things could be done more easily and cheaply in Singapore. The situation changed dramatically in the late 1980s, however, when Singapore's booming economy in effect outpaced its population growth, and this tiny island republic of 3 million people began to experience severe labor shortages—particularly in the labor-intensive manufacturing sector. All of a sudden, companies began to look to Indonesia and Malaysia, and Batam was once again mentioned as a possible site for industrial development.

Much to their credit, it was Singapore's own government which took the lead in convincing all parties concerned that Batam could be made viable. In 1989, Singapore's deputy Prime Minister, Goh Chok Tong, proposed the linkage of Johor (in southern Malaysia), Singapore and the Riau Islands in a synergistic "Growth Triangle"—a free-trade economic zone that would benefit all three areas. In the words of Singapore's Minister for Trade: "Given the right policies and the willingness to work together, all three can prosper much more together than individually." This idea was enthusiastically received and several multi-billion-dollar joint ventures between private Indonesian and government-owned Singaporean concerns were signed within the following months.

These days, Batam's idyllic tranquility is shattered by the incessant buzz of chain saws and the thud of pile-drivers as stretches of virgin jungle are cleared to make way for massive industrial estates, tourist resorts and residential towns. Thousands of Singaporeans make the quick, 25-minute hop across the straits in high-speed hydrofoils every day, and Batam seems destined to become practically an extension of its better-developed neighbor—as more and more companies move the labor-intensive portion of their operations here.

The immediate plan is that Singapore is to provide expertise and investment to establish basic infrastructure and primary ventures in industry, commerce and tourism that will enable the island to achieve a certain "critical mass" in the eyes of private investors. After that, Batam's natural advantages of cheap land, labor and energy will propel its development, and will in turn feed back into Singapore's own high-tech service economy.

Careful planning, huge investments

The key to Batam's success is seen in careful planning, and much of the island has already been carved up for various projects. The entire east coast is being developed into a modern container facility known as Asia Port that will accommodate ships of up to 150,000 tons. Next to it, Hang Nadim International Airport (named after a 15th-century admiral of Malacca's war fleet who ruled the island) is being expanded to handle jumbo jets.

In the center of the island, a self-contained 500-ha industrial park complete with housing estates for workers is being built—the basic

Opposite: *Batam has a well-developed road network.* **Below:** *Feverish construction work continues around the clock all over the island.*

JILL GOCHER

infrastructure of roads, water, sewage, telecommunications and electricity for this project alone is costing US$600 million. So far, 29 corporations, including many Japanese, American and European firms, have already set up manufacturing operations in the park's first phase (50 ha), which is now complete.

Tanjung Uncang peninsula, at the western tip of the island, will serve as a complex for the processing of timber, rubber, palm oil, tin, bauxite, petroleum and other Sumatran resources. Reservoirs and water treatment plants are in place, and an excellent network of roads crisscrosses the island.

Perhaps the jewel in the crown, however, is the planned "New Town" at Batam Centre —an entire city with office blocks, markets, shopping centers and suburban residental neighborhoods that is springing up around the beautiful bay of Teluk Tering, facing across to Singapore. This will be the island's administrative hub, with a polytechnic institute and training center planned.

Indonesian red tape is being slashed for investors, and foreigners commute from Singapore with a minimum of fuss—there are even plans afoot to start a helicopter service. Factory workers, many from the poorer regions of Indonesia such as Java, have started flooding in and live in purpose-built housing a few minutes' walk from their worksite.

Much of the capital needed to realize Batam's ambitious plans will come from abroad, and the Batam Industrial Development Board—an autonomous body that has been given a free hand by Indonesia's President Suharto—is bending over backwards to attract investors. Cash-rich firms plan to use Batam as a manufacturing base in the heart of Southeast Asia, currently the world's fastest growing region economically. A little-advertised attraction is the fact that manufacturers are able to capitalize on the Indonesian Generalized System of Preferences (GSP) allowances for export to the United States, the EEC and Japan. In 1986-7, Indonesia used less that 40 percent of its GSP allocation for the EEC, which allows 10 to 16 percent tax relief on a wide range of products.

Meanwhile, Batam is already becoming a popular tourist getaway. In 1990, more than half a million Singaporeans took the ferry across to Batam to relax, shop, eat and buy duty-free liquor and cigarettes. The island's northeast coast around Nongsa is earmarked as a massive, 350-ha tourist resort that will transform it, along with nearby Bintan, into Singapore's playground. A dozen or more luxury hotels and four golf courses are scheduled to open here by 1993.

Batam's main attraction is its unspoilt beaches, but *kelong*-style seafood restaurants built on stilts over the ocean are also popular. Batam's best known attraction, however, is Radio Ramako—a pop station whose 24-hour "Amazing Zoo" and "Coast 100" broadcasts

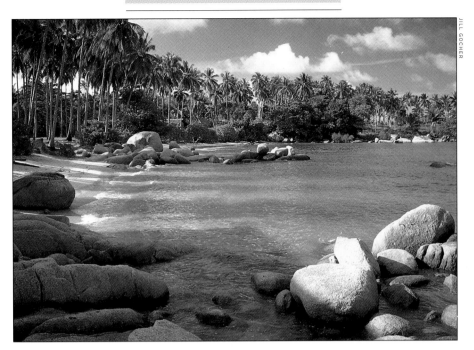

are much beloved by Singaporeans. Their blend of fast music and faster-talking DJs has indeed given Singapore's staid, state-controlled radio station a run for their advertisers' money, and the latter has been forced to counter with a similar 24-hour pop station called "Perfect Ten." More than 100 loyal listeners troop into Radio Ramako every day to meet the DJs and tour the modest facilities.

A day trip to Batam

Apart from the beaches and the seafood restaurants there's really not much to see and do on Batam. It is interesting, nevertheless, to drive through the jungles, visit the coastal Malay kampongs, and imagine what these places will all look like in a few years.

A good starting point is at the ferry landing in **Nagoya**—formerly known as Lubuk Baja ("Pirates' Waterhole") and today a busy trading town largely populated by Chinese. It is impossible to get lost here as there are only 3 main streets; have a quick look around at the shops and the market, then stop in at Vihara Budhi Bhakti Buddhist temple on the eastern outskirts of town, where busloads of Singaporean worshippers fill the air each day with the pungent smoke of incense.

A few km to the southeast of Nagoya is **Batam Centre**, site of a massive commercial and residential development. A drive around this beautiful bay will give you an idea of the scale of things to come. Continue on to the northeast coast at **Batu Besar** for a seafood lunch. This is a pleasant Malay fishing village set on a sandy beach, with several seafood restaurants built on long piers out over the water. The food is excellent, though the prices are strictly Singaporean (see "Riau Island Practicalities"). The airport is close by and jets roar past every few minutes; after lunch, walk down the coast through swaying palms past typical Malay-style houses on stilts.

After lunch, if the weather is fine, head north to **Nongsa** for a swim on the safe, sandy beaches by the new luxury hotels. At Nongsa Beach Hotel you can hire jet scooters, and most of the others rent snorkeling equipment. The waters are crystal clear and there's plenty of shade.

Late in the late afternoon, head for the ferry terminal at **Sekupang** on the northwest coast. If you have time, loop south across the island past the 100-year-old banyan tree just opposite the Batam Industrial Park construction site. Your final stop could be Batam's Radio Ramako station just outside Sekupang, which welcomes visitors—but leave a bit of time before boarding the ferry for Sekupang's excellent duty-free shops. Here you can buy practically everything, from Swiss Cherry Brandy at S$45, to dried salted anchovies (*ikan bilis*) at only S$12 a kilo!

— *Periplus Editions*

Above: *One of Nongsa's fine beaches.*

BINTAN

Sleepy Island on the Edge of Change

For several centuries Bintan played a pivotal role in Malay history. It was here, in the early 16th century, that the deposed ruler of Malacca took refuge after the Portuguese had driven him from his city. The inhabitants of Bintan at this time were not in fact Malays, but *orang laut* sea nomads who were fiercely loyal to the king. Thereafter the court moved several times—to Johor and to Lingga—but a branch of the royal family eventually returned to settle on Pulau Penyengat, a tiny island just off the southwest coast of Bintan. This was where, at the beginning of the 19th century, Thomas Stamford Raffles sought and received permission to lease the nearby island of Singapore for the British crown.

In the 19th century, Penyengat became an important center for Malay and Islamic scholarship. Imams from faraway Mecca taught in the royal mosque, and over 60 major works of Malay literature were composed here. Even today, something of the royal atmosphere remains in these tiny islands, and it is not difficult to imagine oneself transported back in time a hundred years or more to a slower, more elegant age.

Like neighboring Batam, Bintan is now the focus of multi-billion-dollar development schemes that are designed to drag the island into the 21st century within the next several years. These include a huge industrial park and a mega-resort with 20 luxury hotels and 10 golf courses. Direct jetfoil services from Singapore will start in 1992, meaning that the commute across the straits will be cut in half to about 45 minutes. Believe it or not, some 7.4 million tourists are projected to visit Bintan by the year 2000! At the moment, however all of this is but a gleam in the eyes of planners and investors, and the Bintan you see today is much as it has been for centuries—a rustic and sparsely-inhabited island with a few scattered fishing villages and several old Chinese trading settlements on the coast.

Tanjung Pinang

The largest town and main point of entry on Bintan is Tanjung Pinang ("Areca Palm Cape") —a picturesque, predominantly Chinese trading community that spreads across low hills bordering a sheltered bay on the island's southwestern shore. This is a delightful place to visit, if only on a weekend jaunt from Singapore. You can make a leisurely inspection of the town on foot—starting from the clock tower in the middle of Jl. Merdeka, Tanjung Pinang's main street.

Shipping agents, goldsmiths, restaurants and cassette shops line both sides of this broad and busy avenue. Directly opposite the clock tower is Vihara Bhatra Sasana temple, featuring a statue of Kuan Yin—the Chinese goddess of mercy—in the central altar. From the temple, walk north along Jl. Pasar past the central market place; villagers come in

from the countryside on weekends to sell pots of wild honey here—advertised by cages full of angry, buzzing bees—as well as seasonal fruits and vegetables. Sometimes fire eaters selling patent medicines will put on a show for the crowd.

Duck into a rabbit warren of little alleyways to your right. This is Pasar Baru, the "New Market," where tiny stalls sell clothes and plastic household goods. At the back, next to the water's edge, is a huge fish market where boats unload their daily catch of swordfish, sharks, groupers, squids, prawns, shellfish and dark, plump mangrove crabs.

Heading further north on Jl. Pasar, the street becomes an elevated walkway leading through a maze of wooden houses and shops built on stilts out over the mouth of the Riau River. Little gangways lead off to scores of houses on either side, and at high tide the sea rushes in so that you are standing just above the surface of the water. On both sides are small provision shops and foodstalls selling dried salted fish, prawns, crackers, clothing and steaming bowls of Chinese noodles; at the end of the walkway is Pelantar II pier.

Just before the end, duck down a narrow gangway to your left that leads to a small Chinese temple. Color photographs of visiting trance mediums piercing themselves with swords and spike balls cover one wall of the temple. Just in front is an open-air theater for Chinese opera performances that perches

out over the harbor. Beneath the opera stage you can see brightly-painted dragon boats that are brought out once a year for the midsummer festival races.

At the end of the main pier (Pelantar II), you can catch a sampan or motorboat across the wide mouth of the Riau River to **Senggarang**, visible just opposite. You disembark here at the end of a long jetty in Kampung Cina leading to long walkways that run for several km and connect hundreds of houses built on stilts above the water. Most of the houses are inhabited by Teochew Chinese; you can peek in and see the family altars as you walk gingerly down the long and rotting planks to a number of shops at the end.

Once onto dry land, turn left and follow a concrete pathway to the Aw clan house—the ruins of a 2-story temple whose crumbling walls are completely suspended in mid-air—held there by the aerial roots of an ancient banyan tree. Set directly beneath the ruins is a new concrete box structure that has been erected by a wealthy Aw clansman from Medan to house the ancestral altar.

Continue along this same path past a salt warehouse to Vihara Dharma Sasana, a compex of three temples set side-by-side facing the estuary. The temple in the middle has an ornate roof crowned by a pair of dragons and is said to be 200 years old; unfortunately, its beautiful wooden doors have been crudely repainted during a recent restoration. In the hallway is a tank of live turtles, and a stone tiger leaps out of the wall. The temple has an air of austere serenity, in contrast to the newer and more cluttered temple to its right. The smallest of the three shrines is dedicated to Toa Pek Kong, the deity of the soil who is synonymous with luck; people come here to

Opposite: Sunset over Tanjung Pinang harbor.
Above, right: Sampans shuttle passengers from Tanjung Pinang to Senggarang and Penyengat.
Above, right: Tanjung Pinang street scene.

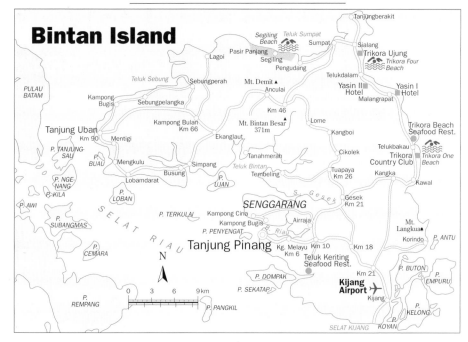

make offerings before building a house.

Back in Tanjung Pinang, stroll up to the top of the hill in the late afternoon—to the colonial-style Catholic Church on Jl. Diponegoro. From here, you obtain a splendid view out across the town and over the bay to Penyengat. On the shore just below the hill is Jl. Hang Tuah—a favorite spot for local residents to take in the evening air in a small park with a sculpture of a giant seashell and sea cows (dugongs) cast out of concrete.

Touring the island

A short ride to the eastern edge of Tanjung Pinang brings you to the **Kandil Riau Museum** on Jl. Katamso, a privately-owned establishment with a dark, dusty interior housing a rich collection of local artifacts and memorabilia from the 18th and 19th centuries. Among the things you will see here is part of a Chinese junk from the Ming period, a Malay cannon, wind instruments and ceremonial drums (nobat) formerly used to install the Bugis viceroys, and a dinner plate owned by Raja Haji—a local Bugis leader who was killed fighting the Dutch at Malacca in 1784. Old swords and paintings of the Bugis-Malay rulers adorn the wall.

Several km further east you can stop in **Kampung Melayu** (km 6) and pay homage to the grave of Sultan Sulaiman, the first ruler of the restored 18th-century Bugis-Malay kingdom. From here you can walk down to the water's edge and hire a sampan to take you up the **Riau River** ($10 for a half day) to the graves of Daeng Marewah and Daeng Cellak—Bugis brothers from Sulawesi who helped recapture the kingdom from Raja Kecil, a Minangkabau adventurer. The boatmen know all the sites; stop along the way at Kota Piring ("Plate Fort") on a tiny island in midstream—built in the 18th century by the Bugis ruler, Raja Haji. The popular name derives from the many Chinese plates that were once set into the walls; little remains today apart from a few broken embankments. Bring hats, drinks and sunblock.

About two hours and 60 km east of Tanjung Pinang are the white sands of **Trikora Beach**. Stretching for 10 km up and down the eastern coast of Bintan, this series of lovely beaches is as yet undiscovered by Western tourists, though there is a small hotel here and much bigger ones are planned nearby. During the week the beaches are completely deserted; on Saturday afternoons groups of noisy Singaporeans troop in, followed on Sunday mornings by the local crowd from Tanjung Pinang. By early Sunday afternoon, however, the crowds disperse and the beach is tranquil for another week.

Trikora actually has four main beaches that are numbered from south to north. Of these, Trikora Four—the last one as you travel up the coast—is particularly recommended. After lunching at the Trikora Beach Restaurant (Rumah Makan Pantai Trikora) in Telukbakau, continue up the main road until you reach a sweeping, sandy-white shoreline stretching as far as the eye can see—framed by swaying palms and foaming breakers. Wonderfully safe for children, the bottom slopes out very gradually so that 50 feet from shore you are only in up to your waist.

Kuta Beach has *nothing* on this place. Small stalls by the creek sell fresh coconuts, snacks and fruits, as well as simple meals on weekends. Pick your way over a mountain of trash and swim well away from the creek, as it empties raw sewage into the ocean. The main drawback though is sand fleas, which can leave bites lasting for days—but a smelly concoction of coconut oil and onions is said to keep them (and your companions) at bay. With more time on your hands, you can continue along this road to **Segiling Beach** on the north coast. This is where a huge, multi-billion-dollar beach resort is planned to shoot up in the mid-1990s.

On the way back, cut inland via the main road, which skirts around **Mt. Bintan Besar** —the island's highest point at 371 m. Several historical and legendary figures are believed buried here, including Wan Empok and Wan Malini—two old widows whose rice harvest turned to gold when the first Malay ruler descended atop the hill. Hang Nadim, the famous 15th century Malay admiral, is also said to be buried here. A guide can be hired locally if you want to climb the hill, which is overgrown with secondary jungle and has a trail that is difficult to follow. The ascent takes about an hour if you are fit; legend has it that a dragon awaits on the summit.

Offshore islands

From Tanjung Pinang you can catch ferries to the neighboring islands. Rempang and Galang are two sizeable islands to the south and west of Tanjung Pinang. Both were used after WW II as detention centers for Japanese soldiers, who complained bitterly about the Robinson Crusoe-like conditions. Today Rempang is a camp for Vietnamese boat people, administered by the UN. Pulau Mantang, south of Bintan, is home to several hundred *orang laut*, many of whom still lead a semi-nomadic existence. Buton (named after the Sultanate of Buton in southeast Sulawesi), Siulung and Kelong are inhabited by a few Malay-Bugis families who depend on the sea for their livelihood.

After days or even weeks exploring these islands, where things have changed so little over the past century, it is quite a shock to crossover the narrow straits to gleaming, modern Singapore. It's hard to imagine that this too was but another island dotted with tiny fishing villages not very long ago.

— *Periplus Editions*

Above: *The Chinese temples at Senggarang.*

PULAU PENYENGAT

Tiny Cultural Capital of the Malay World

Pulau Penyengat ("Wasp Island") is a sliver of an island out in the bay just opposite Tanjung Pinang. During the 19th century this tiny island—just 2,500 m by 750 m—was home to about 9,000 people and became for a time the cultural capital of the Malay world. Some 60 literary works were composed here, including the famous *Tuhfat al-Nafis*, a Bugis-Malay history by Raja Ali Haji, and the island's rulers were famed throughout the region for their Islamic piety and learning.

In the late 18th century Penyengat was an outpost in defensive works thrown up around Bintan by a Bugis viceroy known as Raja Haji. In this period the Malay sultanate of Johor was controlled by a line of Bugis rulers who had usurped the throne and were absorbing other Bugis into the Malay elite through marriage and acculturation. In 1804 the Johor ruler, Sultan Mahmud, gave Penyengat to his Bugis wife, Raja Hamidah, as part of her dowry. In doing so, he effectively divided the island realm in two—her son thereafter ruled the Riau Islands from Penyengat, while his half-brother ruled in Lingga to the south.

It was this division between rival brothers in Lingga and Penyengat that was so cleverly exploited by Raffles in 1819. In return for the protection of the British crown and a sizeable stipend, Raffles convinced the Penyengat prince to grant him the island of Singapore in perpetuity. Partly as a result, the period that followed was a "Golden Age" for Penyengat. Ruled by a sophisticated Bugis elite and supported financially and politically by the British, Penyengat drew upon the rich Muslim Malay cultural heritage and attracted scholars from as far away as Mecca.

About 2,000 Malays now live on Penyengat, many of them tracing their ancestry back to the Bugis-Malay nobility of the 18th and 19th centuries. This is a fascinating place to visit—not only to view the lovely mosque and the remains of several 19th-century colonial-style mansions that reflect the prosperity of the island's former rulers, but also to breathe in the relaxed air of aristocratic Malay village life. A network of paved pathways crisscrosses the island, and with a bit of imagination you may think you have stepped into a time warp as you stroll around the island.

Although the main settlements in the 19th century were on the far side of Penyengat,

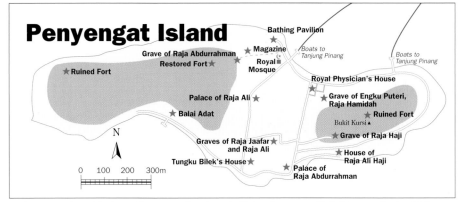

Penyengat Island

Bathing Pavilion

Grave of Raja Abdurrahman ★
Restored Fort ★
★ Magazine
■ Royal
Mosque
Boats to
Tanjung Pinang
Boats to
Tanjung Pinang

★ Ruined Fort

Royal Physician's House

Palace of Raja Ali ★
★ Grave of Engku Puteri,
Raja Hamidah
★ Balai Adat
★ Ruined Fort
Bukit Kursi ▲

N

★ Grave of Raja Haji

Graves of Raja Jaafar ★
and Raja Ali
★ House of
Raja Ali Haji
Tungku Bilek's House ★
★ Palace of
Raja Abdurrahman

0   100   200   300m

facing away from Tanjung Pinang, today they face the town and may be reached in 15 minutes by motorized sampan from Tanjung Pinang's main pier. Late afternoon is the best time to visit, as it can be extremely hot at midday. Moreover, the afternoon sun casts a warm, romantic glow over the ruins and the mosque that makes them even more appealing. Start around 3:00 pm and allow several hours to walk around the island.

A walking tour

There are two main piers on Penyengat—ask to be dropped at the one to the left (east). At the end of the pier, a path to the right leads through an attractive *kampung* bordering the shoreline; unfortunately, many of the charming wooden houses are now being replaced by whitewashed concrete ones. A few hundred meters down on the left is a path leading to the covered grave of Engku Puteri, also known as Raja Hamidah—the original Bugis "owner" of Pulau Penyengat. Her grave is considered *keramat* (miracle working) and is visited by people who ask for help or make a wish by tying a yellow cloth over the headstone (yellow is the color of Malay royalty).

Buried outside the mausoleum is the 19th-century scholar and historian, Raja Ali Haji, a grandson of Raja Haji and author of the *Tuhfat al-Nafis* ("The Precious Gift"), a comprehensive history of the Malay world from the 17th to 19th centuries that served to justify the usurpation of the Malay throne by his Bugis ancestors. He is also well-known on Penyengat for his *gurindam duabelas*, 12 short poems of Islamic inspiration.

Return to the main path and continue on past the ruins of the court physician's house (only the outer walls remain). Turn left here onto a path which leads across the island, and left again to climb up Bukit Kursi ("Chair Hill"). On top of the hill is the grave of Raja

Haji, who controlled this area in the 18th century but was killed at Malacca by the Dutch in 1784. His remains were allowed to be brought back for burial in the 19th century, on condition that the grave was not to become a pilgrimage site. The grave of a revered Muslim scholar, Habib Syaik, was therefore placed alongside it so that Raja Haji's grave could be visited without arousing suspicion. Near to the tomb is an authentic 18th-century Bugis gravestone shaped like a huge egg.

Continue on to the southern shore of the island, to have a look at the remains of Raja Abdurrahman's palace. To the east is the former house of Raja Ali Haji, while to the west you will find a 2-story mansion which once belonged to Tungku Bilek ("Lady Room"), so-named because she spent all her time in her room. It stands forlornly in a compound by the sea and looks like an English country home, complete with wrought-iron decoration above the main gate. Further west you pass the new Balai Adat cultural hall used on ceremonial occasions, and a small fishing village. Facing the open sea to the south, this is where the island's 19th century inhabitants lived; at a later date the Dutch compelled the rulers to move to the Tanjung Pinang side, where they could keep a closer eye on them.

Walk back to the north shore from here along the main path which crosses the island past Raja Ali's palace. Make a slight detour along the way to visit the graves of Raja Jaafar and his son, Raja Ali, who is remembered for his strict adherence to Islam. He forbade gambling and cockfighting, the mixing of unmarried men and women, and the wearing of gold and silk. He paid visiting religious scholars to teach at the mosque, and even instituted a dawn watch to ensure that people arose for morning prayers. His covered grave,

Opposite: *Malay houses lining Penyengat's shore.*

painted a pale yellow, has a tranquil atmosphere, with two water tanks outside.

Raja Ali's palace and mosque

The stately palace of Raja Ali further down this path has fallen into ruin and been overgrown by jungle, but is slowly being restored. The southern entrance has a spendid split gate with huge swirls faintly visible on the sides incorporating European, Arabic, Javanese and Indonesian motifs. A canal once lead up here from the sea, but was filled in to prevent mosquitoes. You can climb around the grounds and up the guard tower for a view, but be careful not to fall into the royal loo!

Walk out of the gates and on to the yellow-and-green Royal Mosque at the end of the lane. Completed in 1844, the mosque is supported inside (in the Javanese style) by four huge pillars and has four Moghul minarets, reached by steeply-winding staircases. The roof has 13 cupolas that look like they belong on a European castle, and from a distance the entire complex looks a bit like the palace of Snow White at Disneyland.

Thousands of egg whites were mixed with lime to produce the fine cement that the mosque is constructed of. The magnificently carved cupboards at the entrance contain a valuable library of Islamic books from India, Cairo, Mecca and Medina. A beautiful 17th century Quran is displayed in a glass case; notice the glass chandelier and the intricately carved *mimbar* or pulpit in the main chamber. This mosque was an important center of Muslim Malay learning in the 19th century. (Be modestly dressed when entering—wear long trousers or skirts; no bare arms.)

A small path to the right of the mosque ends at the communal well. To your left here is an attractive, whitewashed stone bathing pavilion. If no one is using it, peep inside to see the well and the stone seats. Then return to the mosque and turn right up a broad, leafy path just after the shops. A hundred meters up on your right you will find an 18th-century powder magazine in whitewashed stone, looking like a small jail. This exquisite building was used to store gunpowder for the island's three forts.

Walk farther up the hill to a large cemetery and look for the tomb of Raja Abdurrahman, the 5th Yamtuan Muda (Bugis viceroy), who originally commissioned the building of the mosque. Continue up the steps on the left hand side of the cemetery and you arrive at an impressive stone fort. This was built in the late 18th century by Raja Haji to fend off a Dutch attack on the Riau River in 1873. Two cannon found during the recent restorations greet the visitor. The fort offers a splendid view of Bintan and the straits to the east. From here it is a short walk back to the pier by the mosque, for the 15-minute boat trip back to Tanjung Pinang.

— Periplus Editions

KARIMUN

Westernmost Island in the Riau Chain

Karimun is a languid, out-of-the-way island with a colorful past. During the Srivijaya period (7th to 13th centuries) and under the later sultanate of Malacca (1400-1511) it was a strategic base occupied by boat-dwelling *orang laut* who helped the Malay ruler control access to the straits. During the 18th and 19th centuries, Karimun was occasionally claimed by those wishing to challenge the authority of Riau's kings. A Minangkabau *lebai* (mosque official) laid claim to it in the latter part of the 18th century, pompously behaving like "an independent sovereign." Sultan Husein of Singapore sent his people here to mine tin in the 1820s, but under the terms of an 1824 treaty between the Dutch and the British, the island reverted to Dutch rule and his men were forced to return home.

Visiting Karimun

Karimun lies about 60 km due west of Batam and is not on any travel itineraries. There's little to do here apart from wandering about the main town of Tanjung Balai, or exploring the lush countryside. Much of the island is hilly and covered in jungle, making a mountain bike one of the most practical and enjoyable ways of getting around. If you don't have a bike, the next best way to get around is on ancient, swaying buses which ply the island's bumpy tracks. The buses cover just the populated southern part of the island; to travel up north means hiring a car and driver.

Tanjung Balai is the main entry point—a pleasant little town on the southeastern tip of the island. Like many other trading towns in the Riau Islands, it is largely populated by Teochew Chinese. The island's main road runs west of here along the coast past a secluded cove to **Meral**, site of an imposing Chinese clan house, now crumbling with age.

From Meral, the road continues to **Pantai**

Left: *The royal mosque on Pulau Penyengat.*
Right: *A woman in the Tanjung Balai market.*

Pelawan, a sandy beach on the west coast, through scattered village settlements and clove gardens set in rolling, forest-clad hills. Carpets of cloves are laid out to dry in the sun by the roadside and their sweet smell hangs in the air. The cloves vary in color from lime green to rust brown, depending on the stage of drying.

As Karimun guards the southern entrance to Asia's most important waterway, it is not surprising that an ancient Sanskrit inscription has been found. The inscription is carved on a large granite outcropping at **Pasir Panjang** on the island's northwest coast, and is unusually cryptic. It simply reads: "The illustrious feet of the illustrious Gautama, the Mahayanist, who set the sphere in motion." This has been taken to refer to an armillary sphere —an instrument used to determine the position of the planets—supposedly given to a local *orang laut* chief named Gautama as a sign of favor by the ruler of Malayu (Jambi) or Srivijaya (Palembang). In fact the inscription is more likely a piece of ancient graffiti left by a passing Buddhist monk, and simply refers to Gautama Buddha, founder of the Buddhist religion. The Buddha's "footsteps" are said to ascend the rock to the left of the inscription in a series of natural, water-worn indentations. Even today the steps are venerated by *orang laut* who bring offerings of food and white flags here.

— *Periplus Editions*

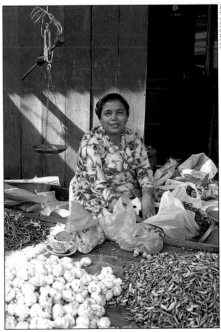

LINGGA ARCHIPELAGO

Enchanting Islands to the South

The Lingga Archipelago is a scattered group of islands that straddles the equator some 50 to 150 kilometers south of Batam and Bintan —about 10 hrs from Tanjung Pinang by slow ferry. The two main islands are Lingga and Singkep; to their north lie a number of smaller ones, of which Sebangka and Bakung are the largest. These make the perfect getaway for diehard romantics: few people here speak English and the foreign visitors you meet can be counted on the fingers of one hand.

The boat ride to Dabo on Singkep Island —the main port of call in the Lingga group— is a particularly enchanting one. The ferry leaves Tanjung Pinang in the late morning and never leaves sight of land as it weaves in and out amongst countless isles set in a calm, shallow sea. Isolated *kelongs*—fishing huts on stilts—jut far out into the ocean; beneath them are huge suspended traps. Scattered

houses, often little more than a few planks, cling to the water's edge and break the monotony of an endless series of tiny, sandy coves with gently swaying palms. Late in the afternoon come the first hazy views of Mt. Daik, a large mountain on Lingga Island that has three jagged teeth at its summit, one of which appears to have broken off at the base. Visible from afar, the mountain is immortalized as a symbol of permanency in Malay poetry, and the island of Lingga actually gets its name from Mt. Daik's remarkable profile (*linggam* means phallus in Sanskrit).

As the evening lengthens, the sea turns a deeper steel blue and the setting sun illuminates a sky filled with ragged grey and white clouds. The boat chugs onward past darkening islands with rocky, jungle-clad shores. Small fires glimmer in the fields behind the settlements, and the muezzin's call to prayer drifts faintly across the water. Darkness falls suddenly—you are now just minutes from the equator—and the houses onshore become twinkling islands of indistinct light.

Visiting Singkep and Lingga

Singkep is a small, flat island pockmarked with huge open-cast tin mines that have been worked now for a century and a half and are all but exhausted. The main town of **Dabo** lies at the foot of a steep hill which makes for a pleasant climb in the early morning. The vegetable and fish markets are close to the harbor and are also best visited early in the morning, when local fishing boats disgorge their catch. Pantai Batu Bedaun, a pretty white-sand beach fringed with palms, is an easy 4-km motorcycle ride south of the town.

The neighboring island of Lingga was the home of Sultan Mahmud, the last effective ruler of the Malay Riau sultanate, who moved his court here in the early 19th century because he feared Dutch retaliation for a pirate attack that he had instigated. The island is lush and spacious, dominated by the towering

and jagged peak of Mt. Daik (1,164 m).

The open-sea crossing in a small boat from Dabo to **Daik** is exhilarating—you are tossed and sprayed by foaming waves. The journey ends in a muddy creek which winds with mysterious intent up through a dense mangrove swamp. The town itself is like something straight out of a Joseph Conrad novel, with little wooden houses that cling precariously to the riverbank.

An hour and a half to the north of Daik on foot are the remains of Sultan Mahmud's palace, which was built a considerable distance from the sea so as to be protected from frequent piratical raids. The island was formerly defended by several earth-and-stone forts bristling with cannon. The best time to visit the palace is the early morning, unless you don't mind the midday heat.

To one side of the *camat* district offices as you leave the town are two huge bronze cannons which date from the late 18th century. The one on the left is *pecah piring* ("the plate breaker") while the one on the right is *padam pelita* ("the lamp extinguisher"). Both names refer to the cannons' fierce reports when fired. A flag in front of the offices flies from a pole set in a cast-iron base bearing the inscription: "W. Macfarlane and Co. Saracen Foundry Glasgow."

Further out of town is Mesjid Jamik, the royal mosque, which is even older than the one on Penyengat. The floor of the mosque is

made of cool white marble, and the great drum which hangs at the entrance dates from the 19th century. Inside is a beautifully carved *mimbar* produced by the same craftsman who made the one at Penyengat. The story goes that he was later put to death so that no other ruler could own such a beautiful piece of work. Behind the mosque is the grave of Sultan Mahmud, which is still visited by those seeking his *berkat* (blessings).

The path to the palace crosses a cool mountain stream with a deep pool, just perfect for a midday swim after the long, hot walk from town. Further down the trail on the left is Bukit Cengkeh ("Clove Hill"), on whose serene and tranquil summit lie the graves of later Malay rulers. The path continues along the old road, now barely visible under the undergrowth, to Robat—site of a Bugis nobleman's grave that is surrounded by an iron fence and partly roofed.

After passing through thick undergrowth the trail brings you at last to the palace site at Damnah. The last sultan to inhabit this place, Abdul Rahman, was deposed by the Dutch in 1911 and died in Singapore in 1930. The palace was built entirely of wood, and only the foundations and the elegant circular stone staircases remain. In front of the foundations is the vegetation-clad remains of the *balairong*, a pavilion where the ruler received visitors. At the rear is a key-shaped royal squat toilet complete with stone-lined cess pit, and nearby are the foundations of a huge harem the sultan was building at the time of his ouster. According to the Dutch, Abdul Rahman was a "sensual and extravagant" sort; a sign, in Indonesian, simply announces these as the "44 unfinished rooms."

— *Periplus Editions*

Opposite: *Muslim Malay residents of Dabo, on Singkep Island.* **Above, left:** *The enchanting 10-hour ferry ride from Tanjung Pinang to Dabo.* **Above, right:** *The village of Daik on Lingga.*

Riau Island Practicalities

Includes Batam, Bintan, Karimun and the Lingga Archipelago. S = single, D = double, AC = air-conditioned. Prices in US dollars.

The best way to see the Riau Islands is by boat. First take the ferry from Singapore's Finger Pier, where a bewildering variety of crafts departs all day for Sekupang or Batu Ampar on Batam, or direct to Tanjung Pinang on Bintan. Visa-free entry is granted at all three places and you can catch boats from here to the other islands—provided you have plenty of time (schedules are practically non-existent in many areas!). Be aware that ferries are mobbed on weekends, and that strong winds and sudden squalls make the seas choppy in November and December.

Batam

Telephone code is 0778.

GETTING THERE AND AWAY

By air. Hang Nadim Airport may one day rival Jakarta as an entry and exit point in Indonesia. Since jet fuel for domestic flights is subsidized, it is cheaper to travel to Batam and take the ferry than to fly direct to/from Singapore. Tickets can be bought from airline offices and agents (cash only) or at the airport (Visa, Mastercard). Garuda flies to Saigon twice a week ($252). Merpati flies from Jakarta 3 times a day ($95) and daily from Bandung ($105), Medan ($80), Bangka ($65), Pekanbaru ($38) and Palembang ($50), and twice weekly from Padang ($54) and Pontianak ($70). Sempati flies many of these routes (same fares), and to/from Kuala Lumpur (Malaysia) twice a week.
Garuda: Pasero Bldg, Batu Ampar, tel: 58620.
Merpati: Komplek Jodoh Squire, Blok A/1, tel: 57388, 57288. **Sempati**: Jl. Imam Bonjol Blok 1/6, Nagoya, tel: 58285.
By sea. Ferries to Sekupang leave every half hour from Singapore's Finger Pier starting at 7:30 am until about 7:30 pm. The trip takes 30 min and the fare is $10 one way, $15 return. Children under 7 are free. Ferries to Batu Ampar are a bit less frequent but the same price and you land closer to the beach. Boats to Karimun, Kundur and other exotic, out-of-the-way islands depart from the wooden pier next to the Sekupang terminal. Fast ferries to Tanjung Pinang also leave hourly from Kabil, on Batam's east coast (see "Bintan" below).

GETTING AROUND

The only way to get around is by taxi; these can be hired everywhere; you'll be approached as you step off the ferry. They don't have meters, so you have to bargain on a per trip basis. Sample fares from Sekupang to: Nagoya ($4-$6), Hang Nadim Airport ($6-$7), Kabil ($6-8). You can also charter taxis by the hour: 5 hrs ($18), 8 hrs ($30).

ACCOMMODATION

Batam is not for budget travelers, though prices are "reasonable" by Singapore standards. The cheapest hotels are **Ramayana** and **Batam Jaya** in Nagoya ($35). Better though to stay at one of the self-contained beach resorts with pool, disco and sports facilities. The poshest ones are at Nongsa, on Batam's northeastern tip. Most hotels have their own restaurants and karaoke bars. All add 15 percent tax and service. On weekends they are full, but on weekdays you'll have the beach to yourself. Book through a travel agent in Singapore, who will arrange ferry tickets, transfers and a tour, plus get you a discount on the room.
Batam Fantasy (140 chalets) Tanjung Pinggir, Sekupang. On the northwest coast. Seaside chalets and a thatched-roof *kelong* restaurant on the beach, open till midnight.
Batam Island Country Club, Tanjung Pinggir. $30-$55. Squash and tennis courts, golf.
Batam View (196 rooms) Jl. Hang Lekir, Nongsa, tel: Singapore 2354366, Batam 22281. Next to a 36 hole golf course. Poolside barbecue. Japanese, Thai, Chinese, Indonesian and Western cuisine. $65 up to $150.
Greenville (48 cottages) Jl. Kuta Laut, tel: 58282. Batak, Balinese and Malay-style cottages on a hilltop facing across to Singapore.
Hilltop. Jl. Ir. Sutami 8, Sekupang, tel: 22482, fax: 22211. Karaoke lounge, disco. $55-$110.
Nongsa Beach, Nongsa. $60 to $100. Water scooters can be hired for $50 an hour.
Turi Beach (156 rooms) Nongsa, tel: Singapore 2355544, Batam 21543, 22375. Elegant "Balinese-style" thatched-roof chalets, a white sand beach and a private island. $75 to $200 (add 20 percent on weekends).

FOOD

If you're waiting for the ferry in Sekupang, **Pondok Batam** on the hill just behind the terminal serves honest, home-cooked meals in unpretentious but clean surroundings. The BBQ chicken, crisp fried *tempe* and delicate fish curry are excellent; about $4 for 2 persons.

The best place to eat seafood is in the big beachfront restaurants at Batu Besar. The largest and most popular is **Selera Wisata**. Getting a seat and a waitress can be a problem, but the food is delicious. The pepper crab is particularly good—swimming in black pepper and garlic, fried so hot that the shell disintegrates. But one crab for $6.50? The tiny *krapau* fish are $4 each and a small can of beer is $1.20! Expect to spend $20 to $25 for two.

Chinese coffeeshops in Nagoya serve the

usual noodle and rice dishes. **Dju-Dju Coffee Shop** in Kompleks Bumi Indah serves clay pot dishes. **Pujusera Nagoya** is a large food and entertainment center, open from 4 pm till sunrise. Tiny restaurants serve seafood while bars like Midnight Cowboy and Bali Indah play loud rock music. Hostesses sit and chat for the price of a beer; at one end is a dance hall where you can gyrate after buying a book of hostess tickets. This is one town that doesn't roll up the sidewalks at sunset.

Bintan (Tanjung Pinang)

Telephone code for Tanjung Pinang is 0771.

GETTING THERE

By sea. Fast Auto Batam ferries make the direct open-sea crossing from Singapore's Finger Pier at 10 am and 2 pm daily (2.5 hrs/$28). Other companies run ferries via Batam that take longer but offer a more scenic journey through the islands. Alternatively, hop any ferry to Batam ($10) and take a taxi ($5) to Kabil, on the east coast, where there are hourly speedboats ($8) and ferries ($4) to Tanjung Pinang. If you are on a very tight budget, take a fishing boat from Kabil to Tanjung Uban ($1.50) on Bintan's west coast, then a bus to Tanjung Pinang ($1).
By air. Merpati and Sempati have daily flights from Jakarta ($90) and Pekanbaru ($48). Tiny SMAC and Deraya fly twice weekly to Dabo ($38), Palembang ($56) and Jambi ($60). Kijang Airport is 12 km from town; taxi is $3. Merpati: Jl. Bintan 44, tel: 22046. Sempati: Jl. Bintan 9, tel: 23177. SMAC: Jl. A. Yani, Batu Lima, tel: 22798. Deraya: Jl. Bintan 46.

GETTING AROUND

Bemos take you in and around town for Rp250. You can also hire local motorbike taxis (you sit on the back), called *ojek*, which cost Rp400. Buses leave hourly from 7 am to 4 pm daily for Tanjung Uban ($1). Shared taxis to Trikora Beach leave from the bus depot next to Bank Duta from 7-11 am ($2). Old Holden taxis can be hired for $3-$5 per hour. You can find them at the main pier and on Jl. Merdeka around the clock tower. You can also rent motorbikes from Info Travel on Jl. Samudra near the main pier, $13 a day. A crash helmet and a tank of petrol is provided: no license required, but they want a photocopy of your passport. Shared taxis to Trikora leave from the bus station before noon ($2 a person) or hire one for the day for $30.

ACCOMMODATION
Expensive (above $20)
While there are not yet any luxury hotels on Bintan, you can get comfortable AC rooms for $20 to $40 in more than a dozen *wisma* (middle range hotels) that cater to weekend visitors from Singapore. The older ones are in town, newer ones are in the suburbs. Rates below are for weekends, you can get lower rates during the week when the hotels are empty.
Asean, Jl. Gudang Minyak, tel: 22161. $28-$43.
Baruna, Jl. Bakar Batu 27, tel: 21483. $20-$28.
Garden Hotel, Jl. Gatot Subroto 282 km 5, tel: 22344. Attractive place 10 minutes from town; bungalows on a landscaped hillside. $35-$43.
Pinang Island Cottage, Komplex Rimba Jaya 133, tel: 21307. $28.
Pringgodani, Jl. Brigjen Katamso km 2.5, tel:

Tanjung Pinang

not to scale

N

Rowboats to Senggarang Pelantar II
Chinese Temple
Pelantar I Riau Holiday Indah
Water Village (on Stilts)
JL. PASAR

Ferry
to Singapore & Batam
Pelabuhan International (Main Pier)
JL. PASAR IKAN
H. Tanjungpinang
Market (Pasar Baru)
Pelantar III
Night Market (Food Stalls)
Boats to Penyengat
Clock Tower
Bemo Terminal
Osaka Shipping
Taxi Terminal
Money Changer
Chinese Temple
Pelni Office
Mutiara Cinema
Info Travel
Ayodia Ship
Post Office
Bank Duta
to Pelantar IV
Park
Gembira Cinema
Bus & Taxi
Night Market
Bung 3-D
Johnny
Wisma Riau
Merpati
H. Surya
Deraya
Kaca Puri
Sempurna Jaya
Bank BNI
Sempurna Inn
Mosque
Telecoms Office
Church
to Kandil Riau Museum

21753. $20-$28.

Riau Holidays Indah (50 rooms) Jl. Pelantar II 53, tel: 22644. Built on stilts right over the Riau River. $26 to $35. The food is awful and the bar an insult to civilized drinking, but a private jetty at the front overlooks the water and more than makes up for the hotel's shortcomings—this is the perfect place to sit and watch the world go by. In the evening, sea eagles dive for fish as the sun sets behind Penyengat.

Sampurna Jaya (77 rooms) Jl. Yusuf Kahar 15, tel: 21555. $33-$40 S, $39-$45 D, $78 suite with breakfast, AC, private bath and hot water. The restaurant serves excellent Indonesian and Chinese dishes; the set lunch ($10) and dinner ($12.00) are particularly recommended.

Wisma Riau (40 rooms) Jl. Yusuf Kahar. Older place with large, dark rooms and a pleasant but inefficient staff. $12-$35 S, $17-$44 D. All with private bath, better ones have AC and TV.

Budget (under $10)

Three guesthouses in the heart of town on Jl. Lorong Bintan II, off Jl. Bintan, offer cheap digs for backpackers. **Johnny's Guesthouse** at the far end of the alleyway is run by a pleasant Malay family ($1.50 per night, coffee or tea included). You will probably meet Johnny as you step off the boat; he's reliable and honest and will help with onward tickets. If Johnny's is full, try **Bung Homestay** or **3D Homestay** nearby. **Lobo Guesthouse** at Jl. Diponegoro 8 offers similar accommodation. **Sempurna Inn**, Jl. Yusuf Kahar 707, tel: 21533, is a cheap hotel with basic services. $7 fan, $11 AC.

FOOD

Eating out in Tanjung Pinang is a delight. The food is fresh and cheap, and there's great variety. Try a typical local breakfast at **Pagi Sore** on Jl. Merdeka—a long, dark coffeeshop with marble-top tables. The roti prata (Indian fried bread) is delicious and the coffee is strong.

For lunch, **Gampang Ingat** on Jl. Teuku Umar serves excellent gado-gado and soto ayam. It is run by two pleasant Christian Chinese girls (closed Sun). **Sempurna Inn** at Jl. Yusuf Kahar 707 is the best Padang place in town. Spotlessly-clean, serves delicately-flavored fish as well as the usual beef and chicken curries. **Bali** on Jl. Merdeka is less refined but still good. Try the dendeng (slivers of sun-dried meat in chili), the ayam kuah (chicken in mild coconut sauce) or the dark and spicy rendang.

In the evenings head for the **Night Market** on Jl. Pos. By day a busy bus and taxi depot, at night it magically transforms into an open-air market. Here you can get fat crabs, juicy squid, succulent prawns, sate and gonggong—a small shellfish steamed and served with a delicious sweet, spicy sauce. Oyster omelettes, fried on platters over a blazing fire, are crisp outside, the oysters still rare inside. Finish off with a bowl of black rice pudding (bubur hitam) topped with chilled, salted coconut milk—the stall furthest from the bank serves the best. Prices are low: a bowl of peppery fish soup with rice is 40 cents, while a dish of tender charcoal-grilled squid costs just $1. The only problem is knowing where to begin!

A short bemo ride, 2 km from town, is **Meja Tujuh** ("Seven Tables") on Jl. Tugu Pahlawan, a night market specializing in sate and martabak. A little before Meja Tujuh on the right is **Selera Rasa**—a cosy, open-air grilled chicken place. A whole chicken costs $4; try the bumbu kecap (sweet soy) and bumbu rujak (spicy marinade). A bowl of sayur asam (vegetables in tamarind broth) compliments the meal.

The best known seafood restaurant is **Teluk Keriting** (Jl. Usman Harun 15), a 15-min bemo ride from town. You are greeted by large Ninja Turtles, a miniskirted rhino and a carousing tiger clutching a can of beer. Dine under the stars at the end of the pier, caressed by cool sea breezes. Fresh prawns, crab, squid and kangkong with beer will set you back $5-$6 a head—the most expensive items are ikan krapau ($25 a kg) and lobster ($23 a kg).

SERVICES

There is an authorized money changer on Jl. Pos. The **Post Office** on Jl. Merdeka is open from 8 to 8 except Fri (to 11 am) and Sun (to 1 pm). The **Perumtel** office on Jl. Hang Tuah is open 24 hours for long distance phone calls.

Pelayaran Lokal Ayodhia at Jl. Samudra 1 and **Osaka Shipping** at Jl. Merdeka 43 are excellent places to buy boat tickets and get reliable information. **Info Travel** at Jl. Samudra 3 arranges hotels, tours and motorbike rentals. The **Pelni** office is on Jl. Ketapang.

Riau Holiday Tour in the Riau Holiday Hotel (tel: 21812) runs a city tour to the Chinese temple at km 8, the museum, the seashell monument and the market (2 hrs/$15 for 2 people), also tours to Senggarang ($7), Penyengat ($12) and Trikora ($34, lunch included).

TRIKORA BEACH

The best time to visit is April to Oct. From Nov to March the beach is hit by SE monsoons.

Trikora Country Club (17 rooms), 37 km from town, overlooks a rocky bay with small sandy coves. Pleasant rooms with tiled floors and veranda: $32-$48 weekdays, $35-$56 weekends. The restaurant serves fresh seafood and the hotel rents snorkeling gear ($3 a day), windsurfing boards ($3 an hour) and tennis courts ($5 an hour). The pool can be used by non-guests for $2. Overnight deep-sea fishing trips can be arranged for parties of 6 or more.

Pantai Trikora restaurant is 2 km up the road at Teluk Bakau (39 km)—a small, unobtrusive place serving magnificent pan-fried ikan unga goreng straight from the sea ($5), and lightly steamed baby crabs ($2.50 a kg). Better still, try the delicious black crab ($5 a kg), all washed down with ice cold beer. A pier behind the restaurant leads to small tables by the sea. **Pak Yasin** runs two budget guesthouses further north, one at Malang Rapat (46 km), the other 4 km further north just before Teluk Dalam (this one is better). Basic chalets are $4-$5 depending on the season, with simple meals. Get there by shared taxi leaving the bus depot in Tanjung Pinang at 7 am daily. The bungalows are right on the beach—the only drawback is the sandflies, which can be repelled with mixture of onions steeped in coconut oil.

ONWARD PASSAGE

From Tanjung Pinang you can catch boats to almost anywhere. A boat to Dabo on Singkep Island, for example, leaves twice a week (Fri, Sun at 11:00/$17.50). A comfortable Pelni passenger ship departs for Medan every other Fri at noon ($15-$35 depending on the class). To Jakarta, Pelni has a weekly sailing (Sat at noon/$30-$45) and another one every other Tue at noon ($16-$55). There are many agents in Tanjung Pinang but the best and cheapest is **Osaka Shipping**, Jl. Merdeka 43. The manager, Raymond Chin, speaks good English and will sort out the intricacies of these travel arrangements for you.

The boat to Pekanbaru via Selat Panjang (40 hrs/$8 deck, $10 bunk) is a midnight adventure up the Siak River, with the boat's spotlights trained on dense rainforests reaching down to the water's edge; you arrive at 3 am. Boats to more distant destinations do not follow any fixed schedule, but leave when they have enough cargo and passengers.

Karimun (Tanjung Balai)

A direct ferry to Tanjung Balai, the main town on Karimun, leaves from Singapore's Finger Pier at 1:30 pm daily ($23, $40 return) but you'll need a visa. Otherwise go first to Sekupang on Batam, where entry is visa-free. Boats to Karimun depart from the wooden jetty alongside the terminal (2 hrs/$8).

Holiday Karimun has clean rooms with AC and TV for $23. The restaurant serves marvelous seafood—the *ikan kerapu goreng* (deep fried grouper) is in a class all its own, and the Szechuan-style *udang cabe* (prawn with dried chili) is a must, as are the *kepiting cabe* (chili crabs) and *kangkong terasi* (water spinach with fish paste). **Wisma Gloria** is a whimsical, rambling hotel with tropical gardens, perched on a hilltop overlooking the sea and town; $4 to $9.

A visit to the Sanskrit inscription at Pasir Panjang can be combined with a visit to Pantai Pelawan. Charter a taxi ($17 for 4 hrs) to the granite quarry and ask for permission to see the inscription, which is in a concrete bunker at the foot of a cliff. On the return journey, stop at Pantai Pelawan (20 km), a scrubby beach with murky water. Shortly after the beach to the left

is a village of young Javanese ladies—Karimun's main attraction for many Singaporean visitors. There is also a waterfall at Bukit Anak (18 km).

Lingga Archipelago

The Lingga Islands are for the adventurous. If you don't mind sleeping on the floor of a small cargo boat or setting out in a tiny, overloaded sampan as a tropical squall approaches, you will thoroughly enjoy these beautiful islands, with their friendly and courteous people.

The Sumbawa II and Sejahtera Indah both sail direct from Tanjung Pinang to Pancur on the north coast of Lingga Island ($3). You arrive around 9 pm and stay overnight before continuing on to Daik the following morning. Choose a berth well away from the engine. Another boat, the Sabar Menanti, occasionally sails from Tanjung Pinang to Daik; inquire in T.P.

The more roundabout way to reach Daik is via **Dabo** on Singkep Island, aboard a wooden boat called the Hentry—(10 hrs/$8 including a simple meak of *ikan bilis*, peanuts, vegetables and rice). During the windy season (Sept-Dec) the boat docks at Sungai Buluh, 45 km up the coast, where you are hustled into a minibus for the 50-min ride to Dabo ($1.25). Ask to be dropped at Penginapan Sri Indah, a clean hotel 5 minutes' walk from Dabo harbor. $3 S, $6 D. The more expensive Wisma Timah is up the hill. There are foodstalls in Dabo behind the hotel plus the usual *warungs* selling *mie goreng*; none is recommended.

From Dabo, the daily boat to **Daik** leaves when the tide is in; inquire at the jetty. Return or onward tickets from Dabo can be arranged at the harbormaster's office on the right, shortly before the jetty bridge. The journey to Daik (2 hrs/$1) can be rough in the windy season.

There is just one hotel in Daik. Rooms are clean enough (don't examine the bathrooms too closely), but hot and noisy. $2.50 a night. The coffeeshop down the road (south) serves good coffee and rolls; a restaurant up the road has tasty fried chicken. (Daik is so small the coffeeshops are known by the names of their owners!) Sulaiman, a local *becak* driver and shoe repairer will seek you out. He's an excellent guide and will show you everything, including a delightful bathing pool 20 minutes from town. You can visit the mosque, ruined palace and royal tombs in a day. To see the forts at Bukit Cening and Pulau Mepar, start early and add another day.

Return to Dabo on the daily boat or hop onto a motorbike taxi (*ojek*) to **Resun** (25 min/ $1.25). From here catch a *pom-pom* (small motorboat) amidst sacks of fruit and trussed chickens and glide through a vast mangrove swamp to Pancur (50 cents) to catch the Sumbawa II (Tues, Sat) or Sejahtera Indah (Mon, Thur) back to Tanjung Pinang.

MAINLAND RIAU

Rainforests, Rivers and Malay Villages

Mainland Riau, with its three great rivers—the Inderagiri, Kampar and Siak—is way off the beaten tourist track. Initiative, time and a working knowledge of Indonesian are essential. While there is a fair system of roads (the best link the city to the harbor at Dumai), the Trans-Sumatran Highway bypasses the province and travel in most areas is still by riverboat. This is a slow process and creature comforts are few, but you get to explore seldom-visited villages offering glimpses of traditional Malay life. Below are a few highlights.

The Siak palace

Riau Province is proud of its historical role in the development of Malay culture. There are many beautiful mosques and important grave sites, but most will interest only Malay visitors. The old royal palace at **Siak Sri Inderapura** is definitely worth a visit from Pekan-baru, however. The journey downriver by speedboat takes 2 hours and the return trip by bus or taxi another 3 hours; you can also stay overnight here in a small *losmen* built over the river (see "Practicalities").

The palace was built in 1889 by Sultan Abdul Jalil Syafuddin, the 11th of 12 sultans who ruled Siak from 1725 to 1945. Moorish arches and minarets give the palace a strong Indian Moghul look, as was the style in colonial times. The palace was refurbished in 1989, exactly a century after its construction, and the large front lawn and main building are meticulously maintained. Although the gold crown and the sacred kris have been removed to Jakarta's national museum, the rest of the furnishings are still there. Life size figures of the sultan and his courtiers sit in the reception area. Large photographs of the last sultans—oriental potentates who formed part of the Dutch establishment—decorate the walls. Much of the decor is European. A big attraction is the large German music player, said to be one of only two left in the world, whose perforated metal disks tinkle Beethoven, Mozart and Strauss tunes which vibrate wonderfully throughout the palace.

West to Bukittinggi

If you are traveling west of Pekanbaru on the main road to Bukittinggi you can stop at **Air Tiris**, near Bangkinang on the Kampar River, to have a look at the Mesjid Jamik mosque.

KAL MULLER

Built without nails in 1901, this multi-tiered wooden structure has ornate carvings. Sagging with age, it is now reinforced with nails and the original shingled roof has been replaced by corrugated metal sheets. Outside the mosque is a large, mysterious stone that is said to move around under its own power.

Further west, on the border with West Sumatra about 135 km from Pekanbaru, are the ruins of **Muara Takus**. It is said that this ancient city was so large that a cat could wander from roof to roof for 3 months before

reaching the last house. The ruins, which are scattered across several square kilometers, date from the 11th or 12th century and were surrounded entirely by an earthen wall. The best preserved building is the tall, slender Mahligai stupa, which has been completely restored. The temples of Muara Takus are probably royal graves; it is said that the last ruler was transformed into an elephant, and when the moon is full, his descendants gather to pay homage to their departed ancestor. (See "Minang Highlands" in WEST SUMATRA.)

Jungle wildlife

The vast rainforests of Riau are a haven for animals, though their habitats are increasingly threatened by logging and plantations. It is estimated there are between 1,100 and 1,700 elephants and 100 to 200 tigers, plus a few hundred rare Sumatran rhinos. All of these animals, however, have developed a very healthy fear of humans. Your best chance of seeing elephants in the wild is to visit remote Danau Pulau Besar and Bawah to the south of Siak Sri Inderapura. You can get there during the dry season by chartered jeep. Pulau Berke, a small island at the mouth of the Rokan River opposite Bagansiapiapi, is home to a large variety of birds. You can get to Pulau Berke by road or by boat from Dumai.

It is also possible to see a fair amount of wildlife in the 2,000-ha protected forest of **Bukit Suligi Reserve**, at the western edge

of the province near the source of the Siak River. This is a field-training camp for forestry students from around Sumatra, with dorm-style accommodations for young visitors and rooms for married couples. There is abundant wildlife in the reserve—tapirs, honey bears, deer, boars, civet cats and the odd tiger. More commonly seen are spider and howler monkeys. In the dense forests it is also possible to see argus pheasants, and on the edges of the swamps, wild pigs and deer come to graze on rattan fruits ripped down by elephants. Birds include hornbills, mynas and jungle fowl. Early morning and late afternoon are best times for seeing the animals.

Surfing the Kampar River

Under the pull of the full moon, giant tidal waves sweep 60 to 70 km up the Kampar River, from Ketam Island to Kuala Panduk village. The waves can reach 2 m high, rushing upriver for 3 hours before running out of steam. (See Somerset Maugham's description of a similar tidal wave in *Borneo Stories*.) Often 6 or 7 consecutive waves appear like a snake slithering up the river. The waves are low near the mouth and rear up as the river narrows. A fearsome roar and misty spray accompanies these *bono* (the local name for the waves), and young men sometimes "surf" them in small canoes, swept along at 10 knots an hour. The *bono* can best be viewed from the riverbank at Teluk Meranti village, about 8 hrs down the Kampar from Pangkalanbaru, 20 km south of Pekanbaru. There is a smaller *bono* on the lower reaches of the Rokan River, up from Bagansiapiapi. This *bono* is considered a weaker female force while the larger one on the Kampar is male: the two are supposed to merge somewhere far inland.

— *Kal Muller*

Opposite: *Logs bound for Pekanbaru's huge plywood mills.* **Above, left:** *A local riverboat.* **Above, right:** *The palace at Siak Sri Inderapura.*

Pekanbaru Practicalities

Most prices in US dollars. AC = air-conditioned. Telephone code is 0761.

Pekanbaru is the capital of Riau Province. Once a small river port at the highest navigable point on the Siak River, today it is a booming oil town with an international airport. The city is divided in two by the Siak River: on the north bank are shops, hotels, banks and the port; to the south are government offices and the main bus terminal. The climate is hot and humid.

GETTING THERE

By air (international). Garuda (offices on Jl. Sudirman, tel: 21026) flies from Singapore 4 times weekly ($92). Sempati flies once a week to/from Melaka (Malaysia) for only $55. Pelangi Air flies weekly to/from Kuala Lumpur ($70).

By air (domestic). Plenty of connections from most cities in Sumatra. Merpati (offices on Jl. Cokroaminoto, tel: 23558) has 3 daily flights to/from Jakarta ($102) and daily flights from Medan ($55), Batam ($38) and Tanjung Pinang ($46). There are also 4 weekly Merpati flights from Palembang ($64) and 3 from Padang ($25). Sempati (local offices at Jl. Sisingamangaraja 3, tel: 21382, 24907) also offers daily flights to/from Jakarta ($102) and Tanjung Pinang ($46) and 6 weekly flights to Batam ($38). SMAC (local offices on Jl. Sudir-

man, tel: 21726) has frequent flights to Rengat ($21), Dumai ($24), Jambi ($43), Tanjung Pinang ($42), Batam ($38), Singkep ($62), Karimun ($38) and Medan ($95).

By bus. You can take a bus from Bukittinggi (6 hrs/$3 for AC), which is the closest point to Pekanbaru on the Trans-Sumatra Highway, about 175 km away. All the way from Jakarta takes 34 hrs ($22 AC).

By minibus. Three companies run minibus services to and from Bukittinggi and Padang, leaving every 2 hours during the day. They pick you up and deliver you right to the door (7 hrs/$7). Call for a pick-up. Kopsi, tel: 25050. Garuda Taxi, tel: 22151. Riau Taxi, tel: 24897.

By sea. Crowded (but cheap) ferries and more comfortable (but expensive) speedboats sail up and down the Siak River between Pekanbaru and the Riau Islands (see "Getting Around" below and also "Riau Islands Practicalities").

GETTING AROUND

You can easily walk around the city. For trips out of town by road, contact one of the tour companies listed below or charter a minibus with driver, about $70 a day (call companies mentioned above). Much of the province's travel is still by water along the major rivers, however. From Pekanbaru you can travel down the Siak River to Bengkalis or Selat Panjang, where you can change for various destinations, including boats going up the Kampar, Inderagiri and Rokan Rivers. The various prices listed below reflect speed and degree of comfort.

By boat/ferry. These are slow and crowded but cheap. To Selat Panjang on Tebingtinggi Island daily: 12 hrs (bunk $7, deck $6). To Tanjung Pinang 3 times weekly: 40 hrs (bunk $12, deck $9.50). To Karimun 3 times weekly: 24 hrs (bunk $10.50, deck $8.50). To Batam 3 times weekly: 40 hrs (bunk $18, deck $14).

By speedboat. Speedboats are owned and operated by the military police (tel: 23779, 22736). Book and pay a day ahead or in the early morning. A boat departs downriver daily at about 11 am bound for Siak ($4), Sungai Apit ($5.50), Pakning ($8) and Bengkalis ($8). Another boat leaves at around 12 pm headed for Siak ($11) and across to Selat Panjang ($16), where you can get a connecting speedboat to Batam ($14). You can charter a speedboat to Siak for $140; overnight there for $165.

TOURS

Kota Piring Kencana travel agency (Jl. Sisingamangaraja 3, tel: 221382, 24907) organizes custom tours off the beaten track, such as canoe and rafting trips on the Subayang River and visits to Riau's more remote tribal areas. **Inti Angkasa Dewa** travel agency (Jl. Sudirman 370, tel: 21074, 23179) offers day tours to Bukit Suligi Reserve, the Sebanga elephant training center, to Siak and to the ruins at Muara Takus. Cost is $20 a person, minimum of 4 persons. **Setia Tour** (Jl. Sam Ratulangi 30A, tel: 22674) is a big company running tours out to North and West Sumatra.

ACCOMMODATION

Thanks to the oil industry and a booming economy, Pekanbaru offers good hotels along with lots of cheaper places to sleep.

Expensive ($30 and up)

Indrapura International (103 rooms) Jl. Dr. Sutomo 86, tel: 25233, fax: 21465. $25 up to $100. A 4-story hotel with an excellent restaurant, swimming pool, disco.
Mutiara Panghegar (150 rooms) Jl. Yos Sudarso 12A, tel: 23102, 23637, fax: 233380. Top place in town. Offers views over a sea of rusting rooftops and the Siak River. $42 to $110. Has the best restaurant in town, serving European, Chinese and Indonesian food.
Sri Indrayani (54 rooms) Jl. Bangka, tel: 24244, fax: 21509. $21 to $68.
Tasia Ratu (53 rooms) Jl. W. Monginsidi 10, tel: 33225, fax: 25912. $29 to $58.

Moderate ($15-30)

Afri (15 rooms) Jl. Setiabudi, tel: 22090. $14 for an AC room.
Badarussamsi (32 rooms) Jl. Sisingamangaraja 71, tel: 22475. $9 to $25. A sprawling hotel in a quiet area. Simple Indonesian meals served.
Kendedes Sri (24 rooms) Jl. Hang Tuah, tel: 31198. $22 to $33, bar and restaurant.
Rauda (35 rooms) Jl. Tangkubanperahu 4, tel: 33372. $14 to $29. Restaurant has inexpensive Indonesian food.
Riau (20 rooms) Jl. Diponegoro 34, tel: 22986. $11 to $22; restaurant and bar.

Budget (under $15)

Several cheap *losmen* can be found on Jl. Nangka, near the bus station. For AC and a bit more money, try one of the following:
Anom (43 rooms) Jl. Gatot Subroto 3, tel: 22636. $8.50 to $14. Clean. Good restaurant serves inexpensive Chinese meals.
Bunda Wisma (20 rooms) Jl. Prof. Dr. M. Yamin 104, tel: 21728. $7.50 to $22.
Sinda, Jl. Pepaya 73, tel: 23719. Close to the bus station in a quiet area. $7 to $11, some with AC. The restaurant serves good Indonesian/Minang food.
Yani (15 rooms) Jl. Pepaya 10, tel: 2367747, 25283. Pleasant, homey atmosphere. $8 for room with fan, $14 with AC, both with private bath and a good breakfast.

EATING

Most of the better restaurants are in the bigger hotels (see above). For Western and Indonesian food, try the **Ky-Ky** on Jl. Sudirman. Pleasant interior and decor. Steaks $3-$5, shrimp $4, sandwiches $1-$2, Indonesian meals, $2-$3. The **Kota Piring** on Jl. Sisingamangaraja offers steaks (including venison) for $4-$5.50, hamburgers for $1.50, salads for 60 cents and Indonesian dishes for $1.50.

For Chinese food, the **Medan** on Jl. Juanda is considered the best in town: "Mandarin and Szechuan, U.S. and International Style." A fantastic selection in AC comfort, including a "red hot" section with stewed and steamed just about anything; most dishes are $2-$3. Go with friends so you can sample lots of goodies.
Jumbo on Jl. Juanda is another Chinese place specializing in seafood sold by the "*ons*" (100 gms): shrimp $1.40, fish $0.80-$1.40, lobster $1.75; crab $1.75 each.

Among the better Padang restarants are **Sari Bunda 88** on Jl. Gatot Subroto in front of the Anom Hotel, and **Mitra Sari** on the same street. For Javanese-style goat *sate* and marrow soup (*soto sungsum*), try **Tambang Rejo** on Jl. Setia Budi, where you can fill up for $3.

ACTIVITIES

It is said that the better hotels can arrange a round of **golf** at Caltex's 18-hole course just outside of town. There is a large **Provincial Museum** 4 km north of town on Jl. Sudirman, built but not yet open at press time. Next door to the museum are several traditional houses. Ask to find out if it is functioning yet.

EXCURSIONS

All major towns around the province have simple, cheap *losmen* accommodation. You can go downriver from Pekanbaru by ferry or speedboat to **Siak Sri Inderapura** to see the palace (see "Getting Around" above), and the riverside restaurant and *losmen* is right at the jetty (18 rooms, $2 a night). From the dock area it is a short walk to the palace.

It is also possible to get to **Bukit Suligi Reserve** by public transport. Take a bus headed west to Bukittinggi as far as Rantau Parangin (just after crossing the Kampar River) and change for a *bemo* headed north to Tandun village. From Tandun, there are occasional trucks and other vehicles on the track leading west into the reserve, or it's an easy 9-km hike. Accommodations here run $3 a night, simple meals are $1, and an Indonesian-speaking guide can be hired for $6 a day ($3 half a day) to show you around.

Muara Takus is not far from here, but you have to go back to the main highway, travel west to Muaramahat, then turn right (north) to the ruins via Kototengah village along a well-marked road.

To see the *bono* (tidal waves), first travel 20 km south from Pekanbaru by land to Pangkalanbaru on the Kampar River, then hire a speedboat down to **Teluk Meranti** (7-8 hrs/$160). You can stay in the *kepala desa's* house, but allow several days around the full moon to make sure you see them.

— *Kal Muller*

PART VII

Introducing Jambi

The sparsely-inhabited province of Jambi comprises a lowland basin of dense jungles, peat bogs and swamps about the size of Switzerland (53,435 sq km)—all of it drained by a single river system, the mighty Batang Hari and its tributaries. The latter is Sumatra's longest river, "a cruel, whitehot pool of fire" that rises on the slopes of Mt. Rasam (2,585 m) in West Sumatra and snakes eastward for some 800 km to the Straits of Malacca. The river's major tributaries—the Tebo, Tabir, Merangin, Tembesi and Asai—pass through gold-bearing rocks yielding tiny gold granules after heavy rains. People still pan for gold here, and the fabled Svarnabhumi ("Land of Gold") of classical Indian texts may have referred to these upriver regions.

The Batang Hari estuary was the site of an ancient port known as Malayu. Early 7th century Chinese sources indicate that a ruler with 5,000 troops lived here, and by the late 7th century the trade had developed sufficiently to attract the unwelcome attention of nearby Srivijaya (Palembang). In 686, Srivijaya conquered Malayu.

By the early 10th century, a vast complex of Hindu-Buddhist shrines, tanks and canals arose at Muara Jambi, 26 km downstream from the present-day capital. After an Indian attack on Srivijaya in 1025, Malayu reasserted itself for a time, but then came under Javanese domination after 1275. Remnants of the ancient court appear to have moved upriver, to the western highlands, and place names with Buddhist associations are still common in the Kerinci area. The name Malayu itself probably means "hill people" (from the south Indian words *mala* "hill" and *ur* "people"), and Indian influence is evident also in the name of Jambi's greatest river—Hari being an avatar of the Indian god Vishnu.

Islam established itself at Jambi in the 16th century. According to legend, the sultanate was founded by a Turk with the curious Malay title of Paduka Berhala ("His Excellency the Idol"). His son, Orang Kaya Hitam ("The Black Aristocrat"), threw off the yoke of Javanese rule just as Dutch traders appeared on the scene, in the early 1600s.

Dutch relations with Jambi were never very smooth. In 1707 they established a post at the mouth of the Batang Hari to control the pepper trade, but were driven out in 1734. Following the treaty of 1833 this post was reoccupied, but not until 1901 was the area placed under direct Dutch rule, and military action in the hinterland continued until 1916.

Today Jambi's booming economy is based on forestry and plantation agriculture. Products include timber, plywood, rubber, palm oil, copra, coffee and tea. Jambi's 2 million inhabitants are very mixed, concentrated in a few major towns along the rivers. About 1,000 Kubu people inhabit the forests, steadfastly resisting attempts to settle them into permanent communities (see "The Kubu").

Apart from a few fertile highland areas in the far west, Jambi consists of low undulating hills, peaty plains and swamps near the coast. The lowlands are only moderately fertile and receive heavy rainfall throughout the year, making them ill-suited for food crops. Jambi imports much of its rice from Riau and Java.

Jambi's rainforests once abounded in wildlife. Today the bears, deer, elephants, tapirs, tigers and other species are threatened by encroaching forestry concessions, oil palm plantations and transmigration settlements. There are two major reserves: the Kerinci-Seblat National Park in the west (40 percent of which lies in Jambi) and a small, swampy coastal area known as Kuala Berbak, 3 hours downstream from Jambi town. Here, on a branch of the Batang Hari, migrating birds pause to rest between October and December.
— *E. Edwards McKinnon*

Overleaf: *Dense jungle around Lake Kerinci.*
Opposite: *A coconut harvester and his well-trained assistant. Both photos by Alain Compost.*

THE KUBU

Primitives of the Lowland Rainforest

Writing in the 1920s, the Dutch colonial ethnographer Van Eerde noted that he could find no greater cultural contrast in Indonesia than between the highly civilized people of Bali—with their lavish costumes, elegant dances and elaborate religious ceremonies—and the primitive Kubu tribesmen of southern Sumatra, who wandered naked in the jungle, lived in simple huts and foraged for food.

Half a century later, members of these two ethnic groups actually found themselves living next to one another in a Jambi transmigration project. The Balinese had been forced to leave their beloved island because of land shortages, while the Kubu had been compelled by government policies to exchange their "miserable existence in the wilderness" for transmigration settlement houses, plots of farmland and a year's free supply of food.

Much as Van Eerde had predicted, the contrast could not indeed have been greater. While the Balinese were delighted to have the opportunity of building a new future in a new land, the Kubu sullenly and steadfastly refused all assistance. "No, thank you!" they said. "We Kubu prefer the forest. We consider ourselves part of the forest and we prefer to live in freedom. We are not attracted to village life, with its many regulations and officials." Coming from primitive forest dwellers, this is a surprisingly "aristocratic" attitude.

Indigenous hunter-gatherers

The Kubu are southern Sumatra's original inhabitants. As traditional hunters and gatherers, they have inhabited the lowland tropical rainforests of Jambi and South Sumatra provinces for centuries, where they survive by gathering an enormous variety of edible forest products, and by hunting wild game—several species of deer, large lizards, boar, tapirs, honey bears, monkeys, birds and, in the past, even elephants. The one animal they do not hunt is the tiger, due to a special relationship between the Kubu and the tiger.

Apart from this, the Kubu eat wild tubers, fruits, leaves, fish, shellfish and smaller animals such as turtles, snakes and rats.

The Kubu use only a long spear to kill their prey. Dogs are used to chase the quarry and exhaust it so that they can kill it with the spear. Bows and arrows, blowpipes and other weapons are unknown to them, but they do make many types of traps and snares to catch smaller animals.

Such a lifestyle requires a high degree of mobility, which in turn limits the size of Kubu groups. The temporary camps consisting of simple huts which they erect in the forest seldom house more than about eight families. Moreover, the composition of such groups changes rather quickly since its members often move to join other groups or start new groups of their own.

A threatened way of life

Until several decades ago, most of southern Sumatra was still covered in virgin jungle. Villages with surrounding agricultural fields were only to be found on the banks of the large rivers that meander lazily through the lowland swamps, and in the highland valleys. But in recent years the entire landscape has changed dramatically. Logging, mining and plantation agriculture have opened up many lowland areas, while the construction of the Trans-Sumatra Highway has brought a flood of migrants from overpopulated Java, Bali and Madura.

All of these factors have contributed to the destruction of the lowland rainforest environment in which the Kubu live. With the destruction of the forests, many plants and animals essential for their survival are also disappearing, and the process of cultural and physical extinction—predicted already for several decades—seems now to have become irreversible.

Though unable to stop the invading farmers, bulldozers and chainsaws around them, the Kubu have nevertheless managed to adapt their way of life to the deteriorating circumstances. Against their nature they have adopted agriculture on a limited scale—they clear small plots of forest land for the cultivation of upland rice, corn or root crops. Moreover, these fields attract animals such as deer and pigs, which may be hunted with greater efficiency.

Right: *This Kubu man, an indigenous hunter and gatherer by nature, has to work as a daily laborer for village farmers in order to survive.*

Most Kubu now live in close contact with village farmers without becoming or wanting to become village dwellers themselves. They settle on farmers' fields where they can hunt freely, and often they work as daily laborers —assisting at harvest time or cutting trees and opening new fields in the forest. They also gather and trade forest products like honey, rattan and various types of tree resins. Their handicrafts—baskets and fish traps— are increasingly in demand. In exchange, the Kubu receive rice, tobacco, salt, hardware (spearheads, axes, bush knives), medicine and cotton loin cloths (which have long ago replaced their old barkcloth ones). Increasingly, however, the Kubu also request flashlights, guns, radios and other products, and the debris scattered around their forest huts bears silent witness to an increasing contact with the outside world. In addition to the familiar husks, shells and bones of game are now found discarded batteries, empty tins, bottles and plastic trash.

Due to these changed circumstances a kind of economic symbiosis has developed between the Kubu and the farmers, in spite of the fact that both groups remain far apart socially. The villagers—sedentary Muslims with a sense of belonging to a new and developing Indonesia—show little respect or sympathy for the "half naked, omniverous, uncivilized Kubu" who cling to such an archaic and disorderly way of life.

For their part, the Kubu still consciously reject village life. The heavy work in the fields, the restricted freedom of movement and the numerous obligations and duties imposed on villagers in the form of mandatory schooling, development and political activities, and *gotong royong* (communal exchanges of labor) frighten the Kubu. And so they continually resist the pressures and temptations of the outside world that would force them to become settled villagers.

This explains also why the Kubu never accept houses in transmigration settlement areas and why they soon leave resettlement villages built for their "development and civilization" by the government or by missionary organizations. They prefer the freedom of the forests, living on the margins of civilization as odd-job laborers in nearby farms.

Only when this possibility is taken from them do they appear more openly in the outside world—as beggars in logging camps, at bus terminals or along the roadways. Perhaps one can look upon this as a modified and "modernized" form of hunting and gathering with money, food and cigarettes as its aim, but it is a way of life which the Kubu have not chosen for themselves. What is required is not simply the protection and conservation of their original environment but a fundamental reconsideration of the fate and future of the Kubu people.

— Gerard Persoon

Bustling Tidal Port on the Batang Hari

The modern provincial capital of Jambi combines the old prewar city, seat of the former Jambi sultanate, with a new administrative center at Telanaipura ("city of Prince Telanai") just to the west. It has a total population of some 300,000—a diverse mixture of Malays, Minangkabaus, Arabs, Chinese, Banjarese, Buginese and Javanese. This is a major tidal river port with a booming economy (palm oil, timber, plywood, rubber) and an interesting blend of old and new lifestyles.

A floating population lives on rafts (similar to those at Palembang) over the Batang Hari at Solok Sipin, just west of the city, and traditional wooden houses stand atop high pillars not far from the modern business center. A new mosque occupies the site of the former Istana—the palace of the sultan overlooking the river. A reconstructed Malay *adat* house, the Mayang Mangurai, has a permanent exhibit of ethnographic materials, including looms. The Provincial Museum has a small but interesting collection of archaeological artifacts from the Jambi region. There are several bronzes, including an unusual late Chola-style *dipalaksmi* temple lamp recovered from the banks of the lower Batang Hari.

The Muara Jambi remains

Covering over 1,500 ha, the site of the ancient port of Malayu, with its *candi* and *menapo* or brick-built temples and canals, is located some 26 km downstream from the modern capital, on the opposite (north) bank. This is the largest archaeological complex in Sumatra, with a small but interesting site museum—accessible by chartered speedboat or waterbus from Jambi (take the regular waterbus service bound for Muara Sabak and Kampung Laut, then scramble up the high river bank to a well-marked path leading to the site museum and ruins).

The full extent of the site and its associated riverine settlements is not yet known. Restoration of three main structures—Candi Tinggi, Candi Gumpung and Candi Kedaton, the last with an unusual fill of small white river pebbles—has been completed. Among the recoveries at Muara Jambi is an exquisite but headless Prajnaparamita image in East Javanese Singosari style, similar to that in the National Museum in Jakarta, dating from the early 13th century. Exploration, excavation and restoration continue under pressure from expanding agriculture in a battle against time.

Muara Jambi is thought to have been attacked and destroyed in about 1377. According to legend the last ruler of Muara Jambi, Prince Telanai, was fearful of a soothsayer's prediction that his son would bring disaster to himself and his realm. Consequently, on the birth of a son he put the boy with a letter into a chest which was thrown into the sea. The chest was washed up in Siam, where the Sumatran prince was adopted by the ruler and brought up at the royal court. Eventually the young prince returned to Jambi with a great Siamese army, killing his father and sacking the city. Whether there is any truth to this legend is not known but Siamese bronze Buddha images have been found in Jambi and a stone Sukhothai Buddha fragment was found during the course of excavations at Muara Jambi.

Much further downstream, at the mouth of the Kuala Niur—a southerly branch of the Batang Hari—the island of **Pulau Berhala** can be reached by speedboat in about 45 minutes from the village of Nipah Panjang. This tiny island, with its unspoilt white sand beaches, interesting rock formations and simple fishing villages, is reminscent of the islands of Bangka or Belitung. A 200-m hill dominates the island and has long been used as a navigational landmark by seafarers; it appears on 15th century Chinese sea charts.

Excursions to the hinterland

With the completion of the middle sections of the Trans-Sumatran Highway, including a 210-km feeder road from Muarabungo to the west, and the surfacing of the 260-km oil road from Palembang to the south, the city of Jambi is no longer as isolated from the rest of Sumatra as it once was. Land access to the north is still difficult, but the recent construction of a bridge over the mighty Batang Hari (said to be the largest bridge in Southeast Asia) opens the way for better road links with neighboring Riau—meaning that Jambi's economy should grow even more rapidly over the next decade.

With a bit of time on your hands, you should head west to the Kerinci Valley via Muarabungo and Bangko, a full day's drive away. The village of **Rantau Panjang** on the Batang Tabir, 30 km north of Bangko, has a number of traditional houses decorated in tricolor black, white and red motifs. Nearby are a number of early Islamic graves.

Just outside the mosque at the town of **Karang Berahi**, on the Batang Merangin some 25 km east of Bangko, is an Old Malay inscription written on stone in the Tamil

Opposite: *Butterflies in the jungles of Jambi.*
Below: *A mosque on the Batang Tebo, just to the north of Muarabungo.*

KAL MULLER

Grantha script which dates from the year Saka 608 of the Buddhist calendar, or AD 686. The lower part of the stone is carved into a lip where sacred water from ablutions poured over the stone and were collected and drunk by the assembled chiefs. In Malay fashion they "drank" the curse which would kill them if they broke the oath of allegiance to the Datuk or ruler of Srivijaya. Apparently a practical person, the Datuk backed up the magic of the curse with force of arms.

The Kerinci Valley

The highlight of this trip is the beautiful but isolated Kerinci Valley in the Bukit Barisan range at the western edge of Jambi province, overshadowed to the north by an active volcano of the same name. At 3,805 m, Mt. Kerinci is Sumatra's highest mountain. The name may in fact derive from the Tamil word *kurinci*, meaning a hilly tract.

The area is steeped in history and was once an important source of gold. Megalithic Bronze Age remains have been found here, along with traces of Buddhistic influence and early second millennium imported Chinese ceramics. Village names such as Sanggar Agung may indicate the persistence of Buddhist religious affiliations until fairly recent times. The area was finally subdued by Dutch force of arms in 1903.

Charles Campbell, who visited the area from Moko Moko in 1800, after an arduous climb taking four days, described the inhabitants as "below the common stature of the Malays, with harder visages and higher cheek bones, well knit in their limbs, and active; not deficient in hospitality, but jealous of strangers." They dwelled "in hoards, many families being crowded together in one long building." The longhouse in which Campbell stayed was 230 feet in length and housed 25 families. Such houses have long since disappeared, now replaced by individual Malay-style family dwellings. The people were growing "excellent tobacco, also cotton and indigo," as well as the "potatoe" which had been introduced some years earlier. Kerinci is now an important rice producing area.

Three routes lead into the valley and small town of **Sungaipenuh** the *kapubaten* administrative center and focus of the 1.4-million-ha Kerinci-Seblat National Park (see "Kerinci-Seblat" in WEST SUMATRA). One road links it with Jambi via the narrow valley of the Batang Merangin from Bangko, a second leads north past Mt. Kerinci through the government-owned Kayo Aro tea estate into

West Sumatra, and a third climbs quickly over the western edge of the Bukit Barisan to the coast via Tapan, also in West Sumatra.

Picturesque **Lake Kerinci**, 783 m above sea level and some 42 sq km in area, is surrounded by mountains. Once plagued with an infestation of water hyacinths (*Eichhornia crassipes*), control methods are now having some positive effect.

Mt. Kerinci, sometimes called Mt. Indrapura, dominates the valley to the north and is accessible by 4-wheel drive vehicles. Here too is the 6,000-ha state-owned PTP VIII Kayu Aro tea estate. A 16-km nature trail running up to the summit can be covered in about 5 hours. There is an overnight camp at about 3,000 m; the balance of the distance to the summit with its crater lake can be covered in about an hour and a half.

The village of **Pondok Tinggi** has a large, ornately decorated (carved and painted) timber mosque built in 1874—said to have been constructed without the use of a single iron nail. Here too is an enormous *bedug*, a horizontally-suspended drum used instead of a muezzin to call the faithful to prayer in very old Javanese mosques—a practice that dates to pre-Islamic Hindu-Javanese temples (much like the *kulkul* in Balinese temples).

Important megalithic remains, accessible along tracks suitable only for 4-wheel drive vehicles, are to be found at several locations. At **Desa Kunun**, some 6 km south of Sungaipenuh, is a 1.5-m-long stone known as the Batu Gong. At Desa Muak in Gunung Raya district south of the lake, some 30 km south of Sungeipenuh, is the Batu Bergambar or "picture stone"—a stone carved with animal and spiral relief motifs which was moved from its original location to a new site in the village in 1960. Here also is a fallen menhir known as Batu Patah, the "broken stone." At **Desa Pondok** in the same area, 35 km south of Sungaipenuh, is another decorated stone with spiral reliefs 3.85 m in length.

Danau Gunung Tujuh is a lake covering some 1,000 ha near the peak of Mt. Tujuh, about 50 km north of Sungaipenuh. At 1,996 m above sea level it has interesting flora and is said to be the highest freshwater lake in Southeast Asia. Temperatures at the nearby resthouse drop to 7 degrees C during the evening. Further north, on the border of West Sumatra's Solok Regency, is the 45-m high Telun Berasap waterfall.

— *E. Edwards McKinnon*

Right: *The diminutive and shy Sumatran rhino.*

SUMATRAN RHINO

The Elusive, Endangered 'Pocket' Rhino

The two-horned Sumatran rhino (*Dicerorhinus sumatrensis*) is a direct descendant of the prehistoric Woolly Rhinoceros that roamed the earth some 40 million years ago. This "pocket rhino" is the smallest of the world's five rhino species and displays an aptly Asian personality—being far less aggressive than its African counterparts. It is a harmless vegetarian that exhibits a certain charm: the young are known to bleat and squeak like lambs.

The Sumatran rhino is a shy, solitary wanderer—extremely difficult to observe in the field. At least one researcher was obliged to study it almost entirely through plaster casts of the beast's footprints.

Rhinos "speak" through smell—leaving urine squirts and communal dung piles as "notice boards" for other rhinos. For instance different scents indicate to a male whether or not a female is in heat or pregnant.

On the edge of extinction

The Sumatran rhinoceros is on the edge of extinction. Only about 800 survive worldwide, 700 in Sumatra itself. For centuries, the rhino has been hunted for its horn and other body parts prized in Asian folk medicine. In his *History of Sumatra*, Marsden stated that "The horn is esteemed an antidote against poison, and on that account formed into drinking cups." Today it is in demand as a fever tonic in traditional Chinese medicine (not as an aphrodisiac, as commonly believed). The rhino's unfortunate tendency to follow known trails make it vulnerable to pit-trap poaching—the hunter simply sits and waits.

Equally threatening is the steady cutting of the rhino's lowland forest habitat. This has forced most rhinos into rugged upland areas, despite their need for swampy mud-wallows to coat their hides against parasites and dry-cracking. Individuals are now too scattered to form viable breeding populations, and the Sumatran rhino's long-term survival is seriously in question.

In 1985 a captive breeding program was launched. Twelve Sumatran rhinos were distributed amongst zoos in Indonesia, Britain and the United States, and the long wait for offspring is on. Sumatran rhino pregnancies occur only every four years, last 16 months, and result in a single calf.

— *Ilsa Sharp*

ALAIN COMPOST

Jambi Town Practicalities

Prices in US dollars. S = single, D = double, AC = air-conditioned. Telephone code is 0741.

Jambi town lies on the southern banks of the Batang Hari. About 6 km to the west is the new administrative center of Telanaipura. To the southwest is Kotabaru ("New Town"), the new residential and office satellite.

GETTING THERE

By air. Merpati has 2 daily flights from Jakarta (1 hr/$70) and one from Palembang (25 min/ $25). Fly to and from other destinations via Palembang. SMAC has flights to Batam, Medan and Pekanbaru. Sultan Thaha airport is about 7 km south of the city, $2.50 by taxi. Merpati/ Garuda office: Jl. Dr. Wahidin 95, tel: 22303.

By car. It takes 28 hours to reach Jambi from Jakarta by car. Roads are good; the 260-km stretch up from Palembang has been resurfaced and is excellent, taking only 4 hrs.

By bus. Takes 30 hrs from Jakarta's Kalideres Terminal. Buses arrive/depart at Jambi intercity terminal outside of town on Jl. Prof. Dr. M. Yamin. A local minibus brings you into town. Cost for AC bus is $18. When leaving they pick you up in town if the ticket is purchased beforehand from an agent. Non AC is cheaper, $13.

By sea. Cargo ships with limited passenger berths travel from Jambi to Riau, where you can catch ships for most other ports. Check at the Pelni office for schedules and fares: Jl. Cut Nyak Dhien, tel: 24311 (close to the port).

GETTING AROUND

Walking is the best way to poke around the *pasar* (market), which is not very big. You see more and meet people, who are always willing to try out their English. Shopping is the local favorite pasttime, so the *pasar* is always busy.

Dokars are horse-drawn carts, a pleasant way to explore further afield, available near the telecom tower. Take care how you get onto the cart, which is delicately balanced and can tip up if you put too much weight on the back step.

Taxis are available in Jl. Mr. Asa'at—a variety of cars with drivers who speak a little English and enjoy giving tours for a price. State your route and agree on the fee in advance.

Oplet/minibuses are available from the *oplet* terminal in town, near the fruit market, to all areas around Jambi. Destinations are designated by color. Fare Rp150 Red-airport, green-jelutung, blue-Sipin/Telanaipura, yellow-Kotabaru

INFORMATION AND TOURS

The Tourist Office is in Kotabaru, near the mayor's office. They try to be helpful, and get so few tourists they may even show you around personally. You can arrange a custom tour in a car, van or bus from the following companies: Jambora Kencana, Jl. Gatot Subroto, tel: 23926. Jayapura Jayaraya, Jl. Damar 54, tel: 23369. Aquavita Jaya, Jl. Gatot Subroto, tel: 23647 (next to Hotel Abadi).

ACCOMMODATION
Expensive (above $20)

Abadi (25 rooms) Jl. Gatot Subroto 92-98, tel: 24054, 23065. The top hotel in Jambi. A new wing has been added at the rear overlooking the river. Good value for money $13 up to $47 for a deluxe room. AC, color TV, fridge, carpeting, modern bath, conference facilities, restaurant and karaoke bar.

Matahari (40 rooms) Jl. Sultan Agung 67A, tel: 24610. Out of town. $6.50 to $30 for a suite. Color satellite TV, AC, hot water, fridge, fan.

Surya, Jl. M. Thamrin 48, tel: 25399, 26558. Large, comfortable rooms, some with a view of the river at the back. Clean, modern bathrooms with AC, hot water, color satellite TV, phone. $15 to $25. Discounts available. Other facilities include video games in foyer, disco, karaoke, restaurant and covered parking.

Moderate and budget (under $20)

Kartika Jaya, Jl. Dr. Sutomo 32, tel: 26816, 22699. TV, disco, bar. $9 up to $21 for VIP.

Pinang, Jl. Sutomo 9. Close to shops, basic accommodation for $6 to $23.

Sederhana, Jl. Dr. Sutomo (next to Bank Rakyat Indonesia), tel: 24365, 22786. Comfortable, clean rooms, AC, tiled floors. $10 to $20 with AC; $6 to $10 with fan.

Wisma Cattleya (10 rooms) Jl. Prof. Dr. Soedewi 7, Sipin, tel: 22232. Nice, quiet place with AC and fan rooms.

FOOD

Jambi has great variety because of its mixed population and excellent seafood because of its proximity to the river and the sea.

Indonesian. Safari Restaurant, Jl. Dr. Wahidin, serves a wide variety of Indonesian dishes. Ayam Yogya, Jl. Abdul Muis 58, tel 26360, is a quiet place with outdoor seating specializing in Javanese fried chicken. Simpang Royal on Jl. M. Thamrin and Sari Bundo on Jl. Dr. Sam Ratulangi have good Padang food.

Chinese/seafood. Terkenal at Jl. M. Asa'at 124, tel: 22931, has an extensive menu of delicious Chinese dishes. Aneka Rasa (Kebun Jeruk) on Jl. Empu Gandring (turn right after the police station in Sipin) has good seafood and Indonesian dishes. Sangkuriang at Jl. Prof. Dr. Sumantri Bojonegoro 43, Sipin, tel 22406, has Sundanese style grilled fish, prawns, squid and chicken. Happiness at Jl. Cokroaminoto 17, tel: 22606 has a broad menu of inexpensive dishes. Sari Wangi, a little out of town on the way to the airport has great sizzling hot plates and seafood, always very popular. Inernational, Jl. Mr. Asa'at 34, tel 24897, has delicious food in a noisy Chinese atmosphere. Sit in the AC room upstairs.

Local specialities. Morning or night, ask a local to take you to their favorite noodle place. After the cinema, drive down to the river and sample fresh corn on the cob grilled over hot coals with a bit of sweet soy brushed on. Another treat which is inexpensive and filling is *martabak*—a sweet, thick pancake with peanut and sugar filling or cheese. There is also a savory *martabak* —a thin crisp pastry cooked on a large circular hotplate with a potato, egg and spicy minced goat (*kambing*) curry filling. This is cooked by Indian families in front of Chinese restaurants along Jl. Sultan Agung. Sit on the sidewalk under the stars enjoying a tasty meal.

SHOPPING

Look for the distinctive local batik, a craft from Java that has developed its own local "royal Malay" designs and colors. Try the handicrafts center, **Sanggar Batik Dan Kerajinan**, about 4 km from the town center at Jl. Prof. Dr. Sri Soedewi Masjchun Sofwan 18, Telanaipura.

NIGHTLIFE

Very little goes on at night as most people stay home and watch TV. There are a number of cinemas which have been refurbished and show some fairly recent action films. **Caesar Palace** is a bar and karaoke bar, pleasant to relax in at night with a drink and a sing along. **Hotel Kartika Jaya** has a disco that is the IN place to be for young people who like loud music. **Hotel**

Surya has a disco on Fri and Sat nights, karaoke on Thurs and Sun nights.

SERVICES

Banks are plentiful around the central market. Most will change traveler's checks and foreign currency; you have less trouble with US dollars than others. International and intercity calls can be made from the **Telecoms Office** at the base of the relay tower, which is can be seen from anywhere around the market. The **Post Office** is on Jl. Sultan Taha, the road beside the river, not far from the Governor's residence. Open 8-2 daily, until 12 noon Fri, closed Sun.

SPORTS

Badminton, table tennis, basketball, waterpolo, judo, karate, gymnastics, tennis and aerobics are all popular, with facilities available at the Sports Hall, Gelanggang Olah Raga in Kotabaru. The public swimming pool on Jl. Slamet Riyadi is olympic size, with pleasant surroundings. No food is available within the pool complex so bring your own. It is very well supervised, clean and has swimming coaches available.

HEALTH

Doctors and dentists are easily found (ask at your hotel) and most speak some English. There are 3 hospitals in town: Rumah Sakit Umum, Jl. Jend. Suprapto, tel: 22364. Rumah Sakit DKT, Jl. Ramattaher. Rumah Sakit Bersalin Theresia (Maternity), Jl. Dr. Soetomo, tel: 23119. Reliable chemists (*apotik*) are Apotik Jambi, in the Plaza, tel: 23205, and Apotik Aria, Jl. M. Thamrin, tel: 24019.

— *Glyn Luntungan*

PART VIII

Introducing South Sumatra

Like the delicate skeleton of a tropical leaf, South Sumatra's enormous network of rivers drains an area the size of Ireland (103,688 sq km). Five mighty rivers, a dozen major tributaries and a thousand small, winding streams link the scattered settlements of this vast and sparsely populated province. At Palembang, most of the larger rivers join the longest and broadest one—the meandering, slow-moving Musi. The story of the Musi is the story of South Sumatra's land and people.

The river rises at the western edge of the province as a small, sparkling stream deep in the jungle-clad Bukit Barisan range near the towering peaks of Mt. Dempo (3,159 m) and Mt. Patah (2,817 m). Leaving the cool uplands, the Musi tumbles and rolls through the foot-hills past scattered coffee plantations and fields of corn and rice cleared and planted by pioneer settlers. Reaching the plain, it slows to a gentle lope, then to a sluggish crawl—winding across the gently-sloping plain to the steamy marshes of the eastern seaboard. Tiny villages line the banks, where on moon-lit nights young Malays row their boats past sleepy waterfront houses.

A thousand years ago, Palembang was the capital of the mighty maritime kingdom of Srivijaya, whose trading network extended to Southern Thailand, the Malay Peninsula and the shores of Java. The town's name derives from *limbang*—to pan for gold—and Palembang's early prosperity was probably founded on river gold. According to ancient travelers' accounts, the ruler's palace contained a pool connected by a narrow canal to the Musi—source of the king's immense wealth. Into this pool every morning he threw bars of gold, which lay shimmering like goldfish beneath the surface of the water. Across the river in the early morning drifted the delicate scent of incense from the monasteries of Palembang, where more than a thousand monks lived and studied Buddhist scriptures.

Today, the river is dominated by Palem-bang's famous Ampera Bridge. Shortly upstream from it, the Musi is joined by its two main tributaries, the Ogan and the Komering. It then swells to several hundred meters in width; ships up to 10,000 tons regularly make the 100-km journey from the coast to Palembang's Boom Baru harbor. The banks of the Musi are lined with houses on stilts; some stand meters above the water at low tide.

South Sumatra is the homeland of the Malay people and the ancient cradle of Malay culture. The ancestor of all Malay rulers is believed to have descended from the heavens on Bukit Seguntang, a small hill to the north of Palembang. (A second Bukit Seguntang is also found by the village of Pariangan in the Minang Highlands.) Now devout Muslims, the Malays absorbed many Indian beliefs during the first millennium AD, deepening and enriching a native belief system which included the veneration of natural objects such as rocks and trees, and a belief in the existence of spirits which must be propitiated. Several 7th-century inscriptions from Palembang are heavily Sanskritized and much of the ritual and special vocabulary used in later Islamic Malay courts is Indic in origin.

Palembang was the most important center of trade in Southeast Asia for more than three hundred years—from the late 7th to the early 11th centuries. Then, as now, the city spread for many kilometers along the banks of the Musi. While the king lived ashore, his subjects made their homes on the water, manning a huge fleet that provided the basis for Srivijaya's control of the straits. Few relics have survived from this era, but more than 24 archaeological sites have been identified, including the ancient palace, and the future thus promises many exciting disoveries.

— *Ian Caldwell*

Overlead: *The rocky shoreline of Bangka Island. Photo by Jill Gocher.* **Opposite:** *Girl in traditional Malay* adat *costume. Photo by David Booth.*

PALEMBANG

Bustling City Astride the Musi River

Palembang is a sweltering, bustling industrial and communications center seldom visited by foreigners—that is trying hard these days to upgrade its image. With over a million inhabitants, it is Sumatra's second largest city (after Medan) and the sixth largest in Indonesia (after Semarang). Its booming economy is based on coal mining, plantation agriculture, oil refining and fertilizer production.

Palembang straddles the 600-m wide Musi River at a strategic point just below the confluence of major tributaries providing access to the vast Sumatran hinterland. Despite its new-found oil wealth, Palembang is a city with a 1,300-year history, steeped in Malay culture and site of the ancient Buddhist Srivijayan empire. It still produces some of finest textiles and lacquerwares in Indonesia, and a number of city residents live out over the water—just as they did many centuries ago.

The old palace precincts

The city's main landmark is **Ampera Bridge** —built by the Japanese as a war reparation by order of Soekarno and inaugurated by him with great fanfare in 1964. At the time it was Southeast Asia's longest bridge and the central span between the imposing twin towers neatly hoisted up and down to allow ships to pass. Now, alas, it is stuck.

Running north from the bridge is Jl. Sudirman, Palembang's main street, joining with Jl. Merdeka at a large roundabout in front of the **Mesjid Agung** or Royal Mosque —built by Sultan Machmud Badaruddin I in 1740 and recently restored to its former splendor. This area was the former capital of an Islamic kingdom which warred periodically with the Dutch, until the last sultan— Ahmad Najamuddin—surrendered and was exiled to Banda Neira in 1825.

Start your tour of the city at the **Museum Sultan Machmud Badaruddin II**, facing the Musi River just west of the northern end of the bridge. The museum building, with its imposing semi-circular staircases, is a curious blend of colonial and traditional Malay architecture. It was constructed by the Dutch in 1823 on the site of the former sultan's palace (after the latter had been razed by attacking Dutch forces), and served for many years as the official Dutch Residency. It is presently being refurbished with a traditional *keraton* (palace) interior upstairs, complete with royal sleeping and living chambers. Downstairs are restaurants serving Palembang specialities. The Tourist Information Center is at the back, next to a new open-air theater where you can watch traditional Malay dances (see "Palembang Practicalities").

To the rear of the museum is the new **Art Market**, 15 miniature pavilions where you can watch local craftsmen at work on delicate gold or silver *songket* brocades and intricate red-and-black lacquerwares—the latter being

a craft introduced to Palembang from China, perhaps as early as the Srivijayan period. Also produced here are finely woven baskets, *tikar* mats, and seashell souvenirs.

Walk from the museum toward the river and turn right onto Jl. Keraton—through the old fruit market where ladies in batik sarongs and headscarves sit amidst piles of bananas, melons and papayas. The view of Ampera Bridge is impressive, but don't step into the road or you are likely to be run down by an *oplet* or *becak*! About 500 m west of the museum is the old **Benteng Kuto Besak** fortress, surround by a 3-meter high, filthy-grey (previously whitewashed) wall. Built by the sultan in 1797, it is now used by the army and entry is forbidden. From the front gates you can however see the elegant old buildings.

The Musi River

A little further upriver is a boarding point for river taxis that ply the Musi. To experience the true flavor of Palembang, a trip along the river is a must. Head downriver past a group of houseboats lining the opposite bank just before Ampera Bridge. After the bridge, move over to the north bank to see the brisk floating market known as **Pasar 16 Ilir**. River activity peaks at about 11 am, but fortunately there are no traffic jams yet.

One km further downstream, on the left, is Palembang's main harbor, **Boom Baru**. Two km further on is the massive, state-owned Pusri Fertilizer Plant—said to be the largest in Asia. Immediately past this is **Pulau Kemaro**—a small, untidy island that hosts a large Buddhist temple and the grave of a Chinese princess. The princess is said to have been sent to marry the king of Srivijaya. When she arrived, boats were sent ashore with large ceramic pots. The king expected to find gold and jewels inside, but in the first one he found only preserved vegetables. This made him angry, and he ordered the pots thrown into the river. Seeing this, the princess jumped in too and drowned. But some of the other pots broke open, revealing that they were indeed full of gold. The princess was buried on this island, and the temple erected nearby is considered particularly efficacious in dispensing good fortune.

Traditional rumah limas

The new **Museum of South Sumatra** 5 km north of town has a collection of mysterious megalithic statues from Pasemah, including a famous one depicting an ancient warrior with a bronze drum astride an elephant. There is also a 150-year-old *rumah limas* or traditional Palembang-style house that was transferred here from the city. Unfortunately many of the original furnishings have been transferred to Jakarta's Taman Mini Indonesia, but there is still a fine display of ceremonial clothes, hunting, farming and fishing implements, and traditional coffee preparation. Open Tues-Sat 8-12 am and 1-4 pm; Sun 8-12. Closed Mon.

Two other well-preserved examples of *rumah limas* remain in Palembang—Rumah Hasyim Ning (at Jl. Pulo, 24 Ilir) and Rumah Bayumi (off Jl. Mayor Ruslan), both still occupied. They can be visited if you make arrangements at the tourism office in back of the Sultan Machmud Museum.

—David Booth

Opposite: *Lovely* rumah limas *interior.* **Above, left:** *Life on the Musi.* **Above, right:** *Ampera Bridge.*

PALEMBANG SIDETRIPS

Journey to the Western Highlands

Tourism is in its infancy in South Sumatra, and there are few established routes or facilities outside of Palembang. The province's many natural attractions can nevertheless easily be reached by public transport or by chartering an air-conditioned car or minibus. The highlights are a visit to the Pasemah Plateau—site of mysterious ancient megaliths (see following section)—and to lovely Lake Ranau, a huge crater lake on the border with Lampung. Both are situated in the rugged volcanic highlands at the western edge of the province, which means a full day's drive from Palembang each way on some rather rough roads. Lodgings and food are very basic, but these inconveniences are more than compensated for by the scenery and by a refreshing sense of serendipitous discovery that accompanies you along the way—not to mention the extraordinarily friendly people you meet.

West to Lahat

The winding, potholed main highway leading west of Palembang runs for the first 50 km through a flat, swampy plain past pretty *kampung* villages with wooden houses on stilts. Children wash and swim in the murky water; men fish from small canoes with nets and spears, and women prepare rice or hang their laundry. Padang restaurants by the roadside are open 24 hours for the convenience of passing motorists. From time to time your driver will slam on the brakes, screeching from a breakneck 100 kph to a sedate 10 kph past isolated police checkpoints.

As the terrain gradually rises out of the swampy lowlands, you enter a thickly forested area dotted with charming country villages whose fine wooden houses and fenced gardens are surrounded by flowering bougainvilleas. Ox-drawn carts lumber along and well-fed cows graze by the roadside.

The first large town is **Prabumulih**, about 2 hours and 96 km from Palembang. This is an oil town and rail junction, and lies in the center of a pineapple-growing area—you can buy some of the sweetest pineapples you've ever tasted, for less than ten cents! The road forks here. If you are headed down to Danau Ranau, turn left (south) toward Baturaja. For Pasemah and Sumindo turn right for Muaraenim, a town 85 km west of Prabumulih.

The road west to **Muaraenim** brings you

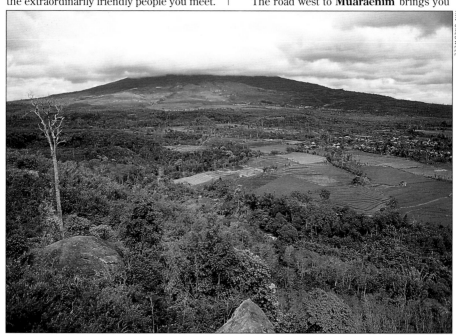

through dense oil palm groves and pretty villages, with roadside stalls selling pineapples, melons and papayas. After about 40 km you reach a turn-off to the right for **Pendopo**, where the region's oil was first discovered in 1899. Today, the wells in this South Sumatran basin are the most productive in all of Indonesia. The roads around here are very bad, however, so expect slow going.

Muaraenim is the next stop, a quiet town at the confluence of the Enim and Lematang rivers that is a good place to stopover for the night, as it has a reasonable, air-conditioned hotel (Hotel Rene). The road forks again, and you turn to the right (west) for Lahat and Pagaralam, the the left (south) for Baturaja. The nearby town of Tanjung Enim, 13 km south of here, is the site of Indonesia's largest open-cast coal mine.

The road from Muaraenim west to Lahat (43 km) is good, passing from the eastern plains into the foothills of the Bukit Barisan, with sweeping views of paddy fields and the winding Lematang River. Stones are collected from the riverbed in tiny villages here to be sold to contractors; coffee and rice are grown on the fertile hillsides and sun-dried on rattan mats by the roadside. About 11 km before Lahat, stop by the river to admire the view of **Mt. Serelo**, an oval-shaped peak topped by a narrow, finger-like protrusion (also known as Bukit Tunjuk or "Finger Hill"). There is a path leading up from the village of Sukacinta,

and this is a popular outing for local youths.

The medium sized town of **Lahat** is the next stop, a road junction on the Trans-Sumatran Highway that is the jumping-off point for visits to Pagaralam in the Pasemah region (see "Pasemah Highlands"). The road up to **Pagaralam** is especially beautiful—shortly after leaving Lahat, it climbs up to a plateau offering views down across to the Lematang River which wends its way through a valley at the foot of an almost-vertical cliff face. Dramatic mountain vistas unfold after the village of Pulau Pinang—with lofty ridges and peaks in all directions as far as the eye can see.

The Sumindo Highlands

On your way back to Palembang, or if you are heading southward to Lake Ranau or Lampung, you can make a scenic full-day's detour into the Sumindo Highlands—a lush and extremely beautiful region accessed via a winding mountain road south of the main Lahat-Pagaralam highway. This is a sparsely populated, coffee-growing region of tiny highland hamlets. Set off early and allow time for stops to take in the breathtaking scenery. Public transport is unreliable, so charter a

Opposite: *A visit to the Pasemah Plateau around Pagaralam, in the shadow of towering Mt. Dempo, is one of the highpoints of an excursion to the western highlands.* **Below:** *Entrance to the Goa Putri ("Princess") caves west of Baturaja.*

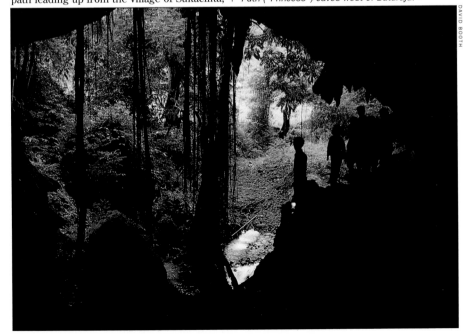

DAVID BOOTH

minibus and pack a picnic lunch, as no restaurants are to be found along the way.

Turn south at Tanjung Tebat, about halfway (30 km) between Lahat and Pagaralam, just near the hairpin bend. The road climbs gently from here to the village of Kota Agung, offering good views of Mt. Serelo to the east. At Kota Agung, turn left to Muaratiga (14 km), then take the right fork in Muaratiga toward Pulau Panggung.

Past Muaratiga the road deteriorates, with potholes the size of bathtubs. Don't be put off by this, because this is where the views start. Steep grades afford superb panoramas of mountain ridges and hillsides thick with durian trees, some 20 m tall. Fresh durians here cost only 25 cents—the same fruit in Jakarta costs ten times as much. Sculpted rice paddies greet you as you whiz round the bends; villagers laden with bundles of firewood strapped to their backs pass you on the road.

Continue on to **Pulau Panggung**, passing through dense rainforests one minute and emerging the next onto open, green carpets of mature rice waving gently in the breeze beneath rolling hills. After Pulau Panggung, where shops sell drinks and provision, the road narrows and zigzags round sharp, blind bends. Small patches of forest are being cleared for coffee plantations here and coffee beans lie on large rattan mats. The 1.5 hour drive to Sugihwaras is simply spectacular.

About 2 km before Sugihwaras, the road

descends steeply; keep an eye out to your right for the 80-m-high **Tenang Waterfall**, set against the mountain ridges. A new, 500-m road leads in to a parking lot and you then walk 1 km to a bamboo suspension bridge over the river; another 500 m brings you to the crashing falls, the largest in the province. Back on the main road at Sugihwaras, you can turn left for Muaraenim and Palembang, or right towards Baturaja and Lake Ranau.

Gua Putri caves

If you are heading south, you may want to stop at the Gua Putri caves. The trek through these fascinating caves, at **Padang Bindu** on the main road 35 km west of Baturaja, is not for the faint-hearted. Strong shoes with anti-slip soles are a must, as the rocks are very slippery in places. Guides with lamps and torches will accompany you and provide detailed explanations (in Indonesian) of legends associated with the caves.

The main chamber is about 150 m long and 15-20 m at its widest point. The ceiling is 12 m high in some places, and as little as 1.5 in others. Hundreds of bats hang from the roof; as the light disturbs them, they swish past you like arrows. Underground rivers here feed the Ogan River. To explore very deeply in the caves, you must be slim and supple to squeeze through the gaps between the rocks. Legends tells of a king who formerly had his palace in the cave, and each cavern has its own story. Stalagmites and stalactites with interesting shapes all figure in the tale—here is a waterfall, there a throne surmounted by an umbrella.

Spectacular Lake Ranau

For most people, the highlight of any visit to South Sumatra's western highlands is Lake Ranau—a shimmering crater lake set in the ancient caldera of Mt. Seminung (1,340 m), an active volcano straddling the border with Lampung Province. The lake is 16 km long and 9 km wide, and has a depth of 300 m. The climate in these highlands is deliciously cool, and the remote setting offers lush vegetation, crystal clear waters and delightful excursions to a nearby waterfall, a hot spring and an island in the lake. Although it is popular with locals on the weekends, the lake has not yet been developed for tourism and you thus have the feeling much of the time of having

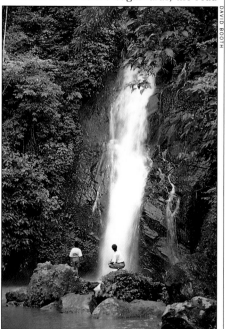

Left: Tenang ("Tranquility") Waterfall, at the edge of Lake Ranau. **Right:** A view across the mirror-smooth waters of the lake at sunset.

stumbled into your own "private paradise."

Banding Agung on the northern shore is the main lakeside farming and fishing community, and has several clean, inexpensive *losmen*. The people here are all farmers who raise cash crops like coffee, tobacco and cloves. Some rice is also grown, as well as succulent pineapples, bananas and avocados that are sold locally for only 5 cents a kilo. The lake teems with fish, which are caught and charcoal grilled in small restaurants by the shore. In the early evening, local fishing canoes are reflected on the lake's mirror-like surface against a brilliant golden sunset, with the mountains silhouetted behind.

Kota Batu on the southeastern shore is Ranau's other tiny town, but has no accommodations. Between these two towns lies Wisma Pusri Ranau, a small state-owned hotel. The manager, Pak Suwarso, speaks good English and is an excellent source of information; he is also a superb cook and enjoys meeting foreigners.

There is plenty to do around the lake. A 15-minute walk from Wisma Pusri through a patch of forest and past coffee groves and rice fields leads to Subik Waterfall—a 25-m cascade tucked into a gentle recess in the rocks by the edge of the lake.

Another excursion, this time across the lake by rented motorboat ($5 per hour from Wisma Putri or Banding Agung), brings you to a hot spring at the foot of Mt. Semuning.

The only evidence of the springs from the lake is a small stream of water trickling down a gently sloping rockface. After the journey across the lake, a refreshing swim or paddle around the spot where the hot and cold waters mix is bliss. Choose your own water temperature, but be careful of the hot sand by the rockface. Snorkeling here is also a delight, and large inner tubes can be brought along for non-swimmers.

Across from the hot springs is a small islet known as **Pulau Marisa**. According to local legend, the island appeared one night as the failed solution to a love triangle. A pretty young princess named Putri Aisah had two suitors—Sipahit Lidah ("Bitter Tongue") and Simata Empat ("Four Eyes"). To solve her dilemma, she promised to marry whichever one could manage to build a bridge across the lake, from the hot springs to Banding Agung, in a single night. This island was the only part of the bridge completed by the time the sun arose, so both suitors were rejected. It is just 5 minutes by boat from the hot springs—here you can lunch in the shade of palm trees and catch up on some lost sleep.

If you are in the mood for something more adventuresome, you can organize an expedition to the summit of Mt. Semuning. There is also an elephant training school in the vicinity, and you can hire the elephants for a "safari" through the jungle.

—David Booth

PASEMAH PLATEAU

Mysterious Megalithic Remains

Some of Sumatra's most remarkable megalithic remains are found on the remote Pasemah Plateau at the western edge of South Sumatra—a wide and fertile grassland plain surrounded by an almost impenetrable wall of mountains. The plateau stretches for 70 km in a northwest to southeast direction along a cleft within the Bukit Barisan range, at the foot of dormant Mt. Dempo (3,159 m). In the early centuries of the Christian era, this plateau was the home of a flourishing Bronze Age megalithic culture.

Pasemah's main town is **Pagaralam** (710 m). Scattered around the town are dozens of megaliths—upright stones arranged in neat groups or rows, troughs with carved human heads, terraced platforms, stone mortars, dolmens (stone tables), painted cist graves sunk into the ground and numerous carved stone figures. Many of the better stones have

been moved to museums in Jakarta or Palembang; the most famous Pasemah figure is the magnificent Batu Gajah or Elephant Stone —now in the Museum of South Sumatra in Palembang—which depicts an armed warrior mounting (or perhaps subduing) an elephant. But many more stones still stand where they were originally placed—in the fertile fields and gardens surrounding Mt. Dempo.

Who built these megaliths—and why? Local legends attribute them to a magician known as Lidah Pahit ("Bitter Tongue") who, it is said, could turn people and animals into stone. One of the images at Tinggi Hari is regarded as a petrified princess (Batu Puteri). The story goes that the princess once met Lidah Pahit. He asked her where she was going, but she was too proud to answer, so he turned her into stone.

A more scientific theory is that the megaliths are the work of an ancient people who lived here between AD 0-500. Several carvings depict armed warriors carrying huge Dongson bronze drums, which arrived in the archipelago in the first centuries AD. None shows signs of the Indian influence, which was to lead, in the 7th century, to the rise of great Indianized trading kingdoms such as Malayu and Srivijaya along the courses of the great rivers nearer to the coast. Many of the carvings celebrate military prowess, and point to an unsettled, warlike society.

Often, the carvings are so worn that is dif-

IAN CALDWELL

ficult to know whether they depict men or women. Women are often dressed in a sort of poncho that is tied under the arms. Children wear only a girdle. Men—perhaps engaged in war or hunting—wear a girdle with a loincloth over it and on their wrists and ankles are large metal rings or bracelets. Several figures wear broad, flat bands around their knecks (similar rings were worn in Nias in the 19th century as a mark of distinction among head-hunters).

Men carry short, broad swords with long

hilts and pommels, and a close fitting headdress ending in a peak at the back. Van der Hoop, a pioneering Dutch aviator-turned-archaeologist who studied these ancient remains in the 1930s, thought they were protective helmets made of bronze or iron. They are also strikingly similar to the Javanese *blankon*—a close fitting cloth cap with a projecting rear knob. Most surprisingly—considering the warlike nature of the carvings—there is no evidence of the use of bows and arrows.

Visiting the megaliths

A megalith depicting a man subduing a headless elephant can be found next to the Taqwa Mosque on the road between Losman Mirasa and the Pagaralam town center. Next to the elephant is a *lesung batu*, a giant mortar half buried on its side.

Walking in the opposite direction from the Mirasa, a left turn onto Jl. Tanjung Aru before the Hotel Dharmakaya brings you after 2 km to **Kampung Tanjung Aro**. Turn right at house no. 106 and walk 50 m to a pair of cist graves—a bamboo fence encloses the site, now partially filled with water.

On the same street, locate house no. 90 to see another *lesung batu*. Then, with the cist graves to your back, walk 50 m to an amazing set of carved rocks scattered among the rice fields. One has a bas relief of a man wrestling a giant serpent. The setting is spectacular, with Mt. Dempo in the background.

The most impressive group of megaliths and cist graves is found just past the village of **Tegurwangi**, 6 km from Pagaralam. Here, 4 human figures squat on a river bank 50 m from the main road (one has almost fallen in!). The heads are clearly defined—with thick lips, bulging eyes and heavy brows. On their backs they carry large, bulky objects. Originally they stood on a platform with their backs to each other, facing the four cardinal directions. Close by and set in the midst of rice fields are 3 recently-opened cist graves. Inside one is the drawing of a *naga* (dragon) and a human figure with a long, orange nose —now badly faded.

A remarkable 3-m-high figure of a warrior has been carved into a rockface close to Tegurwangi. Walk 100 m back down the road and ask directions to **Batu Balai**. A brisk, 15-minute trek through the rice paddies brings you to a large, rocky outcrop—the carving is on the lower left face. The warrior's plumed headdress is similar to those worn by dancing figures depicted on Dongson bronze drums of the first millennium AD.

Berlubai, 3 km from Pagaralam, has a number of interesting megaliths. Ask at the village chief's house (*kepala desa*) to see the *batu gajah* ("elephant stone"), and hordes of schoolchildren will accompany you through fields cultivated with rice, chili peppers and tomatoes, to an enormous rock carving of a warrior wresting an elephant to the ground. The man is wearing anklets and his right wrist is protected by a small shield. On the return journey, ask to see the three standing figures that are smaller versions of those found at Tegurwangi.

— *Ian Caldwell*

Opposite: *Painting of a warrior in a recently-opened cist grave near the village of Tegurwangi.*
Above, left: *A group of figures on a riverbank, also near Tegurwangi.* **Above, right:** *A warrior astride an elephant near Berlubai.*

Palembang Practicalities

Includes Lahat, Pagaralam (Pasemah Plateau), Baturaja and Lake Ranau. Prices in US dollars. S = Single, D = Double, AC = air-conditioned. Telephone code for Palembang is 0711.

Palembang is bisected by the Musi River. The northern bank is known as Ilir, the southern as Ulu. The two are linked by the imposing Ampera Bridge, but everything of importance—hotels, shops, offices and sights—is on the north (Ilir) side. To see the unique Palembang handicrafts and get into the history and culture of this old city, you need 3 days.

GETTING THERE

By air. From Singapore, there are direct Garuda flights on Mon, Tues, Thurs and Sat ($113), but it is cheaper to take the ferry from Finger Pier to Batam ($11), a taxi to Batam airport ($6) and then fly from Batam on Merpati ($51).

Merpati operates six daily flights from Jakarta ($54); one per day from Medan ($103), Padang ($63), Jambi ($26), Pangkal Pinang ($25) and Bengkulu ($37); daily except Fri from Batam ($51) and Bandung ($63); daily except Tues and Fri from Bandar Lampung ($34). Both airline offices are in the Sandjaja Hotel.

For the 13-km journey from the airport to the city either take a blue airport taxi for $5 or walk 2 km to the main highway and catch a minibus to town for Rp300.

By bus. Express buses go direct to Palembang from Jakarta (24 hrs), Jambi (4 hrs), Lampung (10-12 hrs), Bengkulu (12 hrs) and Padang. For a bus with AC, you pay up to $15 whereas the non-AC buses start at $6.50. Have a look at the bus first; you generally get what you pay for. Most bus offices in Palembang are on the main highway on the outskirts of town. To get into the city, hop onto a minibus (usually a Kijang) for Rp150.

By minibus. To and from Bandar Lampung, book a door-to-door AC minibus with reclining seats, karaoke and snacks for $12 each way (9 hrs). Call Eka Travel for pick-up: 51924 in B.L.; 27263, 24396 in Palembang.

By train. From Lampung, the comfortable, AC Sriwijaya Express night train takes 9 hrs and costs $6 (standard), $10 (executive). If you are on a tight budget, take the Rajabasa instead at $2; no AC (and often no seats). Beautiful scenery, but don't expect prompt departures. From Lubuk Linggau and Lahat, daily service on the Sindang Marga day train costs $3.50 and $3, respectively.

You arrive in Palembang at Kertapati station south of the river. The 4-km trip into the city takes 10 minutes by minibus, Rp150.

INFORMATION AND TOURS

For tours with knowledgeable English and Dutch-speaking guides, contact **Wisin Tours**, Jl. Veteran 173. They can also assist with side-trips outside Palembang. Also inquire at the **Tourist Information Office** in back of Sultan Machmud Badaruddin II Museum.

GETTING AROUND

Becaks. The most pleasant form of transport for short distances, up to 2 km, is the *becak*. These can be found anywhere in the city, but cannot travel on main throughfares; going across town thus takes you down quaint sidestreets you would otherwise miss. Fares range from Rp300 to Rp1000 (50 cents), depending on the distance and mood of your driver. Bargain hard and agree on the price first.

Public transport. For longer distances, take a minibus (called *taxi* or *oplet*) or a city bus (*bis kota*) running on set routes. Fares are Rp150 for any distance. *Oplet* routes are indicated by color, and they stop at fixed points; all run from the big roundabout north of Ampera Bridge. Ask at your hotel for specific routes. *Bis kota* only ply the main roads, e.g. Jl. Sudirman, Jl. Veteran, Jl. Kapt. Rivai. Buses and minibuses stop running at about 9:30 pm, so a late night out could result in some unplanned exercise on the way back.

Taxis. Hotel taxis (old and unmarked, some with AC) can be chartered for $2.50 an hour, min. 2 hrs, and it seems that any private car can be rented as a "taxi." Always available by the roadside on Jl. Sudirman at night, and you can negotiate lower prices during quiet periods.

ACCOMMODATION

Palembang is a very big city geared to business rather than tourist travelers. A good hotel is essential to an enjoyable stay. The pleasure—and relief—of collapsing in an AC room is not to be missed after a grueling day of hot *oplet* rides. Budget for 3 nights in a good hotel and worry about the expenses later. Discounts of 10-30 percent are often available for the asking, especially if you ring up first or ask at the airport booth.

Expensive ($30 and up)

All hotels in this category have AC, TV with in-house video and hot water. Add 21 percent tax and service to the prices below.

King's (137 rooms) Jl. Kol. Atmo, tel: 310033, fax: 310937. $33 S, $40-$50 D, deluxe room $60, suites $75-125. Most expensive in Palembang; a newer hotel, central for shopping. The decor is simple, but tasteful. Best coffeeshop in Palembang, serves special snacks as you watch the huge video screen.

Lembang Jl. Let. Kol. Iskandar. Newly opened; just round the corner from King's, with the

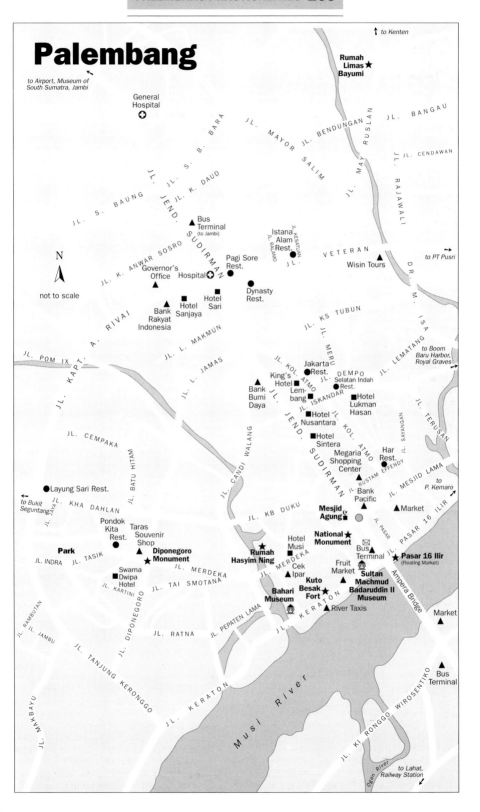

Palembang

to Airport, Museum of
South Sumatra, Jambi

↑ to Kenten

**Rumah
Limas ★
Bayumi**

General
Hospital ✚

JL. S. B. BARA
JL. MAYOR SALIM
JL. BENDUNGAN
JL. MAY. RUSLAN
JL. BANGAU
JL. CENDAWAN
JL. RAJAWALI

JL. S. BAUNG
JL. JEND. SOSRO SUDIRMAN
JL. K. DAUD
JL. KESATUAN
JL. RAJAMO

N

not to scale

Bus
Terminal ▲
(to Jambi)

Istana
Alam
Rest.

VETERAN

JL. K. ANWAR
JL. KAPT. A. RIVAI

Governor's
Office ▲
Hospital ✚

Pagi Sore ●
Rest.

Wisin Tours ●

to PT Pusri →

DR. M. ISA

Bank ▲
Rakyat
Indonesia

Hotel ■
Sanjaya

Hotel ■
Sari

Dynasty ●
Rest.

JL. POM IX
JL. L. MAKMUN
JL. L. JAMAS
JL. KS TUBUN
JL. LEMATANG

to Boom
Baru Harbor,
Royal Graves →

JL. CEMPAKA

JL. BATU HITAM

JL. CANDI WALANG

Jakarta ●
Rest.
King's
Hotel ■
Lem- ■
bang
Bank
Bumi
Daya ■

JL. KOL. ATMO
JL. MERU
JL. ISKANDAR

DEMPO
Selatan Indah ●
Rest.

Hotel ■
Lukman
Hasan

JL. KOL. ATMO

JL. TERUSAN

Hotel ■
Nusantara

Hotel ■
Sintera

Megaria
Shopping
Center

Har ●
Rest.

JL. SAYANGAN
JL. MESJID LAMA

to
P. Kemaro

JL. JEND. SUDIRMAN

JL. RUSTAM EFFENDY

Bank
Pacific ●

Market ▲

Layung Sari Rest. ●

to Bukit
Seguntang →

JL. JAYA
JL. KHA DAHLAN

Pondok
Kita ●
Rest.

Taras
Souvenir
Shop ▲

Diponegoro ★
Monument

JL. KB DUKU

Mesjid
Agung ☾

JL. PASAR
JL. PASAR 16 ILIR

Pasar 16 Ilir ▲
(Floating Market)

Market ▲

Park

JL. INDRA   JL. TASIK

Swarna ■
Dwipa
Hotel

JL. KARTINI

JL. MERDEKA

JL. TAI SMOTANA

Hotel
Musi ●

Cek
Ipar ▲

**Rumah ★
Hasyim Ning**

**National ★
Monument**

Fruit
Market

Bus ✉
Terminal ▲

**Sultan
Machmud
Badaruddin II
Museum**

Ampera Bridge

JL. RAMBUTAN
JL. JAMBU

JL. DIPONEGORO

JL. RATNA

JL. PEPATEN LAMA

JL. KERATON

**Bahari
Museum** ⌂

**Kuto
Besak ★
Fort**

▲ River Taxis

Market ▲

JL. TANJUNG KERONGGO

JL. MAKBAYU

JL. KERATON

Musi River

Bus ▲
Terminal

JL. KI RONGGO WIROSENTIKO

Ogan River

to Lahat,
Railway Station →

same owners. $36-$55 D, suites at $100. Restaurant, 24-hour coffeeshop, fitness center, beauty parlor and convention center.

Sandjaja (144 rooms) Jl. Kapt. A. Rivai, tel: 310675, fax: 313693. A modern hotel with two wings, the higher one with deluxe rooms. $32-$39 S, $43-$49 D, suites at $105. Standard rooms face a noisy street or a wall, superior ones face the pool. Good coffeeshop with reasonable prices. The Sriwijaya Restaurant on top offers good views of the city, and a chance to practice your singing if you like karaoke. Large swimming pool, fitness center, beauty salon, shopping arcade with Garuda/Merpati offices.

Swarna Dwipa (70 rooms) Jl. Tasik 2, tel: 28322, fax: 28999. In a quiet residential area 2 km west of downtown, with a touch of colonial Palembang. Overlooks an artificial lake and small park. Good value at $27-$44 S, $32-$50 D, suites at $100. Pay a bit extra for a room overlooking the park. There is a modern wing and a colonial wing; the latter is best but only has deluxe rooms. Service is excellent. The buffet-style breakfast is a bargain at $3. Happy hour in the colonial bamboo bar from 5-7, with drinks at half price. Pool, fitness center and beauty salon.

Moderate ($10 to $30)

Few good alternatives in this range. If you can afford it, stay at the Swarna Dwipa (or slum it and save). **Hotel Sari** at the corner of Jl. Sudirman and Kapt. A. Rivai (tel: 23319) has 35 rooms from $7 to $24, breakfast included; Padang restaurant in foyer, popular with Indonesians. The **Nusantara** on Jl. Let. Kol. Iskandar is quiet and clean, on a sidestreet close to the shopping district; 15 rooms: $7 with fan, $12 with AC. The **Sintera** at Jl. Sudirman 38 (tel: 21618) has rooms from $7 to $20.

Budget (Below $10)

For the cheapies, try **Lukman Hassan** on Jl. Let. Kol. Iskandar; $3 to $4. The **Asiana** on Jl. Sudirman charges the same; clean and basic.

EATING

All top hotels have good restaurants serving Western and Indonesian food. Hotel Sandjaja's **Sriwijaya Restaurant** on the top floor has good Chinese food and panoramic views of the city, but is only open after 4 pm. **King's Palace** (above King's Hotel) serves some of the best Chinese cuisine in Palembang, but with blaring pop singers after 9 pm and a disco from midnight to 2 am; expensive.

For a quieter evening in pleasant surroundings, try the **Seguntang Restaurant** at the Swarna Dwipa. Have a pre-prandial drink at the bar. Good food but expensive. The place comes alive on Fri nights when expat oilmen roll into town; the bar is a popular watering hole. There is a set course Western and Asian dinner nightly, $3 inclusive. The breakfasts are great: corn-flakes, eggs, croissants, fruit and good coffee.

For tasteful decor, excellent Chinese food and superb service (they even stir your coffee for you), try **Selatan Indah** on Jl. Let. Kol. Iskandar. Large portions and delicious prawns; go up to the second floor.

Sudi Mampir on Jl. Merdeka, and **Mahkota Permai** (with two branches on Jl. Mesjid Lama, 24 Ilir, and Jl. Let. Kol. Iskandar in front of the Timbul Jaya Hotel) both serve reasonably-priced Palembang dishes. Palembang food is served cold on many small dishes, and as with Padang food you pay only for what you eat. Try the local specialities—like *pempek*, *model*, *takwan*, *lakson* and *burger*.

Suwito on Jl. Demang Lebar Daun serves good *sate kambing*. For the cheapest and best *sate*, however, go to **Layung Sari** at the west end of Jl. Kapt. A. Rivai—10 sticks for 75 cents and a large beer for $1.30.

Har on Jl. T. P. Rustam Effendi serves Indian Muslim food like *martabak*, *dal cha*, *roti prata* and mutton soup.

For something different, head for **Istana Alam** at the eastern end of Jl. Veteran, about 2 km from Jl. Sudirman. Sit in privacy in your own bamboo hut near a miniature waterfall, or by the big aquariums inside. Music nightly with Indonesian and western pop songs. Excellent menu. Ring the bell for service.

If you are a karaoke fan, try the **Jakarta** on Jl. Kol. Atmo for Chinese "steamboat." Food is cheap. There are also many Padang restaurants in town. **Pagi Sore** on the corner of Jl. Sudirman and Jl. Veteran is one of the biggest.

SHOPPING

Palembang is particularly famous for its textiles and unique red-black-and-gold lacquerwares. Don't leave town without some.

Textiles

Songket is a cotton or silk fabric, usually in a single color, overlaid with a floating design in gold or silver threads. Most of the weaving is done at home by women on backstrap looms.

Before the war every Palembang girl was expected to wear a self-woven *kain* (wrap-around skirt) and *selendang* (shoulder scarf) on her wedding day. Unmarried girls wore *songket* as a head-covering.

There are 16 traditional designs, mostly named after flowers— like *bunga cina* (Chinese flower), *bunga jatuh* (fallen flower), *bunga tabur* (drum flower) and *bunga intan* (diamond flower). Pricewise, *songket lepus* is the most expensive, *bunga cina* the next and *bunga intan* a little cheaper.

Jumputan pelangi (meaning "rainbow") is tie-dyed cloth for which Palembang is famous. It is prepared using Chinese silk or fine local cotton. Small beans are tied into the cloth, and the knots are dipped in different dye baths. The result is an intricate geometric pattern of stars, circles, diamonds and paisley on a red, green or purple background. Some of the best pieces have a dark maroon or purple background.

As with *kain songket*, *pelangi* comes in sets—a *kain* (approx. 180 x 90 cm) and *selendang* or shawl (200 x 40 cm) range from $25 to over $100, depending on the quality of material and workmanship. Be warned that the colors may run on the cheaper ones.

Prada (meaning "gilded") is a type of batik, usually on fine silk, distinguished by intricate designs in gold paint—often triangular. These are rarely produced today, though expensive antique pieces can sometimes be found.

To see *songket* weavers at work, go in the morning to **Cek Ipar** at Jl. Ilir Syuro 141, 4 km from the roundabout. Catch a brown minibus from Jl. Rumah Bari and ask to be let off at Cek Ipar. The selection is good, but if you have time go to **Songket Husin Rahman**, a small shop a little way back from Cek Ipar where the prices are lower. Wealthy Jakartans shop at both these places so the prices are high. Not much change out of $75 for a *kain* and *selendang* set. *Prada* is also sold at both places.

A good place to shop for these textiles and other local artifacts is **Taras** on Jl. Merdeka. See the owner, Pak Hamid, who speaks good English and can provide useful information on getting around Pelambang. Open till 8.30 pm. Try also **Songket Palace** in the Megaria Shopping Center on Jl. T.P. Rustam Effendi, and **Sumatra Shopping Center** in Pasar Ilir. Both have a variety of local fabrics. For the cheapest *songkets*, take a bus to **Tanjung Batu** where they are made, about 70 km south of Palembang. Ask at the tourist office for directions.

Lacquerwares

The introduction of lacquerware to Palembang can probably be traced to gifts brought to the king of Srivijaya by Chinese emperial envoys. Palembang lacquerware is distinguished by distinctive gold-and-black designs on a deep red background. All designs relate to Chinese and Indonesian folklore. The large *jilin* or golden phoenix is associated with a life free of problems; the lion signifies strength; flowers signify beauty; letters and scrolls stand for Buddhist learning; butterflies are for the joys of the night —love, sleep and sweet dreams.

The lacquer process is complex, requiring 10 steps from start to finish, involving 3 or more people. Work on a single piece can take 4 days. The most complex items are reproductions of Srivijayan period furniture and tall jars.

The first stage involves sealing the wooden core with red ochre, rubbing it down and coating it again. After the second rub-down the craftsman draws the design. Then the background is painted with China ink. The unique local lacquer is made from ant's nests mixed with methylated spirits in a proportion of 2 to 1, left to stand for 3 days. The murky brown liquid is filtered and 3 successsive coats are applied; each one dried in the sun and gently rubbed smooth with sandpaper. Finally, 2 more coats are applied, this time with a thinner mixture of ant's nest to spirits at 1 to 2. After drying again in the sun the product is ready.

Most pots are of mahogany but ceramic, which is cheaper, is also used. Prices range from $5 for a small sugar bowl up to $1,000 for a 1.8 m pot. The best mahogany is from Sebalik village up the Musi River, near Gasing Laut. There is significant demand in Palembang for reproduction lacquered furniture, bordered by scroll-like flowers in gold.

For a wide selection of quality lacquerwares, go to Palembang's **Serelo** area where many shops sell a range of antique and craft items. **Mir Senen International** at Jl. H.M. Amin 39 is a good starting point. See the owner, who speaks good English and can take you to local craftsmen and designers. Try also **Mekar Jaya** on Jl. Slamet Riyadi, which probably has the largest selection of lacquerwares in Palembang, and if you go before 4 pm you can see the craftsmen at work behind the shop.

Rattan products

The *tikar* mats produced here originate in a small village outside Palembang called Gasing Laut. The mats are distinguished by simple red-and-green checked designs and are produced by women at home. A good place to start is **Mir Senen International** (see above). For a wide range of rattan handicrafts and furniture, go to Kampong 2 Ilir and 3 Ilir. **Siti Zahara** on Jl. Cut Nyak Dhien 16 Ilir Barat II, 3 km from the city, has excellent but expensive rattan furniture and can arrange export.

Shellcrafts

The latest craft to arrive here is shellcrafts. Lampshades, wall hangings, plaques, ashtrays and many other items are produced using delicate, opaque shells. The factory moved here from the Philippines in 1990, and already employs over 700 people. The shells are from Surabaya, East Java, and must go through various processes: washing in acid, cutting, heating over charcoal until they are translucent, then dipping in hydrogen peroxide so they can be shaped into boxes. Painting is done with natural varnish. Finished goods are exported to Italy and sold in local department stores.

To see the craftsmen and women at work and buy at wholesale prices, go to **Kerang Indah Rattan and Shells Handicrafts**, Jl. Tanjung Banten 127, 16 Ulu. Cross the Ampera Bridge to the south and turn left to Plaju. Continue for 2 km and turn right for about 500 m. Ask for Pak Sudjono or Jaime Taguba, the Philippine consultant.

Antiques

For a good selection of antiques—from porcelain cups to old grandfather clocks—and a wide selection of local hunting and farming implements, visit the antique shops in the Serelo area. Try **Sriwijaya Antique and Art Shop** at Jl. H.M. Amin 43. A short walk brings you to Jl. Faqih Jalahuddin—a narrow street with old buildings lined with antique shops. Hard bargaining is required as well as a tight grip on your wallet!

NIGHTLIFE

Don't expect much in the way of nightlife. Apart from a good range of restaurants, there are two discos. The best is **Dynasty** on Jl. Veteran (operated by the Jakarta Dynasty, reputedly the largest in Southeast Asia), which is small but has good lighting and music. $1 cover during the week, $2.50 on weekends. Closed Mon.

There are also two nightclubs, but not the kind you would take your mother to. King's Hotel has a small, dark nightclub with live music and hostesses. Rian Cottages on Jl. Kol. Burlian at km 7 on the airport road is similar. If you like karaoke, try the **Jakarta Restaurant** on Jl. Kol. Atmo or the **Sandjaja Hotel**.

Dance performances

South Sumatra is famous for its music and dance, but unless you are invited to a wedding, it is hard to see a traditional performance. However, daily tourist performances of the best known dances are held at the open-air theater behind the Sultan Machmud Badaruddin museum. Most are ritual dances. The traditional costumes, employing *songket* fabrics and diamond-studded necklaces (*kalung*) and crown (*mahkota*) are unique to Palembang. The make-up alone takes 2 hours to put on.

Gending Sriwijaya is a formal welcome dance. Different regions have variations, but all wear costumes called Aesan Gede, consisting of a head piece, *songket* sarong, necklace and other adornments. Dana is a special folk dance for celebratory occasions, and is performed by young people in the *kampung* (village). Lilin (candle) or Dian (lamp) dances are performed at harvest time to honor the Rice Goddess.

CULTURAL EVENTS

On National Day, August 17, the **Bidar boat races** are held on the Musi River in traditional longboats similar to the Chinese dragon boat races—in 20 m long sculls with 50-60 oarsmen to a boat. **Wedding ceremonies** with full traditional dress are rare now as only wealthy families can afford them. Ask at the tourist office or check with the owner of Mir Senen International art shop (see above) to find out if one is taking place.

Lahat

Intercity buses depart from Palembang's Pasar Burung terminal on Jl. Mesjid Lama. Takes about 4 hours and costs $3. The Sindang Marga train from Palembang's Kertapati Station leaves at 8 pm daily, $3; problem is, you travel at night and miss the wonderful scenery.

ACCOMMODATION

The following are on Jl. Mayor Ruslan III, minutes from each other. **Nusantara**: best in Lahat for rooms with AC, ($17-$25) but worst for non-AC rooms ($5$9). **Permata**: $10-$13 D with AC and TV, from $4 with fan, breakfast included. **Losmen Simpang** and **Simpang Baru**: Good clean places with character; $3.50 D; $5 with fan; $8 with TV and private WC; $15 with AC.

Pagaralam (Pasemah)

A cool mountain town at the foot of Mt. Dempo. Visitors to are few and far between, so you may be asked to report to the police; purely a formality. This is the perfect base to explore the Pasemah region and its mysterious megalithic culture. Huge stone mortars, underground stone graves and giant carved stone figures dating from the first millennium are found here. Few services are available, however, and it is even difficult to change money. There are no money changers and the banks won't accept foreign currency. If you are stuck, Ny. Rivai at Losmen Mirasa will help you, but it is best to bring enough rupiah along.

GETTING THERE AND AROUND

Pagaralam can be reached by bus from Palembang (8 hrs) or Bengkulu (5 hrs). If you are coming up or down the Trans-Sumatra Highway, change up at Lahat—2 hrs east of Pagaralam by bus. Local *bemos* charge Rp100 for any distance. To see the megaliths, charter one for $12-$15 a day, depending on hours and distance. Arrange this at your hotel, set out the route and agree on the price with the driver in advance.

ACCOMMODATION

Dharmakarya is the biggest hotel in Pagaralam; 54 rooms in a pleasant garden on the edge of town with duck ponds and bamboo bridges. $4 to $13, plus service and tax. **Losmen Mirasa** is similarly priced, but is closer to town and has better food. The owner, Nyonya Rivai, is an efficient and knowledgeable lady who will organize transport, food and guides. The rooms at the back are delightfully quiet and the home-cooked meals are served in the family dining room. The coffee is grown on Ny. Rivai's own plantation.

EATING

There are plenty of hole-in-the-wall restaurants around the central market and mosque. **Dua Putra** on Jl. Mayor Ruslan has the usual rice and noodle dishes. **Hotel Dharmakarya** offers acceptable Indonesian food. But Ny. Rivai's cooking at the **Losmen Mirasa** has few rivals: honest, delicious and reasonably priced, served in an attractive dining room at the back. Cold beer and a convivial atmosphere.

VISITING THE MEGALITHS

There are only two megaliths in **Pagaralam** that you can walk to. The ones at **Tegurwangi** are accessible by local transport. To visit all the other sites, it is necessary to charter a vehicle and a guide. A *bemo* with a driver can be hired for $15; a guide will cost $5 a day. Ask at your hotel or at the Camat's office. Many of the megaliths are off the beaten track and are hard to find on your own. You will need good walking shoes and a hat. Bring lunch and drinks. The sites are looked after by local villagers and it is necessary to sign a visitors book at each site. A donation of Rp1.000 is greatly appreciated, as these people are responsible for the upkeep and yet receive no money from the government.

Pak Mirin, who works at the Camat's office, is an excellent guide. Ny. Rivai will phone him and make the necessary arrangements. He speaks passable English and is good company.

CLIMBING MT. DEMPO

Charter a bemo to **Tampung Tiga**, above the tea plantation, for $10 or go on Sunday when there are regular *bemos*. Stay overnight with the *kepala desa*, who will arrange a guide. You can get up an down in one day if you are fit. Or you can camp near the top in the valley between the two peaks (Dempo and Merapi), and climb to the summit early the next morning. Good walking shoes and a thick sleeping bag and a waterproof sheet are necessary, as temperatures drop sharply at night.

Baturaja

This is the jumping-off point for visits to Lake Ranau, but is best treated as a transit point if at all possible. To get there, take a bus from Palembang's Pasar Burung terminal ($3-$5), or call a private minibus company and be picked up from your hotel and dropped at your destination in Baturaja: $10 in an AC Kijang. Call **234 Travel**, tel: (071) 23416. The Sriwijaya night train also departs Palembang daily at 8:30 pm, $6 AC or $11 executive; the local Rajabasa day train departs at 8:35 am, $1.50.

For information and assistance in Baturaja, see Pak Djaudin at **Restaurant Megaria I**, Jl. Serma Zakaria 453. He can arrange chartered minibuses at $25 a day plus petrol.

ACCOMMODATION

Lodgings here are overpriced and not very nice, and you are best off heading straight for Lake Ranau. **Hotel Horison**, Jl. HS Simanjuntak 5, tel: 20332, is the best. Dark and dingy rooms with AC upstairs for $10-$13; brighter but noisy rooms without AC downstairs, $6-$9. **Hotel**

Kencana II, Jl. Akmal 820, tel: 20858, has room from $3.50 to $9.50 with AC. All very clean—best value in town.

Banjarsari Hotel and Resturant is a place 16 km from Baturaja on the road to Muara-enim, in the countryside at the foot of the hills. Has new, clean rooms: $13 with AC and $8 without. A refreshing and relaxing place to stay, halfway to Gua Putri caves.

Lake Ranau

Most visitors come down from the Trans-Sumatra Highway via Baturaja or Martapura. It is also possible to come up from Lampung via Liwa on the road to Krui (see "Lampung Sights").

From **Baturaja**, catch a minibus at the terminus in front of the large mosque and National Monument and ask for "Ranau" ($1); 3-4 hours on a very bad road. The bus may go direct to **Banding Agung** or you may have to change first at Simpang Sender. From the latter, there are regular buses to B.A. (Rp500), but only infrequently to Wisma Pusri (Rp1000). Minibuses can be chartered from Baturaja for $25 a day (see above).

ACCOMMODATION

There are two places to stay near the lake: the small town of **Banding Agung** on the northern shore and on the southeastern shore around **Wisma Pusri**—a hotel operated by the huge fertilizer plant in Palembang but open to the public. The latter is nicer but more expensive.

Seminung Permai Hotel, Jl. Akmal in Banding Agung, just before the shore. Very clean and good value. $4-$5 D. Breakfast $1, dinner $2.

Wisma PU/Polri. Overlooking the lake in Banding Agung, a government-owned *losmen* with huge rooms that sleep 2 or 4, $5-$8. Run-down and not very clean.

Wisma Pusri is a state-owned hotel with the best view of Lake Ranau. It's worth paying a bit more here for the location, the food and the service. $8 D standard, $13 for suites with AC. All very clean. Good breakfast with fresh fruit grown in the manager's garden, $1.50. Lunch and dinner ($2.50) always features two meats or meat and lake fish cooked over coffee wood charcoal. Tell the manager, Pak Suwarso, what you want and if it's available he'll prepare it for you. He also arranges barbeques on the lawn in front of the hotel overlooking the lake.

Gunung Putri is the other hotel in this area, between Wisma Pusri and the waterfall. Beautifully situated by the lakeside, surrounded by gardens, but disappointing once you get inside. Run-down, with small rooms, a bit overpriced even at $5.

—David Booth and Nancy Caldwell

BANGKA AND BELITUNG

Magnificent Beaches and Azure Seas

Bangka and Belitung are two verdant islands lying in the placid South China Sea to the east of Sumatra. Geologically they are more closely related to Malaya and Borneo than to Sumatra—forming part of the older, non-volcanic core of the Sunda Shelf. Though seldom visited, they in fact possess some of Southeast Asia's finest beaches, as well as offering refreshing sea breezes and an easy escape (only half an hour by plane) from Palembang's heat and congestion.

Bangka and Belitung are best known as the "tin islands"—part of a rich vein of tin ore running from here up through the Malay Peninsula to southern Thailand, which has historically furnished much of the world's supply of this versatile mineral. As in Malaya and Thailand, the mines here were developed during the 18th and 19th centuries using contract coolie labor imported from China.

Decades of mining have transformed the landscapes of these islands. Densely jungled hills have given way to scrubby forests dotted with small lakes called *kolong*—huge, water-filled cavities where tin has been mined. Despite centuries of large-scale exploitation, the islands are still sparsely populated. Bangka, with 11,615 sq km, has a population of 500,000, while Belitung, with an area of 4,000 sq km, has just 150,000 inhabitants.

Chinese coolie miners

Sea, forest and iron products were the islands' principal exports before tin was discovered on Bangka in 1710. A late 7th century Srivijayan stone inscription found at Kota Kapur testifies to the island's ancient links to Palembang. From the 14th to 17th centuries, the entire area (including Palembang) came under Javanese influence.

When the Dutch East India Company learned of the tin deposits, it cleverly signed contracts with the Sultan of Palembang for deliveries of ore to Batavia (Jakarta)—which was in turn traded to China in exchange for tea, silks and porcelain. Mines in Mentok and along the north and east coast of Bangka were controlled by the sultan through Chinese Muslim agents living on the island.

Tin deposits throughout Southeast Asia usually lie close to the surface, and mining and smelting can be carried out with simple tools and unskilled labor. However, the sultans soon abandoned attempts to work the mines with local recruits and began bringing in coolies from China. Ingenious Chinese mining techniques increased production and the Chinese soon organized themselves into cooperatives (*kongsi*) which developed new mines, managed labor, smelted and sold the ore, and shared in the profits. Although the colonial government took over the island and ran the mines as a state enterprise after 1819, technology and the organization of labor remained in the hands of the Chinese for another century.

The establishment of colonial rule here in fact created serious problems for the Dutch. Colonial bureaucrats were incompetent or corrupt, and between 1819 and 1851 local uprisings repeatedly threatened Dutch rule. When the Dutch extended their control over the *kongsis* after 1850, mortality among the Chinese laborers increased dramatically and they too rose up against their masters.

Bangka thus had two reputations during the 19th century. For the Dutch it represented a lucrative source of income. But for the Chinese, working conditions were notoriously poor and recruitment from China became increasingly difficult. The early coolies were mainly hardy, hard-working Hakkas from a poor and mountainous region of southern China's Guangdong Province. Many stayed on the island and married local women once their contracts were up, and Hakka displaced Malay as the main language in the mining communities. Their descendents, the local-born or *peranakan* Chinese, lived in much the same way as the local people—preferring to farm, fish or clerk for the Dutch rather than work the mines.

In the 1850s a Dutch mining company—the Billiton Maatschappij—opened mines on neighboring Belitung, also importing Chinese labor. By the 1920s, Bangka and Belitung between them had 130,000 Hakka Chinese residents, and by 1930 the Chinese formed nearly half of Bangka's total population and about two-fifths of Belitung's. Dutch-appoint-

Right: *Striking rock formations border pristine white-sand beaches on both Bangka and Belitung.*

ed Chinese officers managed the mines, and were granted in return the lucrative right to sell opium and provide other profitable services. Some became immensely wealthy and erected opulent mansions which may be seen today. Relations between the Chinese and the indigenes have always been good, a fact that all Bangkans are proud of.

Working conditions improved after the mines were mechanized in the 20th century. During the Great Depression, many coolies were laid off and some returned to China. Today only a quarter of Bangka's inhabitants are Chinese; on Belitung only an eighth. The work force in the mines is now made up of local people and Indonesian migrants. The state-owned mining company, Tambang Timah, controls most of the production, although some mines are leased to foreign concerns and local entrepreneurs. While the tin on Belitung has become scarce, mining and pepper continue to dominate the economy of Bangka. Additional income is provided by coconuts, cloves, cocoa, rubber, forestry and fishing. The islands' natural beauty is also being tapped for tourism now, and several large-scale resorts are planned.

Visiting Bangka

Bangka's administrative capital and main port of entry is **Pangkalpinang**, a bustling town of about 100,000 on the island's east coast. Start at the Post Office here and walk south along Jl. Jend. Sudirman to see the city. The mayor's residence, the town square (now a playing field) and many houses date back to the colonial period when the Dutch mining company controlled the island's economy.

There is a small museum belonging to Tambang Timah, the state mining company, near its headquarters at the intersection of Jl. Jend. A. Yani and Jl. Depati Amir, but it is only sporadically open. The Chinese temple on Jl. Mayor Haji Muhidir is in the middle of the business district and was built in the 1830s, when the first mines opened in this part of the island. At that time the town area was a maze of digging sites.

Bangka's best beaches are on the island's northeastern shores (see "Tin Island Practicalities"). The main road to the area leads north of Pangkalpinang through Baturusa to Sungailiat and Belinyu, about 2 hours away by car. Many sideroads to the right along the way end at lovely, white-sandy coves.

Some 10 km north of Pangkalpinang you enter **Baturusa** ("Deer Rock"), and on the right is an early-19th century Chinese temple (*klenteng*)—but alas, it has been extensively renovated. A few houses in this area are still built in the traditional manner, roofed with thatch and walled with bark, but most are of brick and cement. The lakes you pass are the flooded pits of open cut mines.

There is another temple in **Sungailiat** ("Clay River"), 20 km north, with a bell dated

1864 that was cast in China in Foshan, northern Fujian Province. In **Pemali**, just past Sungailiat, is a hot spring and an open pit mine worked with heavy equipment.

From Sungailiat to **Belinyu** is another 50 km, and here a small track to the left leads you to the village of Panji, site of a 200-year-old Chinese temple (although the present building is newer). The grave (dated 1795) of its founder—a tin magnate named Bong Kiung Fu or Kapitan Bong—once lay near the temple, but has been relocated inside the nearby ruins of a *benteng* or fort built in the 18th century for protection against frequent pirate raids. From a nearby stream, now silted up, a magical white crocodile is said to have ruled over the area. With a little urging, the old and nearly toothless caretaker at the fort will provide a story or two about the site.

Bangka's west coast

Mentok on the west coast was Bangka's original capital—strategically facing across the Bangka Strait just opposite the mouth of the Musi River which leads up to Palembang. Mentok is said to have been founded by Chinese in-laws of the Sultan of Palembang at the beginning of the 18th century, just as tin was being discovered here. Tin mining quickly took off, but the mines in the Mentok area gave out a century later, whereupon mining activity shifted to the north and the east. The Dutch used Mentok as the capital until 1913,

then moved it to Pangkalpinang.

Mentok is about 120 km (3 hours) from Pangkalpinang. In the town's harbor across from the tin smelting plant stands an old lighthouse that guides vessels through the treacherous Bangka Strait. This and an old fortress at its base are said to have been built by the British during Raffles' tenure in Java, between 1812 and 1817. During WW II, the Japanese used the fort to house Allied prisoners-of-war, many of whom died here.

Mentok's mid-19th century mosque is constructed in the traditional Palembang style; immediately adjacent to it is an even older Chinese temple, probably built in the 1830s. The proximity of the two symbolizes Bangka's history of tolerance. The town's large Rumah Mayor was the luxurious home of two former Chinese officers, a father and a son by the name of Tjoeng. The vast veranda with its imposing columns reflects the family's former wealth, which derived from a traffic in opium and coolies. The interior fittings, especially the family altar, show that money was no object in the attempt to recreate an ostentatious Mandarin lifestyle on Bangka.

Hire a local guide to take you up a hill north of town to see the graves of the Chinese Muslims who founded Mentok, and who came there from Siantan in the South China Sea. Bangkans claiming the titles *abang* (for men) and *yang* (for women) are descended from them. The Tjoeng family erected elabo-

JILL GOCHER

rate tombs decorated with hand-printed tiles.

On nearby **Mt. Menumbing** (445 m) is the guesthouse where President Soekarno, Vice President Hatta and other nationalist leaders were housed after being captured by the Dutch toward the end of the revolution. The place was surrounded by a barbed wire fence until United Nations observers and journalists arrived and began focusing world attention on the plight of the hostages. The guesthouse is open to the public.

Traveling overland after dusk, you will see family altars illuminated by the glow of electric candles in traditional Chinese homes.

Visiting Belitung

For many centuries, Belitung's rock-studded coastline and offshore island with hundreds of tiny coves made it a perfect pirates' nest. The island lay on the fringe of powerful Sumatran and Javanese kingdoms, but was so poor that they rarely, if ever, took any interest. In 1822, five pirate boats captured the Dutch ship *Anna Maria* and sold the captain and navigator to the chief of Sijuk, on the island's north coast. The two men remained for several years as slaves until they were rescued by a Malay nobleman, who paid a ransom of 2 balls of opium. Other Dutchmen were apparently enslaved at Burung Mandi on the east coast. No one knows what became of them, but when the Dutch finally seized control of the island, a Dutch-style building was found there.

Today, most visitors to Belitung come to laze on the island's excellent beaches. The capital and main port of entry is **Tanjung Pandan** ("Pandanus Cape") on the west coast. Next to the tin company (P.T. Timah) offices in the center of town is the house of the former *kapitan* or head of the Chinese community, Ho A Joen. Unfortunately, the building has been renovated, but the Ho family altar still stands inside the house.

Head south from here to the town's Chinese quarter. Three Chinese mansions formerly lined the main street, but only one remains. It houses a small museum with family photos and antiques. The road continues from here past a bustling morning fish market down to the harbor, where Bugis sailing craft load pepper and kaolin for Java. Turn west (right) to the beach; this is where Tanjung Pandan's best houses once stood overlooking the sea. The beach offers a splendid view of Kalmoa Island to the west, and the sunsets here are particularly lovely.

On a hillside south of town is a *benteng* (fort) from which the Depati (native ruler) of Belitung directed his struggle against the Dutch. From the fort you have a view of the mouth of the Berutak River, teeming with crocodiles.

Beaches and pirate coves

Belitung's best beaches are on the northern shore facing the South China Sea—reached via a scenic road that hugs the coast north of the capital. At **Tanjung Kelayang**, 35 km from Tanjung Pandan, glistening white sand beaches are bordered by photogenic rock formations, and the water is as deep blue as the sky. From here you can walk 2 km east along the shore to Tanjung Tinggi—past secluded coves with idyllic beaches where you can swim and sunbathe in absolute privacy. Bring along a picnic lunch.

Boats can be hired to a group of tiny offshore islands where more spectacular beaches await you. A lighthouse and a sea turtle hatchery are found on **Langkuas**, the island farthest from the shore. On the beaches or amongst the trees along the north shore, look for tiny black stones known as Billitonites—said to be bits of fallen meteors.

Other good beaches are found at the southwestern tip of the island on Gembira Bay just south of Membalong, about 60 km from Tanjung Pandan. From here (also from Tanjung Pandan) you can hire a boat to **Mendanau Island**, where pirates are said to have hidden their loot in caves tucked in amongst the coastal rock formations.

On the east coast of Belitung, **Burung Mandi** ("Birdbath") is another former pirate hang-out. An attractive Chinese temple perches on a bluff overlooking the sea here and is dedicated to the Chinese Goddess of Mercy, Guan Yin, who is frequently supplicated for advice and assistance—especially in the hopes of conceiving a son. The beach below the temple is not as white as some but is a wonderful place to watch the sunrise.

Burung Mandi is 90 km east of Tanjung Pandan, north of the town of Manggar. Two roads connect Tanjung Pandan to Manggar, both passing up and over **Mount Tajam**—the highest peak on the island, which has a refreshing spring, waterfall and lake at its summit. Also here is the *kramat* or holy grave of Datuk Gunung Tajam, who is said to have brought Islam to the island from Aceh in the 16th century.

— *Mary Somers Heidhues/Myra Sidharta*

Opposite: *Smoking fish on the island of Bangka.*

Tin Island Practicalities

Includes Pangkalpinang, Bangka Beaches, Tanjung Pandan, Belitung Beaches. Prices in US$. S = Single, D = Double, AC = air-conditioned.

Pangkalpinang (Bangka)

Telephone code is 0717.

Bangka's beaches are among the finest in Indonesia. The island also has good hotels, and the place is just waiting to be "discovered."

GETTING THERE

By air. Merpati flies from Jakarta 3 times a day (1 hr/$56). Sempati flies from Jakarta on Tues and Fri (same fare). Merpati has daily flights from Palembang ($23). Sempati flies from Batam on Tues, Wed and Thurs ($50). Deraya flies from Belitung every Wed, Fri, Sat ($20).

The airport is 6 km south of town on the road to Koba. Taxi drivers crowd around as you step outside. Bargain hard; a ride into town should cost $3. To the beach hotels it costs $8 (Parai Tenggiri) and $15 (Remodong) but if you have advance bookings they pick you up.

By sea. Every 2 weeks, a Pelni passenger ship sails from Jakarta to Mentok on Bangka's west coast ($18), thence to Tanjung Pinang (on Bintan Island, opposite Singapore) and Belawan (Medan). It turns around there and traces the same route in reverse.

Bangka

Ferries (9 hrs/$4) and jet foils (3 hrs/$11) travel up and down the Musi River and across the Bangka Strait between Palembang and Mentok twice daily. Jet foils depart Palembang at 08:30 and 10:00. From Mentok, a 3-4 hour bus ride brings you to Pangkalpinang, Sungailiat or Belinyu. There is also a ferry from Palembang to Kayu Arang, on Bangka's north coast (near Belinyu), close to the beach resorts and only an hour from Pangkalpinang. A ferry also travels to Pangkalpinang from Tanjung Pandan (Belitung) every Wed and Sun (10 hrs/$7).

GETTING AROUND

Pangkalpinang is small enough to explore on foot. The main street, Jl. Sudirman, runs north-south, and everything is here—restaurants, bakeries, shops, banks, airline offices and travel agents. Stop in at **DBS Tour & Travel** (no. 10) to inquire about tours and car rentals.

Old buses and minibuses run all over the island and are cheap (under $1 to anywhere on the island) but service is infrequent, once or twice in the mornings only between main towns (the exception is between Mentok and Pangkalpinang). If you have time this is fine; otherwise hire a car on a per-trip or per-day basis. Rates are negotiable. Expect to pay $25 a day for local explorations and up to $75 a day if you are touring around the island.

ACCOMMODATION

There is no shortage of hotels in Pangkalpinang but none is very nice and you are better off on the beach resorts. The best in town is the **Menumbing** (65 rooms) Jl. Gereja 5, tel: 22991,22992. $8 to $24; the cheaper rooms at the back are pleasanter. If this is full, try the **Wisma Jaya II** (10 rooms), Jl. Mangkol 10, tel: 21656, offering private bath and TV for $15-$19 S, $19-$24 D. The staff at **Wisma Jaya I** (10 rooms) Jl. Depati Amir 8, tel: 21696, are friendly and helpful—but the rooms are small and dimly-lit. The restaurant features lively rock bands on Sat night. $10-$38. The cheap, but new and clean **Bukit Shofa** (23 rooms) Jl. Masjid Jamik 43, tel: 21062, has small rooms with *mandi* for $3.50 to $5.

EATING

Bangka offers a wide variety of delicious, fresh seafood. Chinese restaurants abound and larger towns have many streetside Chinese foodstalls—always good for a bowl of steaming noodles. Wild boar or monkey meat—a local cure for rheumatism—are occasionally served.

Restaurant Asori on Jl. Kampung Bintang is the best place for seafood. Try their crabs in oyster sauce and steamed prawns. Another good seafood restaurant is **Tirta Garden** on Jl. Lembawai; the place is pleasanter but the food not as tasty. **Bukit Raya**, on the road to the airport, also specializes in seafood. Sweet and savory bread rolls, pastries and croissants are sold in the **French Bakery** on Jl. Sudirman. Try the rolls stuffed with shredded dried fish (*sambal lingkung*)—they taste much better than they sound! The **Dutch Bakery** across the road offers more substantial fare.

SHOPPING

The studio of **Tjoeng Khoen Foe**, Jl. Sudirman 3 (tel: 22581), sells miniature boats, Malay houses and other objects of beaten tin. **Peltin**, the smelting firm, has a shop at the airport selling pewter crafts. Although it is less pure than Tjoeng's tinwares, the pewter is lead-free, cheaper and more durable, and there is greater variety. *Akar bahar* is the root of a mangrove plant—fashioned by coastal villagers into walking sticks, bracelets and other accessories. The bracelets are believed to cure rheumatism. Local farmers around Kelapa (on the road to Mentok) supplement their income by weaving high quality, colorful Muslim hats and baskets which are available in Pangkalpinang's market.

Bangka Beaches

Most visitors come to Bangka for the gleaming white beaches. Hakok Beach, 33 km north of Pangkalpinang (also known as Parai Tenggiri Beach), boasts a spectacular rock-studded bay and the island's biggest hotel. Within walking distance is long and sandy Matras Beach. Romodong Beach is past Belinyu on the north shore—clear, calm waters and endless sands. Book in advance to ensure a room and an airport pick-up. Add 15.5 percent tax and service to the prices below.

Parai Beach (100 rooms) is Bangka's newest resort—modern bungalows in an idyllic setting. Swimming pool, shops, disco, watersports and convention facilities. $45-$60 S, $55-$75 D; $15 surcharge on weekends. A 3-day, 2-night package is available at $90 per person, twin occupancy, including breakfast and hotel transfers. For $110 they throw in some island excursions with lunch. You can book in Jakarta at Wisma Abadi 29-31, Jl. Kyai Caringan, tel: (021) 356025, fax: 356383 or through their Bangka office in Sungailiat, Jl. Pahlawan XII no. 41, tel: (0717) 92133, 92134, fax: 92155.

Romodong Beach (10 cottages) has pleasant AC cottages in a landscaped garden facing the sea. The beach is broad and the sand is incredibly fine; in less than a minute you can swim out to a rock and sunbathe on your own little island. The restaurant serves good seafood. Cottages are $23 to $43. Busy on weekends; book in Pangkalpinang at Jl. Bukit Intan I/147, tel: (0717) 21573; or in Jakarta at Greenville Blok Bi/21, tel: (021) 5604150, fax: 594469.

Tanjung Pandan (Belitung)

Telephone code is 0156.

Belitung's beaches, if anything, are even nicer than those on Bangka, and there is more to see and do here. The main problem is that hotel and travel facilities are not yet as well developed, but this should change soon.

GETTING THERE AND AROUND

Merpati flies from Jakarta daily ($55) and from Palembang on Thurs and Sun ($45). Deraya flies from Pangkalpinang (Bangka) on Sun, Tues, Wed, Fri and Sat ($20). A taxi from the airport to town is $4. A ferry also crosses the Gaspar Strait from Pangkal Balam (Bangka) every Wed and Sat (10 hrs/$7).

Tanjung Pandan is small enough to explore on foot. *Bemos* take you anywhere in town for Rp200. Rent an old Holden for transport to the beach or across the island for $20 to $30 a day, depending on the distance.

ACCOMMODATION

The best hotel is **Martani** (45 rooms) Jl. Yos Sudarso, tel: 432, with clean and spacious, AC rooms for $13-$26; smaller rooms with fan for $6 to $9. **Wisma Dewi** on Jl. Srivijaya is a rambling old family mansion with 12 simple, clean rooms. It has a warm, cosy atmosphere and a good restaurant at the rear. $8.50 to $11 with AC and shower, breakfast included. **Wisma Timah** on Jl. Melati is the tin company's guesthouse. If they are not full, the 2-bedroom cottages can be rented for $15 including meals.

EATING

Belitung's speciality is Chinese seafood. **Pasir Putih** on Jl. Sudek (behind Wisma Dewi) is the best restaurant. Try their *ikan ilek panggang* (charcoal-grilled fish), served with freshly sliced chilis, or the *cumi bakar* (grilled cuttlefish). Padang-style food can be found at **Bagadang** on Jl. Srivijaya, open 24 hours.

Belitung Beaches

The west coast beaches around Tanjung Pandan have brown sand and are polluted, so head for the north coast or down to the southwest. **Tanjung Kelayang**, 27 km north of town, has the best beaches on the island. If you have a car, stay for the sunset. To get to Tanjung Kelayang by public transport, take a minibus to Tanjung Binga (24 km), where you can catch another one to the beach. You can stay at the **Kelayang Beach Hotel**, which has 14 large rooms with showers for $7.50 to $10. A new luxury hotel with 216 rooms and 89 cottages is scheduled to open late in 1992.

Sixty km south of Tanjung Pandan, reached via a bumpy road, a white sandy beach lines Gembira Bay. Take a minibus to **Membalong** (45 km) where you can get another to "Teluk Gembira." As yet, there is no hotel here, and unless you hire a taxi, you will have to start back by early afternoon.

— *Amir Sidharta and Sandra Hamid*

PART IX

Introducing Bengkulu

Bengkulu is the smallest and least populated of Sumatra's provinces—with fewer than a million people living in an area of 21,168 sq km—yet its historical and natural charms rival those of any other part of this huge island. The province encompasses a 500-km-long stretch of unspoiled sandy coastline fringed with casuarina trees. From the sea, the land ascends rapidly to the lofty peaks of the Bukit Barisan. Tigers, elephants and rhinos still roam its pristine jungles, where the exotic rafflesia and wild orchids bloom.

For 140 years Bengkulu was Britain's sole colony in Southeast Asia. Established as an alternative source of pepper after the Dutch seized control of Banten in the 17th century, the tiny British outpost on this sparsely-populated coast never amounted to much, as pepper's importance in the world economy soon declined and Bengkulu lay too far off the major trading routes to offer much else. From 1685 to 1825, reports of the East India Company record continual tales of dismal commerce, boredom and early death on this malarial coast, where months could pass without sighting a ship or news from home.

Fort York, the first British base, was built here in 1685, and in 1715, Fort Marlborough was constructed 2 km away. The British found the local Rejang people "indolent" and began punishing their rulers. When William Dampier was at Bengkulu in 1690, he found two local rulers in the stocks "for no other reason but because they had not brought down to the Fort such a quantity of Pepper as the Governour had sent for." Despite the protests of home authorities, similar treatment continued to be meted out during the 18th and early 19th centuries.

Bengkulu was briefly shaken out of its torpor during the governorship of Thomas Stamford Raffles (1818-1824), but in 1825 the colony was surrendered to the Dutch in exchange for undisputed British influence in the Malay Peninsula and Singapore. During his residence in Bengkulu, Raffles undertook the naval explorations which led to the founding of Singapore. The satisfaction he felt on seeing his new colony flourish was tempered by the sad fact that three of his four children died in Bengkulu. The precise whereabouts of their graves is unknown.

British influence was restricted to the narrow coastal plain. The mountainous hinterland was annexed by the Dutch after a series of military campaigns in the 1850s. At the end of the 19th century the Dutch discovered that Bengkulu's mountains contained rich deposits of gold, and Bengkulu rapidly became the largest gold-producing area in the Dutch East Indies.

Bengkulu's people consist of four main groups. The Rejang are mountain dwellers and form the majority. They are subdivided into two populations—the highland Rejang and the Rejang Pesisir who have moved down to the western lowlands. In the south dwell the Serawai, who are related to the Pasemah people who live in the highlands around Pagaralam and Mt. Dempo. Many of the residents of the capital are Malays.

The region has been inhabited since prehistoric times, as is shown by the discovery of stone tools in the northern area, and megalithic structures and ancient drums of Dongson type in the south. The isolated island of Enggano off the south coast was the home of a separate group of people, distantly related to inhabitants of the Mentawai Islands further north. The Engganese, long protected by their remote location, were decimated by smallpox and other diseases introduced by Western visitors in the late 19th century, and soon afterwards their traditional culture was destroyed; the island is now almost deserted.

—*John Miksic*

Overleaf: Rafflesia arnoldi, *the world's largest flower; a meter across. Photo by Alain Compost.*
Opposite: *Bengkulu woman. Photo by Steve Teo.*

BENGKULU SIGHTS

In Search of a Somnolent Colonial Past

Bengkulu is essentially a colonial town—it was founded by the British in 1685 and occupied by them until 1825 (they called it "Bencoolen"), when the Dutch took over, staying up until the Japanese invasion in 1942. It still seems much as it was described then—quiet and tidy. A walking tour is the best way to explore what remains of Bengkulu's colonial past. Start early in the morning, as the heat can be quite unbearable during the day.

Begin at the western end of Jl. Jend. A. Yani, next to the cupola-roofed memorial to Thomas Parr—the unpopular governor of Bengkulu who was stabbed to death and beheaded (probably by Bugis mercenaries) in 1807 while resting at his garden house, 5 km from the fort. Parr had trained in Bengal and was accustomed to unquestioning obedience from a submissive and subjugated people. Once in Bengkulu, he attempted to re-

duce the power of the "Bugis Corps" which had been recruited to supplement the East India Company's forces. After Parr's assasination, a few local rulers who were under suspicion were blown from the guns and several villages were burnt in vengeance. However, relations between the British and Indonesians were not always this bad, and the large Eurasian population led to Bengkulu being dubbed "a regular Batavian colony" by a British critic, meaning that there was "too much mixing of races."

Fort Marlborough

Continue down Jl. A. Yani to Fort Marlborough. The fort was built by the British East India Company between 1713 and 1719, and was carefully restored between 1977 and 1984. Its plan is rectangular, measuring 240 by 170 meters, with projecting bastions on the four corners.

Fort Marlborough was built to replace Fort York. William Dampier, who served as gunner at Fort York, nevertheless declared it to be the most irregular piece of defensive work he had ever seen. "It would moulder away every wet season and the Guns often fall down into the Ditches." And impressive as the fort looked, it fell to the enemy on the only two occasions in which it was attacked—the first time in 1719 by a local uprising, and the second in 1760 by a passing French fleet.

The outer wall is surrounded by a dry

moat. As well as protecting the fort from attack, this moat—according to India Office records—prevented the sentries from sneaking off to the nearby *kampung* to buy toddy, the powerful alcoholic drink made from the sweet sap of palms!

After 1825, Fort Marlborough was used by the Dutch until the Japanese invasion of 1942. After Japan's surrender, it was briefly occupied by the police of the fledgling Republic of Indonesia. The Dutch reoccupied the fort during their attempt to crush the Indo-

nesian revolutionary forces, but in 1950 it was restored to the police, who continued to use it until the mid-1980s. The fort is now open to the public as a museum.

The fort's main entrance faces south, and is protected by a barbican (a double wall). As you enter the outer defenses, you are greeted by the elaborately inscribed tombstones of British officers who served here, including that of Thomas Parr—now worn smooth by the elements. Both the northern and southern entrances were formerly accessed by crossing small wooden bridges. A door on the east side also led out to the Indian soldiers' quarters. There is no rear wall—an earthen rampart defended the fort.

The fort's massive wooden gates open onto a peaceful, manicured courtyard. On one side is the cell in which Soekarno was briefly held in the early days of his exile; on the other is a small museum. Climbing up to the ramparts affords a good view of the town and the sea. A tall tower originally stood over the north gate, but collapsed due to repeated earthquakes. There were no buildings inside the fort; soldiers' quarters, kitchens, offices, guardrooms and stores were all built into the walls. Some of these rooms are now used for displays illustrating the history of the fort, including artifacts discovered during the recent restoration. Poignant graffiti adorn the wall of one room that was used as a prison.

The area around the fort has a brooding and melancholic air, especially in the evenings—almost as if the sad ghost of Raffles still paces the ramparts, scanning the horizon for the sails of the Fame, a ship which was to deliver him and his ailing wife, Sophia, from Bengkulu. The former **British Residency** is just across from the fort, set back a little from the main road. Now derelict and crumbling, it is surrounded by warehouses and occupied by stray dogs. About 200 m to the north is a point of land called Tapak Paderi, providing beautiful sunset views over the sea. The open square southeast of the fort dates from the time when the British laid out the settlement.

Leaving Fort Marlborough, walk to the old **Chinese quarter** which is located around Jl. D. I. Penjaitan, just behind the British residence and close to the Parr monument. Here, rows of two-storied old wooden shop houses with ornately-carved balconies line both sides of the street. These buildings were all constructed in 1926 after the quarter was destroyed in one of the earthquakes which periodically afflict the province.

The European cemetery

From the fort, a pleasant, 15-minute walk brings you to an obelisk on Jl. Letkol Santoso in the southeastern part of the town, erected over the remains of Captain Robert Hamilton, "who died on the 15th of December 1793 at the Age of 38 Years in Command of the Troops." (Hamilton apparently had an affair with a local girl!)

From here walk a few hundred meters north to the old European cemetery. Most of the British graves date from the late 18th and early 19th century; the later graves are Dutch. During the period of British rule, there were never more than a handful of European wo-

Opposite: *Fort Marlborough, constructed by the British between 1713-19 and now fully restored.*
Above, left: *One of the fort's old cannons.*
Above, right: *Tombstone of a British officer.*

men in Bengkulu and some of the tombstones are affectionately telling: Captain Thomas Tapston's "was erected to his Memory by his much afflicted friend, Nonah Jessminah." Unfortunately, many of the graves have been vandalized. Raffles' three children who died in Bengkulu are possibly buried here, though their gravesites are unknown until this day.

Soekarno's house

A short walk to the east will bring you to the house where Indonesia's first president Soekarno, his first wife, Inggit, and his adopted daughter, Ratna Juami, were exiled by the Dutch from 1938 to 1941. The house is located on Jalan Soekarno-Hatta, in the district called Anggut Atas. On the verandah is the trusty bicycle that Soekarno used while courting his second wife, Fatmawati, then a local Bengkulu belle (Soekarno was in his late thirties at that time). In wooden cabinets are his books, mostly in Dutch, and his clothes. Faded pictures of the family adorn the walls. The house is open 8 am to 2 pm Tues to Thurs, Fri 8-11 and Sat 8-12. There is a small admission charge.

Fort York

Fort York, built in 1685, stood about 2 km north of Marlborough, on the south bank of the Bengkulu River. The area is now called Pasar Bengkulu in memory of the time when the town's main market lay near the fort. No traces of the old brick fort can be seen, but archaeologists have discovered the foundations of the walls and artifacts used by the fort's inhabitants on the hill where a primary school and slaughterhouse now stand. From the hill you can look down on a landing where local fishing boats sell their catch on the riverbank early in the morning.

The provincial museum

The provincial museum, which is in the southern suburbs of town in an area called Padang Harapan, has extensive collections ranging from prehistoric stones and ancient bronze drums to wooden models of traditional houses. Other displays include traditional Engganese textiles and looms. Of special interest is the batik cloth made in Bengkulu called *kain besuruh*, with designs incorporating Arabic calligraphy and the Majapahit sunburst.

There are also displays of imported ceramics and of *tabut*—towers made of wood and paper used in a local ritual of the same name. Each year on the 10th of Muharram, the first month of the Muslim year, the towers—some as tall as 10 m—are borne in procession through the town in honor of the Prophet Muhammad's grandson, Husein, who fell at the battle of Karbala in Iran in AD 680.

This ceremony is a remnant of earlier Shiite influence, though Bengkulu—like the rest of Indonesia—now follows the Sunni school of Islam. There are two small shrines in the town where those who are to take part in the *tabut* go to burn candles and make requests. If their petitions are granted they will sponsor the construction of a *tabut* tower. The museum is open 8-2 pm Tues to Thurs; 8-11 am on Fri and Sat; closed Mon.

Natural attractions

There are three main places of natural interest on the fringe of Bengkulu town. One is the beautiful, 7-km-long beach which begins at Pantai Nala and continues south, where its name changes to Pantai Panjang Gading Cempaka. Gading Cempaka was a legendary princess whose skin was as fair as ivory (*gading*) and as fragrant as frangipani (*cempaka*). Swimming here is generally safe, but large waves and a strong undertow make it necessary to exercise caution. Signs are erected at the safest swimming spots.

Another spot which attracts nature lovers is a lake called **Danau Dendam Tak Sudah** ("Lake of the Never-Ending Grudge") which lies about 8 km southeast of the town. This lake is surrounded by low hills, above which you can see the peaks of the Barisan mountains in the distance. At the northern edge of the peaty water is a nature reserve where a particular variety of wild water orchid flourishes, the *Vanda hookeriana*.

The small island of **Pulau Tikus** ("Rat Island") lies about 5 km off the coast of Bengkulu. The island measures only 60 by 100 m, and is part of a much bigger coral reef which lies beneath it. In the colonial period, ships anchored to the lee of this reef to be safe from storms raging in the Indian Ocean beyond. Large iron anchors are still set in the reef. Snorkelers and scuba divers report that it is exceptionally rich in marine life.

Bengkulu sidetrips

Bengkulu has many attractions for travelers who wish to see Sumatran nature in its pristine state. Most of these lie in the Barisan Mountains, and can be reached along a winding road which leads, via Kepahiang, to the large town of Curup.

In November the huge *Rafflesia arnoldi* blooms along the banks of streams in the primary forest. The most accessible sites for viewing the world's largest flower are the areas near Taba Penanjung, Bengkulu's official rafflesia reserve on the main Bengkulu-Kepahiang road. Visitors should call at the forestry office in Bengkulu to find out whether any giant flowers are in bloom.

Curup, 85 km northeast of Bengkulu, is an attractive, cool hill town in the Barisan mountains where local agricultural products are sold in the town's market. The town is connected to Bengkulu by a good paved road climbing up through the forests in Barisan mountain and offering spectacular view of Bengkulu city and the Indian Ocean. Major crops are rice, coffee and vegetables such as carrots and cabbage. Rice mills driven by water power can still be seen in many areas of the Tebong Valley around Curup.

A few kilometers outside Curup is a hot spring, **Suban Air Panas**, a popular weekend spot. In ancient times the spring appears to have been a religious site, for on a low rise near it is a base for a statue and a crude Siva *lingga*. A few meters further up the slope is another stone carved into a rectangular shape —connected with a legend about a princess named Puteri Swangka. Another ancient remnant is a large, flat stone called Batu Panco that was possibly used as a meditational spot by religious ascetics. From Curup a road leads north to Muara Aman—center of the gold mining industry during the colonial period. Along the way it passes a lovely mountain lake, **Danau Tes**, famous locally for its scenic beauty and for being the largest lake in Bengkulu.

There are several active volcanoes in the province. Behind Curup towers Bukit Kaba, 1,937 m high, with two main and 12 subsidiary craters emitting sulphurous gases. The most serious eruption occurred in 1845, when 150 people were killed.

Bengkulu also has two major parks. In the north, near Seblat, Mt. Bukit Gedang forms part of the huge **Kerinci-Seblat National Park**. This park, which is Indonesia's largest, is home to rare wildlife such as the Sumatran elephant, rhinoceros and tiger, as well as more common animals like deer, birds and monkeys. (See "Kerinci-Seblat Park" in WEST SUMATRA). In the south, the **Bukit Barisan Selatan National Park** includes the region of Kaur Timur. Besides elephants, tigers and crocodiles, this park contains the Sumatran mountain goat and the slow loris.

In the sub-district of North Bengkulu, 114 km off the coast, lies **Enggano Island**—with its numerous coral sea gardens, sparkling seas and lovely beaches. However, the coastline is swampy and the only way to get there is to take a boat which operates irregularly from Bengkulu. Once you are there, there is no other way of getting around on the 29 by 18 km island except on foot!

— *John Miksic*

RAFFLESIA

World's Most Magnificent Flower

What a wonderful plant is rafflesia! Several of its species have large flowers, but only *Rafflesia arnoldi* opens to a diameter of 90 cm, thus ranking as the largest flower in the world. This species is named after its discoverers, Sir Thomas Stamford Raffles and his botanist friend, Dr. Joseph Arnold, who died shortly after the discovery from a bout of malaria.

Sumatrans call it by various names—the Sun Toadstool, the Stinking Corpse Lily and Devil's Betel Box are some of the more colorful terms ascribed to rafflesia. It is the most specialized of all parasitic plants, having no stem, no leaves and no roots. Apart from the flower, the plant consists only of fungal-like strands within the stem of its host, a wild vine called *Tetrastigma*.

Parts of these strands starts to expand and small orange-brown, cabbage-like flower buds break through the bark of the vine.

These buds take one to two years to blossom; a 15 cm rafflesia bud will take 2 to 3 months to flower. Buds are more frequently seen than flowers.

When the bud opens, there issues forth a horrible stench of carrion, irresistible to the flies and beetles which swarm inside, crawling over the hidden sexual parts beneath the spiny plate in the center of the flower. One flower of each sex has to be open in the same area for successful pollination.

The flower stays in bloom only for about a week, then it withers and collapses into an unpleasant, fetid heap, with the fruits buried somewhere near the bottom. Small rodents, insects, deer or pigs, investigating this pile, may inadvertently get the seeds stuck on their feet. It seems incredible that any of these seeds could manage to find their way to the right sort of vine, where they lodge in fissures in the bark.

The Sakai people of southern Sumatra believe that an infusion of the flowers is an aphrodisiac (for men only!). The plant is also used in *jamu*, the traditional Malay herbal cures. An extract from the bud is given to women after childbirth, to shrink the womb and to restore the figure, and is widely believed to confer youth and beauty.

— *Anthony Whitten*

Below: *Inside the rafflesia, where a powerful stench attracts insects necessary for pollination.*

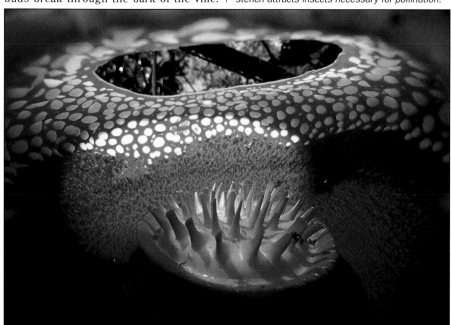

Bengkulu Practicalities

Most prices in US dollars. Telephone code for Bengkulu town is 0736.

Bengkulu has two distinct seasons: cool and wet (Jan to March) and hot and dry (Aug to Dec). During the hot season, the weather can be quite oppressive. The town is remarkably pleasant. It's best to stay at Pantai Nala, a 10-min *bemo* ride or 25-min walk from the town. The swimming isn't much, but the beach has a windswept, melancholic air which recalls the city's maritime past.

GETTING THERE AND AROUND

Merpati flies to Bengkulu daily from Jakarta ($67) and Palembang ($39). The airport is 14 km from the city; *bemos* can be chartered to take you to your hotel for $3. **Merpati Office** is in Hotel Asia, Jl. A. Yani 922, tel: 21119.

Buses approach Bengkulu from three directions, all of the challenging: from Padang via Muko-Muko in the north (20-30 hrs/$5), from Pagaralam via Manna in the south (full day), and from the Trans-Sumatra Highway at Lubuklinggau in the east (5-7 hrs/$3). The latter is by far the easiest route, as the condition of the other roads is appalling. The trip up from Jakarta along this route takes about 24 hrs ($7).

Bengkulu Town is small enough to walk around. *Bemos* (called *taksi*) travel around town on fixed routes charging Rp150. You can charter them to most places in town for Rp500; to the airport or Danau Dendam Tak Sudah costs $1. Jeeps can be chartered for trips out of town for $15 to $20 a day; ask at your hotel.

ACCOMMODATION

Nala Seaside Cottages, Jl. Pantai Nala 133 (tel: 21855) has 5 pleasant wooden chalets overlooking the beach, about 3 km from town. $12 S, $15 D with non-working AC, cold water and breakfast. The restaurant serves decent food and expensive beer. If you need a guide, Rozi, who works here, is knowledgable and helpful. **Pantai Nala Samudera** is next door (tel:31722). An up-market but less attractive beach hotel with rooms for $25 and up. Both accommodations are a 10 minute *bemo* ride from town. **Hotel Asia** on Jl. Ahmad Yani 922B (tel:21901), is right in the center of town and has large clean rooms for $12-$25 (AC). **Wisma Marlboro** on Jl. Prof. Hazairin 1 (tel: 31004), is 5 minute's walk from Hotel Asia, with spacious rooms for $9 (AC). Recommended. **Wisma Balai Buntar**, Jl. Khadijah 122, tel: 31254, has decent rooms for $11. Quiet and central.

For budget travelers, the **Wisma Rafflesia**, Jl.

A. Yani 95, the **Surya**, Jl. Abidin 26, or the **Mesalena** on Jl. Berlian, have rooms from $3.

EATING

The **Nala Seaside Restaurant** at the hotel of the same name offers *cap cay* (mixed vegetables), *ikan bakar* (grilled fish), spaghetti and salads. Western steak dishes can be ordered in advance. 15 percent tax and service. **Hotel Asia** has a dreary restaurant serving very cold beer.

Several restaurants can be found along Jl. Suprapto, among them **Nasi Kapau**, **Simpang Raya** and **Sari Bundo**, all of which serve Padang food, and the **Gandhi Bakery and Ice Cream Parlor**. If you're tired of Sumatran cooking, **Citra Restaurant** on Jl. Sudirman serves Chinese and Javanese food. Try the *ikan bakar* (grilled fish) with a cold beer. Delicious!

Excellent food is found at the **Rumah Makan Srikandi** at Jl. Ahmad Yani 331, across the street from Hotel Asia. Ask for *makanan biasa*, their standard meal, which includes a salad of cabbage and cucumbers, a minestrone-like soup of corn and beans in broth, and succulent fried chicken (*ayam goreng kalasan*) piping-hot from the kitchen, all for $1.50. There are four or five other small restaurants opposite Hotel Asia; all serve decent food. The **Sari Rasa** serves cold Bir Bintang for $1.25.

SHOPPING AND SERVICES

Bengkulu is not noted for its shopping. Polished river stones, woven baskets and local batik can be bought at **Gedung Kerajinan** (Handicraft House) next to Nala Seaside Cottages. Javanese batik clothing can be purchased at reasonable prices from **Danar Hadi** in the town center.

The **Post Office** is at Jl. A. Yani 38, open 08:30-12:00 and 13:30-16:00 Mon through Thurs, and 08:30-11:30 on Fri. Long distance phone calls can be made at the **Perumtel** office, Jl. Suprapto 155, tel: 38222; open 24 hrs.

Change money at **Bank Bumi Daya** on Jl. Indra Caya, around the corner from the post office. The **Tourism Office** has recently moved out of town—ask the taxi driver for "Bekas Wisma Haji Lama." The **Indonesian Forestry Service** (PPA) is at Jl. Mahoni 11. Get your permit here to visit the national parks, and ask if any rafflesias are in bloom in the vicinity.

LEAVING

The flight to Palembang leaves at 09.00 daily; to Jakarta at 12.30 and 15.00 daily. Buses depart from the *terminal bis* which is 9 km from the town's central Pasar Minggu market by bemo. Padang can be reached in 20 hrs ($5), Jakarta 24 hrs ($7), Lubuklinggau 6 hrs ($3), Palembang 18 hrs ($5) and Bandar Lampung 18 hrs ($5). From the harbor it is possible to catch vessels to Jakarta or Enggano Island.

—Jay Goodfriend

PART X

Introducing Lampung

Lampung is one of the most interesting, and yet least known provinces of Indonesia. It occupies the southernmost tip of Sumatra— separated from Java by the shallow Sunda Straits, that are less than 30 km wide at their narrowest point. Lampung has consequently been the area of Sumatra most influenced, socially and economically, by its densely populated and politically powerful neighbor.

Until the early decades of this century Lampung, like most of Sumatra, was very sparsely populated. Due mainly to a flood of immigrants from Java, it has had one of the highest population growth rates in Indonesia in recent years, and is now the most densely populated (and poorest) province in Sumatra. In the past two decades, the population has grown from 2.5 to over 6 million people living in an area of 33,307 sq km.

Only one in ten of Lampung's present inhabitants is descended from the original population, which comprised three distinct groups: the Orang Abung or mountain people who practiced headhunting and remained in isolation until the 19th century; the Orang Pubian who inhabited the eastern lowlands; and the Orang Peminggir or peoples of the south coasts around Lampung and Semangka Bays, who probably came under the suzerainty of Palembang-based Srivijaya, and were later Islamized through influence from Java.

According to local legends, all these people have a single ancestor, Si Lampung, from whom the province derives its name. Their descendants today speak two closely-related languages, Komering and Lampung, but due to the influx of migrants, even more people here now speak Sundanese or Javanese.

Life in Lampung was probably always unsettled—especially along the coasts, which were susceptible to piratical slave raids. Many early settlements were protected by earthen ramparts and thorny bamboo hedges. Two inscriptions of the mighty Srivijayan empire attest to a direct involvement in the late 7th century, no doubt fostered by Lampung's rich resources of gold and dammar (a valuable tree resin). In the 16th century, the Islamic sultans of Banten in West Java gradually took control of the region, conferring the title of *punggawa* (representative) on Lampung chiefs in return for deliveries of pepper grown in the interior. This made Banten the largest and wealthiest pepper port in the archipelago at the time that the first Europeans arrived. The Dutch eventually took over this trade in the late 17th century.

The traditional culture of Lampung reflects indigenous beliefs overlain by Hindu-Buddhistic and Islamic influences. A strong megalithic tradition continued until fairly recent times; the *pepadon* or ritual throne used by Lampung chiefs appears to have had megalithic origins, and ancient stone sculptures show the ancestors with symbolic motifs that suggest sacrificial rites. The influence of Dongson bronze kettledrums is also apparent in the spirals, curves and stylized human and animal figures of the sacred Lampung "ship cloths." These ubiquitous fabrics played an important role in ritual and marriage ceremonies, and rank among the world's most striking traditional textiles.

Rapid changes have taken place over the past century. Beginning in Dutch times, migrations were encouraged as a means of relieving Java's population problems. This was stepped up in the 1960s and '70s through government transmigration programs (which have now stopped). Today only about 20 percent of Lampung's forests remain—some, like Way Kambas Reserve, now designated as special wildlife areas. Most other areas are cultivated with wet-rice *sawah* or groves of oil palms, rubber, coconut, coffee and cloves.

— *E. E. McKinnon/K. H. Picard*

Overleaf: *Herding wild elephants into the Way Kambas Game Reserve. Photo by Max Lawrence.*
Opposite: *Enjoying a swim. Photo by Jill Gocher.*

SHIP CLOTHS

Rare Ritual Fabrics of Lampung

The three peoples native to Lampung—the Abung in the north, the Pubian in the center and the Peminggir along the southern coast —are all famous for a distinctive form of textile that commonly features geometric ship motifs. These extraordinary fabrics are collectively known as "ship cloths" and are prized the world over by textile collectors.

The production of these striking cloths— usually of cotton but sometimes of silk— dates back to an era when a lucrative pepper trade flourished in Lampung. The collapse of the pepper trade in the last century brought about the demise of many local traditions— including the time-consuming production of these ritual cloths, which have not been woven for over 100 years. Nowadays such fabrics are rare collector's items, costing a small fortune when they can be found at all.

By their form and function, the cloths may be divided into two categories: *tampan* and *palepai*. The former are small and square in shape, measuring no more than a meter across; the latter are long and narrow, averaging 3 meters in length and half a meter in width. The ornamentation of the two is quite different—*tampan* often have very precise, even abstract motifs, whereas *palepai* normally depict solid, easily recognizable objects. The decorative style of both displays a clear affinity with Bronze Age designs found on Dongson kettledrums (see "Prehistory"), especially the stylized double spirals, meanders and hook-and-key motifs on the borders.

Tampan and *palepai* were woven by identical techniques—single-colored supplemental wefts were applied to a plain weave foundation. The biggest job was to count out the threads needed for the intricate patterns before mounting them on the handloom. Peminggir women made *palepai* as well as *tampan*; Pubian and Abung women made *tampan* only.

Ritual uses

The Peminggir are organized in patrilineal descent groups or *suku*. Four or more of these *suku* constitute a so-called *marga*. Their members have a number of titles, of which the Penyimbang, descendants of the founder of a *suku* or *marga*, are the most important— representing an aristocratic class privileged to own *palepai*.

The long *palepai* cloths are employed in all life-cycle rites that a Penyimbang undergoes: birth, circumcision, marriage and death. Apart from this, they are used in rites marking the attainment of higher rankings within the elaborate social hierarchy. During such rites, the *palepai* are hung on a wall inside the house and serve to indicate the family's status within its *marga*. Traditionally there were "strong" and "weak" *suku*—classifications based on the relative age, wealth and size of the descent group.

Tampan cloths are similarly used during life-cycle rites—but unlike *palepai*, they are not the prerogative of any particular group. During such rites the initiate often sits on a *tampan*, and ceremonial gifts of food are also wrapped in them. The quantity is what is most important—the more *tampan* one gives, the more one is respected. Whereas *palepai* remain in the possession of a particular *suku* and symbolize the ruling class, *tampan* circulate among descent groups in all levels of society.

Motifs and symbolism

A number of small, clearly recognizable objects are often depicted on *palepai* standing astride the deck of the ship: people, animals, trees and houses. A distinction is usually made between *palepai* having blue and those having red ships. On very rare *palepai* only rows of human figures are shown whithout any ship at all.

The designs of *tampan* are much more diverse and difficult to categorize. The ship motif is, as on the rare *palepai*, sometimes completely missing—in which case the design may consist of a big bird or various small birds, a tree, or other more abstract motifs. Simple rows of human forms are also found on *tampan*.

The ship motif nevertheless predominates on all these cloths—above all symbolizing transition and movement, a notion appropriate to the life-cycle rituals in which they are used. Apart from this, the ship also expresses social structure. The person undergoing the rite finds himself on the border between two phases in life—a time that is considered unsettling and potentially quite dangerous. He is helped along to the next stage by highly structured rituals, in which the society as a whole is represented as a ship carrying its members along.

During marriage rituals, for instance, the bridal couple is borne in a procession in the shape of a ship, in which all *suku* in the *marga* take up prescribed positions. In this way, the newlyweds are brought from a temporarily insecure position on the fringes of society to a secure and stable position within the social fabric.

— *Toos van Dijk and Nico de Jonge*

Below: *A* palepai *of the red ship type.*

LAMPUNG SIGHTS

Scenic Bays at Sumatra's Southern Tip

Though it is possible to fly to Lampung from Jakarta in under an hour, visitors are encouraged to make the 27-km ferry crossing from Merak, at the northwestern tip of Java, to the new ferry terminal at **Bakauheni** at Sumatra's southeastern extremity. The Sunda Strait separating these two huge islands have a certain grandeur and historical significance, and from the ferry you can sometimes catch ominous glimpses to the south of the infamous Krakatau volcano, which erupted with devastating force in 1883—producing tidal waves that killed 35,000 people on both sides of the straits (see "Krakatau").

From Bakauheni, it is an easy 99 km and 2 hours to Bandar Lampung along a broad, fast road. If you have the time, you can break your journey at **Kalianda**, 38 km from the ferry, to visit the old hot sulfur springs at Way Balirang, 3 km above the town. Constructed by

the Dutch, each of its three pools has a different mineral content. There is a small admission charge. There are also two other hot spring pools in the town itself. Also here are the remains of an old fort from which the Indonesian national hero Raden Intan II (1830-1889) harassed the Dutch. His grave, an object of veneration, lies nearby.

The Kalianda area is dominated by Mt. Rajabasa (1,281 m), a dormant volcano whose slopes are dotted with yellow-green clove trees. A scenic road encircles the volcano to the south of the town, passing along the coast though a series of lovely fishing villages.

From the village of **Canti** you can hop a small ferry to the offshore islands of Sebuku and Sebesi. Boats can also be chartered here for the choppy, 3-hour crossing to Krakatau. From Canti you can also climb up to Mt. Rajabasa's summit in several hours. Book a guide first at the Canti pier, register with the local police and get an early morning start.

North of Kalianda, the main road to Bandar Lampung heads inland, but after 9 km a well-marked sideroad to the left leads to a lovely beach at **Merak Belantung**, a sheltered cove off Lampung Bay. This sandy shore is ideal for swimming and sun-bathing, and there are small cottages here for rent and a restaurant offering meals by the beach.

Other beaches line the road much closer to Bandar Lampung, including **Pasir Putih**, 16 km south of the city, where you have spectacular views of Lampung Bay, several small uninhabited offshore islands, and Krakatau in the distance on a clear day. Small boats take you across to a white sand beach on **Condong Island**, which has food kiosks and is only 10 minutes away.

Bandar Lampung

The provincial capital and university town of Bandar Lampung overlooks one of the most scenic bays in the whole of Sumatra. The city was formed recently through an amalgamation of Tanjung Karang, the former colonial administrative center which lies up on a hillside overlooking the bay, and its adjacent port of Teluk Betung down by the water, terminus of the southern Sumatra railway system. Good roads link the capital with all other parts of the province, there are many fine hotels here, and interesting sidetrips can be made using the capital as your base.

The city's main attraction is the **Provincial Museum** on Jl. Teuku Umar, which has a good collection of *kain tapis* embroidered cloth, local musical instruments and wedding costumes. There is also a collection of archaeological finds from Labuan Meringgai (on the east coast) and Sumberjaya (in the northwest), including Dongson bronze drums, Chinese ceramics and carnelian and glass beads—all of which suggest that Lampung was involved in an extensive trading network linking it with eastern Indonesia, India and Indochina some 2,000 years ago.

In the evenings, the **Pasar Mambo** night market near the Teluk Betung harbor has delicious fresh seafood, while the open-air terrace of the **Marcopolo Hotel** up in Tanjung Karang is the perfect place to sit and admire the view as you enjoy a drink.

Eastern Lampung

An excursion to the east of Bandar Lampung leads to the elephant training station and nature reserve at Way Kambas (see "Way Kambas Reserve"), and can be combined with a stop at the fortified prehistoric site of **Pugung Raharjo**, 42 km to the northeast of the city. The latter covers an area of about 30 ha in the midst of pepper, clove and coffee plantations, and has remains dating from at least the 12th to the 17th centuries and probably earlier. Sights here include 13 prehistoric stepped temple mounds (*punden berundak*), a Buddhist statue and the remains of a fortified settlement. Legend has it that water from a spring at the site cures all ills and restores youth, and the area was once considered "haunted." It was uninhabited until transmigrants moved here in the 1950s, which is when the first artifacts were discovered.

To reach the site, take the road northeast from **Panjang** (6 km south of Bandar Lampung). The road climbs away from the bay

Below: *Islets dot the surface of Lampung Bay.*

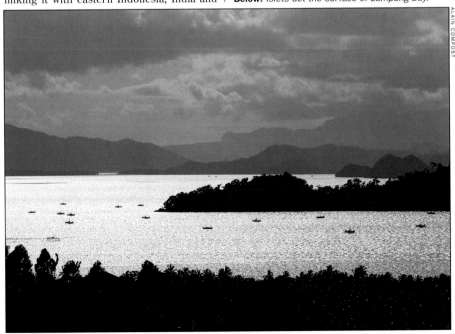

ALAIN COMPOST

and across a broad plain to the Sekampung River valley. Shortly after crossing the river, a left-hand turn at the Jabung crossroads brings you 2 km north to the small site museum. Displays here include a 7th-century Srivijayan "curse" inscription discovered at the village of Bungkuk, and an unusual *bodhisattva* statue. A further 1 km along a paved road brings you to the archaeological site.

The ancient settlement was defended by an impressive series of ramparts and ditches the remains of which still run for 1,200 m along the eastern perimeter of the site and for 300 m along the west. Inside are a number of megalithic structures, including standing ancestor stones and ancient stepped pyramids which were probably used in pre-Islamic religious ceremonies. Many scholars think that such prehistoric mounds, such as those in India, may have influenced the development of later Buddhist monuments such as Borobudur. Other stones found here include mortars, possibly used in rain-making ceremonies, and several grooved *batu bergores*, the significance of which is unknown. Northeast of the complex is another small megalithic group, known as *batu umpak* (pedestals).

To contine on to Way Kambas, return to the main road and head east across a small range of hills to the coastal plain. Turn left at the T-junction and continue on past Jepara to **Tridatu**. The road to the reserve's elephant school is clearly signposted on the right.

The 16-km road into the park takes you through savannah-like country which is home to around 250 wild elephants. At the training school, which has 30 lumbering "pupils," you can watch the elephants being trained and take a short safari around the park. To visit the nearby Way Kanan River, continue along the main road for another 13.5 km. There, you may hire a *perahu* to take you downriver to the simple guesthouse. Some 280 bird species live along the river, so bring along your binoculars (see "Way Kambas Reserve" for more details).

Western Lampung

Most people just can't wait to hop on a bus to begin the long, arduous and often boring (especially in the south) journey up the Trans-Sumatran Highway to Bukittinggi and Lake Toba. In fact, many interesting sights lie in the vicinity of Bandar Lampung, particularly to the west of the city. Here the Bukit Barisan range meets the Indian Ocean and forms two huge bays—Semangka and Lampung—that create a long and incredibly dramatic coastline. The remote and densely forested mountains at the southwestern "heel" of Sumatra, encompassing much of western Lampung, have recently been declared a national park known as **Bukit Barisan Selatan National Park**. The park covers 3,568 sq km all up and down the west coast and mountains of Lampung province, and is the home of

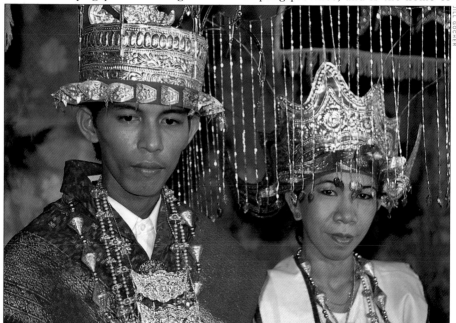

Sumatran tigers, honey bears, elephants, rhinos, bearded pigs, argus pheasants, rare orchids, rafflesias and the *Amorphophallus titanum*—the world's tallest flower.

A scenic road hugs the rocky western shore of Lampung Bay immediately to the southwest of Bandar Lampung, passing tiny coves and islets on the way to the village of **Padang Cermin**. About 35 minutes out of the city, you arrive at the fishing village of Ketapang, where it is possible to hire motorboats to offshore islands. Be aware that this

is also a top-secret Japanese pearl farming area, and security is tight in some places.

Another road heads due west of the city along the upper reaches of the Sekampung River to the town of **Kota Agung**, located at the head of Semangka Bay, about 2 hours away. After 1.5 hours you can stop at the foot of Mt. Tanggamus (2,102 m), where a concrete stairway constructed during the Dutch times leads 1,100 m down to waterfalls formed by the Way Lalaan River. Beyond the first fall, a second, grander fall awaits the visitor. Bring along your swimsuit!

From Kota Agung, it is possible to take a motorized *perahu* down the west coast of the bay to the village of **Tampang**, located at the southernmost tip of Bukit Barisan Selatan National Park, a journey of about 5 hours. From Tampang you can hike across the peninsula through the jungle along a 32-km trail to **Belimbing**. Of historical interest is a 57-m lighthouse overlooking Belimbing Bay, built in 1879 by the Dutch. From atop the lighthouse you have dramatic views of the Indian Ocean, its powerful surf crashing against the coast, and of a disused airstrip built by the Japanese during WW II. Take a guide and plenty of food and water.

The northwest coast

An alternative route into the park starts at **Bukit Kemuning**, 130 km north of Bandar Lampung on the Trans-Sumatran Highway, and cuts westward through the mountains to the traditional fishing village of Krui, on the west coast. The road climbs up through the hills, affording magnificent views. At Simpangsari, about 30 km from Bukit Kemuning, turn off left to visit the megalithic complex at **Sumberjaya**, near the headwaters of the Way Besai, a tributary of the mighty Tulangbawang River. Here rows of large upright ancestor stones and dolmens stand facing nearby Mt. Abung. Imported Chinese ceramics from the 8th to 11th centuries (Srivijayan period), which may have been used in ritual ceremonies, have been recovered at Sumberjaya. Other megalithic complexes can be seen in the immediate vicinity.

Further west, you pass several dammar (resin) collecting villages. At **Liwa** a sideroad forks north to beautiful Lake Ranau (see "Palembang Sidetrips" in SOUTH SUMATRA).

From Liwa the road descends steeply through a pass to the coastal village of **Krui**. Pisang Island, visible to the northwest, is where Lampung's famous *kain tapis* are woven and can be reached by boat. Krui is also known for its pepper. During the British occupation of Bengkulu (1685-1824), a tiny outpost was established here.

In the old graveyard at Krui was a tombstone which was once in English but had been reinscribed in the Lampung script. It commemorated one "Bob Brown, son of James Brown Esq." who was Resident of Krui from 1809 to 1814. A translation of the Lampung script reads: "This is the inscription of the grave of Bab Barawan, son of the Resident Masta Barawan Iskanwayar, from a union with a Lampung woman." The dates are illegible but presumably predate Brown's resignation in November of 1814.

— *E. Edwards McKinnon*

Opposite: *Traditional Lampung wedding costumes show a distinctive Srivijayan Malay influence.*
Above, left and right: *Fishing in Lampung Bay.*

WAY KAMBAS RESERVE

Training an Elephant to Play Ball?

Ear-splitting trumpeting echoes across the forest as a young elephant struggles against stout ropes holding it to a wooden frame—and against the pressure of an immense adult elephant. The young wild elephant is undergoing its initiation into Indonesia's first and only elephant training program—designed to transform it within a few years from a wild beast into a tractable, domesticated creature. The elephant training center (Pusat Latihan Gajah) is at **Kandangsari**, in Lampung's Way Kambas Reserve.

Way Kambas is one of the oldest reserves in Indonesia, declared in 1937. It covers a triangle of marshy lowlands along the eastern coast of Lampung, measuring some 1,300 sq km in area. The habitats at Way Kambas are different from those of other Sumatran parks, as they consist largely of freshwater swamps and include one of the few stands of lowland dipterocarp forests in any Sumatran reserve. The coast is lined with mangroves, nipa palms and casuarinas. It was declared a reserve because of its wildlife, and unfortunately most of the forests within the original park boundaries have been cut. Commercial products such as dammar (a tree resin used in making varnish), timber, honey and animals are still being extracted.

The elephant training program was started in the mid 1980s after much deliberation over what to do about southern Sumatra's wild elephant problem. Over the last 20 years the forests of this region have been cleared to make way for plantations and transmigration settlements. Of all the animals displaced, elephants have posed the most persistent nuisance to the new settlers—trampling crops and even attacking their homes. Villagers complained that while elephants had complete freedom to do as they pleased, they were not allowed to do anything to stop them, as elephants are a protected species.

The solution seemed simple enough. In other regions of South and Southeast Asia, elephants are commonly captured and domisticated. In Sumatra, this practice died out hundreds of years ago—but why not revive it? So in 1985, two Thai elephants and their mahouts were brought in to begin a training program, with the aim of taking animals from the wild and training them to become productive members of the tourism industry. Since it

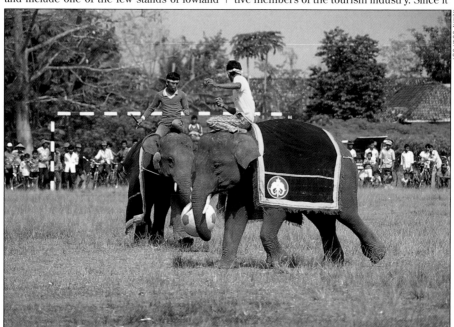

ALAIN COMPOST

began, the program has dramatically raised the profile of the park—from an obscure reserve to a popular place offering "safari" rides on elephant back across the park's flat, open terrain.

In the West, there is a tendency to criticize the use of wild animals to provide amusement and labor for humans. But the alternative for these elephants would probably be a slow death after being caught in a poacher's noose or being poisoned by villagers. They can instead serve a useful purpose in attract-

ing tourists (and their money) to the region, providing jobs and helping to explain to people in concrete terms why there is a need for national parks and reserve areas.

Visiting Way Kambas

The main access to Way Kambas is from the village of **Tridatu**, 10 km north of Jepara. The turn-off to the right is well marked. It takes about 2 hours to drive here from Bandar Lampung, and about 3 hours from the Java-Sumatra ferry terminal at Bakauheni (7 hours altogether from Jakarta). Make sure you arrive during office hours, so that officials at the park office can issue you a permit.

It is estimated there are over 300 wild elephants living in Way Kambas, and this is the best place in Indonesia to see them. After their capture from the wild, the elephants are given twice-daily training classes, at 8 am and again at 3 pm. These classes at the same time provide training for local mahouts, each of whom is assigned his own elephant. It is hoped that looking after an elephant will become a source of pride and income for families in the area, with sons learning to take over from their fathers.

If you intend to stay overnight, there is a simple guesthouse at **Way Kanan**, 13.5 km past the park entrance. The road there is negotiable only by 4-wheel drive vehicles. (If you have no transport of your own, the park wardens will take you to Way Kanan on the

back of motorbikes for a small fee.) The guesthouse at Way Kanan is very basic, and you must bring along all food and eating utensils and to be prepared to cook over an open fire. For most people it is better to make a day trip, timing your visit to coincide with one of the elephant classes at Kandangsari.

Other wildlife abounds in the reserve. Along the road to Way Kanan, agile long-tailed macaques and heavier-set pig-tailed macaques watch you approach before dashing into the bushes, while families of pigs frequently trot across the road right in front of you. In the morning the wild calls of siamangs and dark-handed gibbons ring out in a wonderful morning chorus, adding to the natural concert of a whole host of birds.

From Way Kanan, take a boat downstream to the coast, and ask the driver to turn the motor off so you can drift quietly with the current and see more wildlife. Monitor lizards frequent the river banks, slipping into the river at the slightest disturbance. Giant squirrels and monkeys quickly scamper up trees along the banks, and stork-billed kingfishers with yellow head and red bill take flight in a streak of bright turquoise.

For birders with more time, an alternative route into Way Kambas is via the port of **Labuhan Meringgai**, south of the park. From the port it is a 4-hour boat ride up the coast to the Way Kambas estuary. The river is then navigable for 25 km upstream, and from the boat you can see colonies of herons, storks and waders. During the wet season (Nov to March), higher water levels offer an excellent opportunity to explore swamp areas which are normally inaccessible by canoe.

— *Janet Cochrane*

Opposite: *The Pusat Latihan Gajah (Elephant Training Center) at Way Kambas has become a popular tourist site. Here, trained elephants play a game of soccer.* **Above, left:** *Nipa palms line the Way Wako.* **Above, right:** *A baby elephant walk.*

KRAKATAU

The Day the World Exploded

Like battered teeth knocked from the mouth of Lampung Bay, the islands of Krakatau lie scattered in the Sunda Straits between Sumatra and Java. Greater eruptions have shaken the island—the one which created Lake Toba is thought to have been the largest the world has ever known—but none is a more powerful symbol of incalculable subterranean energy than the explosion which ripped the old island of Krakatau apart in 1883.

The name comes from an old Sanskrit word, *karkata*, meaning "crab" (perhaps referring to the shape of atolls once formed by the volcano's caldera). It lies in the middle of the Sunda Strait, right on the unstable "elbow" where the range of volcanic mountains forming Sumatra turns abruptly eastward to form Java. Ancient Javanese chronicles tell of a mountain here called Kapi, which in about AD 416 "burst into pieces with a tremendous roar and sank into the depths of the earth, and the water of the sea rose and inundated the land." Whether Kapi was Krakatau we shall never know, but geologists have shown that at least one massive eruption of Krakatau took place in pre-modern times.

Prelude

At the end of the 19th century, Krakatau was a fertile and pleasant island, though one which had been long been deserted by human inhabitants. Tropical jungle clothed the slopes of its three peaks—Rakata (830 m), Danan and Perbuatan. This was the spot where European mariners once filled their larders with giant sea turtles, as well as the occasional supplies of pepper and rice which they purchased from small villages along the shores.

The eruption of Krakatau was not unheralded. Beginning in early June, 1883, tremors shook the town of Anyer on the west coast of Java for several days. By the middle of June, puffs of steam and ash were visible above the cone of Perbuatan. But on an island where the earth regularly trembles and dozens of volcanoes frequently emit smoke, few took special notice.

By the end of June, however, Krakatau presented a fearsome sight. Two columns of steam rose from the island, now blanketed with grey ash, and only the bare trunks of large trees remained of the once-luxuriant jungle. The waters surrounding the island churned and heaved, while here and there floated carpets of pumice so thick a man could walk on them. A party of sightseers from Batavia reported a "fiery purple glow, appearing for a short while every 5 to 10 minutes, from which a fire rain fell."

Climax

This overture to one of nature's greatest known cataclysms lasted for 2 months. Finally, early in the afternoon of August 26th, 1883, Krakatau exploded with a series of roars heard round the world—from Rangoon, Burma to Perth, Australia. A pillar of ash and pumice towered 26 km into the sky. Rock and dust rained over the surrounding region, forming a blanket cloud which turned day into night for 150 km in every direction. Ash from the eruption gradually spread throughout the atmosphere, creating spectacular sunsets across the world for two years.

The finale came the following morning, when a gaping maw in the earth's crust—hollowed out by the expulsion of 18 cubic km of ash and rock—collapsed on itself. The sea rushed in and began to boil immediately upon contact with the molten rock, throwing up tsunamis (tidal waves) 10 meters high. The waves could still be detected a day and a half later when they finally rolled against the coast of France.

The devastation around Krakatau was of incredible proportions. All coastal villages facing the Sunda Straits were obliterated. No one knows the exact toll in human lives, though a common figure cited is 35,000. Eyewitnesses described a wall of water "taller than a palm tree" sweeping away everything in its path. In Teluk Betung (now Bandar Lampung), the funnel effect of the narrow Lampung Bay lifted the waves to a height of 30 meters, carrying a Dutch gunboat more than 2 km inland.

When the waves subsided and the dust dispersed, three quarters of Krakatau was gone. The peak of Rakata was still close to its original height, but its northern half had disappeared—sliced off as if by a knife, leaving a

Right: *An aerial view of Anak Krakatau.*

sheer cliff plunging 300 m to the sea below. Two islands, Panjang and Sertung, had been totally re-shaped, while debris from the eruption merged to form islands farther away.

Krakatau remained in a state of geological flux for some time. The new islands disappeared within a few years, but volcanic activity continued below the surface, and in January, 1928, the rim of a new crater arose close to where the vent of Perbuatan had first erupted. Since then, Anak Krakatau ("Child of Krakatau"), has continued to grow, and now stands 150 m high. This "baby island" gives scientists a fascinating opportunity to observe the colonization of plant and animal species on new soil.

Visiting Krakatau

To see Krakatau you need only travel on the ferry from Java and along the southeastern coasts of Lampung. As long as the air is clear, the old peak of Rakata will be visible on the horizon—a low, symmetrical cone about 50 km offshore. Although most people approach the volcano from Java's west coast, an excursion is also possible from **Canti**, a fishing village not far from the Java-Sumatra ferry, lying along the scenic road that encircles Mt. Rajabasa just south of Kalianda. Choose a sturdy boat and a reliable crew—the return journey can take 6-8 hours and the narrow straits can be dangerous in rough weather (expecially December to April).

Visitors land at the island's southern corner, where pine-like casuarinas, hardy colonizers of the shoreline, offer welcome shade. Walk north along the beach until the vegetation thins out, then strike uphill. The succulent plants of the shore quickly give way to clumps of tough grass, but even these only survive on the first few hundred meters.

The slope looks gentle but the going is tough. The fine, black volcanic sand, hot under the tropical sun, gives way underfoot, causing the trekker to slide backwards with each step. Twenty or thirty minutes brings you to the crest of a ridge—the outer edge of Anak Krakatau's crater. From here the view is spectacular. The smouldering cone is in front and a dark skirt of recent lava flows on either side—while behind you the slope you have just climbed spreads out like a fan, delicately edged with young, green vegetation and fringed with a line of surf. The older islands of Rakata, Sertung and Panjang hover in a circle like ladies-in-waiting.

The truly enthusiastic can venture further, down into a scorchingly hot valley where giant misshapen lumps of lava lie as they fell from the sky, and up a rocky path on the other side past sulphur fumaroles to the edge of the inner crater. The view is no better from here, but there is an awe-inspiring sensation in standing next to a void that leads straight into the underworld.

— *Robert Cribb*

ALAIN COMPOST

Lampung Practicalities

Includes Bandar Lampung, Kalianda, Krakatau, Merak Belantung and Krui. Prices in US dollars. S = single; D = double; AC = air-conditioning.

Bandar Lampung

Telephone code is 0721.

Banjar Lampung is actually two towns: Tanjung Karang (the locals simply call it "Karang") up on a hill to the north, and Teluk Betung (called "Teluk") to the south, by the bay. Connecting the two is Tanjung Karang's Jl. Raden Intan, which turns into Teluk Betung's Jl. Diponegoro. A large decorated wall with colorful tiles in *kain tapis* patterns marks the boundary.

GETTING THERE

Merpati has six daily flights from Jakarta. Two leave from Soekarno-Hatta International Airport, the rest from Halim Perdanakusuma (the old airport to the southeast of Jakarta); fare is $28 one-way; the flight takes 55 minutes. Bandar Lampung's airport is at **Branti**, 24 km north of the city. There is a taxi service in the arrival hall. If you are staying at the Sheraton, there is a free transfer service.

You can also travel overland from Jakarta by bus, via the ferry terminal at Merak, where a 24-hour service takes you across to Bakauheni at the southern tip of Lampung. A ferry leaves

every 45 minutes. The crossing takes 1.5-2 hours and costs $11 for cars, 90 cents a person for 2nd class (AC) and 60 cents for 3rd class (non-AC). From the terminal at Bakauheni, Bandar Lampung is only 2 hours away; total traveling time Jakarta-Bandar Lampung is about 7-8 hours. The best way to go is not by bus but by door-to-door taxi. Call **Taxi SB90** for a pick-up, tel: 4898027, 6696194 (Jakarta); 43026, 45026 (B.L.); fare is $12 each way.

GETTING AROUND

Taxis are for hire at $3 an hour within the city; they wait in front of the bigger hotels, particularly the Marcopolo. Negotiate the fare in advance. They can also be hired for day-trips out of the city; bargain hard! There is an Avis car rental desk at the Sheraton for AC cars with English-speaking drivers, $5 per hour (2-hr min) or $42 a day in the city. Excursions outside the city are $52 for first 5 hrs, $8 per add. hour.

Minibuses can also be rented for $80 a day (seats 6) from Femmy Tour and Sahid Gema Wisata (see "Information and Tours" below).

Public **buses and minibuses** are readily available to get around the city. The central terminal is on Jl. Raden Intan in Tanjung Karang. Fare is Rp150-200 within the city; ask at your hotel for specific routes. Damri buses take passengers from here to the Rajabasa intercity terminal, 11 kms north of town, for Rp150. This is where all buses depart for other parts of Lampung and Sumatra.

ACCOMMODATION

Hotels in Bandar Lampung are extremely reasonable. All accept major credit cards and add 21 percent tax and service.

Expensive ($25 and up)

Indra Palace (64 rooms) Jl. Wolter Monginsidi 70, tel: 35119, fax: 62399. A new hotel on a hill above the city, with a panoramic view. $40 S, $44 D, up to $90 for a suite.

Marcopolo (104 rooms) Jl. Dr. Susilo 4, tel: 62511, fax: 54419. An older hotel, on the hill with a splendid view of the bay. Olympic-size pool, helpful staff. $22 S, $28 D, up to $50 for a suite. Best value for money in Lampung.

Sahid Krakatau (94 rooms) Jl. Yos Sudarso 294, tel: 44022, fax: 63589. Right on the beach, with a swimming pool by the bay. A popular business hotel with rooms overlooking the water. $30 S, $33 D, up to $100 for the suite.

Sheraton Inn (113 rooms) Jl. Wolter Monginsidi 175, tel: 63696, fax: 63690. The best in Lampung. Restaurant and bar, swimming pool, well equipped gym and sauna, even a children's playground. Spacious and luxurious. $65 up to $250 for the suite. American breakfast incl.

Intermediate and budget (below $25)

Andalas (35 rooms) Jl. Raden Intan 89, tel: 63432. A 3-storey hotel in the center of town.

$9 to $30. Rooms with AC and color TV for just $12. If you don't need AC, ask for rooms 7 or 8, which overlook a small garden.

Kurnia City Jl. Raden Intan 114, tel: 62030, fax: 62924. Right on the main street in the middle of town, convenient but noisy. Coffee shop, swimming pool, tennis court. Good value. $9 to $15 for AC rooms with color TV.

Kurnia Dua (59 rooms) Jl. Raden Intan 75, tel: 52906. Simpler and less expensive than the Kurnia City. $7 to $10.

INFORMATION AND TOURS

The Diparda **Tourist Indormation Office** at Jl. Wr. Supratman Gn. Mas. 39 in Teluk Betung has a number of helpful brochures and can give you information on getting around on your own. **Sahid Gema Wisata Tours** in the Sahid Krakatau Hotel (tel: 64244, 62167, 62114) offers a series of organized tours for groups of any size. They will take a group of 4 to Way Kambas or Krakatau, for example, for $50 and $64 per person, respectively. They specialize in diving tours and can supply you with a boat, a tank, gear and a guide for $132. The biggest agency in town is **Femmy Tours & Travels**, Jl. Wolter Monginsidi 143, tel: 44911, 44690, who also organize all kinds of custom tours.

EATING AND DRINKING

The Sheraton's **Kebun Raya** restaurant has an excellent Indonesian and European menu. The Sahid's **Rakata** is known for its Chinese seafood by the beach. The **Balenso Bar** in the Indra Palace is Bandar Lampung's premier watering hole, open until 2 am. Also try the **Swiss Pub & Disco**, Jl. Yos Sudarso.

For great Chinese dishes and fresh seafood in the evenings, head for **Pasar Mambo** in Teluk—stalls that open onto the street. Try the Tio Ciu restaurant: delicious crabs, prawns, *kailan* with beef for about $5 a head with beer.

A good place for lunch is **Cookies Corner**, Jl. Kartini 29 (next to Artomoro Dept. Store), run by an English woman and her Chinese husband. Their speciality is salads and burgers, but they have everything from steaks to Chinese and Indonesian dishes at very reasonable local prices, along with iced cold drinks.

If you like singing, try the **Golden Dragon Sea Food and Bar**, Jl. Yos Sudarso, a Chinese karaoke restaurant serving good but expensive seafood, such as squid in sweet sour sauce.

Hot, spicy Padang food is found everywhere in Bandar Lampung. The best is **Simpang Raya**, Jl. Diponegoro 18. Try their delicious chilly squid (*cumi belado*) and grilled spicy chicken (*kelio ayam panggang*). Very reasonably priced. Another good Padang restaurant is **Begadang II**, nearby on Jl. Diponegoro.

On the west end of Jl. Yos Sudarso, stalls selling *martabak* (Indian fried bread with minced mutton and egg) and other snacks set up in the evenings.

SHOPPING

Top of the list for local handicrafts are the hand-woven and embroidered silk *kain tapis* fabrics, and ornaments made from coconut shells. Original *kain tapis*, designed specially for upholstery and curtains, can be bought at **Lampung Art Shop** at Jl. Kartini 12 in Tanjung Karang; you can see the women weaving upstairs.

Kalianda and Krakatau

Stay at the **Hotel Beringin** (8 rooms) Jl. Kesuma Bangsa 75, tel: 2008—an old Dutch house with big clean rooms, large enough for 4. Some have outside baths open to the sky. $2.50 to $3.50, breakfast included. The owner, Pak Akib Yakub, organizes tours for small groups, including a one-day boat trip to Krakatau. **Hotel Sudi Mampir** is one block from Hotel Beringin and has rooms from $3 to $4.

At night the streets around Hotel Beringin are filled with push-carts selling *sate*, *soto*, *nasi goreng*, excellent noodles and *empek-empek* (spicy fish cakes).

Boats to **Sebesi Island** from Canti take an hour and cost 50 cents per person. To **Sebuku Island** takes 2 hours and costs 75 cents. The regular ferry comes back the next day, but you can charter a boat back the same day for $13.

To charter a boat to **Krakatau** costs $90 for a large boat (20 people); $78 for a smaller one (10 people). Ask to see the boat first. The trip takes 3-4 hours each way; you leave at 8 am and return at 6 pm. Ask first how rough the seas are; it can be dangerous from Nov-April.

Merak Belantung

A tiny resort with 4 cottages set in a garden a few steps from the beach. Pleasant atmosphere, $13 per cottage. A good place to stop if you're driving to or from Jakarta. The beach is delightful and overlooks two small islands.

Krui

Krui is 273 km from Bandar Lampung. Buses from Rajabasa terminal north of the city head north all day. Get off at Bukit Kemuning ($1) and change for Krui ($1). The best place to stay in town is **Sempana Lima** (6 rooms) Jl. Kesuma 708, tel: 40. All rooms with private bath, $6 including breakfast. A motherly Sundanese woman runs the place. The family runs a minibus service to Bandar Lampung, departing twice a day, at 6 am and 3 pm ($2).

Stalls selling *sate* and other dishes can be found around the market; nothing very exciting.

Charter a fishing boat to **Pisang Island**, where the *kain tapis* is woven, for $13 round trip. If you take the regular ferry, cost is only 50 cents. Ask at the pier for departure times.

—*Sandra M. Hamid and Eric Oey*

Travel Advisory

Prices in US dollars unless indicated. Information was gathered between January and June, 1991. Prices and schedules change very rapidly, however, so check with a travel agent.

VISA FORMALITIES

Nationals of the following countries are granted entry to Indonesia without a visa for 60 days. Other nationals must obtain a tourist visa from an Indonesian embassy or consulate.

Argentina	Greece	Norway
Australia	Iceland	Philippines
Austria	Ireland	Singapore
Belgium	Italy	South Korea
Brazil	Japan	Spain
Brunei	Liechtenstein	Sweden
Canada	Luxembourg	Switzerland
Chile	Malaysia	Thailand
Denmark	Malta	United Kingdom
Finland	Mexico	United States
France	Netherlands	Venezuela
Germany	New Zealand	Yugoslavia

To avoid any unpleasantness on arrival, check your passport before leaving. Make sure it will be valid for at least 6 months after arrival, and that you have at least one empty page for the stamp. You must also have proof of onward passage, whether return or through tickets, and sufficient money. Employment is forbidden on a tourist visa or visa-free entry. Visa-free entry is not extendable, and is only possible in Sumatra when entering through Batam, Padang, Pekanbaru, Belawan, Palembang, Medan and Tanjung Pinang. At other ports, a visa is required.

GETTING THERE

By air. Medan's Polonia Airport is Sumatra's main gateway—but Batam, Padang, Palembang and Pekanbaru are also now served by international flights (mainly from Singapore). Keep in mind that Singapore is closer to most Sumatran cities than Jakarta, and that Kuala Lumpur and Penang (in Malaysia) are closer to Medan than Singapore. From many cities in Europe or North America, it is cheaper and easier just to buy a ticket to Singapore or Malaysia and purchase a ticket to Sumatra there. For details of flights to each city, check the respective "Practicalities" sections. Cost of a Singapore-Medan RT ticket, for example, is about $175—check the Straits Times classifieds in Singapore or Kuala Lumpur for the best deals.

There are also daily flights to all major Sumatran cities from Batam, the large Indonesian island just below Singapore. It often costs you less to take the ferry across from Singapore's Finger Pier ($11), take a taxi to the airport ($4) and then hop on a plane to your Sumatran destination. The problem is that you cannot book in advance and you often cannot even get accurate information over the phone about flights and ticket availability. So in practice you risk spending the night in Batam, and hotels there are expensive. The island is served mainly by Merpati and Sempati, both flying jets, but also by SMAC and Bouraq prop planes. Check under "Riau Island Practicalities" for more details.

There are also of course daily flights to all major Sumatran cities from Jakarta. From Bali, Yogya and other points in Indonesia you have to travel through Jakarta.

By ship. To get the real flavor of Sumatra, arrive the way people have for centuries—by sea! PELNI, the national steamship line, has a fairly new and comfortable air-conditioned passenger vessel, the KM Lawit, that sails back and forth between Jakarta and Medan every two weeks, with stops at Mentok (on Bangka Island) and Tanjung Pinang (on Bintan Island, just opposite Singapore). You will need to time your movements properly to catch this ship, but if you can, it's cheaper and more interesting than flying. Tickets are available only in the port of departure, however, and cannot be ordered in advance. (See "Practicalities" for Medan, Riau Islands and Tin Islands for boat schedules and prices.) In addition to the PELNI ship, there is also the fast Gadis Langka Suka hydrofoil from Penang to Medan.

By ferry from Riau. An even more adventurous way to get to Sumatra is by local ferry boat. All sorts of crafts ply the Straits of Malacca and the South China Sea, radiating out from Batam and Bintan through narrow channels between the scattered islands of the Riau chain, up the Batang Hari and Siak rivers to Jambi and Pekanbaru. These are generally slow and cheap, but there are a number of faster and more expensive speedboats with twin 100 Hp outboards, as well as some new hydrofoils. Given plenty of time, you can island-hop on slow inter-island ferries from Singapore right down through the Lingga Archipelago to Bangka and Belitung, thence to Palembang or Java. You need plenty of time to do this, and the conditions are not exactly luxurious, but it can be the adventure of a lifetime—like moving through a time warp back to the romantic days of Joseph Conrad! Check respective "Practicalities" for details.

By ferry from Java. The ferry from Java is fast, comfortable and cheap. Don't even think of flying to Lampung from Java unless you really don't have the time to go overland. See "Lampung Practicalities" for details.

Tours. While not generally the way to go, there are some great deals from agents in Singapore and Malaysia. For example, a 5-day 4-night tour of Medan, Berastagi and Toba costs just $300 per person double occupancy including return airfare, hotel and transport. The drawback is that you are stuck with a busload of tourists.

Still, you can't beat the prices and if time is limited you do see quite a bit. Check the classified ads in the papers.

CUSTOMS

On entry a maximum of 2 liters of alcoholic beverages, 200 cigarettes or 50 cigars or 100 gms of tobacco, and a reasonable amount of perfume are allowed per adult. Firearms and ammunition are strictly forbidden. All kinds of narcotics are illegal, and their use, sale or purchase results in long prison terms and huge fines. Advance approval has to be acquired for carrying transceivers, and all movie films and video cassettes have to be cleared by the Film Censor Board. There is no restriction on import or export of foreign currencies, however the export or import of more than Rp50.000 in Indonesian currency is prohibited.

TRAVELING AROUND SUMATRA

Getting around the island is not a problem, but it takes time and endurance, as the distances are very great. The question is how to do it so as to get where you are going with the energy to see something—hopefully also to see something along the way. The two main options are to travel by plane or bus. Trains are found only in the very south, from Lampung up to Palembang, and in the north from Medan to Pematang Siantar (near Toba). Both means of travel have their advantages and disadvantages. A third and much better way to go anywhere is to rent an air-conditioned minibus with driver for several days or even weeks (see below). This way you go where you want to when you want to—and at $70-$85 per day including gas and driver's expenses, this is not expensive when split between 3-5 people.

By air

Air transport is more costly but obviously much faster than traveling by bus on a huge island where the roads are winding and the distances between major points considerable. Only problem is that you don't get to see very much from up there. From Jakarta up to Medan takes two hours by air, however, while the fastest bus will take two days to get there. If time is limited, this is clearly the only way to go—and by international standards it is quite cheap. See "Practicalities" for prices and flight frequencies.

The national carrier is **Garuda**, which has a subsidiary called **Merpati**. All domestic routes —together with many of the old DC-9s and F-28s—have now been turned over to Merpati. In addition, there are four private airlines operating in Sumatra: **Sempati**, **Bouraq**, **SMAC** and **Mandala**. Only Sempati has jets; the others fly creaky old props with fares that are 10 percent lower. Service on all these airlines is pretty good by Third World standards, if still pretty awful by Western ones. The food, when you get any, is terrible, and you may have to wait in line

an hour or more to make or change a booking, but generally you get there in the end. Note the following important points:

• It is difficult to confirm bookings out of a different city than the one you are in. You can buy a ticket and the computer may say you have a booking, but don't believe it until you reconfirm with the airline office in the city of departure.

• Always reconfirm directly with the airline in the city of departure between 24 and 72 hours before your flight, particularly during the peak tourist seasons and Indonesian holiday periods. Your seat may be given away if you reconfirm either too early or too late (or not at all).

• Make bookings in person, not by phone, or buy a ticket through an agent in your hotel and let them do it. (Reconfirmations can be made by phone, however.) Request written evidence of your booking and jot down the name of the person who makes it in case you are later told you don't have a booking.

• Note down the computer booking code, as names have a way of going astray or being wrongly entered. When you change your booking, get a new sticker put on your ticket. *Concrete evidence of your booking is essential.*

• Get to the airport an hour before the flight. As long as you have a sticker, you can often get on even if your name isn't in the computer.

• If you are told a flight is full, go to the airport anyway two hours before departure and ask that your name be entered on the waiting list. Hang around the desk and be friendly to the staff; 15 minutes before departure you will probably get on. Flights are chronically overbooked but rarely completely full.

Long haul bus travel

Traveling across Sumatra by bus is one of the island's quintessential experiences, and you've not really "been there" until you have done at least one stretch of the Trans-Sumatra Highway on one of these huge, careening caravans. The highway is now paved along its entire length, and is mostly in good condition, although during the rainy season there could be landslides and fallen trees that bring you to a halt. Once off this main artery, however, road conditions are highly variable. What may look like a major road on the map can be little more than a bone-shaking potholed track that has rarely, if ever, been resurfaced since it was first constructed during the Dutch colonial times. On the other hand, road construction crews all over the island are making rapid progress and you can find some excellent stretches of newly-paved and very scenic secondary roads.

A number of companies operate so-called "*Non-Ekonomi*" or luxury intercity buses on the Trans-Sumatra Highway that are large, new, air-conditioned and mostly in quite good condition. Competition for business is keen. The general consensus is that ANS (for *Aman-Nyaman-Sejuk* "Safe-Comfortable-Cool") is the best company overall, with connections to all major cities. By local standards their fares are considered a bit expensive: Padang to Jakarta for $25, for example. When you consider that this is a 34-hour ride, though, it isn't that much. Other companies offer similar services, and might charge the same or a bit less. Check them out. Older, non-AC "Ekonomi" buses may cost half the price, but are hot, dirty and crowded, and can add many hours to the journey.

On ANS at least the AC works, the seats are fairly wide and they recline, pillows are provided and there are squat toilets at the back. (The latter are only for peeing, however; other calls of nature have to be attended to during the frequent meal stops. When requested to by male passengers, however, buses will stop at a river. Here, local etiquette allows them to drop trow and squat in the shallows, pulling down their underpants at the last moment.)

Intercity buses depart more or less on time, but invariably arrive later than scheduled. Schedules are in fact very approximate, and actual travel times vary by hours depending on road conditions and traffic (and how the driver feels). Night buses are faster, but you don't see much.

Bus fares also vary greatly. In theory they are regulated, with increments allowed for certain facilites. In practice, you can pay quite different prices for the same facilities. Western faces, moreover, invite surcharges. Check with several other agents of a given company. Most important of all, know what you are paying for, as buses from the same company have different rates depending on the "extras."

Buses are almost always full. If you are on an overnight journey and can afford it, buying an extra seat may help you sleep better. Onboard entertainment is all the rage now, so you often have to suffer through interminable Indonesian tear-jerkers, or even worse—a karaoke singalong. Treat it as a cultural experience. Passengers, usually men, grab the mike to belt out a number—some with remarkably good voices receive an appreciative round of applause from fellow passengers.

Less appreciated by Westerners is the 4:15 am shalat subuh morning call to prayers, coming in loud and clear over the loudspeaker. If a mosque is nearby, the bus will stop to allow passengers to pray. This is often followed by a taped sermon, delivered in Indonesian to mostly sleeping passengers. One 90-minute sermon dwelled on the dangers of "free sex," recommending marriage, sports and study groups as the antidote. All the risqué words—sex, masterbation, genitals, prostitutes—were in English, which drew occasional titters from the few insomniacs who were listening.

Long-haul bus crews usually consist of two drivers who relay each other, plus a helper who cleans out the bus and washes the windows at every stop. At the rest stops they sometimes have special toilets, labelled Khusus Pak Sopir

("Special for Mr. Driver"). The buses do break down, but drivers carry an impressive array of tools and spares, and you are usually on your way after only a short hiatus. Good chance to walk around and stretch your legs.

Health-conscious Westerners will be thankful for the ban on smoking in some AC buses. But the rule is not always enforced, as many drivers are themselves chain smokers. Smokers can have nicotine fits lasting several hours. When the bus finally stops for gasoline, everyone stands around the pumps puffing away madly, oblivious to the "No Smoking" signs posted all around.

The large restaurants where buses stop invariably serve spicy Padang food, with dishes stacked across your table; you pay for what you eat. If you are unaccustomed to spicy food, ask the waiter Apa yang tidak pedas? ("What is not hot?") as the food is brought over. You might ask for a spoon and fork (garpu dan sendok) if you are not yet used to eating with the right hand only—a messy proposal for many foreigners. Sometimes you can get beer-over-ice, and they always have an assortment of bottled drinks and snacks for sale. With your meal you get only hot water.

While the best views are from the front row seats, nervous passengers should avoid them. In the mountains, curves are hair-raising and space on the road is at a premium, especially at the center of the highway—the preferred place to be. Most Sumatran bus drivers take a devil-may-care approach to driving. Top speed, pedal-to-the-metal, hand-on-the-horn style. Never touch the brakes unless they absolutely necessary, and at absolutely the last possible instant. The situation is further aggravated by incessant road works and digging of drainage ditches. Not a few buses end up in them.

The best seats are snapped up where the long-haul buses start, in the provincial capitals. Purchase your ticket a day earlier here to get a better seat (front seat or window on the side with better scenery). Seat numbers are not strictly observed, however, and the same number is often sold twice, so there may be someone in yours when you get there. Polite smiles will (usually) get you your rightful place.

The smaller buses making the "local" runs are no fun, but provide an insight into how the common folk travel. Your luggage goes topside or serves as an extra seat inside. It's hot if sunny, wet if rainy. Diesel fumes are wafting everywhere. Just when you thought no more people could possibly get on, three more pile in, with luggage.

Always beware of an empty bus, which like nature abhors a vacuum. It means long waits, as the bus will not go until more people pile in.

Bus stops can turn into a 3-ring circus. As you get further north, men accost you with collection boxes for their mosque or charity. Blind men with begging bowls chant verses from the

Koran, led around by young boys. Insistent vendors flog a variety of food or drinks in bags.

Tickets are available at the bus terminals, which are always on the outskirts of town, and there are usually a number of buses going your way. Have a look around, check out the seats or the photos if the buses themselves are not present, to see what you are getting. Try to buy a ticket from a counter, but if they are sold out you may have to buy from a scalper. Check the official rate and allow a 10 percent "premium." In some cases these scalpers and touts can be helpful in getting you and your things on the bus, but follow your instincts in judging the "good" ones from the cheats and pickpockets, and check your tickets very, very carefully.

Local buses

Usually old rattle-traps, quite different from the sleek intercity buses. These run along major and minor roads, stopping anywhere to pick up and discharge passengers. Only use them if you are going short distances or are looking for a "local experience," as you do get to see quite a cross-section of village society, including the domestic animals. Fares are ridiculously cheap. Flag one down on the roadside.

Express minibuses

Called "*travel*" these are 6-, 10- or 14-passenger vans, often AC and quite comfortable, that connect major cities and will deliver you right to your destination. They also sometimes pick you up. Most travel only during the day, though on longer routes they may travel at night like the bus. More expensive than the bus but much more comfortable and convenient. Also much safer as they tend not to drive as fast.

Local minibuses

These non-AC vans ("*kol*" or "*bemo*") are the real work-horses of the transport network, going up and down relatively impassable tracks to deliver village farmers and produce. There are no set fares; the conductor, often a small boy, tells you how much, and it isn't much. Flag one down on any roadside. You can also charter them. Just say "charter" and where you want to go, then bargain for the fare in advance.

Car rentals

Sedans or taxis with drivers are available in major cities but are very expensive, and they don't really like to go long distances. Also, you have to return them to the point of rental. More for daytrips or business clients than for touring. In Medan, self-drive cars are available now (see "Medan Practicalities") but unless you have experience driving in Indonesia, it's not a good idea. You'll need a valid international license.

Chartering a minibus

Undoubtedly the best way to tour Sumatra is to rent a minibus with driver. This is especially true if you are traveling with a group of 3 to 5 people. The vans can take up to 7, but you need extra space because you'll be in it for hours, so 6 including the driver is generally maximum. Most travel agents can arrange this for you, and will provide driver/guides who speak English and may even be able to tell you what you are seeing. The bell captain or receptionist in your hotel can also help you find one. It is a very good idea to hire the van for a day around the town first—to make sure that the driver and the vehicle are acceptable.

Set your itinerary. You need to allow the driver time to get back if you are not returning to the starting point, but this usually means an extra day's rental with gas and food money. Rates vary greatly. Bargain and ask around at different places. For a 5-day journey, approximate cost should be around $300 including the driver. You pay for the gasoline (which is cheap; remember—Indonesia is a leading member of OPEC). You'll have to pay the full rental amount in advance, before the trip. You also pay for the driver's food and lodging en route, but he usually sleeps in the van and food is cheap. At the end of the trip, fill up the tank and give him extra money for gas, food and cigarettes along the way.

PLANNING YOUR ITINERARY

Sumatra is so huge, the first thing to realize is that you can never cover the whole island, even if you were to spend several months here. Don't make an impossibly tight schedule, and try not to spend all your time on the road (which is easy to do in Sumatra). Realize that things happen more slowly in Indonesia, and adjust yourself to the pace of people around you. Better to spend more time in a few places and see them at a leisurely pace than to end up hot and bothered; you'll see more this way, not less. Also realize that the long drives take their toll; budget some time for rest and recuperation.

Top places on your list should be Lake Toba and the Minang Highlands. But in fact there are interesting things to see and do everywhere on the island. If you love wildlife and the great outdoors, visit one of the national parks or go hiking in the mountains. All of the volcanoes can be climbed, but you need to be prepared and to hire a guide. Some of the tourist information and forestry (PHPA) offices can be helpful in arranging this, but your best bet is to work through a private travel agent.

If you like beaches, try the Riau Islands or Bangka and Belitung (South Sumatra) or head for just about any place along the west coast. For something truly exotic, visit the western islands (Mentawai or Nias).

ACCOMMODATION

In Medan and other major cities you have several kinds of hotels to choose from, from luxury chains to simple lodges, called *penginapan* or *losmen* (from the French *logement* via Dutch). Once out of the district capitals, however, standards drop dramatically (and so do prices). The big exceptions are of course the well-traveled tourist areas (like Berastagi and Toba). Even in smaller towns, particularly around mining or plantation areas, you can find a clean, AC room with Western-style bath, but in others you'll have to make do with a dingy, mosquito-ridden room. All are very cheap by Western standards, though rates vary widely and so does what your get for your money.

Have a look at the room before checking in. Shop around if you don't like what you see. Always bring along your own towel and simple bedding if you are traveling on the cheap. Small hotels don't usually provide them, and if they do, you don't want to use them. Buy a plastic mosquito net ($4-$5 in any general goods store —ask for a *kelambu*) and hang it up with some string so you can get a good night's sleep. Bathrooms usually have a squat toilet and a *mandi* —a tub of cold water and a bucket to douse yourself with. Bring along your own tissue paper. Ask for boiled water (*air minum*) for drinking and brushing teeth, or buy bottled water.

Advance bookings are necessary at popular places in the Batak Highlands of North Sumatra during peak seasons (July/August, Christmas/New Year and Indonesian national holidays). These places can also be flooded with Singaporean and Malaysian tourists during other periods, around Chinese New Year, for example. Other places are rarely full.

In many hotels, discounts of 10-30 percent from the published rates are to be had for the asking, especially if you have a business card. Booking through travel agencies can also result in lower rates. Most larger hotels add 15.5 or 21 percent tax and service to the bill.

WHAT TO BRING ALONG

Copy all essential documents and numbers: passport, credit cards, plane tickets, travelers' checks, prescriptions. Keep them separately, so that you will have the information if the originals are lost or stolen.

Keep in mind that you will be in the tropics, but that it gets cold in the mountains. Dress light and casual, with natural fibers that absorb perspiration. A sweater or jacket is a must, as is a sturdy pair of walking shoes. Suits and ties are never worn. Don't bring too much, as you'll be tempted to buy clothes here. Most tourists find the local cotton batik shirts more comfortable than what they brought along. Bring at least one long-sleeve shirt and nice skirt or trousers in case you are invited to visit someone's home or have to go to a government office.

In the cities and large hotels you can find Western toiletries, even if your brand may not be available. Contact lens users should be well-stocked with lens solution and eye drops, as these are not easy to find. Certain things, like dental floss and tampons, are non-existent.

LANGUAGE

The national language, taught in school, is Bahasa Indonesia, though local languages are spoken throughout the island. Spend your time on the long flight over learning a few basic words—it gives Indonesians great pleasure to hear a foreigner speaking their language.

In big cities and tourist areas, many people speak English. Some older people speak Dutch. If you are in a bind, look around for someone in their 20s—they are taught English in school and may be able to understand a bit. A small dictionary or phrasebook, available at any bookshop, will help you a great deal in these situations.

Spelling and pronunciation

On the whole, Indonesian is not difficult to pronounce, but the lack of standardized spelling causes problems. As the result of new spelling conventions adopted in 1972, *c* (formerly *tj*) is pronounced as "ch"; *j* and *y* (formerly *dj* and *j*) are pronounced as in English; *sy* is "sh"; *ng* is as in "singer" (never as in "finger"); and *g* is hard, as in "golf" (never as in "gentle").

MONEY AND BANKING

Prices quoted in this book are in US dollars, and were gathered between January and June 1991, when the exchange rate was Rp1950 to $1. The Rupiah is being allowed to slowly devalue and inflation is around 10 percent a year, so prices stated in US dollars are more likely to remain accurate over time. Even so, the prices listed here should be taken merely as indications. Don't be alarmed if certain prices are considerably higher or even lower than stated.

The local currency unit is the Rupiah. There are coins of 5, 10, 25, 50 and 100. Notes come in 100, 500, 1000, 5000 and 10.000. Change all the money you will need at banks in the big cities; once you get out into the country it is difficult to find a bank that gives a good rate, even in tourist areas. Get a supply of smaller bills—Rp1000, 500 and 100—when you change money, as smaller shops and restaurants often don't have change for bigger bills.

Major credit cards are accepted only in the large hotels, restaurants, department stores and shops catering for the tourist trade. You can get money from your cards in major cities (see "Medan Practicalities").

There are no exchange controls so your Rupiahs can be freely converted back to foreign currency on departure, and you are only allowed to take Rp50.000 out of the country.

Tax, service and tipping

Most larger hotels add 15.5 or 21 percent tax and service to your bill. The same practice also applies in some big restaurants. Tipping is not a custom here, but Rp500 appreciated for special services. Rp500 per bag is considered a good tip for roomboys and porters. Taxi drivers will round up to the nearest Rp500 or Rp1000.

SHOPPING AND BARGAINING

Bargaining is an integral part of shopping in Indonesia. This is especially true in small towns and markets. In the cities, in department stores with everything under one roof, you'll see signs saying *harga pas* ("fixed prices") and you don't need to bargain. If you are making big purchases, though, it is always worth asking for a discount. You don't bargain in restaurants.

The key to successful bargaining is to keep smiling. First ask the price and then, on hearing it, feign shock and say *mahal, mahal* ("expensive"). Indonesians appreciate good histrionics. Offer less than half the asking price in a playful manner. The vendor should come down and you should go up—slowly at first to see how far he or she will come down. Don't let on if you really must have an item; point out its (real or imagined) defects in a playful way. Give your best offer and make your way slowly to the door. If it is accepted, there is no turning back; you have to buy. (Some foreigners renege on offers; this is not done and the seller may get quite angry.)

In the end, follow your instincts. There is no "right price." Retailers often mark-up only 10 percent of their cost, and if they can make a bit extra this is a bonus. If you can get a lower price through skillful bargaining, you get the bonus. Don't get angry or upset if someone is asking outrageous prices, or if you see it much cheaper elsewhere. Buy things that you really like and then relax—you probably paid much less than you would have at home.

Be extremely cautious when buying antiques, works of art or expensive items, especially in tourist areas. Most are reproductions, though very good ones (and cheap to boot!). Think carefully about the ethics of encouraging villagers to sell their family heirlooms or cut off a piece of their house so you can hang it up on your wall at home. Don't encourage the wholesale destruction or export of artifacts that have been here for a very long time and have great meaning for the island's inhabitants.

ETIQUETTE

In all social situations, play it safe. The Batak of North Sumatra are notoriously aggressive, and easily offended. Don't horse around, be careful what you say, and don't lose your temper or start insulting people, no matter how badly you may feel you have been treated. You can find yourself in a very bad situation. It's never worth it to hassle about small amounts of money. If you don't like the service, just pay up and leave. Don't try to get your money back or demand your rights or threaten to report to the police. Won't do you much good anyway.

Older men should be addressed as *pak* (*ba-pak* or "father"); older women as *bu* (short for *ibu* or "mother")—these are the equivalents of Mr. and Mrs. Keep the following points in mind:
• Pointing or waving at people is impolite.
• Never receive something (money, etc.) with the left hand, as it is considered unclean. Apologize by saying *maaf, kiri* if you must use your left hand.
• Take off your shoes when entering someone's house. Sometimes the host will stop you, but you should go through the motions until he/she does.
• Dress decently, especially in Islamic areas. For women this means shoulders covered, long skirt or pants. For men, a shirt with a collar and long trousers. Some Sumatrans treat you very badly if you are dressed in T-shirts, halter tops, ragged shorts, etc. At the very least they feel embarrassed. Sarongs and undershirts are fine at home, but when Indonesians go out they put great emphasis on dressing properly.
• Don't drink or eat until invited to, even after food and drinks have been placed before you.
• Sip your drink and don't finish it completely; never eat the last morsels from a plate.
• You are often invited to eat with the words *makan, makan* ("eat, eat") if you pass someone who is eating. This is not really an invitation, but simply means "Excuse me as I eat."
• If someone prepares a meal or drink for you it is impolite to refuse.
• If you are having a cigarette, offer all the men around you one.

FOOD

Cooking styles vary greatly from region to region. Most Sumatran food, however, is very spicy and salty. By Western standards, it is also very cheap. For under $1 in most places, you can get a meal. On the other hand, the island does not really have a banquet tradition. People only eat in restaurants out of necessity when they are traveling or working, for example. The major exception to this is the Chinese, who are fond of eating out. Most Indonesians eat much better at home than outside, and the range of dishes available in restaurants is not great. The best foods are reserved for festivals and ceremonies like weddings.

Padang restaurants are found literally everywhere. In a Padang restaurant you are served a number of meat, fish and vegetable dishes, as many as 15 or 20 different types, on small plates brought to your table. Whatever you eat is tallied up at the end of the meal and paid for, the rest is taken back to the counter.

Javanese restaurants are also common. Here you will find a standard menu consisting of *sate* (skewered barbeque meat), *gado-gado* or *pecel* (boiled vegetables with spicy peanut sauce) and *soto* (vegetable soup with or without meat). Also found are some Chinese dishes like *bakmie goreng* (fried noodles), *bakmie kuah* (noodle soup) and *cap cay* (stir-fried vegetables). Javanese-style fried chicken (*ayam* goreng) is common and very tasty—stewed in coconut cream, coriander and onions and then deep-fried to give it a crispy coating. Then of course there is the ubiquitous *nasi goreng* (fried rice), which is often eaten for breakfast with an egg on top. *Nasi goreng istimewa* means you also get a piece of fried chicken or several sticks of *sate* on the side, maybe both.

In larger towns, you can often find a Chinese restaurant on the main street. They serve a style of cuisine very much assimilated to local tastes. Standard dishes, in addition to the *bakmie* and *cap cay* mentioned above, are sweet and sour whole fish (*gurame asem manis*), beef with Chinese greens (*kailan/caisim ca sapi*), and prawns fried in butter (*udang goreng mentega*). Any of these with a plate of vegetables and rice makes a delightful meal.

POLICE

In just about all hotels or *losmen*, the form you fill out to register is taken to the police by the management, so you don't have to worry about registering yourself. If you get far off the beaten track or stay with someone in a village, the police may come to see you. No problem. They probably want to practice their English. In really out of the way places, people might think you are up to something suspicious. Way out in the sticks, it's always best to explain who you are and why you are there, preventing misunderstandings with the locals and the police. Tell them you just love Indonesia, and be sure to always carry your passport with you.

HEALTH

Have a thorough medical (and dental) checkup before leaving if you are planning to do some serious traveling in remote areas. Ask which inoculations your doctor recommends—tetanus definitely, and a cholera vaccine. Though the latter makes you sick and doesn't eliminate the risk, it can help. A gamma globulin shot, effective for about six months against some strains of hepatitis, may also be worth getting.

Hygiene is a perennial problem in Indonesia. Very few places have running water or sewers. Most water comes from rivers or wells, and raw sewage goes into the ground or into the rivers. Tap water in the big cities is never potable and must be boiled. Dishwashing in restaurants, even fancy restaurants, often involves a quick rinse in a tub and a wipe with a towel.

Not surprisingly, stomach complaints are universal among Indonesians (just look at the billboards advertising stomach remedies!), and it is very difficult to spend much time here without having some problems. In many cases your stomach is just not used to the strange foods and stray bacteria. Make sure you do not get something more serious, like hepatitis or amoebas, by taking the following precautions:

• Drink only bottled or boiled beverages (mineral water, beer, soft drinks, tea, coffee, etc.).

• Never drink or eat ice, no matter how tempting on a hot day, as the water is never boiled. The only exception is in a luxury hotel, but even then it may not be true.

• Eat in restaurants, not in roadside stalls. At least they have running water to wash dishes, whereas stalls use a bucket of dirty water all day—often drawn from the river or canal.

• Don't eat uncooked foods like salads, garnishes or peeled fruits. Buy your own fruits in the market and peel them yourself. Even in a fancy hotel, avoid raw vegetables and salads.

• When you get hit with diarrhea, eat rice with little else (a bit of vegetable soup is good) and drink black tea (a pinch of salt in it helps). It should go away in a day or two.

• Whether you have problems or not when you get back home, it is a good idea to have stool and blood tests done. Some 80-90 percent of all Indonesians have intestinal parasites and these are easily passed by food handlers. They may cause only minor discomfort if you are healthy and have a good diet, but if left untreated they can cause serious damage.

• Clean all cuts, scrapes and bites thoroughly with disinfectant and apply a bandage with a bit of antibiotic cream. Small wounds quickly fester in the tropics. A good antibiotic cream is a must. A handy disinfectant to carry around is Betadine, available in a soap solution from any pharmacy in Indonesia.

Malaria

Malaria is a disease affecting all tropical countries, particularly in rural areas. It is caused by a protozoan, *Plasmodium,* which affects the blood and liver. The vector for the *Plasmodium* parasite is the *Anopheles* mosquito.

Malaria is a big problem in coastal lowland areas of Sumatra, especially in the southeast (Lampung) and on the western islands (Siberut and Nias). You *must* take malaria pills if you trek in these areas. However, pills do not offer full protection. Malaria is a real risk that must be weighed before traveling here. If you are pregnant, have had a splenectomy or have a weak immune system, you should definitely not go to those areas. Consult your doctor as there is quite a bit of controversy about which medications are safe and which are effective.

Doctors and hospitals

If you should happen to fall sick, your hotel or *losmen* could help to find a doctor speaking some English. Doctors and health care are quite inexpensive by western standards, but the quality leaves much to be desired. At least they're familiar with the symptoms and treatment of tropical diseases, which is something your family doctor might have a real tough time with back home.

The Indonesian name for pharmacy is *apotik*; and a hospital is called *rumah sakit.* Some hospitals expect you to pay in advance. Big hotels have resident physicians. In smaller villages they have government clinics, called Puskesmas, which are not equipped to deal with anything serious. Emergency care leaves much to be desired. Your best bet in the event of a life-threatening accident or illness is to get on the first plane back home or to Singapore. Phone your embassy or consulate in Jakarta or Medan for assistance. Medivac airlifts are expensive ($26,000) and most embassies will recommend that you buy special insurance to cover the cost of it when traveling extensively in remote areas.

POSTAL SERVICE

Do not send anything of value by mail—parcels quite often arrive with contents missing or not at all. Parcels sent home have to be inspected at the post office before sealing. Registered letters have a better chance of getting through. Outgoing letters take a long time to leave the country; it's worth paying extra for express (*kilat*) service. Courier services are an alternative, quicker and safer although considerably more expensive. **DHL** is the most reliable international service, but also the most expensive. **Elteha** (LTH), with offices in all towns and cities, is a domestic parcel service that also sends courier packages overseas and is quite reliable. Post restante is efficient but incoming parcel post is a multi-signature affair to clear customs and pay duties, which can take hours.

TELEPHONE

The telephone can be a great source of frustration in Indonesia. Just be thankful when it works at all. Service is improving dramatically, however. Your best bet is to call from your hotel; pay phones outside don't usually work. In big cities, use the pay phones in major hotels: Rp50 or Rp100. Overseas and long-distance calls may have to be placed at the Perumtel telephone office. Long-distance rates are now relatively reasonable by international standards.

Small telephone offices called Warung Telekomunikasi or Wartel for short (literally "telecoms kiosk") are springing up all over. Sometimes they are open 24 hrs, offering long distance calls, telefax service, telex and stamps.

TIME

There is only one time zone in Sumatra, Western Indonesia Time. (GMT +7 hours). Singapore and Malaysia are one hour ahead. Sunrise is around 6 am; sunset around 6 pm.

CALENDAR

The government sets a certain number of legal holidays every year, on both fixed and moveable dates. Most of these holidays are for the major religions practiced in Indonesia. Both the Christian Easter and all the Muslim holidays are based on the moon, so confusion results in attempting to extrapolate several years ahead.

The fixed national holidays on the Gregorian calendar are New Year, Jan. 1; Independence Day, Aug. 17; and Christmas, Dec. 25. Easter, Good Friday and Ascension Day are honored. The Balinese new year, Nyepi, and the Buddhist Waisak New Year are also legal holidays.

Official Muslim holidays are: **Israk Meraj.** When Muhammad ascended on his steed Bouraq. **Idul Fitri.** The end of the Muslim fasting month of Ramadan, also called Lebaran. It is very difficult to travel just before and just after Idul Fitri as just about everyone wants to return to his or her home village to celebrate, then get back to their places of work in the cities. **Idul Adha.** The day of Abraham's sacrifice and the day that the haji pilgrims circle the Kaaba in Mecca. **Hijriyah.** The Islamic New Year, beginning the month of Muharram, when Muhammad traveled from Mecca to Medina. **Maulid Nbai.** Muhammad's birthday. **Note:** The Muslim calendar begins with the Hejira, Muhammad's flight to Medina, in A.D. 622 according to the Gregorian calendar. Early A.D. 1991 corresponds to A.H. 1411. The Muslim calendar is a lunar calendar, and gains 10 or 11 days on the Gregorian calendar each year. Islamic holidays will thus regress 10–11 days a year against to the Gregorian calendar.

ELECTRICITY

Most of Sumatra has switched to 220 volts and 50 cycles, though a few places are still on old 110 lines. Ask before you plug in if uncertain. Power failures are common, and voltage can fluctuate considerably, so use a stablizer for computers and other equipment. Plugs are of the European two-pronged variety.

OFFICE HOURS

Government offices are officially open 8 am to 3 pm, but if you want to get anything done, get there before 11. On Fri they close at 11:30 am and on Sat at 2 pm. In large cities, offices are open 9-5 and shops are open 9-9.

SECURITY

Petty theft is very common; pay very close attention to your belongings, especially in crowded public places. Be sure that the doors and windows of your hotel room are locked at night. If you spend a lot of time walking on the street, use a money belt for valuables instead of a shoulderbag that can be snatched. Moneybelts are a good idea for holding passports and travelers' checks. Big hotels have safety boxes for valuables. If your hotel does not have one, carry all documents along with you. Make sure you have a photocopy of your passport, return plane ticket and travelers' check numbers and keep them separate from the originals. Be especially wary in crowded bus terminals; this is where pickpockets lurk and they are very clever at slitting bags and extracting valuables without your noticing.

Further Readings

ARTS AND CRAFTS

Barbier, J.P. and D. Newton (eds) *Islands and Ancestors: Indigenous Styles of Southeast Asia* (New York 1988).

Barbier, J.P. *Sumatra: The Batak People and Their Art.* (Dallas 1982). Exhibition catalog.

Barbier, J.P. *Tobaland; The Shreds of Tradition* (Geneva, 1983). A rambling discussion of Batak art and culture based on the author's five visits to North Sumatra in the 1970s.

van Dijk, T. and N. de Jonge. *Ship Cloths of the Lampung, South Sumatera* (Amsterdam 1980). Exhibition catalog.

Feldman, J. *The Eloquent Dead. Ancestral Sculpture of Indonesia and Southeast Asia* (Los Angeles 1985). Excellent chapters on Nias and Batak ancestral figures and their symbolism.

Hasibuan, J.S. *Batak Art et Culture* (Jakarta 1985). Lovely photos. An English edition is planned.

Hasibuan, J.S. *Primitive Art of the Ancient Batak* (Medan 1982).

Hitchcock, M. *Indonesian Textiles* (Singapore 1991). A good overview of traditional fabrics. Widely available in Indonesia.

Leigh, Barbara. *Hands of Time: The Crafts of Aceh* (Jakarta). Many illustrations and excellent discussions of how the crafts are made. Available in Jakarta bookshops.

Nias: Tribal Treasures. Cosmic Reflections in Stone, Wood and Gold (Delft 1990). Catalog of an exhibition held at the Museum Nusantara, Delft, with informative articles on sculpture, architecture, festivals, jewelry and folktales.

Niessen, S.A. *Motifs of Life in Toba Batak Texts and Textiles* (Dordrecht 1985).

Taylor, P.M. and L.V. Aragon. *Beyond the Java Sea: Art of Indonesia's Outer Islands* (Washington 1991). Excellent introductory text.

Waterson, R. *The Living House: An Anthropology of Architecture in South-East Asia* (Singapore 1990).

LITERATURE

Ambler, Eric. *Passage of Arms* (London 1959). A thriller about gun-running in Sumatra, by a master of the genre.

Clerkx, E. and W.F. Wertheim. *Living in Deli, Its Society as Imaged in Colonial Fiction* (Amsterdam 1990). A survey of (mostly Dutch) fiction set in North Sumatra during the first decades of this century.

Conrad, Joseph. *Youth* (London 189?). Conrad's first novelette, in which he describes his initial impressions of the Indies, landing at Mentok on Bangka Island as a young seaman.

Lubis, Mochtar. *Harimau.*

Székely, Ladislao. *Tropic Fever* (New York 1937, repr. Singapore 1989). An autobiographical novel by a young Hungarian who worked as a tobacco planter in the Medan area around the turn of the century, it sensitively portrays the hardships endured by coolies and European overseers alike.

Székely-Lulofs, Madelon. *Coolie* (London 1932, repr. Singapore).

Székely-Lulofs, Madelon. *Rubber: A Romance of the Dutch East Indies* (London 1931, repr. Singapore).

PEOPLES OF SUMATRA

Bartlett, H.H. *The Labors of the Datoe and Other Essays on the Bataks of Asahan (North Sumatra)* (Ann Arbor 1973).

Collet, O.J.A. *Terres et peuples de Sumatra* (Amsterdam 1925). Offers a detailed description of flora, fauna, peoples and cultures.

Errington, F. *Manners and Meaning in West Sumatra* (New Haven 1984).

Graves, E. *The Minangkabau Response to Dutch Colonial Rule* (Ithaca 1981).

Hagen, B. *Die orang Kubu auf Sumatra* (Frankfurt 1908). The earliest major account.

Heidhues, Mary F. Somers. *Bangka Tin and Mentok Pepper: Chinese Settlement on an Indonesian Island* (Singapore 1990).

Josselin de Jong, P.E. de. *Minangkabau and Negri Sembilan. Socio-political Structure in Indonesia* (The Hague 1980).

Kipp, R. S. and R. (eds) *Beyond Samosir: Recent Studies of the Batak Peoples of Sumatra* (Athens, Ohio 1983). A collection of essays.

Loeb, E.M. *Sumatra: Its History and People* (Vienna 1935, Singapore 1972, 1989). A systematic study compiled largely from Dutch ethnographic sources; still very readable. The author spent five months on the Mentawais.

Singarimbun, M. *Kinship, Descent and Alliance Among the Karo Batak* (Berkeley 1975).

Snouck Hurgronje, C. *The Achehnese* (Leiden/London 1906). The classic work by a Dutch scholar who greatly influenced colonial policy during the wars with Aceh.

Sopher, D. *The Sea Nomads* (Singapore ?). Excellent description of the *orang laut*, their habitat and lifestyle.

Suzuki, P. *Critical Survey of Studies on the Anthropology of Nias, Mentawei and Enggano* (The Hague 1958).

Tobing, P.O.L. *The Structure of the Toba-Batak Belief in the High God* (Amsterdam 1956, 1963).

HISTORY AND ECONOMY

Bastin, John. *The British in West Sumatra 1685-1825* (Kuala Lumpur 1965). Has a selection of edited letters and reports from the British at Bengkulu.

Bellwood, P. *Prehistory of the Indo-Malaysian Archipelago* (Sydney 1985). A standard work.

Bowen, John. *Sumatran Politics and Poetics:*

Gayo History 1900-1989 (New Haven 1991).

Collis, M. *Raffles* (London, 1966). Wonderfully readable account of a fascinating man; poignantly describes Raffles' years in Bengkulu.

Cunningham, C.E. *The Postwar Migration of Toba-Bataks to East Sumatra* (New Haven 1958).

Dobbin, Christine. *Islamic Revivalism in a Changing Peasant Economy (Central Sumatra, 1784-1847)* (London 1983).

Franke, Wolfgang and Salmon, Claudine. *Chinese Epigraphic Materials in Indonesia, Vol. I: Sumatra* (Singapore 1988).

Gould, J.W. *Americans in Sumatra* (The Hague 1961).

Hal Hill (ed) *Unity and Diversity: Regional Development in Indonesia Since 1970* (Singapore 1990). A mine of information on Sumatra's economy, presented province-by-province. (Bengkulu and Jambi are not covered however.)

Lombard, D. *Le Sultanat d'Atjeh au Temps d'Iskandar Muda 1607-1636* (Paris 1967).

Marsden, W. *The History of Sumatra* (London 1783, 1811). The first scientific study in English of any Indonesian island. Not a light read, but a book you will come back to time and again to learn about the geography, flora, fauna, people and history of the island. Based in large part on the author's observations during an 8-year stay at Bengkulu. The substantially revised third edition of 1811 contains additional material gleaned from informants in Sumatra. Available in a facsimile reproduction from Oxford in Singapore.

Maxwell, J. (ed) *The Malay-Islamic World of Sumatra: Studies in Policies and Cultures.*

Milner, A.C. *Kerajaan: Malay Political Culture on the Eve of Colonial Rule* (Tucson 1982).

Reid, A. *Southeast Asia in the Age of Commerce 1450-1680. Vol. 1: The Lands Below the Winds* (New Haven 1988).

Reid, A. *The Blood of the People: Revolution and the End of Traditional Rule in Northern Sumatra* (Kuala Lumpur 1979). An account of the massacre of the Malay aristocracy in an outburst of pent-up anger during the revolution.

Reid, A. *The Conquest for North Sumatra* (Kuala Lumpur 1969). Highly readable historical account of the Aceh wars.

Schnitger, F.M. *Forgotten Kingdoms of Sumatra* (Leiden 1938, repr. Singapore 1989). As romantically readable as the title sounds; offers a good introduction to the antiquities of Sumatra. Written in a lively, first person style by an amateur archaeologist who himself discovered and excavated many Sumatran monuments. Touches also on legends, folktales and ethnographic details of the island's peoples.

Schnitger, F.M. *The Archaeology of Hindoo Sumatra* (Leiden 1938). A more technical work.

Thee, Kian-wie. *Plantation Agriculture and Export Growth: An Economic History of East Sumatra 1863-1942* (Jakarta 1977).

Wolters, O.W. *Early Indonesian Commerce: A Study of the Origins of Srivijaya* (Ithaca 1967).

Wolters, O.W. *The Fall of Srivijaya in Malay History* (Ithaca 1970).

NATURE AND ECOLOGY

Griffiths, M. *Indonesian Eden: Aceh's Rainforest* (Jakarta 1989).

Holmes, D. and S. Nash, *The Birds of Sumatra and Kalimantan* (Singapore 1990). A brief but comprehensive introduction.

King, B., Dickson, E.C. & Woodcock, M. *Field Guide to the Birds of South East Asia* (Collins). There is as yet no field guide for Sumatran birds, but this book covers the mainland, with a good deal of overlap.

van Marle, J.G. and Voous, K. *The Birds of Sumatra, An Annotated Checklist* (Checklist No. 10 from the British Ornithologists' Union, 1988). All serious ornithologists will need a copy.

Savage, V. *Western Impressions of Nature and Landscape in South East Asia* (Singapore 1984).

Whitten, A., D. Sengli, A. Jazenul and H. Nazaruddin. *The Ecology of Sumatra* (Yogyakarta 1984). An authoritative and richly-documented overview of the island's ecosystems.

Whitten, A. *The Gibbons of Siberut* (London 1982).

GUIDES AND TRAVELOGUES

Burton and Ward. "Report of a Journey into the Batak Country, in the interior of Sumatra, in the year 1824" in *Transactions of the Royal Asiatic Society* 1:485-583 (London 1827).

Dalton, Bill. *Indonesia Handbook* (Chico 1992). The backpacker's Bible, in an all-new, "slimmed down" 5th edition.

Harfield, A. *Bencoolen; The Christian Cemetery and the Fort Marlborough Monuments* (London 1985).

Junghuhn, F. *Die Battakländer auf Sumatra* (Berlin 1847). One of the earliest explorers to the Batak highlands.

Maass, A. *Durch Zentral-Sumatra* (Berlin 1910). A classic work, 2 vols.

Modigliani, E. *Un Viaggio a Nias* (Milan 1890).

Salmon, C., D. Lombard and P. Labrousse, "Guide Archipel III: Palembang et Bangka" in *Archipel 15* (Paris 1978), pp.145-161.

LANGUAGE

Johns, Yohanni and R. Stokes. *Bahasa Indonesia. Langkah Baru: A New Approach.* (Canberra 1977, 1989). The best comprehensive grammar, designed for the classroom.

Barker, John. *Practical Indonesia* (Singapore 1991). The best phrasebook for the traveler; all the Indonesian you need to know. Widely available in Indonesia for about $2.50.

Echols, J.M. and H. Shadily. *Kamus Indonesia Inggris. An Indonesian-English Dictionary. Third Edition* (Jakarta 1989). The only Indonesian-English dictionary worth owning, if rather unwieldy to carry around. Buy it in any bookshop in Indonesia for about $12.

About the Authors

Peter Bellwood is Reader in Prehistory at the Australian National University, and specialises in Southeast Asian and Pacific Prehistory. His books include *Man's conquest of the Pacific*, *Prehistory of the Indo-Malaysian Archipelago* and *The Polynesians*.

David Booth has been traveling for work and pleasure since 1970. His work as a civil engineer took him to West Africa, the Middle East, the Caribbean and Papua New Guinea, whilst most of his pleasure trips were to Southeast Asia. He first visited Indonesia in 1985. Later deciding to settle down here and concentrate on writing, he became an English teacher and moved to Jakarta in 1989.

John Bowen is Associate Professor of Anthropology at Washington University in St. Louis.

Ian Caldwell was educated at the School of Oriental and African Studies in London and holds a doctorate in Indonesian history from Australian National University. In the last ten years he has traveled widely in Indonesia, photographing and studying its pre-Islamic cultures. He is currently lecturer in Malay Studies at National University of Singapore.

Nancy Caldwell was born in India and grew up in Singapore. She has traveled widely in Asia and Europe, where she ran a transport café and worked for a London council. She obtained her BA from the United States, where she studied modern and primitive Indonesian art.

Janet Cochrane has been involved in Indonesia since 1979, including 6 years' work there in conservation, tourism and development, and 3 years as a producer with the BBC Indonesian section. Her most recent project was advising on tourism in Wasur National Park in Irian Jaya. She is director of a tour company, Detours, specializing in wildlife and cultural travel.

Alain Compost was born in France and has lived in Bogor, West Java, for many years. He specializes in nature photography and his work has appeared in many books and magazines, including *Paris Match* and *National Geographic*.

Robert Cribb, an Australian, studied Indonesian history at the universities of Queensland and London. His reseach has included such diverse topics as warlords and opium smuggling during Indonesia's revolution, and the history of environmental protection in Indonesia. He is author of the *Historical Dictionary of Indonesia*.

Richard Davidson studied French and German at Cambridge University before traveling in Asia and Africa as a journalist and safari guide. He spent 6 months in 1991 traveling the length of Indonesia. He is currently writing a travel guide to Vietnam.

Toos Van Dijk, a cultural anthropologist (Free University of Amsterdam), is a researcher at the Centre of Non-Western Studies at the University of Leiden. She is the author of various publications on the material culture of Indonesian peoples. Currently she is preparing her PhD thesis on the symbolic system of the population of the Babar Archipelago, SE Moluccas.

Jerome Feldman is a professor of art history at Hawaii Loa College, specialized in the tribal arts of Indonesia and Oceania. He was educated at the City College of New York, University of Hawaii and Columbia University. His dissertation was on the architecture of Nias and he has edited and contributed to *The Eloquent Dead*, *Art of Micronesia*, *Islands and Ancestors*, *To Speak with Cloth* and *Nias Tribal Treasures*.

Annabel Teh Gallop grew up in Brunei Darussalam. She has been Curator for Indonesian and Malay at the British Library, London, since 1986 and has organized a number of exhibitions, including *Early Malay Printing 1603-1900* (1989) and *Paper and Gold: Illuminated Manuscripts from the Indonesian Archipelago* (1990). She is co-author of *Golden Letters: Writing Traditions of Indonesia* (1991) and is currently working on a doctoral dissertation at SOAS, London University, on Indonesian historical novels.

Jill Gocher is a free-lance photojournalist who studied photography in Melbourne, and has traveled and worked in Asia for over 10 years, contributing regularly to a number of magazines. Her favorite destination is Indonesia, and she has produced guides to Cirebon, Bandung and the Riau Islands.

Beatriz van der Goes studied Cultural Anthropology at the University of Amsterdam. She did field research from 1989-1990 among the Karo Batak of North Sumatra. Presently she is writing her PhD thesis and is a research assistent at the Centre of Non-Western Studies of Leiden University.

Jay Goodfriend is a freelance photographer who splits his time between Indonesia and San Francisco. Since 1986 he has worked on a photo documentary exploring the relationship between culture and land use. He is researching a historical novel set in the Japanese era.

Sandra Hamid was born in Jakarta in 1962. She moved to Bali soon after finishing her degree at the Faculty of Social & Political Science at the University of Indonesia, and worked for a time at the Bali Hyatt. She is now a journalist for *Tempo* magazine, based in Jakarta.

Derek Holmes was born in Kettering, England, in 1938 and graduated in geology at Bristol University in 1960. He has worked in Asia as a land resources consultant since 1963, and in Indonesia since 1974. He is co-editor of *Kukila*, the bulletin of the Ornighological Society of Indonesia, and has authored two popular books covering the birds of Java, Bali, Sumatra and Kalimantan.

Nico de Jonge studied Cultural Anthropology at

the Free Univerisyt of Amsterdam and is now a researcher at the Centre of Non-Western Studies at the University of Leiden. He is the author of various publications on the material culture of Indonesian peoples. Currently he is preparing his PhD thesis on the symbolic sistem of the population of the Babar Archipelago, Southeast Moluccas.

Rita Smith Kipp is Professor of Anthropology at Kenyon College, Ohio, and first carried out field research in Sumatra in 1972-4, when she lived in a highland village in order to write a dissertation on Karo weddings and funerals. She has written articles on Karo kinship and her books include *The early years of a mission; The Karo field* (University of Michagen Press, 1990).

Glyn Luntungan has lived in Indonesia intermittently since 1979, when she first fell in love with the country and its people. She was married in 1984 in Jambi and taught English to many of her friends there before returning to Australia to teach Indonesian for two years. In 1988 she returned to Indonesia to live with her recently widowed mother-in-law in Jambi.

Edmund Edwards McKinnon trained in agriculture at Edinburgh and first came to Sumatra in 1960 as a rubber planter. He has a longstanding interest in archaeology and has traveled extensively throughout the island and other parts of the archipelago. He holds a degree in History of Art from Cornell University and is currently consultant to the Director General of Culture, sponsored by the Ford Foundation. He lives with his family in Jakarta.

John Miksic holds a doctorate in SE Asian history from Cornell University and is lecturer in history at the National University of Singapore. He has spent many years conducting research in Indonesia under the auspices of the Ford Foundation and the Asian Cultural Council.

Kal Muller is a veteran photojournalist whose travels have taken him to more than 80 countries. For the last 16 years he has explored and photographed the Indonesian archipelago. He holds a doctorate in French literature and has written several guides to the more remote islands of Indonesia.

Eric Oey was born in the United States and has degrees in mathematics from Brown University and in Indonesian language and literature from the University of California, Berkeley. He founded Periplus Editions in 1988 and is now based in Singapore.

Gerard Persoon studied Cultural Anthropology at the University of Amsterdam. Through the years he traveled and worked in Indonesia; for instance three years on a development project in Siberut. He now works at the Environmental Centre of Leiden University.

Kunang Helmi Picard is an Indonesian freelance journalist based in Paris. She studied history, law and political science in Bonn, followed by post-graduate studies in London and Hamburg. She now contributes photos and articles to German, French, American and Indonesian publications.

Anthony Reid is Professor of Southeast Asian History at the Australian National University in Canberra. He has published several books and articles on the history of Sumatra. His most recent book is *Southeast Asia in the Age of Commerce, 1450-1680.*

Michael Richardson is the Singapore-based Editor for Asia of the International Herald Tribune.

Nicola Robertson is an English and Drama graduate from Edinburgh University. Founder of Stage International, a group specializing in Eastern European Drama. She is presently writing a play set in the Mentawai Islands.

Gottfried Roelcke graduated in 1975 in geography from Hannover University, where he first befriended a number of Indonesian students. He visited Indonesia in 1977 and has lived in the country since 1982, working as a technical advisor in Samarinda, Padang and now Bandung. Indonesia suits him perfectly, providing plenty of opportunities for photography, hiking, climbing and chatting with nice people.

Reimar Schefold studied cultural anthropology in Basel and Munich and carried out field research on Siberut in 1967-69, 1973, 1978, 1983 and 1988, and among the Toraja of Sulawesi in 1983. He is Professor of Cultural Anthropology at Leiden University and his research in Mentawai has resulted in numerous books and articles, museum exhibitions and a film for the *Disappearing World* series of Granada TV, UK.

Ilsa Sharp is a British-born journalist who has lived and worked in Southeast Asia for 22 years. She runs a writing agency and is an active member of the Malayan Nature Society.

Amir Sidharta was born in Jakarta. He received a BA in architecture from the University of Michigan and is currently a Fulbright Scholar undertaking an MA degree in museum studies at George Washington University.

Edward Van Ness was born in Bloomfield, New Jersey and has taught in Madras, India, at the Akademi Musik Indonesia in Yogyakarta, at Universitas Sumatera Utara and at Oberlin College, and is currently chairman of the music department at Nommensen University in Medan. He is a practicing violinist, violist and conductor, as well as author of several books, including a work on Javanese *wayang kulit.*

Roxana Waterson studied anthropology at Cambridge; her thesis was on the Sa'dan Toraja people of Sulawesi. She is author of *The Living House: An Anthropology of Architecture in South-East Asia*, and presently lectures in anthropology at the National University of Singapore.

Tony Whitten is an ecologist who has lived in Indonesia for nearly 9 years and works with the Ministry for Population and Environment. He is co-author and editor of *The Ecology of Sumatra* and *The Ecology of Sulawesi* and is currently working on another volume in the same series, *The Ecology of Java and Bali.*

Index

Bold **text** indicates the book has a section on this subject.
Bold **numerals** represent pages for a section, article or map. Italicized *numerals* are pages for an illustration. Letters: A, B, J, L, NS, R, SS, and WS. stand for provinces, Aceh, Benkulu, Jambi, Lampung, N. Sumatra, Riau, S. Sumatra and W. Sumatra.